JOURNAL FOR THE STUDY OF THE NEW TESTAMENT SUPPLEMENT SERIES
206

Executive Editor
Stanley E. Porter

Sheffield Academic Press

Has God Not
Chosen the Poor?

The Social Setting of the Epistle
of James

David Hutchinson Edgar

Journal for the Study of the New Testament
Supplement Series 206

Copyright © 2001 Sheffield Academic Press

Published by Sheffield Academic Press Ltd
Mansion House
19 Kingfield Road
Sheffield S11 9AS
England
www.SheffieldAcademicPress.com

Typeset by Sheffield Academic Press
and
Printed on acid-free paper in Great Britain
by Bookcraft Ltd
Midsomer Norton, Bath

British Library Cataloguing-in-Publication Data

A catalogue record for this book is available
from the British Library

ISBN 1-84127-182-9

CONTENTS

Preface   7
Abbreviations   9
Introduction   11

Chapter 1
APPROACHES TO THE INTERPRETATION OF
THE EPISTLE OF JAMES   13

Chapter 2
THE SELF-PRESENTATION OF THE AUTHOR   44

Chapter 3
THE PRESENTATION OF THE ADDRESSEES   95

Chapter 4
READING THE TEXT: JAMES 1.2-18   137

Chapter 5
READING THE TEXT: JAMES 1.19–3.18   158

Chapter 6
READING THE TEXT: JAMES 4.1–5.20   186

Chapter 7
CONCLUSION   216

Bibliography   232
Index of References   244
Index of Authors   258

PREFACE

This book is a revision of my doctoral thesis, supervised by Professor Seán Freyne, and accepted by the University of Dublin in 1996. I am deeply indebted to Professor Freyne for his wise and understanding guidance of my work through the years of postgraduate study and beyond, and for the personal warmth which, as much as his fine scholarship, has been an example to those who have studied under him.

I am also grateful to the examiners of my thesis, Revd Terence McCaughey of the University of Dublin and Professor Philip Esler of the University of St Andrews, for their insightful and constructive comments on my work. Professor Richard Bauckham of the University of St Andrews has also been generous and helpful in his supportive criticism of my thesis, as has Dr Fearghus O Fearghail of St Kieran's College, Kilkenny. Friends and colleagues in the School of Hebrew, Biblical and Theological Studies, Trinity College, Dublin, have also provided greatly appreciated support.

Thanks are also due to Professor Stanley Porter, editor of the JSNT Supplement Series, and to the staff of Sheffield Academic Press for their assistance during the publication process. A number of important works on the Epistle of James have been published in the time between the completion of the doctoral thesis on which this book is based and the publication of the book itself. I have endeavoured to make due recognition of such works in the revision of my own text, but inevitably engagement with some of these works is a little more sparse than the treatment of books which were available to me during the whole period of my research.

Most of all, thanks are due to my family, whose support in many ways has been inestimable. My wife, Shuna Hutchinson Edgar, has lent considerable assistance in the preparation of this book. For this, as well as for the profound personal enrichment her love and inspiration bring to my life, I am most grateful. Particular mention must also be made of my parents, Louise Edgar and the late Robert Edgar, who from an early age encouraged (and funded) me in the love of learning, without which this work could not have been undertaken. To them this book is dedicated in gratitude.

ABBREVIATIONS

ABD	David Noel Freedman (ed.), *The Anchor Bible Dictionary* (New York: Doubleday, 1992)
ACNT	Augsburg Commentary on the New Testament
ANRW	Hildegard Temporini and Wolfgang Haase (eds.), *Aufstieg und Niedergang der römischen Welt: Geschichte und Kultur Roms im Spiegel der neueren Forschung* (Berlin: de Gruyter, 1972–)
Bib	*Biblica*
BN	*Biblische Notizen*
BTB	*Biblical Theology Bulletin*
BZ	*Biblische Zeitschrift*
BZNW	Beihefte zur *ZNW*
CBQ	*Catholic Biblical Quarterly*
CNT	Commentaire du Nouveau Testament
ConBNT	Coniectanea Biblica, New Testament
CRINT	Compendia rerum iudaicarum ad Novum Testamentum
EvQ	*Evangelical Quarterly*
EvT	*Evangelische Theologie*
ExpTim	*Expository Times*
FzB	Forschung zur Bibel
HTKNT	Herders theologischer Kommentar zum Neuen Testament
HTR	*Harvard Theological Review*
IB	*Interpreter's Bible*
ICC	International Critical Commentary
IDB	George Arthur Buttrick (ed.), *Interpreter's Dictionary of the Bible* (4 vols.; Nashville, Abingdon Press, 1962)
IDBSup	*IDB*, Supplementary Volume
Int	*Interpretation*
JBL	*Journal of Biblical Literature*
JSNT	*Journal for the Study of the New Testament*
JSNTSup	*Journal for the Study of the New Testament*, Supplement Series
JTS	*Journal of Theological Studies*
LB	*Linguistica biblica*
Neot	*Neotestamentica*
NICNT	New International Commentary on the New Testament
NIGTC	The New International Greek Testament Commentary

NovT	*Novum Testamentum*
NovTSup	*Novum Testamentum*, Supplements
NTD	Das Neue Testament Deutsch
NTOA	Novum Testamentum et orbis antiquus
NTS	*New Testament Studies*
OTP	James H. Charlesworth (ed.), *The Old Testament Pseudepigrapha* (2 vols.; New York: Doubleday, 1983)
PTMS	Pittsburgh Theological Monograph Series
RHR	*Revue de l'histoire des religions*
RTP	*Revue de théologie et de philosophie*
SBLDS	Society of Biblical Literature Dissertation Series
SBLSP	*Society of Biblical Literature Seminar Papers*
SBT	Studies in Biblical Theology
SE	*Studia Evangelica* I, II, III (= TU 73 [1959], 87 [1964], 88 [1964])
SNTSMS	Society for New Testament Studies Monograph Series
SNTU	Studien zum Neuen Testament und seiner Umwelt
ST	*Studia theologica*
TDNT	Gerhard Kittel and Gerhard Friedrich (eds.), *Theological Dictionary of the New Testament* (trans. Geoffrey W. Bromiley; 10 vols.; Grand Rapids: Eerdmans, 1964–)
TGl	*Theologie und Glaube*
TLZ	*Theologische Literaturzeitung*
TRE	*Theologische Realenzyklopädie*
TU	Texte und Untersuchungen
TynBul	*Tyndale Bulletin*
TZ	*Theologische Zeitschrift*
WBC	Word Biblical Commentary
WMANT	Wissentschaftliche Monographien zum Alten und Neuen Testament
WUNT	Wissentschaftliche Untersuchungen zum Neuen Testament
ZNW	*Zeitschrift für die neutestamentliche Wissenschaft*
ZTK	*Zeitschrift für Theologie und Kirche*

INTRODUCTION

The Epistle of James has suffered more than most New Testament writings, over the centuries, at the hands of its interpreters, whose disposition has frequently tended in a somewhat deprecatory direction. As late as the fourth century, the epistle was listed by Eusebius among those texts whose canonicity was disputed.[1] Even modern critical scholarship (which will be analysed in detail below) has seldom engaged itself in unambiguously expounding the virtues of this epistle: 'The epistle of James is an enigmatic writing'[2] and 'The epistle of James is an oddity'.[3] But the Epistle of James does not deserve such a reputation as the black sheep within the fold of early Christian writings. Rather, as the present work will show, this document not only fits coherently within the diverse and dynamic world of emergent Christianity, but is worthy of being treated as an equal in importance, both historically and theologically, to its more usually favoured companions among the New Testament texts.

That is not to say that the Epistle of James does not pose distinct interpretative problems. The proposed scholarly solutions to basic questions such as literary form, purpose and original setting have certainly not been characterised by much agreement. For instance, it has been suggested that the epistle originated in such various locations as Jerusalem,[4] Rome,[5] Alexandria,[6] Antioch,[7] Syria-Palestine (for instance,

1. Eusebius, *Eccl. Hist.* 2.23.24-25; 3.25.3.
2. P.J. Hartin, *James and the Q Sayings of Jesus* (JSNTSup, 47; Sheffield: JSOT Press, 1991), p. 12.
3. S. Laws, *A Commentary on the Epistle of James* (London: A. & C. Black, 1980), p. 1.
4. F. Mussner, *Der Jakobusbrief* (HTKNT, 13.1; Freiburg: Herder Verlag, 5th edn, 1987), p. 23.
5. Laws, *James*, pp. 25-26.
6. R. Hoppe, *Jakobusbrief* (Stuttgarter Kleiner Kommentar zum Neuen Testament, 15; Stuttgart: Katholisches Bibelwerk, 1989), p. 14.
7. R.P. Martin, *James* (WBC, 48; Waco, TX: Word Books, 1988), pp. lxxvi -lxxvii.

Caesarea),[8] Galilee,[9] or anywhere in the Greek-speaking Jewish Diaspora, with a more precise location not discernible.[10]

This is partly due to the nature of the text itself, as there are naturally issues which cannot be answered conclusively from the relatively sparse amount of information which any document of only 108 verses contains. Some of the apparent difficulty in interpreting James satisfactorily also lies in the influence of interpretative methods and presuppositions which are insufficiently nuanced in vital aspects of their literary, cultural and historical dimensions to be able to provide an adequate framework for the answering of these questions. The brevity of the epistle throws the finite abilities of scholars into all the more sharp relief by its apparent defiance of decisive definition.

The aim of this work is to re-examine the disputed question of the epistle's setting within the social world of emergent Christianity, in particular, through sociohistorical investigation of its context. The distinctive methodological presuppositions of the approach employed here, and the programme for this work, are set out in the final section of Chapter 1, below. To begin, however, a review of the principal scholarly approaches to the epistle is offered in Chapter 1. In this way, methodological presuppositions can be seen to emerge from dialogue with the strengths and weaknesses of previous approaches.

---

8.   J.H. Ropes, *A Critical and Exegetical Commentary on the Epistle of James* (ICC; Edinburgh: T. & T. Clark, 1916), pp. 48-49.

9.   L.E. Elliott-Binns, *Galilean Christianity* (SBT, 16; London: SCM Press, 1956), pp. 45-46.

10.   M. Dibelius, *James* (rev. H. Greeven; trans. M.A. Williams; Hermeneia; Philadelphia: Fortress Press, 11th edn, 1975), p. 47.

Chapter 1

APPROACHES TO THE INTERPRETATION OF THE EPISTLE OF JAMES

Approaches to the Epistle of James have tended to focus on certain key areas of investigation which, when resolved, provide the basis of the author's interpretative stance. These different focuses include stress on the literary form of the document, on the identity of its author, on its relationship to contemporary theological traditions and perspectives, and on the text's reflections of its social world. Each approach, while important, has its own strengths and weaknesses; these can now be examined in a brief review of the work of the most influential representatives of each perspective.[1]

1.1 The Form and Structure of the Epistle of James

Biblical interpretation in the first half of the twentieth century, dominated by the form-critical school, saw the importance of classifying texts in terms of literary form, in order to understand the function and setting of any particular text. Initial classification of James as a letter is supported by the opening verse, which bears the characteristic features of a conventional Greek letter opening: sender, address and greeting formula. A number of scholars, however, argued that this was merely a stylised formula, employed to give a semblance of epistolary form to an otherwise non-epistolary document.[2]

---

1.   For reviews of research on the Epistle of James, see in particular the lengthy analysis of T. Penner, *The Epistle of James and Eschatology* (JSNTSup, 121; Sheffield: Sheffield Academic Press, 1996), pp. 15-103. Cf. also W. Popkes, *Adressaten, Situation und Form des Jakobusbriefes* (Stuttgart: Katholisches Bibelwerk, 1986), pp. 9-49; P.H. Davids, 'The Epistle of James in Modern Discussion', *ANRW* 2.25.5, pp. 3621-45; R.B. Edwards, 'Which Is the Best Commentary? The Epistle of James', *ExpTim* 103 (1992), pp. 263-68; H. Paulsen, 'Jakobusbrief', *TRE*, XVI, pp. 488-95.
2.   See, e.g., Ropes, *James*, pp. 6-15; Dibelius, *James*, pp. 1-3.

1.1.1 *The Epistle of James as a Diatribe*

Ropes proposed that the Epistle of James should be classified as a diatribe, a form of popular Hellenistic moral discourse, used in particular by Cynic and Stoic preachers and philosophers, drawing abundant parallels between the Epistle of James and the characteristics of the diatribe style.[3] There are, however, problems with assigning this text to this literary type. The epistle also exhibits significant differences from many of the preserved Graeco-Roman diatribes.[4] Many of the stylistic features which Ropes cites as examples of this style are not exclusive to the diatribe. Instances of such characteristics as quotation, rhetorical questions, analogy and comparison can easily be adduced from other types of literature. Ropes's argument is based upon the cumulative effect of single parallels, and does not present an argument for viewing the text *as a whole* as a diatribe. Thus, for instance, while the principal trait of the entire diatribe was its dialogue character, this is not a strong feature in the Epistle of James, where the mood is far more peremptory. Certainly, many common features of the Hellenistic moral address can be discerned, but they do not mark the whole text so thoroughly as to justify this designation as the document's literary type.

1.1.2 *The Epistle of James as Paraenesis*

Of decidedly greater significance and influence is Dibelius's denotation of the textual character of the Epistle of James. In his view, the text consists of a collection of diverse sayings, lacking any clear thematic unity throughout the 'epistle', with three slightly larger, but also unrelated, diatribe-like treatises at the centre of the composition (2.1-12; 2.14-26; 3.1-12). Essentially, the document is an almost random assortment of largely traditional exhortations and instructions, which reflect both Jewish and Hellenistic Christian piety, and which can be classified as paraenesis.[5] He cites four basic, related features of paraenetic literature which he finds present in the Epistle of James, namely, eclecticism, lack of continuity, repetition and the general rather than specific applicability of the admonitions.

There are several further consequences of this classification.[6] Due to the eclectic, traditional and thematically discontinuous nature of

---

3. Ropes, *James*, pp. 9-10.
4. Ropes, *James*, pp. 15-16.
5. Dibelius, *James*, pp. 1-11.
6. Dibelius, *James*, pp. 21-34, 45-47.

paraenesis, the Epistle of James cannot be said to disclose any distinctive theological standpoint; authorial individuality is largely indiscernible. Because of the traditional quality of the admonitions, little can be said of the environment of the author or of an occasion giving rise to the text. At most, the Epistle of James represents the piety of a Christian, ethically-oriented, Hellenistic Judaism ('liberated diaspora Judaism'[7]); nothing more can be adduced about the origins of the text, apart from the general compiling of a collection of exhortations.

Since its first publication in 1920, Dibelius's commentary has been extremely influential.[8] He is obviously correct in noting that the Epistle of James consists largely of moral exhortations and that the text is composed in a rather aphoristic style, with a preference for short, pointed sentences. Nevertheless, there are fundamental difficulties with his position, especially in the light of methodological developments beyond form criticism.

First, the nature of the so-called paraenetic texts, with which Dibelius parallels the text, is problematic. In view of the conspicuous dissimilarities between such texts as the Pastoral Epistles, the sayings of Jesus, portions of Tobit, Hebrews and the Pauline Epistles, Hermas and *Pseudo-Phocylides*, 'paraenesis' must be seen as a rather vague and

7. Dibelius, *James*, p. 43 (citing Bousset).

8. Among longer works on the Epistle of James, W. Schrage, 'Der Jakobusbrief', in W. Schrage and H. Balz, *Die katholischen Briefe* (NTD, 10; Göttingen: Vandenhoeck & Ruprecht, 1973), pp. 5-58, and R.A. Martin, 'James', in R.A. Martin and J.H. Elliott, *James, 1 and 2 Peter, Jude* (ACNT; Minneapolis: Augsburg, 1982), pp. 7-51, stand particularly close to Dibelius. His views are frequently recounted with blanket acceptance; see, e.g., V.P. Furnish, *The Love Command in the New Testament* (London: SCM Press, 1973), pp. 175-82; N. Perrin and D.C. Duling, *The New Testament: An Introduction* (New York: Harcourt, Brace, Jovanovich, 1982), pp. 372-75; W.G. Kümmel, *Introduction to the New Testament* (London: SCM Press, 1966), pp. 284-92. Even scholars who depart from other aspects of Dibelius's analysis often accept his formal analysis as their own starting point; see, e.g., K.-G. Eckart, 'Zur Terminologie des Jakobusbriefes', *TLZ* 89 (1964), cols. 521-26; J.-L. Blondel, 'Le fondement théologique de la parénèse dans l'épître de Jacques', *RTP* 111 (1979), pp. 141-52; B.S. Easton, 'James', *IB* XII, pp. 3-74 (18): 'extraordinarily informative, especially and uniquely as regards the literary form of the epistle'. Interestingly, F. Mussner has revised his earlier view, influenced by Dibelius, of the epistle as paraenesis with no clear thematic unity; see F. Mussner, 'Die ethische Motivation im Jakobusbrief', in H. Merklein (ed.), *Neues Testament und Ethik* (Freiburg: Herder, 1989), pp. 416-23 (420-23), in contrast with Mussner, *Jakobusbrief*, pp. 58-59.

general term. As such, its usefulness as a designation of literary genre becomes questionable. This becomes all the more clear when one supplements the form-critical examination of basic textual units with a redaction-critical view of the composition of the whole text.

Second, the language of the Epistle of James does not support the portrayal of an author whose role in the composition of the text is unimportant. The text is written in a uniform level of good quality Greek. Certainly differences in rhetorical style are evident between various sections of the epistle, but the quality of the language is consistent throughout. That the author of the Epistle of James was so fastidious as to allow only traditions which reached a certain linguistic standard entry into the compilation is hardly a convincing suggestion. If, however, the Greek text was written or redacted by its author, and represents, at least on the surface, the author's linguistic expression, then it clearly raises the question as to whether the Epistle of James is really as discontinuous in other respects as Dibelius argued.

Thus, third, Dibelius's depiction of the Epistle of James as lacking structural coherence (apart from the use of 'catchwords') can be called into question. There is a degree of circularity about his arguments in this respect: the characteristics of paraenetic literature are lack of continuity in thought and the repetition of identical motifs at different places within the writing. Each of these features serves to justify the other. Thus, because the Epistle of James is a paraenetic text, and lacks continuity in thought, the recurrence of an already-mentioned theme *must* represent the random repetition of the same traditional motif. Vice versa, because it is a paraenetic text, and the repetition of identical motifs is a feature of such texts, the recurrence of the same theme in the Epistle of James illustrates its lack of continuity in thought. These features of paraenetic literature rule out a priori the reprise and development of the the same themes within the whole text.

Fourth, Dibelius's assertion that the Epistle of James is of general applicability, rather than addressed to any specific situation can also be shown to be arbitrary. Even interpreters who wish to retain the term 'paraenesis' in relation to the text's literary type frequently renounce this ban on the discernment of a possible life-situation for the document.[9] Inasmuch as certain themes are clearly of importance for the

---

9.   Cf., e.g., Mussner, *Jakobusbrief*, pp. 22-24; Hoppe, *Jakobusbrief*, p. 12; Hartin, *James*, pp. 20-21; L.G. Perdue, 'Paraenesis and the Epistle of James', *ZNW* 72 (1981), pp. 241-56.

author, it is legitimate to see these as reflecting the situation of origin of the epistle and the environment of the author and/or the addressees.

In the end, the classification of the Epistle of James as paraenesis is unsatisfactory. The text does not meet the criteria, which, according to Dibelius, are characteristic of paraenetic literature. In fact, the term 'paraenesis', as demonstrated by its supposed representatives, is too vague to function effectively as a definite *genre;* rather, it could, at best, serve to describe the *function* of certain texts, that is, as 'general exhortations of an ethical or practical nature'.[10]

1.1.3 *The Epistle of James as a Letter*

The other important designation of the literary genre of James is that of letter.[11] Obviously, such a classification involves a rejection of the arguments of Ropes and Dibelius against the presence of epistolary characteristics in the Epistle of James. Francis reassesses the possibility that this text may indeed show features of epistolary convention, with particular attention to the opening and closing paragraphs. An examination of several letters presented in the works of Josephus and Eupolemus, the letter of Demetrius in 1 Macc. 10.25-45, the Pauline Epistles and a number of Hellenistic papyrus letters displays a common feature in the use of a doubled opening statement, introduced by a thanksgiving/rejoicing/blessing formula, which also raises and restates the significant themes of the letter. His analysis finds the Epistle of James compatible with this, seeing Jas 1.2-11 and 1.12-25 as 'carefully balanced thematic statements' which introduce 'main argumentative interests of the epistle'.[12]

The closing paragraph of the Epistle of James also displays epistolary features: restatement of themes (5.7-11), which, coupled with eschatological exhortation, forms a common element in much early Christian epistolary literature. Further, Francis points out that the phrase, 'above

---

10. D. Schroeder, 'Paraenesis', *IDBSup*, p. 643 (who does not refer to paraenesis as a genre). W. Popkes, 'James and Paraenesis, Reconsidered', in T. Fornberg and D. Hellholm (eds.), *Texts and Contexts: Biblical Texts in their Textual and Situational Contexts* (Festschrift Lars Hartmann; Oslo: Scandinavian University Press, 1995), pp. 535-61, also rejects Dibelius's generic use of the term, in favour of a functional definition.

11. F.O. Francis, 'The Form and Function of the Opening and Closing Paragraphs of James and 1 John', *ZNW* 61 (1970), pp. 110-26.

12. Francis, 'Form', p. 118.

all' (πρὸ πάντων), followed by a health wish, or an oath formula, are frequent characteristics of Hellenistic epistolary endings. Thus, 5.12 opens with πρὸ πάντων, followed by a prohibition of oaths, and reference to the health of the recipients (5.13-16). Concern with prayer (5.15-18) is also a common aspect of the conclusion of early Christian letters.[13]

The strength of Francis's presentation is that it puts forward the feasibility of viewing the text as a structurally integrated whole. His examination of similar features in other letters shows that the Epistle of James can be seen to reflect accepted epistolary convention. The fact that many of the parallels examined by Francis derive from a Hellenistic Jewish cultural milieu (Maccabees, Josephus, Eupolemus, Paul) shows that this convention would have been culturally accessible to the author of this text. A number of weaknesses are also evident in Francis's exposition. While he analyses in detail the form of the opening and closing paragraphs, he does not examine thoroughly the structural or thematic development of the main body of the letter.[14] Also, his analysis is purely formal and, while arguing plausibly that the Epistle of James can be seen as a letter form, he does not provide any explanation of the relationship between the letter form of text, and the character of its contents. Specifically, he does not explain the framing of so much hortatory material in a letter, or the relative lack of personal details, which might have been expected in a letter.

1.1.4 *Summary*
The external structure of the Epistle of James has been portrayed in widely differing terms, which range from a minimally-related assembly of traditional exhortations to a carefully structured whole, comprising exhortation within the overall form of a letter. Of these presentations, the depiction of the text as an integrated unity raises less problems, particularly as this unity can be seen in terms of the form which the text, through its epistolary greeting, explicitly claims for itself.

13. Francis, 'Form', pp. 124-26.
14. The contents of the body of the letter occupy just two pages of his work, pp. 118-20. It is clear from the title of the essay that the focus of attention is the opening and closing sections of the text; nevertheless, it remains a weakness that the presentation of Jas 2.1–5.6 is not grounded in the same kind of detailed analysis.

1.2 *The Author of the Epistle of James*

The association of a given text with a specific figure within the early Christian movement provides supplementary information as to its possible date, location and circumstances of origin, based on our knowledge of that figure from other sources. This has the obvious advantage of allowing the text to be relatively easily assigned to a particular position within the history of early Christianity, and understood in this context. Thus, the identification of the author of the Epistle of James has frequently offered a decisive starting point for the examination of the text.[15] Essentially, there has only been one candidate for the role of author as a decisive interpretative factor in relation to the Epistle of James; the discussion has centred on whether or not the epistle derives from James, 'the brother of the Lord',[16] mentioned as an influential figure in the early Christian community in Jerusalem by Paul (Gal. 1.19; 2.9, 12; 1 Cor. 15.7), and by the author of Acts (Acts 15.13; 21.18), and of whose martyrdom a sympathetic account is provided by Josephus.[17] The attribution of the epistle to James, the brother of the Lord, has traditionally been the dominant view, particularly since Jerome (who also identified this James with James the son of Alphaeus, one of the twelve [Mt. 10.3; Mk 3.18; (and 2.14, codices D and Q); Lk. 6.15; Acts 1.13]). Obviously, for those who reject the possiblity of authorship by this 'historical' James, opting rather for pseudonymous authorship, the actual identity of the author is not a decisive interpretative consideration, although it does raise other questions about the particular trajectory within early Christianity with which the pseudonymous author of the Epistle of James wishes to identify himself.

---

15. A summary of the major historical positions is provided by P.H. Davids, *The Epistle of James: A Commentary on the Greek Text* (NIGTC; Exeter: Paternoster Press, 1982), pp. 2-5.

16. For accounts of James, the brother of the Lord, see especially W. Pratscher, *Der Herrenbruder Jakobus und die Jakobustradition* (Göttingen: Vandenhoeck & Ruprecht, 1987); on the epistle of James, which he holds to be pseudepigraphical, see pp. 209-21. Cf. also R.P. Martin, *James*, pp. xxi-lxvii; M. Hengel, 'Jakobus der Herrenbruder—der erste Papst?', in E. Grässer and O. Merk (eds.), *Glaube und Eschatologie* (Festschrift W.G. Kümmel; Tübingen: J.C.B. Mohr [Paul Siebeck], 1985), pp. 71-104; W. Pratscher, 'Der Standort des Herrenbruders Jakobus im theologischen Spektrum der frühen Kirche', *SNTU* (Series A) 15 (1990), pp. 41-58.

17. Josephus, *Ant.* 20.197-203.

The decisive considerations in favour of seeing the author as James, the brother of the Lord, are summarised most clearly by Mussner in the appendix to the third edition of his commentary.[18] None of these considerations, however, provides compelling evidence for the authorship of the document specifically by James, the brother of the Lord. Rather, they represent reasons why this possibility need not be rejected. Given that there is no conclusive argument in favour of seeing the epistle as a pseudonymous document, dating from the end of the first century, rather than before the death of James, the brother of the Lord, in the year 62 CE, the identification of this James as the author still rests on the assumption that if it is not impossible to envisage him as the author, then it is preferable to maintain this traditional view.

A number of further problems remain. Although the document can be assigned to a date within the lifetime of James, the brother of the Lord, it does not follow that, because he is the most influential figure of this name known to us, it should be attributed to him. In fact, it is difficult to discern a clear picture of James. Certainly, his authority was recognised by Paul (1 Cor. 15; Gal. 2), but while on the one hand, he appears to have accepted Paul's Gentile mission (Gal. 2.9), on the other hand, those associated with him seem to represent stricter Jewish observance (Gal. 2.12). Josephus commends him as an observant Jew, and this portrayal is borne out by the account, clearly with legendary embellishments, preserved from Hegesippus by Eusebius.[19] Acts suggests a moderating figure (Acts 15, 21), but this depiction by the author of Luke–Acts may reflect a desire to display a highly unitary early Christianity. About as much as can be said with certainty is that James was an observant Jew, and an important leader of the early Christian community in Jerusalem. In the end, it cannot be asserted with confidence that the Epistle of James would have been the kind of text which James, the brother of the Lord, 'bishop' of Jerusalem, would have written.

Further, the history of the reception of the Epistle of James in the early church argues against the authorship of the brother of the Lord. Had the epistle been unequivocally associated with this key figure, it seems unlikely that it would have met such reluctant recognition as is

18. See Mussner, *Jakobusbrief,* pp. 237-40 (also pp. 1-11); F.J.A. Hort, *The Epistle of St. James* (London: Macmillan, 1909), pp. xi-xxii; and, at great length, J.B. Mayor, *The Epistle of St. James* (London: Macmillan, 1913), pp. i-lxv.

19. Eusebius, *Hist. Eccl.* 2.23.

witnessed by the comments of Eusebius, as late as the fourth century.[20] In the absence of any more definite link with James, the brother of the Lord, to use his authorship of the epistle as a starting point in the interpretation of the text seems too tendentious to be satisfactory, in spite of Mussner's clear and balanced arguments in favour of the traditional view. Certainly, to go so far as to speak of 'the home bond between James and Jesus' as an influential factor in the shaping of the epistle, as Adamson does, is unwarranted.[21]

An adaptation of the traditional position, which attributes the document to James, the brother of the Lord, has been put forward by scholars such as Martin and Davids. This view argues for a two-stage compositional process, ultimately deriving from the teaching of James, the brother of the Lord, of which certain traditions were collected and edited at a later stage to form our epistle.[22] According to Martin, this compilation was produced in Antioch, after the death of James, and the dispersal of his disciples from Jerusalem.[23] This two-stage theory offers a solution to two objections to direct authorship by James, the brother of the Lord: first, the argument that James would have been unable to write Greek of the quality of that in the epistle; second, the argument that James appears to be a collection of traditional materials.

In spite of its ingenuity, this suggestion of authorship deriving from, rather than directly by James, the brother of the Lord, is highly problematic. Its basic assumption appears to be the desirability of maintaining the insubstantiable link between the epistle and the figure of James, the brother of the Lord. To do this, an even more insubstantiable transmission and compilation process is proposed. The hypothesis is too speculative and lacking in evidence to be satisfactory.

Neither of the positions which take the identity of the author as the fundamental interpretative key for the epistle can be seen to rest on conclusive evidence in favour of this identification. It is impossible to establish whether or not the epistle originated from James, the brother

---

20. Eusebius, *Hist. Eccl.* 2.23.25; 3.25.3.

21. J.B. Adamson, *The Epistle of James* (NICNT; Grand Rapids: Eerdmanns, 1976), p. 18.

22. See Davids, *James*, p. 12.

23. R.P. Martin, *James*, p. lxxvi; cf. *idem*, 'The Life-Setting of the Epistle of James in the Light of Jewish History', in G.A. Tuttle (ed.), *Biblical and Near Eastern Studies* (Festschrift W.S. LaSor; Grand Rapids: Eerdmans, 1978), pp. 97-103 (102-103).

of the Lord. In this case, it is preferable simply to leave the question open, rather than run the risk of allowing excessive interpretative influence to such a tendentious consideration as authorship is in relation to the Epistle of James. That is not to say that questions of authorship are entirely to be neglected; further investigations relating, not to the explicit identity of the author, but rather to the implied role of the author within the text and its social world will be examined below.[24]

1.3 *History of Traditions*

A further means of locating the interpretative key to the Epistle of James has been the investigation of connections between the epistle and conceptual or theological traditions current in Judaism. The establishment of such links to a defined tradition of thought provides the ideational background against which the expression of the Epistle of James becomes most easily understandable.

1.3.1 *The Epistle of James and the Wisdom Tradition*

The importance of the contacts between the Epistle of James and the well-developed Jewish theological tradition of wisdom has been asserted frequently, most strongly by U. Luck[25] and R. Hoppe.[26] This tradition is generally seen as represented by those works which portray the order of creation and of human behaviour through the concept of wisdom—so, for example, Proverbs, Ecclesiastes, the Wisdom of Solomon and Sirach. The possession of God's wisdom enables human conduct in accordance with God's demands; most explicitly, in Sirach, this wisdom is closely identified with the Jewish Law (Sir. 24). Particularly important are passages in the epistle where wisdom is explicitly mentioned, in terms similar to those of the 'wisdom literature': Jas 1.2-18//Sir. 2.1-18//Wis. 6.12-21; Jas 3.13-18//Wis. 7.22-30.

The specific strength of both Hoppe's and Luck's presentations is that they establish firm connections between the Epistle of James and

---

24. See below, Chapter 2; following the analysis of the text, a verdict on the possible identity of the author is offered in Chapter 7, §7.3.1.

25. U. Luck, 'Weisheit und Leiden: Zum Problem Paulus und Jakobus', *TLZ* 92 (1967), cols. 253-58; *idem*, 'Der Jakobusbrief und die Theologie des Paulus', *TGl* 61 (1971), pp. 161-79; *idem*, 'Die Theologie des Jakobusbriefes', *ZTK* 81 (1984), pp. 1-30.

26. R. Hoppe, *Der theologische Hintergrund des Jakobusbriefes* (FzB, 28; Würzburg: Echter Verlag, 1977).

its Jewish theological conceptual background. To interpret the text against such a conceptual background allows it to be viewed within a broad frame of reference, which can both clarify specific ambiguities of the text itself and make possible the comparison of the text with other texts, which may be viewed on a similar basis, hence Hoppe's comparison of the epistle with the synoptic gospel traditions,[27] and Luck's examination of the relationship between the Epistle of James and the works of Paul.[28]

A number of difficulties should also be mentioned. That such different texts as Proverbs, *1 Enoch*, the Qumran literature and the early Christian texts are working with a uniform concept of wisdom is belied by even a surface comparison of these texts. Indeed, significant differences can be noted even between the roles attributed to wisdom in Sirach and in the Wisdom of Solomon. To treat these as if they comprised a single, undifferentiated trajectory is methodologically imprecise. That is not, of course, to deny that wisdom is an important theological concept in Judaism, and or that it is a significant expression within the Epistle of James, but too simplistic a view of this 'wisdom tradition' may provide only a blurred background against which to view the text.[29]

Second, the intensity with which the governing role of wisdom is identified in those sections of the text which are deemed to be important, is suspect. In fact, wisdom (σοφία) is mentioned in only two passages, Jas 1.5 and 3.13-17, but is traced through a network of 'catchwords' into other passages. So, 'the wisdom from above' (ἄνωθεν) in 3.17 is equivalent to 'every perfect gift from above' (ἄνωθεν) in 1.17, which is further equivalent to the 'word of truth' (λόγος ἀληθείας) in 1.18 and to the 'implanted word' (ἔμφυτος λόγος) in 1.21, and so on.[30] When this connection with wisdom is established through the paralleling of phrases from other early Christian documents, the procedure is even more problematic, as it would seem to presuppose an unacceptably

---

27. Hoppe, *Hintergrund*, pp. 119-45.

28. Luck, 'Jakobusbrief', pp. 176-79; 'Theologie', pp. 20-30.

29. On the diversity of wisdom traditions in Judaism at this time, see M. Hengel, *Judaism and Hellenism: Studies in their Encounter in Palestine during the Early Hellenistic Period*, I (London: SCM Press, 1974), pp. 206-207; on the pervasive presence of the 'wisdom' in virtually all Jewish writings, see J.L. McKenzie, 'Reflections on Wisdom', *JBL* 86 (1967), pp. 1-9.

30. Hoppe, *Hintergrund*, pp. 50-51.

static understanding of semantics. Thus, for example, the fact that Paul uses the phrase 'Lord of glory' (κύριος τῆς δόξης) in his depiction of Jesus Christ as the wisdom of God in 1 Cor. 2.6-9 cannot be used to argue that the author of the Epistle of James does the same thing.[31]

Third, the identification of wisdom as the conceptual key to the epistle within the framework of Jewish theological tradition involves a stress on certain sections of the text which are most amenable to this interpretation, most noticeably Jas 3.13-18 (wisdom from above), 1.2-12 (wisdom, faith and endurance in testing), 1.17-25 (implanted word/word of truth = baptism = saving wisdom), and 2.14-26 (faith perfected in works = wisdom). This means that very substantial portions of the text are relegated to a subsidiary position for the understanding of the whole text. According to Hoppe, this is because they contain largely traditional materials and do not significantly illustrate the author's theological perspective.[32] He also sees 1.2-12 as largely traditional, but finds this passage very useful in his examination of the author's viewpoint. This procedure suggests that Hoppe is working with an interpretative axiom which simply brackets out all those sections of the text which do not immediately lend support to his arguments as 'traditional', and therefore not demanding much interpretative attention. Even if these elements are traditional, that, in itself, is not a valid reason to ignore them. A comprehensive and adequate understanding of the epistle must surely involve examination of the whole text, and not just those parts of it which suit a particular viewpoint.

In the end, it must be accepted that wisdom is an important concept in the Epistle of James, and that the most immediate context in which this should be viewed is that of Jewish belief. Yet, while wisdom is indeed a significant motif in the Epistle of James, it is not the only theme, and also not the all-controlling question of the epistle.[33]

1.3.2 *The Epistle of James and Sirach*
The close relation of the Epistle of James to Jewish writings in which the theme of wisdom is particularly important is given further explica-

---

31. Hoppe, *Hintergrund*, pp. 75-78; Luck, 'Theologie', p. 22.

32. Hoppe, *Hintergrund*, pp. 2-17.

33. Cf. the criticism of Luck and Hoppe in E. Baasland, 'Der Jakobusbrief als neutestamentliche Weisheitsschrift', *ST* 36 (1982), pp. 119-39 (136 n. 21); also H. von Lips, *Weisheitliche Traditionen im Neuen Testament* (WMANT, 64; Neukirchen–Vluyn: Neukirchener Verlag, 1990), p. 437.

tion by H. Frankemölle, who believes the epistle to be rooted in the reception of Sirach within early Christianity. Although the thematic unity of the text is first of all established on the basis of the internal analysis of the epistle itself,[34] the key themes of the epistle are to be traced to the author's reception and reworking of Sirach. This dependence is established, according to Frankemölle, through a comparison of the significant number of keywords which occur in the opening section of the text, Jas 1.2-18, with other Jewish and early Christian writings; the greatest frequency of parallels occurs in relation to Sir. 2.1-18 and 15.11-20.[35] These include testing (πειρασμοί, Sir. 2.1), being proved worthy (δοκιμάζομαι, Sir. 2.5), patience (ὑπομονή, Sir. 2.14), faith (πιστεύω, Sir. 2.6, 8, 13), lowliness (ταπείνωσις, Sir. 2.4, 5) reward (μισθός, Sir. 2.8), God as creator (Sir. 15.14), deception (πλανάω, Sir. 15.12), sin (ἁμαρτωλός, Sir. 15.12; ἁμαρτάνω, 15.20), death (θάνατος, Sir. 15.17), and deeds (ἔργον, Sir. 15.19).[36] It is furthermore striking that both the author of the Epistle of James and Sirach highlight the central theme of patience under testing at the start of their texts, in Jas 1.2-18 and in Sir. 2.1-18.

While these parallels between the Epistle of James and Sirach are striking, the conclusion that the author is thereby directly dependent on Sirach remains problematic. First, all the instances cited by Frankemölle constitute parallels of a single word, or of a combination of concepts; there are no clear examples of a closer verbal correspondence between the two texts. In view of the author's ability both to quote the LXX (cf. Jas 2.8; 2.23; 4.6) and to echo both the LXX and the traditions of the sayings of Jesus, this lack of direct allusion to the text of Sirach is remarkable, if it really was as fundamental to the composition of the text as Frankemölle suggests.[37] Second, while the theme of patience under testing is a key theme in the Epistle of James, this concern is secondary in Sirach, where it occurs not at the start of the

34. H. Frankemölle, *Der Brief des Jakobus* (Ökumenischer Taschenbuch Kommentar zum Neuen Testament, 17; Gütersloh: Gütersloher Verlagshaus, 1994), p. 196; *idem*, 'Zum Thema des Jakobusbriefes im Kontext der Rezeption von Sir 2.1-18 und 15.11-20', *BN* 48 (1989), pp. 21-49 (35).

35. Frankemölle, *Jakobus*, pp. 190-94; *idem*, 'Thema', pp. 34-36.

36. See the table in Frankemölle, *Jakobus*, pp. 193-94; *idem*, 'Thema', p. 49.

37. It is also worth noting that the two key passages in Sir. 2.1-18 and 15.11-20, comprise 28 verses in all, which is considerably larger than any of the other texts which Frankemölle parallels to Jas 1.2-18.

text, but following the opening, and much more important, assertion that all wisdom comes from God (Sir. 1.1-30). Third, when viewed as an independent whole, there are crucial discrepancies in the basic outlook of the two writings. In particular, the strong sense of eschatological expectation which marks the Epistle of James is entirely lacking in Sirach. The idea of testing as the instruction of God's wisdom (Sir. 4.17) expresses an entirely different view of wisdom and testing to that of Jas 1.2-18. The dualistic view of the universe as hostility between allegiance to God and allegiance to the devil (Jas 3.15-17; 4.4, 7) is not only lacking, but is also consciously resisted by Sirach (e.g. Sir. 21.27). While points of contact certainly exist, such fundamental differences make it difficult to accept that the author of the Epistle of James is principally informed by Sirach. Fourth, in his insistence on the dependence of the Epistle of James on Sirach, Frankemölle at times lays extraneous stress on similarities with Sirach, when other traditions stand much closer to the concerns of James. Thus, for example, the parallels in Sirach to Jas 5.1-6[38] are of considerably less importance than the reception of prophetic traditions (cf. the allusion to Isa. 5.9 in Jas 5.4); in fact, it is questionable if there is any influence at all of Sirach in these verses. Thus, although it is clear that the Epistle of James draws extensively on Jewish traditions, Frankemölle's thesis that Sirach stands explicitly first among these traditions cannot be accepted.

1.3.3 The Epistle of James and Early Christian Tradition
Another channel in the investigation of the Epistle of James has been the examination of the links between this text and other texts from the emergent early Christian tradition. In this way, it is hoped to establish the theological setting and perspective of the text in relation to the immediate context in which it was shaped,[39] that is, the emergence of definitive self-expression, and of an authoritative tradition in the early Christian movement.

---

38. See Frankemölle, *Jakobus*, pp. 649-50, 654-55, 659-60.

39. A Jewish, pre-Christian origin, later interpolated with Christianizations, was proposed by F. Spitta, *Zur Geschichte und Literatur des Urchristentums* (Göttingen: Vandenhoeck & Ruprecht, 1896), and by L. Massebieau, 'L'Epître de Jacques, est-elle l'oeuvre d'un chrétien?', *RHR* 32 (1895), pp. 241-83. This proposal, however, has received very little scholarly acceptance. For an extensive refutation, see Mayor, *James*, pp. cxciii-ccv.

1.3.3.1 *The Synoptic Gospels.* In view of the the striking number of parallels which have been adduced between the Epistle of James and the synoptic gospels, it is clear that this relationship must be taken seriously in any evaluation of the epistle. Kittel listed some 26 correspondences between the text of the Epistle of James and the sayings of Jesus, none of which, taken singly, would provide substance for a convincing argument in favour of seeing an influential contact between the Epistle of James and these sayings traditions, but, when taken as a whole, these resonances are too frequent, and too consistent, to be satisfactorily explained in any other manner.[40] These points of contact are all in the nature of allusion, rather than direct quotation, which led Kittel to suggest circumstances of origin for the epistle prior to the framing of authoritative written traditions (such as the gospel texts) of the sayings of Jesus, which could be quoted as Scripture.[41]

A similar view is taken by L.E. Elliott-Binns, who proposes that these apparently close connections between the Epistle of James and the sayings of Jesus suggest that the epistle originated among the early Galilean Christian community, stressing the teaching of Jesus, with less interest in teaching about him or in the events of his life.[42] In recent years, the most extensive treatment of James along this line of approach is that of P.J. Hartin, in his examination of the Epistle of James and 'Q', the supposed sayings source, common to Matthew and Luke. Hartin stresses strongly the literary and theological character of both the Epistle of James and 'Q' as Jewish wisdom. His analysis of the textual relations between the Epistle of James and the reconstructed 'Q' text concludes that James knew the version of the 'Q' document which was further developed in the Matthean community and eventually incorporated into Matthew's Gospel (Q^{Mt}).[43]

While the relationship between the Epistle of James and the synoptic

40. G. Kittel, 'Der geschichtliche Ort des Jakobusbriefes', *ZNW* 41 (1942), pp. 71-105.

41. Kittel, 'Ort', pp. 91-94. The manner of allusion to dominical sayings was examined further, and contrasted with that of later Christian texts in a subsequent essay: G. Kittel 'Der Jakobusbrief und die apostolischen Väter', *ZNW* 43 (1950), pp. 54-112. Kittel, like most others who place importance on links with the sayings of Jesus, attributed the epistle to James, the brother of the Lord.

42. See Elliott-Binns, *Galilean Christianity*, pp. 45-49. Elliott-Binns believes that the attribution to James is secondary.

43. See Hartin, *James*; pp. 220-40 summarize his position on the development and relationship of the communities and texts.

gospels clearly must be taken seriously, a number of problems with the perspectives outlined above remain. The relationship between the epistle and the gospel traditions does not necessarily imply an early date for the epistle; if Mark, Matthew and Luke were written in the period 70–90 CE, and if more time is then allowed to elapse before they became 'Scripture', then the epistle could have been written at any time during, or prior to this period.

Hartin's arguments on the relations between 'Q', the Epistle of James and the Jewish conception of wisdom raise further problems. First, he works with a deceptively narrow view of the 'wisdom tradition', in which he sees the Epistle of James and 'Q' as rooted, and with an overstated presentation of the role of wisdom in James.[44] Second, his handling of the gospel traditions is problematic. His confident use of reconstructed hypothetical texts (as 'Q', and certainly the two further developed editions, 'Q^{Mt}' and 'Q^{Lk}', are), as if they were verified, extant, ancient sources (as the gospels are), is excessive. Third, some of his findings seem to rest as much on bias as on critical argument; for instance, the closeness of Jas 2.5 to Mt. 5.3, 5 is taken as evidence of the author's knowledge of 'Q^{Mt}', while the equivalent closeness of Jas 4.9 to Lk. 6.25 is taken to demonstrate that James did not know 'Q^{Lk}', although no argument is presented to show why this is so.[45]

1.3.3.2 *Subsequent Christian Writings.* In her commentary, Laws draws on similarities between the Epistle of James and the Shepherd of Hermas, written in Rome during the first half of the second century, as a key to placing the text within the context of the early Christian movement.[46] These similarities are mostly in the form of certain common concerns, and a common use of certain unusual words.

These contacts with Hermas, as well as similarities with 1 Peter and 1 Clement, lead Laws to conclude that the epistle is best seen as representing the Christianity of a Roman community, apparently towards the end of the first century. This, however, is problematic. While it does seem likely that the author of Hermas was familiar with the Epistle of James, he shows a markedly different perspective from this text in relation to certain important concerns, most strikingly in his far more

44. See the criticisms of a constricted identification of the Epistle of James with the wisdom tradition, above, §1.3.1.

45. Hartin, *James*, pp. 149-52.

46. Laws, *James*, pp. 22-26.

accomodating treatment of the rich (Hermas, *Sim.* 2). As this theme is particularly rooted in the exigencies of practical existence, it does not seem to indicate a shared social world, or, at least, a similar attitude to a possible shared social environment. Moreover, while Laws's view that a document is most likely to be known in its place of composition is not entirely inaccurate, the assumption that the Epistle of James should be interpreted as *originating* in Rome at the end of the first century, because it was known in this context, is unsatisfactory. The evidence for this is too tenuous.

This raises a general problem with using relationship to a particular conceptual tradition as the decisive consideration in settling upon an interpretative starting point. Certainly, texts will show specific conceptual affinities with each other. They draw on the resources of tradition, of existing shared understanding, in order to express meaning. As such, every text can be seen as part of an ongoing tradition. It is, however, insufficient to analyse a given text on the grounds of possible literary-conceptual relationships, as the text—and especially a text from the ancient world—represents not an exercise in abstract reflection or speculation about certain concepts, but an attempt to appropriate the traditional resources for meaning within a specific social context and environment, to which these concepts are now applied. Meaning is always expressed amid real-life situations, not in a social vacuum. Thus, any analysis of conceptual-theological correspondences must also take account of the particular social setting and circumstances towards which a particular tradition or concept is addressed, according to the manner in which it is taken up in a particular text.

1.3.4 *Summary*

The investigation of the connections between the Epistle of James and Jewish and/or early Christian conceptual traditions is a useful and essential aspect of the interpretation of the epistle. This process provides an entrance towards understanding the ideational background upon which the author of the epistle draws. Attempts to force the epistle into the framework of a narrow portrayal of a particular tradition (e.g. wisdom, as represented by Proverbs–Sirach–Wisdom—which themselves are quite different—without any attention to the importance of wisdom in apocalyptic literature) are, however, unsatisfactory. Further, an examination of concepts and literary expressions as abstractions, rather than as related to the precise circumstances of origin of the text, intrinsically rooted within a continually changing and developing social environment, yields an inadequate frame of reference for the understanding of the text.

1.4 *The Social Setting of the Epistle of James*

As the preceding comments have indicated, an evaluation of how the text fits into the setting in which it functioned as a piece of meaningful communication should play a significant role in the interpretation of a text like the Epistle of James.

1.4.1 *From Literary Type to Social Setting*
The designation of the Epistle of James as paraenesis is accepted by L.G. Perdue,[47] but with the modification to Dibelius's view that, while individual precepts are of general applicability, entire paraenetic texts (such as he believes the Epistle of James to be) do have social settings in which they originate and continue to be used.[48] He suggests that paraenesis forms a vital element of a rite of passage, involving the imparting or reiteration of norms from an experienced teacher to an inexperienced audience. A time of prospective separation of teacher from student—such as the impending death of the teacher—provides a common setting for such instruction, to the effect that the potential threat to the security of the audience posed by the teacher's departure/ death is overcome by the leaving of a 'bequest' of important teaching.[49]

While Perdue's work does put forward some interesting reflections on the social functions of ethical exhortation, there are difficulties in his move from literary type to social setting. Not least are the problems involved in seeing paraenesis as an actual genre, and in assigning the Epistle of James to this classification.[50] Furthermore, the manner in which he attempts to relate paraenetic texts in general to a certain type of life-setting is far too mechanical. The Epistle of James does not read very well as a 'bequest' of important teachings, given by a teacher to those from whom his separation, probably by death, is imminent. Further, the examples which underlie the choice of this life-setting are not

47. See Perdue, 'Paraenesis and James'.
48. L.G. Perdue, 'The Social Character of Paraenesis and Paraenetic Literature', *Semeia* 50 (1990), pp. 5-39.
49. Perdue, 'Paraenesis and James', pp. 247-51.
50. See above, §1.1.2.

convincing: Tobit 4 and 12 are firmly rooted within the book's fictitious narrative context; the *Testaments of the Twelve Patriarchs* are indeed presented as 'testaments', but this again is a literary fiction. It is not altogether plausible to suggest that Seneca decided to commit suicide, and then spent two years writing a 'bequest' in his letters to Lucilius. While it is plausible that a relation between literary type and social setting exists, neither the literary type nor the social setting, suggested for the Epistle of James by Perdue, is convincing.

1.4.2 *From Text to Social World*

The project of using the exegesis of passages within the text which contain indications of sociohistorical conditions, in order to relate the text to a general social context, is set out by Maynard-Reid,[51] who, however, stops short of an exhaustive analysis of these issues, choosing rather to confine himself to an examination of the theme of poverty and wealth in the Epistle of James.

Maynard-Reid concentrates his exegesis on four passages which explicitly mention the rich-poor theme: Jas 1.9-11; 2.1-13; 4.13-17; 5.1-6. His analysis demonstrates the deep concern of an early Christian leader (whom he believes to be James, the brother of the Lord) with issues of social justice as an indispensable dimension of true religious commitment, in accordance with God's 'option for the poor'. There are, however, two main problems with his work. First, his entire focus on the theme of poverty and wealth is one-sided. Certainly, this is an important issue in the epistle, but an examination of considerations other than economic ones would yield a more balanced overall picture. Second, in spite of his awareness of the cultural and social discontinuities between the first century and the present day, he at times makes too easy use of terms which derive more properly from modern economics, often in a value-laden manner, for instance, speaking of 'the exploitation of the urban capitalists'[52] of the poor.

1.4.3 *From Text to Community*

Another avenue of interpretation is to examine the assumptions about the kind of early Christian social group, which are either directly related, or implied, in the text of the epistle. From the nature of the

---

51. P. Maynard-Reid, *Poverty and Wealth in James* (Maryknoll, NY: Orbis Books, 1987), pp. 4-5.
52. Maynard-Reid, *Poverty*, p. 22.

epistle's injunctions, Burchard sees a basic ethical principle of brother-
liness, within a relatively egalitarian community situation.[53] The term
συναγωγή (2.2) indicates the community assembly, into which outsiders should be welcomed as equals, and in which care for the needs of
the poor should be undertaken.[54] The presence of well-to-do members
in the community is indicated in 4.13-17; they are exhorted not to self-
impoverishment, but to the doing of their affairs under the will of God,
which would thus include almsgiving.[55]

Burchard's conjectures about the characteristics of the community
which the Epistle of James presupposes illustrate usefully the extent to
which such social information can be found in the text, by contrast with
those interpreters (such as Dibelius) who argue that the epistle contains
little or no such information. More caution could be urged, however, in
relation to the force with which he appears to relate all possible indica-
tors of social circumstances to the life of the community. For instance,
it is not immediately apparent that 4.14-17 should be read to imply an
injunction to almsgiving within the community on the part of better-off
members.

An examination of both the implied social conditions and of the kind
of community suggested by the text is carried out by W. Popkes in his
work on the situation, addressees and form of the Epistle of James. For
him, although the addressees belong to a range of social backgrounds,
the most significant is an ambitious middle-ranking class.[56] The community problems attacked by the author bear a certain resemblance to
those faced by Paul, especially in 1 Corinthians: an apparently libertine
tendency, which exalted the value of a faith which is minimal in content
(Jas 2). Such a position, he argues, would be possible for a group like
the God-fearing Gentiles, associated with the Hellenistic mission in
Acts.[57] There is little indication of sacramental development, rather, the

53. C. Burchard, 'Gemeinde in der strohernen Epistel: Mutmassungen über
Jakobus', in D. Lührmann and G. Strecker (eds.), *Kirche* (Festschrift Günther
Bornkamm; Tübingen: J.C.B. Mohr [Paul Siebeck], 1980), pp. 315-28.

54. Burchard, 'Gemeinde', pp. 322-26.

55. Burchard, 'Gemeinde', pp. 326-28.

56. Popkes, *Adressaten*, p. 90; M. Sato, 'Wozu wurde der Jakobusbrief geschrieben?: eine mutmassliche Rekonstruktion', *Annual of the Japanese Biblical
Institute* 17 (1991), pp. 55-76 (63), also sees the majority of the text's addressees as
an economically ambitious middle class.

57. Popkes, *Adressaten*, pp. 53-91.

stress in the Epistle of James is on 'the word' (1.18-22), with a correspondingly important role for teachers (3.1)—a situation which, for Popkes, suggests the designation 'early protestantism'.[58]

There is, however, a number of problems with this depiction. First, the socio-economic portrayal of the community as middle class and socially upwardly mobile is too simplistic and anachronistic. Although the Hellenistic age was one of economic expansion, opportunities for social advancement, such as his description suggests, were exceptional rather than commonplace, and are much more typical of the modern, (post-)industrial economic system. Likewise, an ecclesial description of the epistle which sees it as representative of an 'early protestantism' simply interpolates an anachronistic designation into a context in which it is more confusing than clarificatory.

Second, the links he establishes with post-Pauline churches are tenuous. The author of the Epistle of James shows little, if any, explicit concern with the central condition of Paul's position—the death and resurrection of Jesus Christ. Faith, love, freedom, wisdom and so on are terms shared by Paul and the Epistle of James, but are certainly not unique to these two writers. Even in the much-discussed case of faith, works and justification (Jas 2.14-26) the terms do not appear to have a particularly Pauline nuance. Further, if one views the development of Pauline thought and community in the trajectory from the undisputed Pauline Epistles to the Pastoral Epistles, the problems which the Epistle of James is proposed to be addressing do not immediately emerge, except when this text is already inserted into this context to illustrate them.

1.4.4 *Summary*

The possibility of locating the Epistle of James within some sort of situational context, towards which the text's comments were directly addressed, is a necessary element in the understanding of the writing. Portrayal of the social context, however, should be appropriate to the first-century world and its culture, which was very different from contemporary society, both in its social organisation and its perceptions of reality. Care must also be taken not to derive social data too mechanically from the text. A sensitive approach to the way in which a text functioned as a piece of communication between author and addressees,

58. Popkes, *Adressaten*, p. 119.

within a particular situation, should yield a controlled appreciation of the manner in which the text encodes social and cultural information.

1.5 *Rhetorical Interpretation of the Epistle of James*

To examine a text from a rhetorical perspective involves looking at the manner in which the text is styled in order to communicate certain meaningful information within its social context.

1.5.1 *The Polemical Dimension of the Epistle of James*
The careful stylistic and compositional unity of the Epistle of James is the starting point for M. Hengel's attention to the polemical overtones of the epistle, which, in his view, forms a strikingly sharp attack on an unnamed opponent, to be identified as Paul.[59] Thus, the possible anti-Pauline tendency of 2.14-26 is indeed a direct attack on Paul's teaching of justification by faith. The 'traders' of 4.13-16 are not actual travelling merchants, of whom there is little evidence in Christian groups at this time. Instead, they form a figurative indictment of Paul's missionary strategy of travelling, like a merchant, on long, preplanned journeys (cf. Rom. 15.24) for the purpose of winning converts.[60] For this, he required the financial support—even if he did not demand such support, he accepted it when offered (cf. Phil. 4.10-20)—of well-to-do members of his communities; hence, the uncompromising censure of the rich (especially Jas 5.1-6).[61] Likewise, the warning about presumptuous teachers (3.1) thus falls into place as a reference to Paul.[62]

This interpretation has the advantage of seeing the epistle as a stylistically and conceptually unified whole, utilising conventional strategies for a particular purpose within a particular setting. Ultimately, however, Hengel's position requires more elasticity of evidence than it is judicious to accept.[63] This view of the epistle relies fundamentally on

59. M. Hengel, 'Der Jakobusbrief als antipaulinische Polemik', in O. Betz and G. Hawthorne (eds.), *Tradition and Interpretation in the New Testament* (Festschrift E. Earle Ellis; Grand Rapids: Eerdmans, 1987), pp. 248-78 (253).

60. Hengel, 'Polemik', pp. 255-59.

61. Hengel, 'Polemik', pp. 262-64.

62. Hengel, 'Polemik', pp. 260-61.

63. Virtually all commentaries deal with the question of the relation between the Epistle of James and Paul's activity and thought. See, e.g., Mussner, *Jakobusbrief*, pp. 12-19; Frankemölle, *Jakobus*, pp. 461-74. Particularly helpful are Baasland, 'Jakobusbrief', pp. 127-33; G. Boccaccini, *Middle Judaism: Jewish Thought 300*

seeing Jas 2.14-26 as a rejection of Paul's teaching of justification by faith. This, however, is not clearly so. Paul argued that justification by faith, without works of the Jewish Law, was possible (Rom. 3.28); the Epistle of James does not speak of works of the Jewish Law, but of a minimalist claim to faith which lacks practical consequences (Jas 2.14-17). Moreover, the specific bone of contention between Paul and James recounted in Galatians appears to have been the table fellowship of Jewish and Gentile Christians (Gal. 2.11-13); there is no mention of this theme in the Epistle of James. There is no clear indication, either in Paul's writings (cf. Gal. 2.9), or in Acts (cf. Acts 15.12-19), that James actively opposed Paul's Gentile mission, and certainly not as vehemently as Hengel's interpretation necessitates. From Gal. 1.19 and 2.9, it appears that James was one of the Jerusalem apostles who had most contact with Paul. It is thus highly unlikely that he could simply have misunderstood Paul. If he then understood Paul's position, and rejected it with the force which Hengel suggests, it is very difficult to see how Paul could have achieved any influence, and the situation depicted in Galatians and in Acts would be entirely impossible. Hengel's solution in the end raises more problems than it solves.

1.5.2 *The Epistle of James as* Hortatio

The analysis of E. Baasland shares the view that the Epistle of James forms a coherently structured unity, which, in his opinion, fits the literary category known as *hortatio*. He marks out the structural development of James corresponding to this literary type, principally according to Aristotle's description of rhetoric. Thus, 1.2-15 forms the introductory *exordium*, linked by a *transitus* (1.16-18) with 1.19-27, the *propositio*. This is followed in 2.1–5.6 by the *argumentatio*, which can be subdivided into the *confirmatio* (2.1-13; 2.14-26; 3.1-10a), *transitus* (3.10b-12) and *confutatio* (3.13–4.6; 4.7-10; 4.11–5.6). The *peroratio* in 5.7-20 is marked by thematic recapitulation, corresponding to the opening *exordium*.[64]

Baasland also examines the thematic development of the epistle and its argumentative purpose within its historical setting. He draws atten-

---

BCE–200 CE (Minneapolis: Augsburg/Fortress Press, 1991), pp. 213-28; L.T. Johnson, *The Letter of James* (AB, 37A; New York: Doubleday, 1995), pp. 58-65.

64. See Baasland, 'Jakobusbrief', pp. 118-23; also *idem*, 'Literarische Form, Thematik und geschichtliche Einordnung des Jakobusbriefes', *ANRW* 2.25.5, pp. 3646-86 (3649-59).

tion to the two contrasting ways of life portrayed in the Epistle of James—the way of the righteous and the way of the sinner. The author's exhortations draw on the presentation of the God-human relationship in Jewish wisdom writings, but with a strong eschatological concern, similar to that of the proclamation of Jesus in the synoptic gospel traditions.[65] Baasland concludes that the text, as an instruction-speech in letter form, fits best into a diaspora situation, where Jewish Christians form a majority of the addressees, and contacts with the Jewish synagogue community remain quite close, so that Jews in general can be seen as a kind of secondary intended-reader group.[66]

Baasland's analysis of the form and structural development of the entire text as a coherent and integrated whole yields helpful insights, such as the introductory functions of the first chapter (*exordium* and *propositio*), and the degree of correspondence between this and the concluding *peroratio*. Some of the details of his breakdown of the letter remain open to question. For instance, it is not immediately apparent that either 1.16-18 or 3.10b-12 form a *transitus,* except on the grounds that the address ἀδελφοί must mean the beginning of a new section or subsection, which is not entirely convincing. Nevertheless, the broad contours of Baasland's presentation of the structure of the Epistle of James remain illuminating.

1.5.3 *The Epistle of James and Communication Theory*

W. Wuellner approaches the Epistle of James by drawing extensively on modern studies of rhetoric and text-pragmatics.[67] He complains that most modern scholarship has a static view of text, and a conception of meaning which is correspondingly oriented towards semantics. He argues for a semiotically-oriented means of interpreting the text, which will do justice to the functional nature of the text's meaning as part of a communication process, focusing on the rhetorical integration of text type, style and argumentation as appropriate to the purpose of the text.[68] The argumentation of the Epistle of James falls within a process of inner-church polemic; the goal of the text-process is the transformation

---

65. Baasland, 'Literarische Form', pp. 3664-71; *idem*, 'Jakobusbrief', pp. 123-27.

66. Baasland, 'Literarische Form', pp. 3673-79.

67. See W.H. Wuellner, 'Der Jakobusbrief im Licht der Rhetorik und Textpragmatik', *LB* 43 (1978), pp. 5-66.

68. Wuellner, 'Jakobusbrief', pp. 5-20.

of certain values on the part of the recipients.[69] Wuellner analyses the text itself in three major parts: an introduction (1.1-12), the main body of the argument (1.13–5.6), and a conclusion (5.7-20). The *argumentatio* can be divided into six sections of approximately equal length, which in turn fall into contrasting positive and negative subsections.[70]

Wuellner's rhetorical-critical examination is taken up (with small modifications) by J.H. Elliott, and used as the basis of his investigation of the epistle from the social-scientific perspective of holiness and purity.[71] Elliott relates the traditional concern with holiness and purity as characteristic of the divine cosmic order to the concern with wholeness stated in the opening verses (1.2-4), and developed by means of a series of seven negative/positive contrasts in the body of the letter (in which he includes 5.7-11 and 5.12). In his view, the author addresses 'issues of fragmentation and wholeness on correlated personal, social, and cosmic levels of existence'.[72] He traces the personal (e.g. 1.5-7, 14-15, 19-20), social (e.g. 2.1-4, 6-14) and cosmic (e.g. 1.2, 12, 13-15, 17-18) dimensions of the contrasting elaboration of the themes of wholeness/unity and incompleteness/division.[73]

A number of important points emerge from this kind of rhetorical analysis of the epistle. First, as the purpose of any text must be to communicate something, it is surely helpful to adopt an approach to the text which views it as part of a dynamic communication process. Second, when the whole epistle is viewed from this perspective, there is in fact little difficulty in interpreting the text as a coherent and integrated unity, displaying consistent thematic, structural and stylistic development. Third, this approach allows the evaluation of the form of the whole text as an integral part of the communicative process, drawing attention, in this respect, to the importance of the introductory and concluding sections of the epistle. Fourth, in setting out the argumentative goal of the text within a framework of active communication,

69. Wuellner, 'Jakobusbrief', p. 21.

70. Wuellner, 'Jakobusbrief', pp. 35-57. Binary oppositions within the epistle are also used as the basis for interpretation in the brief article by K.D. Tollefson, 'The Epistle of James as Dialectical Discourse', *BTB* 21 (1991), pp. 62-69.

71. J.H. Elliott, 'The Epistle of James in Rhetorical and Social-Scientific Perspective: Holiness-Wholeness and Patterns of Replication', *BTB* 23 (1993), pp. 71-81.

72. Elliott, 'Epistle of James', p. 71.

73. Elliott, 'Epistle of James', pp. 78-79.

stressing the importance of the theme of unity within the text, this approach facilitates the fitting of the text into an appropriate situation within the social dynamics of early Christianity. Likewise, the further development of the analysis by Elliott, using the tools of the social sciences, draws attention to the importance of being able to relate the findings of textual analysis of the epistle to the key cultural conceptions of reality of the time.

A number of criticisms may also be made. First, although the pre-script is formulated 'to the twelve tribes in the diaspora', it is not certain that this means that it is actually a circular letter to the dispersed public of all Christians. It is equally possible, and perhaps more likely, that a much more specific situation than that of all Christians was envisaged by the author as the goal of the text. Also, Wuellner does not really make clear how he arrives at the situation in which he locates the epistle. As the crucial issue of the unity of Jew and Gentile is never explicitly mentioned in the epistle, he may be attributing excessive weight to the implied Christendom of 'the twelve tribes'. Further, his analysis is entirely directed to the internal rhetoric of the epistle itself, with only superficial reference to the social dynamics of the wider early Christian movement, as indicated by other New Testament texts. Particularly in view of the apparent contacts between the Epistle of James and the synoptic gospel traditions, attention to these areas might yield a more nuanced view of the situation of the epistle.

1.5.4 *Summary*

As an interpretative starting point, a rhetorical perspective has proved the most fruitful of those examined above. This perspective offers the 'fullest' view of the text, seeing it not simply as a literary structure, the work of a particular author, an example of thought developments within a particular tradition, or a reflection of social context. Rather, this approach integrates the literary form and composition of the text and its thematic development, as purposeful communication within, and appropriate to, a specific context.

1.6 *Methodological Presuppositions of this Work*

This section begins by giving a summary of the methodological pre-suppositions used in this examination of the Epistle of James. This is followed by an outline of the structure of the argument, in terms of its development in Chapters 2 to 7.

1.6.1 *Language as Communication: Text and Context*

Language is above all a medium of social interaction. Thus, the emphasis in the interpretation of a text will fall on the functional nature of language, that is, on the use of language as a sign-system to express and exchange meanings between people.[74] These meanings which are shared and expressed by language are always contextual.[75] They are rooted in a particular social and cultural context, in which they are accepted as comprehensible by those who are familiar with the society's understanding of itself and of the world in general as a meaningful reality.[76]

Research in the field of sociolinguistics has suggested that any text will show a number of characteristic features of contextual orientation. First, a text encodes the significant cultural processes and phenomena, which are experienced by those who realise this culture in their every-day lives. Second, a text encodes statuses, roles and role relationships between the participants (that is, author/sender and addressees/recipients) in the communicative exchange, of which it is the medium. Third, the whole text is coherently realised through certain culturally conventional linguistic and stylistic forms.[77]

These insights highlight the need to examine the sociocultural dimensions of any text, focusing on the cultural norms and social processes

74. Examination of language as a system of social interaction is undertaken in the specialist domain of sociolinguistics; see, e.g., M.A.K. Halliday, *Language as Social Semiotic* (London: Edward Arnold, 1978), especially Chapters 6 and 7, pp. 108-51; M.A.K. Halliday and R. Hasan, *Language, Context and Text* (Oxford: Oxford University Press, 1989).

75. See Halliday and Hasan, *Language, Context and Text*, pp. 5-11.

76. The 'classic' text on the perception of reality as socially constructed and mediated is P. Berger and T. Luckmann, *The Social Construction of Reality* (Garden City, NY: Doubleday, 1967); cf. P. Berger, *The Social Reality of Religion* (London: Faber & Faber, 1969), pp. 3-28; in relation to the interpretation of the New Testament, see, e.g., J.H. Elliott, *What Is Social-Scientific Criticism?* (Minneapolis: Fortress Press, 1993), pp. 36-37; B.J. Malina, *Christian Origins and Cultural Anthropology* (Atlanta, GA: John Knox Press, 1986), pp. 1-12.

77. See Halliday and Hasan, *Language, Context and Text*, p. 12; Halliday, *Language as Social Semiotic*, pp. 108-113; 142-45; cf. Elliott, *Criticism*, pp. 53-54.

and phenomena within which the text functions as an instance of meaningful communication.[78] In this respect, the insights of approaches which draw on the social sciences to provide heuristic models for the investigation and clarification of the social world of early Christianity are particularly helpful.[79]

When interpreting a text which originates in a sociocultural context different to that of the interpreter, it is vital that the interpreter is aware of the manner in which reality may be perceived differently by the members of such a different context. The biblical texts give expression to the self-understanding of the members of a cultural context, which is distant in time, and usually also in space, from that of the modern interpreter. It is therefore important that the social values and norms of behaviour (inasmuch as these can be reconstructed) which were operative in the ancient eastern Mediterranean, including the Jewish world in which earliest Christianity emerged, should be taken into account in the attempt to understand these texts.[80] Such values and norms would include the central social organizational markers of kinship and status, the concepts of honour and shame as the pivotal standards of conduct and prestige, self-perception in terms of dyadic, socially-embedded (rather than individualistic) personality, the view of both material and social goods and resources as limited, and the patron–client system of social exchange.[81]

78. As V.K. Robbins, *Jesus the Teacher* (Philadelphia: Fortress Press, 1984), p. 6, comments: 'A socio-rhetorical approach…analyzes the text as a strategic statement in a situation characterized by "webs of significance" containing an intermingling of social, cultural, religious and literary traditions and conventions in the Mediterranean world'. The present work, while sharing many of Robbins's interests, is not, as such, derived from Robbins's socio-rhetorical methodology.

79. Elliott, *Criticism*, provides an extensive examination of the methodology of social-scientific interpretation of biblical texts, including a comprehensive bibliography. As social-scientific methods have been fruitfully employed in biblical studies for several decades, there is scarcely any need to offer a detailed theoretical justification for the use of social-scientific perspectives in this work; see Elliott, *Criticism*, pp. 9-16.

80. See Elliott, *Criticism*, pp. 37-49; B.J. Malina, *The New Testament World: Insights from Cultural Anthropology* (Louisville: Westminster/John Knox Press, 2nd edn, 1993), pp. 1-7, 23-24.

81. Malina, *New Testament World*, gives a thorough introduction to cultural values and norms in the ancient Mediterranean world, including: honour and shame, pp. 25-50; dyadic personality, pp. 51-70; limited good, pp. 71-93; patron–client

In addition, the choice of rhetorical, formal and stylistic conventions used in the text can play an important role in articulating its socially-rooted meaning. Thus, it is important to appreciate the social implications of the literary conventions of the time in the process of author/audience communication: what does the expression of this material in this manner imply about how, according to the socio-literary norms of the ancient world, the text could have functioned? These considerations draw attention to a text's rhetorical dimension, that is, to the way in which the author of a text expresses him/herself, so as to have a particular effect upon, or to elicit a particular response from, the addressees.[82]

Also important is an appreciation of the role and status of religion in this context. The concept of religion as an isolated social institution, which can be viewed separately from other social institutions, is foreign to the ancient world. Rather, religion was inseparably interrelated with the political-legal and economic subsystems, with the cultural values and norms, with ideological patterns of persuasion, and so on. In short, religion was thoroughly integrated within the whole of life.[83] In fact, a very important role of religion in this context is to provide a framework within which the whole of life is consistently integrated as meaningful and coherent. In this light, religion is concerned with the way in which social reality is perceived as coherently ordered within a cosmic framework of ultimate reality.[84]

1.6.2 *The Programme for the Present Work*
The task is now to utilize the interpretative presuppositions set out above, by applying them to an examination of the Epistle of James.

---

relationships, pp. 81-82. Cf. also the relevant chapters in R.L. Rohrbaugh (ed.), *The Social Sciences and New Testament Interpretation* (Peabody, MA: Hendrickson, 1996), and in B.J. Malina and J. Pilch (eds.), *Biblical Social Values and their Meaning* (Peabody, MA: Hendrickson, 1993).

82. See Elliott, *Criticism*, pp. 54-55, 72-75; cf. K. Berger, *Exegese des Neuen Testaments* (Heidelberg: Quelle & Meyer, 1984), pp. 91-107, 117-27, 234-39.

83. See J.H. Elliott, 'Social-Scientific Criticism of the New Testament: More on Methods and Models', *Semeia* 35 (1986), pp. 1-33 (13-16); Elliott, *Criticism*, p. 57.

84. See P. Berger, *Social Reality*, pp. 26-52; Berger and Luckmann, *Social Construction*, pp. 110-21; cf. the discussion of sociological views of religion in relation to early Christianity in G. Theissen, 'Sociological Theories of Religion and the Analysis of Early Christianity', in G. Theissen, *Social Reality and the Early Christians* (Edinburgh: T. & T. Clark, 1992), pp. 231-56, and 'Some Ideas about a Sociological Theory of Early Christianity', pp. 257-87, in the same volume.

Chapter 1 has provided a review of the principal scholarly approaches which have been used to interpret the Epistle of James, drawing attention to their respective strengths and weaknesses. This overview of scholarly opinion serves to set the scene, in terms of the current state of research on the Epistle of James, for the specific investigations of the following chapters.

Chapters 2 and 3 examine the issue of the way in which the relationship between the participants in the communicative exchange is encoded in the text. Chapter 2 focuses on the self-presentation of the author within the text, both directly, through explicit self-designation (§2.2), and indirectly, through his self-identification with authoritative socioreligious traditions which he draws on in the composition of the text (§2.3). Chapter 3 then turns to the other side of the text's communicative exchange, the addressees, and examines the way these are depicted by the author (§3.2). The later part of Chapter 3 develops the findings of this examination, testing the proposal that the author presupposes a shared basic world-view between himself and the addressees, but challenges what he sees as inconsistency and wavering in the addressees' identification with this view. This is carried out through the analysis of one of the key verses which indicate such a concern, Jas 2.5, within its context.

Chapter 4 tests the findings of the previous chapter through an investigation of the opening subsection of the text. This analysis is carried further in Chapters 5 and 6, which together examine sequentially the remainder of the text of the epistle. These chapters also contain brief analyses of the literary composition of the sections of the epistle under examination. Finally, Chapter 7 sets out the investigative conclusions of this work in terms of the social location and function of the Epistle of James as an instance of purposeful and meaningful communication within the complex social world of early Christianity.

Throughout this investigation of the communicative exchange represented by the Epistle of James, care will be taken to present readings of the text which are sensitive to the sociocultural context of the ancient eastern Mediterranean world. In this way, it is hoped to avoid some of the pitfalls of inadvertently importing inappropriate frameworks of reference from the modern world, and at the same time to open up new insights on the text, which some more traditional methods may have overlooked. The aim is to see the text communicate in a fresh and dynamic manner, through reading it, with the aid of sociocultural models, in terms of the values and presuppositions of the kind of social world in which it originated. It is thus hoped that this reading of the Epistle of James will contribute to a deeper understanding and appreciation not only of this text's place within the social world of earliest Christianity, but also of that social world itself.

Chapter 2

THE SELF-PRESENTATION OF THE AUTHOR

2.1 *Introduction*

This chapter will focus on the role of the author, not primarily as com-
poser, but with regard to the social implications of his self-presentation
within the text. In this respect, there are two important aspects to be
considered. First, the manner in which the author explicitly identifies
himself, through the use of terms directly describing his role and status,
will be analysed. Second, the author's self-identification in relation to
cultural norms, standards and theoretical bodies of knowledge, that is,
his self-location in relation to socially authoritative traditions, will also
be examined.

2.2 *The Self-Presentation of the Author*

This section will examine how the author depicts himself within the
text, in terms of the typical roles of the contemporary social environment. The Epistle of James has relatively few explicit references to the
author's self-perception and role. In fact, there are only two such
references of significance, the self-designation in the epistolary
greeting, 'slave (δοῦλος) of God and of the Lord Jesus Christ' (1.1),[1]
and the self-inclusion among the teachers (διδάσκαλοι) in 3.1, through
the use of the first person plural verb in the following subordinate
clause, 'not many should become teachers...knowing that we are all the
more liable for judgment' (μεῖζον κρίμα λημψόμεθα).

---

1. S.R. Llewelyn, 'The Prescript of James', *NovT* 39 (1997), pp. 385-93, suggests that Jas 1.1 is a secondary addition to the text. This position, however, has no
support in the textual tradition, and little internal evidence from the text itself, and
must be judged unconvincing.

2.2.1 *'Slave of God and of the Lord Jesus Christ'*. The significance of this self-designation has sometimes been dismissed as an imitation of 'the Pauline pattern of evoking apostolicity immediately in the opening address'.[2] This, however, is a problematically simplistic interpretation. Apart from the fact that there are no good reasons to give such primacy to the Pauline Letters,[3] the terms of the opening greeting in the Epistle of James, when examined closely, are substantially different from those of Paul. In Rom. 1.1 and Phil. 1.1, Paul describes himself as a 'slave of Jesus Christ' (δοῦλος Ιησοῦ χριστοῦ); elsewhere, when a self-designation is used it is 'apostle'. Nowhere does Paul use either slave or apostle with the double correlation found in James, '...of God and of the Lord Jesus Christ'. Paul typically uses the unconventional letter-greeting, 'grace and peace', while James employs the usual Greek greeting, χαίρειν.[4] Thus, the Pauline Letters should not be seen as the literary background from which the self-expression of Jas 1.1 derives. Acquaintance with a similar, or shared cultural environment is enough to explain the use of the term 'slave' (δοῦλος) as a self-designation by both authors, independently of each other.

This word in Greek generally designates the role of intrinsic service of the slave in relation to the master. Although some slaves were able to achieve more favourable standing, as a designation of servitude within Graeco-Roman society, the term does not in itself depict particularly positive or prestigious status.[5] The use of the word to designate

2.   J.L. White, 'New Testament Epistolary Literature in the Framework of Ancient Epistolography', *ANRW* 2.25.2, pp. 1751-56 (1752).

3.   Cf. K. Berger, 'Hellenistische Gattungen im Neuen Testament', *ANRW* 2.25.2, pp. 1031-378 (1333-34).

4.   Jas 1.1 corresponds exactly to the usual Greek letter-opening formula: A to B, greetings (χαίρειν). The classic treatment of the Greek letter form is F.X.J. Exler, *The Form of the Ancient Greek Letter: A Study in Greek Epistolography* (Washington: Catholic University of America, 1923), especially with regard to the opening (χαίρειν) and closing (ἔρρωσο) formulas; also H. Koskenniemi, *Studien zur Idee und Phraseologie des griechischen Briefes bis 400n. Chr.* (Helsinki: Suomalaien Tiedeakatemie, 1956). Cf. also W.G. Doty, *Letters in Primitive Christianity* (Philadelphia: Fortress Press, 1973), pp. 1-19. On the body of the letter, see in particular, J.L. White, *The Form and Function of the Body of the Greek Letter* (Missoula, MT: Scholars Press, 1972).

5.   See D.B. Martin, *Slavery as Salvation* (New Haven: Yale University Press, 1990), pp. 22-49.

relationship to God is not particularly common in Greek literature,[6] but occurs frequently in the LXX, as the translation of the Hebrew עבד.[7]

As well as its general use for those who obey God, the word is used of figures whose relationship to God is particularly exemplary, such as Moses, Joshua, David and the prophets.[8] When God is viewed as the supreme, universal authority, then the metaphor of slave presents itself naturally with reference to those under this authority, of whom complete obedience is demanded. The particular use of the term עבד/δοῦλος for those whose fulfilment of this demand of service is especially worthy of note follows in an extended sense from this.

The use of this word as a self-designation in relation to God by the author of the Epistle of James is clearly derived from the LXX use of δοῦλος for עבד. Whether this use of δοῦλος in 1.1 represents a particular claim to special status, like that ascribed to such figures as Moses, David and the prophets,[9] or is simply a profession of humility, identifying the author among the servants of God in general,[10] is more difficult to resolve. Certainly this word represents the subordination of the author to the supreme authority of God, and, as such, the acknowledgement, in traditional terms, of his appropriate status. This acknowledgement may not be a deliberate claim to special esteem, analogous to that merited by the great figures of Israel's past, but it still entails a certain claim to authority. The author has set himself in the correct place within the overall order of the universe, by placing himself under the supreme authority of God.[11] The self-designation 'slave of God' invokes God's authority behind the author's activity. Like the prophets and others who

---

6.   See D.B. Martin, *Slavery*, pp. xiv-xvi.

7.   עבד is usually translated by either δοῦλος (314 times) or παῖς (336 times). There would seem to be a preference for one or other word in many books: παῖς is found more often in the Pentateuch, Chronicles, Proverbs and Isaiah, while δοῦλος is more common in Kings, Psalms and the Minor Prophets.

8.   E.g. 1 Kgs 8.53, 56; 2 Kgs 18.12; 21.8; LXX Ps. 104.26; Mal. 3.24 (Moses); LXX Josh. 24.30; Judg. 2.8 (Joshua); 1 Kgs 8.24-26; 14.8; LXX Pss. 88.4, 21; 131.10; Ezek. 34.23 (David); 2 Kgs 10.10 (Elijah); 14.25 (Jonah); 17.13, 23; 21.10; Amos 3.7; Zech. 1.6; Ezek. 38.17 (prophets).

9.   Dibelius, *James*, pp. 65-66; R.P. Martin, *James*, p. 6; Hoppe, *Jakobusbrief*, p. 17.

10.   Ropes, *James*, pp. 117-18. For the use of δοῦλος as a designation for early Christians in general, cf. Acts 4.29; 1 Pet. 2.16; Rev. 2.20.

11.   Cf. P. Gruson (ed.), *La Lettre de Jacques: Lecture socio-linguistique* (Cahiers Evangiles, 61; Paris: Cerf, 1988), p. 13.

were obedient to God, the author, if he is fulfilling the role appropriately, can claim to speak in the name of the Lord (cf. 5.10).[12]

As well as being under the supreme authority of God, 1.1 also designates the author as under the authority of the Lord Jesus Christ:
'Ιάκωβος θεοῦ καὶ κυρίου 'Ιησοῦ χριστοῦ δοῦλος. This precise combination is unique here within early Christian writings,[13] thus the
significance of this double genitive in correlation to δοῦλος, and the
relation to each other of the two elements, God and Lord Jesus Christ,
must be examined more closely.

Vouga suggests that God and Lord should be read in apposition, both
of them being taken to refer to Jesus Christ.[14] While this is grammatically possible,[15] it is highly unlikely. Such a bold identification of Jesus
as God would be exceptional within the New Testament, and would
also create interpretative difficulties with regard to other occurences of
these words in the epistle.

κύριος is the common Greek word for an authoritative person: 'lord'
or 'master'. Its use here recognises the authoritative status, as it does
elsewhere in early Christian literature. κύριος is also the word used in
the LXX and Greek Jewish literature for the divine name יהוה, as the
equivalent of the Hebrew אֲדֹנָי 'lord', which was substituted for the
unutterable divine name יהוה in speech. However, as the secular meaning of both אֲדֹנָי and κύριος, as simply lord or master, remained in full
use, there is no need to see a suggestion of the attribution of ontological
status, equivalent to that of the God of Israel, to Jesus through the use
of κύριος in this verse. On the other hand, the linking of κύριος with
Jesus Christ in Phil. 2.5-11 does indicate that the term, applied to Jesus,
could be given much more than ordinary connotations. Thus, its
significance as a term depicting the authoritative status of Jesus should
not be underestimated. The nature of the authoritative status in relation

---

12. K. Berger, 'Apostelbrief und apostolische Rede: Zum Formular frühchristlicher Briefe', *ZNW* 65 (1974), pp. 190-231, argues that early Christian letters are
fundamentally related to prophetic speech, and also to apocalyptic literature and the
testaments of Jewish heroes.

13. The nearest to this formulation is Tit. 1.1: 'slave of God and apostle of Jesus
Christ'.

14. F. Vouga, *L'Epître de Saint Jacques* (CNT, 13a; Geneva: Editions Labor et
Fides, 1984), pp. 31, 36.

15. Vouga cites παρὰ τῷ θεῷ καὶ πατρὶ (1.27) and τὸν κύριον καὶ πατέρα
(3.9) as instances of similar usages in the Epistle of James, *Jacques*, p. 31.

to God which is ascribed to Jesus is brought out more fully by the
further qualification, Christ (χριστός).

The term χριστός has particular significance as the Greek equivalent
of מָשִׁיחַ or 'anointed one'. As such, χριστός designates one specially
chosen by God. In the canonical Hebrew Scriptures and the LXX,[16] this
term is particularly associated with the monarchy (1 Sam. 12.3, 5; 24.7,
11; 26.9, 11, 16, 23; 2 Sam. 1.14, 16; 22.51; 23.1; LXX Pss. 2.2; 17.51;
88.39, 52), and with the priesthood (Lev. 4.5, 16; 6.15). A particularly
interesting 'messiah' is the Persian king Cyrus (Isa. 45.1), chosen by
God to fulfil God's will among the nations. In the prophet Zechariah's
vision of two olive trees, the priest, Joshua, and the Davidic heir,
Zerubbabel, are portrayed as 'the two anointed [בְנֵי־הַיִּצְהָר] who stand
by the Lord' (Zech. 4.14), suggesting the hope of divinely sanctioned
restoration (Zech. 4.1-4, 11-14; cf. 3.1-10; 4.4-10; 6.9-14).

It is difficult to tell exactly how widespread or consistent the idea of
messiah was in the period of formative Judaism.[17] It plays virtually no
constructive role in Philo, or in Josephus. How consistent or significant
such ideas were within the movement represented by the Qumran
scrolls remains unclear.[18] Two messiah-figures seem to be depicted: a
priestly messiah, or 'anointed one of Aaron', and a royal 'messiah of
Israel'. These seem to be expected to arise as eschatological leaders of
the community, who will preside over its sacred banquet at the consummation of its destiny as the true chosen people of God (1QS 9.10-
11; CD 12.22-23; 13.20-22; 14.18-19; 1QSa 2.11-22). It is probable
that the idea of dual messiahship at Qumran, marking the time of the
restoration of Israel, is derived from prophetic associations of renewed

16. On the use of the term in these texts, see J.J.M. Roberts, 'The Old Testa-
ment's Contribution to Messianic Expectations', in J.H. Charlesworth (ed.), *The
Messiah: Developments in Earliest Judaism and Christianity* (Minneapolis: Fortress
Press, 1992), pp. 39-51.

17. Good presentations of the ambiguity of messianic ideas at this time are
given in J. Neusner, W.S. Green and E.S. Frerichs (eds.), *Judaisms and their
Messiahs at the Turn of the Christian Era* (Cambridge: Cambridge University Press,
1987), and in Charlesworth, *Messiah*. On this question, see particularly the Introduction by W.S. Green, in Neusner, Green and Frerichs, *Messiahs*, pp. 1-14.

18. See J.H. Charlesworth, 'From Messianology to Christology: Problems and
Prospects', in Charlesworth, *Messiah*, pp. 3-35, especially pp. 24-29; L. Schiffman,
'Messianic Figures and Ideas in the Qumran Scrolls', pp. 116-29 in the same vol-
ume; S. Talmon, 'Waiting for the Messiah: The Spiritual Universe of the Qumran
Covenanters', in Neusner, Green and Frerichs, *Messiahs*, pp. 111-38.

priesthood and kingship with a renewed Israel, such as that of Zechariah 4. The presentation of messiahship in other Jewish texts from this period also draws on the idea of eschatological, divinely-raised priest- and king-figures at the restoration of the people of God.[19]

It is apparent that there was no uniform concept of messiah/Christ in Judaism of the time. Where 'messianic' figures are presented, a number of common points may be noted: he appears as a figure who is specially empowered by God; he tends to be associated with the hope of the eschatological consummation and restoration of God's people; he tends to be associated with the fulfilment of God's righteous will among the restored people.

The use of this term in relation to Jesus is quite consistent throughout the New Testament. Thus, it seems safe to say that Jesus was identified as χριστός from an early date; whether this identification was one to which he himself laid claim remains an open question, but, at any rate, the designation appears quite secure for the authors of the New Testament texts. As such, Jesus is denoted as one specially chosen and empowered by God. This view of Jesus most likely had eschatological overtones in the light of the strong eschatological elements in his ministry and in the movement which came into being around him. Thus, 'Christ' could designate Jesus as a special authority figure, who proclaimed and instigated restoration of the people of God, by the righteous doing of God's will. It is highly unlikely that anyone associated with the movement around Jesus could have been unaware of his crucifixion.[20] Thus, the honorific titles given to Jesus must be under-

---

19. The *Testaments of the Twelve Patriarchs* speak of the Lord raising up an eschatological priest-figure descended from Levi (*T. Levi* 18; cf. *T. Reub.* 6.8, ἀρχιερεὺς χριστός), who will rule the eschatologically restored and perfected world, and of a similarly, but less extensively described king-figure of the descendants of Judah (*T. Jud.* 24), who may be meant to be subordinate to the priest (cf. *T. Jud.* 21.1-5), or possibly even identified with him (*T. Benj.* 11.2-4, of MS c, Codex Graecus 731, Vatican Library). The *Psalms of Solomon* make explicit reference to a χριστός (*Pss. Sol.* 17.32; 18.5, 7) as a kingly figure, raised and empowered by God to purge Jerusalem, and to rule the holy people in righteousness.

20. B.J. Malina, 'Christ and Time: Mediterranean or Swiss?', *CBQ* 51 (1989), pp. 1-31 (reprinted in B.J. Malina, *The Social World of Jesus and the Gospels* [London: Routledge, 1996], pp. 179-214), draws attention to the need for a revised view of eschatological ideas in the social context of the ancient Mediterranean world, which lacked the strong orientation towards the future typical of modern industrial and post-industrial societies.

stood in relation to this, although the events themselves are not explicitly referred to in the Epistle of James. Thus, 'Lord' (κύριος), and even more so, 'Christ' (χριστός), must demonstrate the conviction of God's ultimate vindication of Jesus, which is, of course, explicitly recounted elsewhere with reference to the resurrection.

There is no contradiction between being 'slave of God' and 'slave of the Lord Jesus Christ'. Jesus is a figure of special authority and honourable status, chosen and vindicated by God. To be the slave of one implies an equivalent acknowledgement of the status and authority of the other.

Thus, the self-designation 'slave of God and of the Lord Jesus Christ' at the opening of the text can be seen to fulfil several important functions. First, it identifies the author as standing under the supreme authority of God, and of Jesus, to whom, as Lord and Christ, especially honourable status within the universal order of things has been ascribed. Second, by placing himself under this double authority, the author explicitly acknowledges this special authority of Jesus. Third, the contents of the following text are likewise placed under their ultimate authority.

2.2.2 *Teacher* (διδάσκαλος)

In addition to presenting himself as under the unequivocal authority of God and of Jesus in 1.1, the author also identifies himself as a teacher (διδάσκαλος) in 3.1, through the first person plural verb λημψόμεθα, 'we shall receive', following the injunction, 'Not many should become teachers' (μὴ πολλοὶ διδάσκαλοι γίνεσθε). This usage implies that the author includes himself among such teachers. Thus, the significance of this designation within the environment of James must be examined.

2.2.2.1 *The General Use of the Word* διδάσκαλος. In general, the word is used of one who teaches, that is one who gives instruction of particular contents.[21] διδάσκαλος occurs only twice in the LXX (Est. 6.1 and 2 Macc. 1.10), which more frequently uses the participle, διδάσκων, as a substantive, to denote a teacher, especially one who teaches the requirements of living in accordance with the demands of God.[22] The term διδάσκαλος, however, does seem to be one of importance in the Greek writings of the early Christian movement. It occurs 49 times in

---

21. K.H. Rengstorf, 'διδάσκαλος', *TDNT*, I, pp. 148-59.
22. Rengstorf, 'διδάσκαλος', p. 151.

the canonical gospels, 42 of which refer to Jesus as teacher, including the direct address διδάσκαλε 30 times. Elsewhere, the word is used of John the Baptist (Lk. 3.12), teachers in the temple in Jerusalem (Lk. 2.46), and Nicodemus, a Pharisee and 'ruler of the Jews/Judeans' (ἄρχων τῶν Ἰουδαίων, Jn 3.1, 10). This depiction of those who give religious instruction on life according to God's order is consistent with the use of the word-group in the LXX.

The development and precise nature of the role of teachers within Judaism in the first century CE is difficult to evaluate.[23] The extent to which the later rabbinic school system already existed at this stage, particularly prior to the Jewish War, and, consequently, the extent to which rabbinic literature can be seen to reflect accurately the activity of earlier teachers, is open to question. It is likely that some degree of continuity existed, but the existence of the position of Rabbi as an acknowledged teacher in the pre-war period is hard to corroborate.[24]

Apart from Jas 3.1, there are a several significant references to διδάσκαλοι among the early Christian texts. Acts 13.1 refers to prophets and teachers in the early Christian community in Antioch; 1 Cor. 12.28 speaks of ordering the community according to 'first

23. Reconstructions of the development of the Jewish school are offered by Hengel, *Judaism and Hellenism*, I, pp. 78-83, and by R. Riesner, *Jesus als Lehrer: Eine Untersuchung zum Ursprung der Evangelien-Überlieferung* (WUNT NS, 7; Tübingen: J.C.B. Mohr [Paul Siebeck], 1981), pp. 153-99. The optimism with which Riesner identifies the early Christian movement as a Jewish school is doubtful, however, as he fails to take adequate account of certain peculiarities of the movement, such as its itinerant proclamation and miracle-working.

24. Riesner, *Lehrer*, pp. 266-72, argues that Mt. 23.7 indicates the pre-70 CE use of rabbi for Jewish teachers, although as a reverential appellation, and not yet as a formal title. This, however, is doubtful; its occurrence here probably reflects the author's polemic against emergent rabbinic Judaism, rather than being drawn from an early tradition, as Riesner suggests. On this negative significance of the term 'rabbi' within the development of the Matthean narrative, cf. S. Byrskog, *Jesus the Only Teacher: Didactic Authority and Transmission in Ancient Israel, Ancient Judaism and the Matthean Community* (ConBNT, 24; Stockholm: Almqvist & Wiksell, 1994), pp. 284-87. The uncertainty of the degree of continuity between later rabbinic Judaism and the pharisees at the time of the emergence of the early Christian movement, and the pervasiveness of non-scholastic elements in early Christianity also render problematic such 'classic' presentations of early Christianity as a Jewish school as that of B. Gerhardsson, *Memory and Manuscript: Oral Tradition and Written Transmission in Rabbinic Judaism and Early Christianity* (Uppsala: C.W.K. Gleerup, 1961).

apostles, second prophets, third teachers'. In the later Pauline texts, the role of teacher is mentioned along with apostles, prophets, evangelists and shepherds in Eph. 4.11, and in conjunction with the role of herald and apostle in 1 Tim. 2.7 and 2 Tim. 1.11. The *Didache* also refers several times to teachers in chs. 11–15, dealing with the reception and treatment of teachers, prophets and apostles. From the consistent association of teachers with, in particular, prophets (προφῆται) and apostles (ἀπόστολοι), both in Pauline and non-Pauline writings, it is apparent that these roles were closely associated within the early Christian movement. It is not so clear, however, precisely what each of these roles comprised, and how they were related to one another. These questions must be examined in order to clarify the background to the designation 'teacher' (διδάσκαλος) in Jas 3.1.

2.2.2.2 The Roles of Apostles, Prophets and Teachers. In 1886, Harnack put forward the thesis, based largely on the then recently-published *Didache*, that these three roles should not be seen as permanent officials, chosen for office within a particular community, but rather rather referred to persons who operated freely throughout any and all Christian communities, between which they travelled and preached.[25] Their authority was attributed to divine gift (χάρισμα), and consequently they were recognised and received with respect by local Christian groups as they travelled from place to place. This universally acknowledged authority stood over and above that of the local leadership, appointed by and for particular communities,[26] and it played an important role in maintaining affinity between dispersed communities.[27]

This view was rejected by Greeven, who argues, on the basis of Paul's references to these roles in 1 Corinthians 12, that there are no grounds for seeing prophets and teachers as itinerant, supralocal figures whose authority was generally recognised.[28] On the contrary, while apostles do appear to have exercised a travelling ministry (1 Cor. 9.1-5), the

---

25. A. Harnack, 'Die Lehre der zwölf Apostel', TU 2 (1886), pp. 94-137 (96). A review of diverse scholarly understandings of the role of the teacher since the publication of Harnack's arguments is presented by A. Zimmermann, *Die urchristlichen Lehrer: Studien zum Tradentenkreis der διδάσκαλοι im frühen Urchristentum* (WUNT NS, 12; Tübingen: J.C.B. Mohr [Paul Siebeck], 1984), pp. 36-68.

26. Harnack, 'Lehre', pp. 97-98.

27. Harnack, 'Lehre', p. 104.

28. H. Greeven, 'Propheten, Lehrer, Vorsteher bei Paulus', *ZNW* 44 (1952–53), pp. 1-43.

prophets and teachers were clearly defined and recognisable officials performing roles of leadership and instruction within a particular community.[29] An intermediate position has been taken more recently by Aune, who admits the recognition of apostles, prophets and teachers as supralocal and divinely-empowered figures,[30] and while many prophets and teachers may have resided in single communities in which they performed their roles at least some seem to have been itinerant.[31]

In fact, the primary early Christian texts, while consistently associating the roles of apostles, prophets and teachers, do not necessitate that these roles were perceived or performed in all strands of early Christianity as distinct, clearly defined and uniform.[32] 1 Cor. 12.28-31 does not suggest itinerancy as an essential characteristic of prophets or teachers, especially in the light of the subsequent exhortation: 'Strive for spiritual gifts, especially that you may prophesy' (1 Cor. 14.1). The purpose of prophecy in these verses is the edification of the community, and the Corinthians are hardly being urged to seek this in order that they may become itinerants and move out of the community, rather, they fulfil this role within the local assembly (1 Cor. 14.26-32).

In Acts 13.1, however, two of the prophets and teachers are sent out to perform an itinerant ministry (cf. Acts 16.32-41); likewise the prophet Agabus appears twice in the course of travel, between Jerusalem and Antioch (Acts 11.27-28), and between Judaea and Caesarea (Acts 21.10). The *Didache*, a text which is closer in tone to the synoptic gospels than it is to the Pauline writings, envisages prophets and teachers as travelling; otherwise they could not come to the community to teach (*Did.* 11), nor could they settle there if they wished (*Did.* 13.1-2).[33] Nevertheless, if itinerant activity could be expected of such

29. Greeven, 'Propheten', p. 17.

30. D.E. Aune, *Prophecy in Early Christianity and the Ancient Mediterranean World* (Grand Rapids: Eerdmans, 1983), pp. 201-202.

31. Aune, *Prophecy*, pp. 211-17.

32. Cf. Sato, 'Jakobusbrief', p. 64.

33. J.A. Draper, 'Social Ambiguity and the Production of Text: Prophets, Teachers, Bishops and Deacons and the Development of the Jesus Tradition in the Community of the *Didache*', in C.N. Jefford (ed.), *The Didache in Context: Essays on its Text, History and Transmission* (NovTSup, 77; Leiden: E.J. Brill, 1995), pp. 284-312, believes that there is no evidence for itinerant prophets and teachers in the *Didache*; however, the itinerant role of apostles, prophets and teachers is defended in the same volume by S.J. Patterson, 'Didache 11–13: The Legacy of Radical Itinerancy in Early Christianity', pp. 313-29.

figures, obviously it was not utterly essential, as settling in a particular community is also acceptable (*Did.* 13). *Did.* 13.1 only mentions explicitly the possibility of a prophet wishing to settle, but the instruction of the following verse, 'likewise a true teacher is himself worthy, like the workman, of his food' (*Did.* 13.2), suggests an incoming teacher, analogous to the incoming prophet of *Did.* 13.1, as a resident in the community would already have a means of support there.

All three sources, Acts, Paul and the *Didache*, indicate the perception of these roles as being under the special authority of God. Thus, in Acts 13.1-3, it is the Holy Spirit which sets Paul and Barnabas apart among the prophets and teachers in Antioch to be sent out. In 1 Cor. 12.28, the roles of apostle, prophet, teacher and so on are placed by God (ἔθετο ὁ θεός). In *Did.* 11.1-2, a teacher (ὃς ἂν ἐλθὼν διδάξῃ ὑμᾶς) is to be received as the Lord (ὡς κύριον); so also an apostle (*Did.* 11.4). The prophet, once tested and found genuine, is above judgement, being answerable only to God (*Did.* 11.11). Prophets and teachers are described as 'honoured' (τετιμημένοι) within the community (*Did.* 15.2).

Thus, it can be asserted that apostles, prophets and teachers were generally recognised as authorities under the special commission of God; it also seems likely that itinerancy was a common characteristic of the activity of prophets and teachers, as well as apostles, although this is less clear in the case of the Pauline groups, and does not seem to have been a necessarily permanent feature of their ministry. This leaves the question of the relation to one another of the various roles.

2.2.2.3 *The Relation of the Teacher to Other Roles.* The apostle (ἀπόστολος) is probably the most clearly-depicted of these roles in the early Christian literature, being used of one specially appointed and sent out to proclaim the good news (εὐαγγέλιον) of the early Christians. Thus, Matthew 10 recounts the calling together of the twelve disciples by Jesus, their being given special power, and their being sent (ἀποστέλλω, Mt. 10.5) as apostles (ἀπόστολοι, 10.2), to heal and announce the coming of the kingdom of heaven (10.7).

The role of the prophet (προφήτης) appears to be to give instruction for the edification of the community (1 Cor. 14.3-5, 31; Acts 15.32; *Did.* 11.10). This prophetic instruction seems to be particularly associated with inspired speech (*Did.* 11.7-8), which probably marks the principal difference in role between the prophets and the teachers, who are nowhere described as speaking in tongues or in the power of the spirit.[34] In this respect, the importance of prophecy in early Christianity can be seen to be set in succession to traditional Hebrew prophecy and to draw on the expectation of the reawakening of prophecy at a time of God's restoration of the chosen people (Acts 2.17-21; Joel 3.1-5; cf. Mt. 23.29-39). As it is unlikely that prophets only spoke in trance, there would have been some amount of overlap between the activity of prophets and teachers, hence the double designation of the five named in Acts 13.1 as prophets and teachers.

To make any further formal distinction between prophets and teachers is to go beyond the evidence of the early texts. For instance, Friedrich differentiated sharply between prophecy and teaching, arguing that while 'teachers expound Scripture, cherish the tradition about Jesus and explain the fundaments of the catechism, the prophets, not bound by Scripture or tradition, speak to the congregation on the basis of revelations'.[35] This distinction, however, is excessive. It is clear from *Did.* 11.7-12 that the revelations of prophets were subject to evaluation on grounds of Scripture and tradition; moreover, the functions which Friedrich ascribes to teachers are nowhere so depicted in the early texts, but suggest a much more institutionally organized and officially structured body than the early Christianity which emerges from the New Testament and other early texts.

Zimmermann's investigation of the role of teachers, distinct from other roles within the early Christian movement, yields the view that they formed a rabbinate-like circle responsible for the transmission of tradition, subordinate to the apostles and prophets.[36] His results, however, appear conditioned by the fact that, from the start of his investigation, he links the function of the transmission of traditions with these teachers.[37] Filson's depiction of the role of teachers fits the dynamism of the early movement better:

> In the exaltation of the resurrection faith, and with a sense of present spiritual guidance and power, they were far from being mere conservative guardians of a tradition. They preached an urgent and stirring message.[38]

---

34. Harnack, 'Lehre', pp. 131-34.

35. G. Friedrich, 'προφήτης', *TDNT*, VI, pp. 781-861 (854). Cf. Aune, *Prophecy*, p. 217.

36. Zimmermann, *Lehrer*, p. 218.

37. Zimmermann, *Lehrer*, pp. 33-34.

38. F.V. Filson, 'The Christian Teacher in the First Century', *JBL* 60 (1941), pp. 317-28 (321).

He goes on to suggest that the distinction from other roles should not be seen as clear-cut:

> Every leader of the primitive Church was a teacher...certain gradations of prestige and differences of endowment emerged, without being clearly separated, without being isolated in separate individuals and without depending upon formal election or official installation.[39]

While it may be overstated to assert that all leaders were teachers, this more flexible understanding of the function of teachers and their relation to, in particular, prophets is preferable to a narrow view of a fixed and institutionalized teaching office within the early Christian movement, responsible for the careful handing down of traditions.[40] The interpretation of Scripture and the use of traditions relating to Jesus, especially of the words of Jesus, can still be seen as forming an important part of the content of teaching,[41] but this cannot be seen as a fixed tradition to be taught and handed down as such until after the emergence of authoritative stable written sources, such as the synoptic gospels.

It remains to be seen how the self-identification of the author of the Epistle of James as a teacher fits within this general picture of the teacher in early Christianity.

2.2.2.4 The Author of the Epistle of James as a Teacher. To see the role of teacher as one generally recognised as an authority under the commission of God accords well with what has already been seen with regard to the author's self-presentation in 1.1, where, as slave of God and of the Lord Jesus Christ, he sets himself under the supreme authority of God. Moreover, this view of the author as a teacher is suited to the fact that this is the only explicit claim to authority in the whole text, although much of the rest of the text is written in a pressing and imperatival style, which suggests that the author expects recogni-

39. Filson, 'Teacher', pp. 322-23.
40. Cf. H. Schürmann, 'Und Lehrer', in H. Schürmann, *Orientierungen am Neuen Testament* (Düsseldorf: Patmos, 1978), pp. 116-56, who sees teachers largely as charismatic-inspired figures, closely linked with prophets, whose role included the interpretation and transmission of Scripture and tradition; also M.E. Boring, *Sayings of the Risen Jesus* (SNTSMS, 46; Cambridge: Cambridge University Press, 1982), pp. 78-80; M. Sato, *Q und Prophetie* (WUNT NS, 29; Tübingen: J.C.B. Mohr [Paul Siebeck], 1988), pp. 396-97.
41. Cf. Filson, 'Teacher', pp. 323-26.

tion of his right to make these demands and instructions without any further justification. Further, the role of the teacher as one who draws constructively on the traditions of Jewish Scripture and on traditions deriving from the figure of Jesus for the edification and instruction of the early Christian community is in harmony with the relation of the Epistle of James to such socially authoritative traditions. This point will now be examined in more detail in the next section of the chapter.

2.3 *The Relation of the Epistle of James to Authoritative Traditions*

The use of authoritative religious traditions by the author in the composition of the epistle provides a significant indicator of his social location in relation to others who also held these traditions to be meaningful expressions of reality. Likewise, the expression of deviation from the standards or norms of the cultural environment gives evidence of the author's stance over against others who upheld these traditional norms.

The view of the world which is presented in the Epistle of James is one which is fundamentally grounded in the Jewish conception of the order of the universe. The author makes extensive use of Jewish religious tradition in the articulation of his concerns and exhortations in the text. While the basic world-view which is presupposed is Jewish, there are certain distinctive emphases which mark the text as representing the particular interpretation of the Jewish order of life associated with the early Christian movement.

2.3.1 *The Jewish Universe: God as Cosmological Centre*
In the Jewish framework for the perception of reality, the centre and ultimate authority is the one God, whose dealings with the Jewish people and their forebears were recorded in their sacred Scriptures, particularly the law and the prophets. This basic view is explicitly stated in Jas 2.19: 'You believe that God is one'. The fundamental and inescapable nature of this perspective is highlighted by the conviction of 2.19b, that even the demons acknowledge this divine authority: 'Even the demons believe, and shudder'. This fundamental statement about God (εἶς ἐστιν ὁ θεός) is particularly significant in its reminiscence of the opening words of the *Shema*, the Jewish credal prayer recited twice daily,[42] derived from Deut. 6.4-9: 'Hear, Israel: the Lord

---

42. Cf. Dibelius, *James*, p. 159; Ropes, *James*, p. 215; Laws, *James*, p. 125.

our God is (the) one Lord' (LXX: ἄκουε, Ἰσραηλ· κύριος ὁ θεός ἡμῶν κύριος εἷς ἐστιν). The further use in Jas 4.12, in the phrase 'there is one lawgiver and judge' (εἷς ἐστιν ὁ νομοθέτης καὶ κριτής), of the words εἷς ἐστιν is probably a deliberate echo of the statement of 2.19a, and thus also an allusion to the *Shema*. Likewise, the phrase 'until it receives 'the early and late rains' in 5.7 may be an allusion to Deut. 11.14, which speaks of the early and late rains being given by God, and was also a part of the *Shema*. By making links of this kind to such a central element of authoritative Jewish tradition, the author explicitly grounds what he says very firmly in the Jewish view of the universe.[43]

In accordance with this view of God, the world, both human and non-human, is coherently ordered under absolute divine authority. Consequently, the standard for acceptable human behaviour in the world is compliance with this divine order. This idea of positively evaluated human existence as corresponding to God's ordering of the universe is explicitly referred to several times in the Epistle of James.

Thus, for instance, in 1.19-20, the addressees are urged to respond to the author's exhortations according to the standards of God's righteousness, and in 1.27, they are told that to keep oneself uncorrupted by the world and to care for widows and orphans in their tribulation is pure and undefiled religion before God. Similarly, in 3.9, the incompatability of blessing God and cursing fellow-humans, who are in the image of God, is stated. Another negative example, of non-correspondence with God's order is found in 4.4: 'Friendship with the world is enmity with God'. In 4.12, God's supremacy as the giver of the order of existence and as the final evaluator of status in correspondence with this order is asserted: 'There is one lawgiver and judge, who is able to save and to destroy'. Again, in 4.15, the renowned *conditio Jacobaea* states explicitly the necessity of the correspondence of human activity to the will of God, 'if God wills...'

This idea is also expressed through the use of key terms such as wisdom (σοφία, especially in 3.13-18), righteousness (δικαιοσύνη, 1.20; 2.23; 3.18) and law (νόμος, 1.25; 2.8-13; 4.11-12). These terms are closely related to each other within the traditional Jewish expression of God's order in the universe and the demands of this order on human

---

43. On the significance of these allusions to the *Shema* in the Epistle of James, see further D. Hutchinson Edgar, 'The Use of the Love-Command and the Shema' in the Epistle of James', *Proceedings of the Irish Biblical Association* 23 (2000), pp. 9-20.

behaviour. Thus, in 3.13-18, right behaviour and disposition is identified as wisdom,[44] whose origin as the gift of God is expressed through the spatial imagery, 'from above' (cf. 1.5-6), and characterised through the virtue-list in 3.17. Conduct according to this wisdom is explicitly linked with the concept of righteousness in 3.18. Righteousness is used to designate behaviour in accordance with God's order in 1.20, and again in the long discussion of right human conduct in 2.14-26, as well as the related verb, justify (δικαιόω, 2.21, 23-25). Likewise, law as an expression of the standard for human activity approved by God occurs several times (1.25; 2.8, 12; 4.11-12), typically expressed in 1.25, where the person who is not just a hearer, but a doer of the perfect law of freedom (νόμος τέλειος τῆς ἐλευθερίας) is the one to whom favourable status will ultimately be ascribed.

The distinct nuances of this view as it is manifested in the Epistle of James can, however, be identified as representative of the particular emphases of the interpretation of the Jewish world-view associated with Jesus and his movement. This dimension of the text needs to be examined next.

2.3.2 *The Early Christian Perspective of the Epistle of James*
It has already been noted above that the whole text is set under the authority of the Lord Jesus Christ in the opening greeting of 1.1. There is one further explicit reference to the name of Jesus in the epistle, in the exhortation in 2.1: 'Do not hold commitment to our Lord Jesus Christ of glory in ways which show favouritism' (μὴ ἐν προσωπολημψίαις ἔχετε τὴν πίστιν τοῦ κυρίου ἡμῶν 'Ιησοῦ χριστοῦ τῆς δόξης). First, the significance of this verse will be discussed, and then the indications of close contacts between the Epistle of James and the sayings of Jesus will be examined.

2.3.2.1 *'Our Lord Jesus Christ of Glory'*. The identification of Jesus as a divinely approved figure, discussed above in relation to 1.1,[45] is strengthened by the only other explicit reference to him in the epistle, with the attribution 'of glory' (τῆς δόξης) in 2.1. This is a significant

---

44. Von Lips, *Traditionen*, pp. 433-34, outlines the many themes shared between this epistle and other texts in which wisdom plays an important role, while also noting how the handling of such themes in the Epistle of James is distinct from such other wisdom-oriented texts.

45. See above, §2.2.1.

attribution, as 'glory' (δόξα) functions as a key theological expression in Jewish Greek writings. This is largely the result of the use of δόξα in the LXX as synonym for the Hebrew כבוד, a fundamental attribute of God:

> It implies that which makes God impressive to man, the force of [God's] self-manifestation. The more seriously religious reflexion took the idea of Yahweh's invisibility and transcendence, the more this expression for the impressive element in God became an important term in Old Testament theology.[46]

As a designation of the essential transcendence of God's presence, the glory of God, כבוד־יהוה,[47] δόξα received a more powerful sense than in secular Greek, where it denotes honour, renown or reputation; in general in Jewish Greek religious texts, the primary meaning of δόξα is this essential trait of God's presence. This nuance, of course, is closely related to the common sense of the word to mean honour or reputation, designating the supremely honourable status of God within a cultural context where honour was seen as a key measure of one's worth and position.[48] This deepened sense, in a Jewish religious setting, is noticeably taken up by *1 Enoch*, where the phrase 'Lord of glory' (κύριος τῆς δόξης) is frequently used to designate God in the Greek manuscripts of the 'Book of the Watchers' (*1 En.* 22.14; 25.3; 27.3, 5).

The attribution of glory to others becomes a reflection of their essential proximity to God and of God's approval. Thus, glory is attributed to the praised 'fathers' in Sir. 44–50, (Abraham, 44.19; Moses, 45.2; Aaron, 45.20; David, 47.11, etc.). Glory will be God's reward for those who do God's will (*T. Sim.* 4.5; *T. Benj.* 4.1; *Pss. Sol.* 2.31; cf. (Ethiopic) *1 En.* 58.2; 61.8; 62.16; 65.12). The restored holy city of Jerusalem will be clothed in glory (*Pss. Sol.* 11.7; Bar. 5.1-4). Glory is given to the eschatological priest in *T. Levi* 18.7, and to the royal messiah-figure of *Pss. Sol.* 17.31.

The early Christian use of δόξα follows that of the LXX and other Jewish Greek religious writings, in largely using the word as a charac-

---

46. G. von Rad, 'δόξα', *TDNT*, II, pp. 238-39.

47. E.g. Exod. 16.10; 24.16; 40.34-35; Pss. 57.5, 11; 63.2; 138.5; Isa. 42.8; 48.11; Ezek. 10.18; 11.23 etc.

48. On the importance of the sentiment of honour in ancient Mediterranean society, see Malina, *New Testament World*, pp. 28-62; also H. Moxnes, 'Honor and Shame', *BTB* 23 (1993), pp. 167-76.

teristic of God.[49] Its use in relation to Jesus is virtually always in reference to the post-Easter glorification of the risen Christ (Acts 7.55; Rom.
6.4; 1 Tim. 3.16; 1 Pet. 1.11, 21; 4.11, 13; 5.4, 11). Similarly, 'Lord of
glory' (κύριος τῆς δόξης) is used by Paul in 1 Cor. 2.8, to designate
Christ as the revealer of God's eternal wisdom. In the synoptic gospels,
it is used of the coming Son of Man (Mk 8.38; 13.26; Mt. 19.28;
25.31), of the transfigured Jesus (Lk. 9.32), and of his presupposed
future exaltation (Mk 10.37).

In this broad context, it seems clear that the use of 'glory' (δόξα) in
relation to Jesus in Jas 2.1 should be read very much as an expression
of his exaltation. It is an affirmation of his high standing in the God-
derived universal order of things; he is vindicated and approved by
God, and thus is characterised as having particularly honourable standing in proximity to God.[50] Thus, the exalted status of Jesus in proximity
to God, as 'our Lord Jesus Christ of glory', designates Jesus as an
authority-figure of universal importance, within the theocentric Jewish
framework of understanding.[51]

In view of the particularly authoritative status which is attributed to
Jesus in the references to him in 1.1 and 2.1, it is all the more noteworthy that there are only these two explicit references to him in the

49. For a full treatment, see A.M. Ramsey, *The Glory of God and the
Transfiguration of Christ* (London: Longmans, Green & Co., 1949), pp. 23-81.

50. Cf. F. Mussner, 'Direkte und indirekte Christologie im Jakobusbrief',
Catholica 24 (1970), pp. 111-17 (112-13). C. Burchard, 'Zu einigen christologischen
Stellen des Jakobusbriefes', in C. Breytenbach and H. Paulsen (eds.), *Anfänge der
Christologie* (Festschrift Ferdinand Hahn; Göttingen: Vandenhoeck & Ruprecht,
1991), pp. 353-68 (358), suggests that this may include allusion to the eschatological glory which Christians can hope to receive, as well that which Jesus has
already received.

51. It must be noted that the epistle does not use the precise term 'Lord of glory'
(κύριος τῆς δόξης), which is used as a designation for God in *1 Enoch* (22.14; 25.3;
27.3, 5). It cannot thus be argued by analogy to these occurences that the author is
here ascribing ontological divine status to Jesus; whether the author sees Jesus as
sharing in God's own glory, or as being attributed glory as part of his approval by
God (analogous to Sir. 44–50), is not completely clear, but the latter seems more
likely. On the other hand, cf. M. Karrer, 'Christus der Herr und die Welt als Stätte
der Prüfung: Zur Theologie des Jakobusbriefes', *Kerygma und Dogma* 35 (1989),
pp. 166-88 (171-72), who inclines towards the former interpretation. The peculiar
phraseology is perhaps to be explained by the author's frequent use of genitives of
attribution, cf. Jas 1.18, 23, 25; 2.4, 12; 5.15. Neither can 2.1 be explained on the
basis of the use of κύριος τῆς δόξης as a designation for Jesus in 1 Cor. 2.8.

entire text.[52] Other possible references to the figure of Jesus have been suggested by Mussner in the designation 'Lord' (κύριος) in 5.7-8 and 5.14-15, and in the term 'name' (ὄνομα) in 2.7 and 5.14.[53] However, none of these can be taken to refer with certainty to Jesus,[54] rather than to God, who would normally immediately be understood as the referent of an unqualified κύριος as a universal authority-figure in Greek-speaking Jewish thought. Thus, possible references to Jesus such as these cannot be used securely in treating the role of Jesus in the epistle.

Nevertheless, within the text as a compositional whole, the two references to Jesus occur at particularly strategic points: in 1.1, which expresses the grounding authority for the whole epistle, and in 2.1, at the start of the central development of the epistle's key themes. Moreover, the role of Jesus as a particular authority is consistently affirmed in another manner throughout the text, through the frequent allusion to the traditions of the sayings of Jesus. The frequency with which echoes of these traditions occur in the Epistle of James is perhaps even more striking than the relative paucity of actual references to the person of Jesus. This contrasts with, for instance, the Epistles of Paul, in which the words of Jesus seem to be relatively rarely recalled,[55] but in which

---

52. Cf. Vouga, *Jacques*, p. 32.

53. Mussner, 'Christologie', pp. 112-14; cf. Vouga, *Jacques*, pp. 30-32.

54. In the present work, only the phrase 'the coming of the Lord' (ἡ παρουσία τοῦ κυρίου) in 5.7-8 is seen as a likely further reference to Jesus. If this is the case, then it indicates the anticipation of the great eschatological revelation, when Jesus will come again, and at this time his real status and authority within God's eschatological order of the universe will be manifested. See further below, §6.3.1.

55. How far Paul actually knew or used traditions derived from Jesus remains an unresolved question. Bultmann took the view that he knew virtually no sayings of Jesus, which were unimportant for his understanding of Jesus' significance: see R. Bultmann, 'Die Bedeutung des geschichtlichen Jesus für die Theologie des Paulus', in R. Bultmann, *Glauben und Verstehen*, I (Tübingen: J.C.B. Mohr [Paul Siebeck], 1958), pp. 188-213; little use of the sayings of Jesus is also argued by H.W. Kuhn, 'Der irdische Jesus bei Paulus', *ZTK* 67 (1970), pp. 195-320. On the other hand, W.D. Davies, *Paul and Rabbinic Judaism* (London: SPCK, 1955), pp. 136-46, argues that Paul was thoroughly familiar with the sayings of Jesus, and frequently alluded to them; see also N. Walter, 'Paul and the Early Jesus-tradition', in A.J.M. Wedderburn (ed.), *Paul and Jesus* (JSNTSup, 37; Sheffield: JSOT Press, 1989), pp. 51-81. D.L. Dungan, *The Sayings of Jesus in the Churches of Paul* (Oxford: Basil Blackwell, 1971), p. 149, concludes that Paul allusively cites 'a considerable number of Jesus' teachings'. In either case, however, the traditions of

the figure of Jesus himself, as crucified and resurrected, is of great significance. Thus, while the designation of Jesus as 'our Lord Jesus Christ of glory' presupposes the conception of his vindication and exaltation by God, the text suggests a location within early Christianity with close links to those groups who perpetuated the traditions of the pre-crucifixion ministry of Jesus, especially the traditions of his verbal proclamation. The authority of Jesus as one specially appointed and exalted by God is confirmed by the presupposition of the authority of his proclamation.[56] These parallels with the Jesus traditions of the synoptic gospels will now be examined in detail in the next subsection.

2.3.2.2 Resonances of the Jesus Traditions in the Epistle of James. The number of possible points of contact between a text of only 108 verses like the Epistle of James, and the synoptic Jesus traditions, is very striking. Dibelius points to a threefold similarity: first, a formal similarity between, for example, James 1 and 5, and the collections of sayings in Matthew and Luke, as both can be described as paraenetic literature; second, a similarity of style, in the use of short pointed imperatives and of similar metaphors; third, the sharing of the same general convictions of piety. While Dibelius admits that the author must be familiar with such traditions, in his view this acquaintance should not be particularly highly ranked in the assessment of the epistle.[57] Other commentators, however, attach more significance to these connections, which range from close verbal correspondence (Jas 5.12 and Mt. 5.34-37), to the similar use of certain words or phrases (Jas 1.5 and Mt. 7.7//Lk. 11.9; Jas 5.9 and Mk 13.29; Jas 2.5 and Mt. 5.3//Lk. 6.20), to broad thematic similarities (Jas 2.1-13 and Mk 10.17-20//Mt. 19.16-22//Lk. 18.18-23). None of them is exactly identical with the wording of the gospel traditions, and, taken singly, many, perhaps even most, can plausibly be explained as simply sharing a common ethos.[58] Taken as a whole, however, the resonances are too frequent and consistent to be explained satisfactorily as accidents of a common general outlook.

The fact that it is the sayings of Jesus which are represented in the

the sayings of Jesus appear of less importance in Paul's writings than the crucifixion and resurrection of Jesus.

56. Cf. Mussner, 'Christologie', pp. 114-16.

57. Dibelius, *James*, pp. 28-29.

58. As Spitta showed in his argument that James is a Jewish, not a Christian document; Spitta, *Geschichte und Literatur*, pp. 158-78.

Epistle of James does not imply that the author was familiar only with sayings traditions. Outside the gospels, when reference is made to the activities of the ministry of Jesus, it is most frequently to a saying of Jesus, even among the writings of the later 'apostolic fathers', who undoubtedly were acquainted with the gospel narratives of Jesus' deeds (e.g. Polycarp, *Phil.* 2.3; 7.2; 12.3; *2 Clem.* 2.4; 3.2; 4.2; 6.12; 8.5; 9.11; 13.4). That the references to the sayings of Jesus do not correspond exactly to any of those recorded in the gospels is also not a surprise. Allusion as much as citation represents the author's manner of referring to the LXX text.[59] Even if written traditions of the sayings of Jesus had been compiled by the time of the composition of the epistle, either in the form of our gospels, or of earlier, pre-gospel collections, it was not until well into the second century that such works began to be explicitly cited as Scripture.[60] Thus, if the epistle was written before a definitive Greek version of such traditions had been recognised, obviously the author could not quote from it. It is impossible to tell if he does in fact quote from such forms of sayings of Jesus as he was acquainted with, but which differ from those in the gospels. This is certainly a possibility in relation to 5.12, and it has been suggested that other verses of the epistle (e.g. 2.13; 3.18; 4.17) may preserve otherwise unrecorded logia of Jesus.[61]

With regard to the echoing of traditions of the sayings of Jesus in the epistle, rather than citation, comparison with the *Didache* is particularly illustrative. This document shows clear knowledge of the sayings of Jesus, especially of a form similar to that in which they occur in Matthew. In particular, *Didache* 1 is replete with references to the 'sermon' of Matthew 5–7, which approximate to the wording of the gospels, but without reproducing it exactly. Although phrases reminiscent of the gospel sayings are found in almost every chapter, only twice

59. E.g. Jas 1.10 and Isa. 40.6-7; Jas 3.9 and Gen. 1.26; Jas 5.4 and Isa. 5.9; possibly Jas 5.7 and Deut. 11.14; Jas 5.20 and Prov. 10.12.

60. For recent discussions of the issues involved in the debate over the use of written or oral tradition in early Christianity, see H. Koester, 'Written Gospels or Oral Tradition?', *JBL* 113 (1994), pp. 293-97; W.H. Kelber, 'Jesus and Tradition: Words in Time, Words in Space', *Semeia* 65 (1994), pp. 139-67. Koester and Kelber both favour seeing oral tradition as predominant in the early movement.

61. See P.H. Davids, 'Jesus and James', in D. Wenham (ed.), *The Jesus Tradition outside the Gospels* (Gospel Perspectives, 5; Sheffield: JSOT Press, 1987), pp. 63-84 (69).

is this expressly stated to be a saying of the Lord, in 8.2 and 9.5. Interestingly here also, the citation of the prayer of Jesus in Mt. 6.9-13//Lk. 11.2-4, although closest to Matthew's version, does not in fact correspond exactly to either version. Accordingly, the *Didache* would seem to bear witness, on the one hand, to the practice of unattributed reference to the sayings of Jesus, by writers who were obviously thoroughly familiar with the traditions of Jesus' words, and on the other hand, to the possibility of the circulation of such traditions in forms which were not identical to those preserved in the gospels.[62] Thus, it would seem to verify the legitimate possibility of the use by the author of the epistle of traditional sayings of Jesus, which were recognised as authoritative, but which had not yet achieved a static form.

The table contained in the appendix to this chapter sets out points of correspondence between the Epistle of James and the synoptic gospels.[63] The first column shows the text of the relevant verses of the Epistle of James. The third, fourth and fifth columns show the parallel texts of the gospels according to Matthew, Luke and Mark respectively. Matthew and Luke have been placed side by side in order to facilitate comparison of Q material as it occurs in both gospels. The second column shows the source from which the gospel text in question derives.[64] Beneath the symbol for the gospel source in each case is a number, which indicates the closeness of contact between the Epistle of James and the gospel texts. '1' refers to the closest parallels, those which show close verbal and conceptual corrrespondence; '2' designates some degree of verbal and conceptual correspondence, where contact between the Epistle of James and the gospel traditions is likely,

62. Cf. W. Rordorf, 'Does the Didache Contain Jesus Tradition Independently of the Synoptic Gospels?', in H. Wansborough (ed.), *Jesus and the Oral Gospel Tradition* (JSNTSup, 64; Sheffield: JSOT Press, 1991), pp. 394-423, who argues for the use of oral tradition in the *Didache*, rather than dependence on the written gospels.

63. See also Hartin, *James*, pp. 141-42; Mayor, *James*, pp. lxxxv-lxxxviii; Davids, *James*, pp. 47-48; Mussner, *Jakobusbrief*, pp. 48-50; J. Chaine, *L'Epître de Saint Jacques* (Paris: Libraire Lecoffre, 1927), pp. lxiv-lxix; A. Schlatter, *Der Brief des Jakobus* (repr. Stuttgart: Calwer Verlag, 1985 [1956]), pp. 19-21.

64. Q refers to the double tradition, common to Matthew and Luke; this does not presuppose any particular theory as to whether Q was an oral or written text. Mk refers to material deriving from Mark's Gospel. M(Q) and M(Mk) refer to the Matthean redaction of Q and Mark respectively; likewise L(Q) and L(Mk) refer to the Lukan redaction of Q and Mark. M refers to material found only in Matthew; L to material peculiar to Luke.

but not so clearly probable as in the case of those marked with '1'; those marked '3' show more distant verbal and/or conceptual resonances, which, while still worthy of note, may reflect a common ethos as much as contact between the specific traditions in the gospels and the Epistle of James.

From a total of 80 gospel passages, 26 derive from Matthew or Matthean redaction, 24 from Q, 19 from Mark and 11 from Luke. When these figures are broken down in terms of the closeness of parallel, the overall picture can be viewed more precisely, as follows:

	Q	Mk	M(Q)	M(Mk)	M	L(Q)	L(Mk)	L
1	10	5	1	1	1	2	-	-
2	10	2	6	2	3	1	2	1
3	4	12	4	3	5	1	-	4
Total	24	19	11	6	9	4	2	5

When the figures for the redaction of Mark and Q by Matthew and Luke, together with those for the material special to Matthew and Luke, are added together, the figures in relation to the three gospel sources and Q are as follows:

	Q	Mk	M	L	Total	%
1	10	5	3	2	20	25
2	10	2	11	4	27	34
3	4	12	12	5	33	41
Total	24	19	26	11	80	
%	30	24	32	14		

It is striking that half of the closest parallels and 37 per cent of the middle-range parallels are found in Q. Although there are considerably more middle-range parallels with Matthew than with Mark, there are slightly more close parallels to material deriving from Mark than from Matthew (but it must also be noted that 4 of the 5 close parallels to Markan material are also found in Matthew). At any rate, the fact that there is a sizeable number of parallels with material found in the Markan source would seem to render it unlikely that the author of the epistle was familiar only with the sayings preserved in the double tradition. There are also noticeably more parallels, especially in the second and third grades of proximity, to Matthew than to Luke.

The question of the respective dates of the composition of all the texts in question makes closer comparison problematic. It cannot be presupposed that the Epistle of James is later than the other texts,[65] thus, where parallels occur, for instance, with Matthew, this cannot be taken to indicate that the author was familiar with the gospel text,[66] or with the version of Q reflected in this gospel.[67] If the epistle is earlier, points of contact are just as likely, perhaps more likely, to indicate that Matthew was influenced by the Epistle of James, or knew traditions which bore the influence of the epistle's phraseology or concerns, as that the author of the epistle knew specifically pre-Matthean traditions. Indeed, the fact that both the Matthean beatitudes and the Lukan beatitudes and woes show separate points of close contact with the epistle would seem to support its priority over the gospel texts.[68]

The large number of parallels with Q strongly suggests the proximity of the epistle's author to the Q tradents.[69] The attempt to compare the resonances of the sayings of Jesus in the epistle of James with the Q sayings of Jesus is, however, beset with difficulties. On the one hand, there is no text of the sayings of Jesus underlying the echoes of the sayings in the epistle; on the other hand, there is no extant text of Q, thus any comparison has to be with the hypothetical reconstructions of modern scholars. This intangibility of the two items for comparison, despite the best efforts of scholars like Hartin, surely renders the fruitfulness of the undertaking somewhat questionable, or, at least, extremely tentative.[70] A balanced position on the relation of the epistle

65. The results of this work indicate that the epistle should be dated earlier; see below, §7.3.3.

66. M.H. Shepherd, 'The Epistle of James and the Gospel of Matthew', *JBL* 75 (1956), pp. 40-51. His argument that James was familiar with Matthew through hearing the reading of the gospel, but not through reading it himself, hence his imprecise references, lacks convincing evidence.

67. Hartin, *James*.

68. Jas 1.2, cf. Mt. 5.11-12//Lk. 6.22-23 (Q); Jas 2.5, cf. Mt. 5.3//Lk. 6.20 (Q); Jas 2.5, cf. Mt. 5.5 (M[Q]); Jas 4.9, cf. Lk. 6.21 (L[Q]); Jas 5.1, cf. Lk. 6.24-25 (L[Q]).

69. Contrary to the opinion of W.D. Davies, *The Setting of the Sermon on the Mount* (Cambridge: Cambridge University Press, 1964), pp. 403-404, who wishes to play down the importance of parallels with Q, in the light of his view that Q was not primarily a catechetic or paraenetic text.

70. Penner, *James*, pp. 241-53, is similarly cautious in his comparison of the Epistle of James with the Q materials. His analysis stresses the parallels in the eschatological perspective which can be discerned between the Epistle of James and the final form of Q. Cf. also M. Jackson-McCabe, 'A Letter to the Twelve Tribes in the Diaspora: Wisdom and Apocalyptic Eschatology in the Letter of James', *SBLSP*

to the gospel traditions is struck by Davids, who concludes:

> The lack of verbal parallels and the combined similarity to both Matthew
> and Luke point to James's having used the unwritten Jesus tradition
> freely.[71]

This provides the most useful view of the relationship: the author of the
Epistle of James and the authors of the synoptic gospels share traditions
of the sayings of Jesus which have not yet reached the degree of
permanence that would be associated with an authoritative written
form. The concerns of the epistle resemble at times those of both Luke
and Matthew (and Q), but are not elaborated in an identical manner.
The epistle is not specifically dependent on the Matthean or Lukan
development of the Jesus traditions, but like these and other surviving
early Christian texts represents a unique point in the development, use
and transmission of these traditions within the dynamics of the social
world of early Christianity.

Nevertheless, if the attempt to determine the precise lines of relation
between the Epistle of James and the traditions of the sayings of Jesus
preserved in their various forms in the gospels is to be renounced, it
remains clear from the similarities adduced in the table in the appendix
that there are strong correspondences in terms of expression and content. The substance of these is of considerable importance in marking
the distinctive Christian ethos of the epistle. Based principally on the
closest parallels from the table, the most significant of these shared
concerns represented by both the Epistle of James and the gospels are
laid out below.

    1.   *Affirmation of the Lowly or Marginal.* This theme, which is
        one of the most striking in the text, is also an important aspect
        of the Jesus traditions in the gospels. There are close connec-
        tions, both verbally and thematically between the expression
        of the favoured status of the lowly (ταπεινός) in Jas 1.9-11,
        and the saying of Jesus concerning the exaltation of those
        in servile positions and the lowering of status of the exalted

---

33 (1996), pp. 504-17, who draws attention to the fact that the so-called sapiential
and apocalyptic elements, often used as a basis for the differentiation of
compositional strata in Q (see especially J.S. Kloppenborg, *The Formation of Q*
[Philadelphia: Fortress Press, 1987]), are thoroughly integrated in James.

    71. Davids, *James*, p. 50; cf. also Laws, *James*, p. 15.

(Mt. 23.12//Lk. 14.11; 18.4). This theme is also well attested in synoptic texts of Markan origin (cf. Mk 10.43-44//Mt. 20.26// Lk. 22.26; Mk 9.35//Mt. 18.4).

Similarly, there are close links between the affirmation of the status of the poor (πτωχός) as inheritors of the kingdom (βασιλεία) in Jas 2.5, and, in particular, the opening beatitude of Mt. 5.3//Lk. 6.20; less directly, the poor are those to whom the good news is announced in Mt. 11.5//Lk. 7.22. The kingdom image of Jas 2.5 is, of course, a central expression of the proclamation of Jesus in the gospels. This theme is also widely reflected in the gospel narrative tradition in the persistent presentation of the affirmation or restoration by Jesus of the marginal, such as the blind, the lame, the skin-diseased, widows (cf. 1.27), and so on.

2. *Reversal of Status.* Closely related to the affirmation of the marginal is the theme of reversal of status within God's order of things. Thus, ultimately, the lowly brother is exalted (1.9-10), and the poor person is the inheritor of God's kingdom (2.5). Conversely, those who claim exalted status for themselves are abased. In the Epistle of James, it is particularly the rich (πλούσιοι) (1.10-11; 5.1-6), whose earthly security will, ultimately, be overturned. The final transcience of such material well-being is also announced in the gospel traditions, perhaps most notably in Luke, for instance, in the woes which follow the Lukan beatitudes (Lk. 6.24-25), and in the two parables about the fate of a rich man (Lk. 12.16-21; 16.19-31; cf. also Mt. 6.19-21//Lk. 12.33-34). The exhortations to abasement before God in Jas 4.7-10 also fit in this context of status reversal, and again bear verbal similarity to the Lukan beatitudes and woes (Lk. 6.20-26) and the Matthean beatitudes (Mt. 5.3-12).

3. *Eschatological Expectation/Threat of Judgement or Reward.* Linked with the conviction of the ultimate reversal of status within God's order is a strong sense of eschatological expectation, which in turn grounds a sense of the assignment of favourable status to those in harmony with God's order, and the corresponding rejection of those who are out of harmony. The opening exhortation to joy amid testing (1.2; cf. 1.12)

should probably be seen in this light, in the same way as Jesus' followers are urged to rejoice amid difficulties in anticipation of their coming reward in Mt. 5.11-12//Lk. 6.22-23.

This theme is particularly prevalent in the subsection Jas 4.11–5.11, again with noteworthy parallels in the synoptic traditions. The image of the corruptiblity of earthly treasures in the light of eschatological realities (5.2-3) is strongly reminiscent of the contrast between earthly and heavenly treasures in Mt. 6.19-20//Lk. 12.33. The expectation of the final coming (παρουσία, Jas 5.7-8) is expressed in Matthew 24, followed by the great judgement parables of Matthew 25. The same image as is used in Jas 5.9, of the eschatological judge having reached the gates in his final coming, is also found in Mk 13.29//Mt. 24.33. The conclusion of this passage, with the exhortation to endurance in Jas 5.11, again has a close parallel in the eschatological assurance that 'the one who endures to the end will be saved' (Mk 13.13; cf. Mt. 10.22; 24.13; Lk. 21.19). Likewise, the fundamental conviction that judgement is the prerogative solely of God (Jas 4.11-12; cf. 5.9) is found in the sayings tradition in Mt. 7.1//Lk. 9.54-56; it is God who ultimately has the power to save or destroy (Jas 4.12, cf. Mt. 10.28).

4. *Radical Behavioural Demand.* There is also a significant correspondence between the demands for behaviour in accordance with God's order found in the gospel traditions and in the Epistle of James. Thus, Jas 1.22-25 stresses the importance of doing, as well as hearing, what is demanded by God's standards, similar to Mt. 7.24-27//Lk. 6.46-49, the closing paragraphs of the 'sermons' of Matthew 5–7//Lk. 6.17-49. What is entailed in this demand is given key expression through the importance of the love-command (Jas 2.8, citing Lev. 19.18, cf. Mk 12.31//Mt. 22.39//Lk. 10.27). The allusion to the *Shema* (Jas 2.19; cf. Deut. 6.4, combined with Lev. 19.18 in Mk 12.29; cf. Mt. 22.37//Lk. 10.27), which contains the command to absolute love of God (Deut. 6.5) should probably also be seen to bring out this demand.

5. *God's Mercy.* Along with a powerful conviction of impending eschatological judgement and reversal of status in the early Christian view of the world is a strong sense of the mercy of

God, which is most plainly expressed in the Epistle of James in 2.13: 'mercy triumphs over judgment'. Corresponding to this is the demand for mercy in human action, likewise expressed in 2.12-13, which has a number of parallels in the synoptic gospels, perhaps most closely in Mt. 5.7: 'Blessed are those who show mercy, because they will receive mercy' (cf. Mt. 6.14; Lk. 6.36). Dependence on God's mercy again lies behind the confession of sin, healing and restoration in Jas 5.14-20, and in the exhortation to unconditional submission to God in 4.7-10.

6. *God's Giving/Dependence on God.* Again, a sense of radical dependence on God, both as the guarantor of ultimately favourable status to those approved by God, and for the provision of immediate earthly needs is found in both the Epistle of James and in the traditions associated with Jesus in the synoptic gospels. That God is the giver of all good things is stated in 1.17 (cf. Mt. 7.11//Lk. 11.13); dependence on the generosity of God, who gives what is needed to those who ask, is expressed in the exhortation of Jas 1.5: 'Let him ask... and it will be given to him'. This verse bears a close resemblance to the assurance of the sayings tradition in Mt. 7.7//Lk. 11.9: 'Ask and it will be given to you'. The same idea occurs in a negative connotation in Jas 4.2-3, where the addressees are told that they do not receive because they do not ask, and ask wrongly, to spend on their pleasures.

Further, the example of 2.15-16 may reflect the kind of dependence on God on the part of the socially marginal for one's daily needs expressed by the petition for bread in the prayer of Jesus (Mt. 6.11//Lk. 11.3). Dependence on God, rather than on human plans is again exhorted in Jas 4.13-17, reminiscent of Mt. 6.34.

7. *The Effectiveness of Prayer.* Related to a sense of dependence on God is a firm belief in the power of faithful prayer, expressed in 1.5-6 and in 5.13-18. A close parallel in content is found in the interpretation of the cursing of the fig tree in Mk 11.23-24//Mt. 21.21-22 (cf. also Mt. 17.20//Lk. 17.6; Mt. 7.7-8//Lk. 11.9). This particularly fervent view of the effectiveness of faithful prayer is distinctive to the gospel traditions and the Epistle of James.

Thus, in conclusion, it can be asserted with confidence that the Epistle of James is thoroughly pervaded by an early Christian perspective, which closely resembles the ethos of the traditions of the sayings of Jesus in the synoptic gospels. Although it seems impossible to trace the direct lines of contact between the epistle and these traditions with any certainty, the correspondences, both in expression and in content, are virtually indisputable.

2.4 *Conclusion*

This chapter has examined the depiction of the author within the text of the Epistle of James, both through direct self-designations and implicitly through his use of, and self-identification with, authoritative traditions.

1. The author places himself under the supreme authority of God, and of Jesus, who as Lord and Christ, is seen as specially chosen, vindicated and honoured by God. By placing himself absolutely under God's authority, the author implies the divine authorisation of what he says in the epistle.

2. As a teacher (Jas 3.1), he depicts himself as one who carries out an authoritative role within the early Christian movement, a role which was widely recognised as commissioned by God, and which was closely related to those of apostles and prophets. The teacher was one who expounded the will of God for his hearers, often drawing on the resources of Scripture and tradition.

3. This constructive drawing on Scripture and tradition is reflected in the affirmation by the author of the Jewish religious world-view, referring, for example, to the *Shema* (2.19) and the Decalogue (2.11), and in the use of such key terms as law, righteousness and wisdom. This view, however, is also shaped by the influence of early Christian traditions, as is clear from the striking number of resonances in the epistle of the sayings of Jesus preserved in the synoptic gospels. These are particularly to do with such issues as God's favour towards the lowly and marginal, the importance of radical dependence on God, and a strong sense of eschatological expectation, anticipating the judgment of those who are out of harmony with the

demands of God's eschatological order, and the honouring of those who are loyal to God.

4. The large number of points of contact with the sayings of Jesus points towards the proximity of the author to the tradents of these Jesus-traditions. It is difficult, however, to go much further than this in determining the precise relation between the Epistle of James and other extant early Christian texts, such as the synoptic gospels.

Appendix

THE EPISTLE OF JAMES AND THE SYNOPTIC GOSPELS

James		Matthew	Luke	Mark
1.2 πᾶσαν χαρὰν ἡγήσασθε, ἀδελφοί μου, ὅταν πειρασ-μοῖς περιπέσητε ποικίλοις…	Q 1	5.11-12 μακάριοί ἐστε ὅταν ὀνειδίσωσιν ὑμᾶς… ἕνεκεν ἐμοῦ· χαίρετε καὶ ἀγαλλιᾶσθε…	6.22-23 μακάριοί ἐστε ὅταν μισήσωσιν ὑμᾶς…ἕνεκα τοῦ Υἱοῦ τοῦ ἀνθρώπου. χάρητε ἐν ἐκείνῃ τῇ ἡμέρᾳ	
	L(Mk) 2		8.13 …οἳ ὅταν ἀκούσωσιν μετὰ χαρᾶς δέχονται τὸν λόγον…οἳ πρὸς καιρὸν πιστεύουσιν καὶ ἐν καιρῷ πειρασμοῦ ἀφίστανται…	
1.4 ἡ δὲ ὑπομονὴ ἔργον τέλειον ἐχέτω, ἵνα ἦτε τέλειοι καὶ ὁλόκληροι, ἐν μηδενὶ λειπόμενοι.	M(Q) 2	5.48 ἔσεσθε οὖν ὑμεῖς τέλειοι ὡς ὁ πατὴρ ὑμῶν ὁ οὐράνιος τέλειός ἐστιν.		
	M(Mk) 2	19.21 εἰ θέλεις τέλειος εἶναι, ὕπαγε πώλησόν σου τὰ ὑπάρχοντα καὶ δὸς πτωχοῖς, καὶ ἕξεις θησαυρὸν ἐν οὐρανοῖς, καὶ δεῦρο ἀκολούθει μοι.		
1.5 …αἰτείτω παρὰ τοῦ διδόντος Θεοῦ πᾶσιν ἁπλῶς καὶ μὴ ὀνειδίζοντος, καὶ δοθήσεται αὐτῷ,	Q 1	7.7 αἰτεῖτε καὶ δοθήσεται ὑμῖν…	11.9 αἰτεῖτε, καὶ δοθήσεται ὑμῖν…	

James		Matthew	Luke	Mark
1.6 αἰτείτω δὲ ἐν πίστει, μηδὲν διακρινόμενος·	Mk 1	21.21-22 ἐὰν ἔχητε πίστιν καὶ μὴ διακριθῆτε…καὶ πάντα ὅσα ἂν αἰτήσητε ἐν τῇ προσευχῇ πιστεύοντες λήμψεσθε.		11.23 ὃς ἂν εἴπῃ τῷ ὄρει τούτῳ, Ἄρθητι καὶ βλήθητι εἰς τὴν θάλασσαν, καὶ μὴ διακριθῇ ἐν τῇ καρδίᾳ αὐτοῦ ἀλλὰ πιστεύῃ ὅτι ὃ λαλεῖ γίνεται, ἔσται αὐτῷ.
	M(Mk) 3	17.20 ἐὰν ἔχητε πίστιν ὡς κόκκον σινάπεως…οὐδὲν ἀδυνατήσει ὑμῖν.		
1.9-10 καυχάσθω δὲ ὁ ἀδελφὸς ὁ ταπεινὸς ἐν τῷ ὕψει αὐτοῦ, ὁ δὲ πλούσιος ἐν τῇ ταπεινώσει αὐτοῦ,	Q 1	23.12 ὅστις δὲ ὑψώσει ἑαυτὸν ταπεινωθήσεται, καὶ ὅστις ταπεινώσει ἑαυτὸν ὑψωθήσεται. cf. 18.4	14.11 πᾶς ὁ ὑμῶν ἑαυτὸν ταπεινωθήσεται, καὶ ὁ ταπεινῶν ἑαυτὸν ὑψωθ-ήσεται cf. 22.26; 18.14	
	Mk 3	20.26-27 ὃς ἐὰν θέλῃ ἐν ὑμῖν μέγας γενέσθαι, ἔσται ὑμῶν διάκονος, καὶ ὃς ἂν θέλῃ ἐν ὑμῖν εἶναι πρῶτος, ἔσται ὑμῶν δοῦλος·		9.35 εἴ τις θέλει πρῶτος εἶναι, ἔσται πάντων ἔσχατος καὶ πάντων διάκονος. cf. 10.43-44

James		Matthew	Luke	Mark
1.17 πᾶσα δόσις ἀγαθὴ καὶ πᾶν δώρημα τέλειον ἄνωθέν ἐστιν καταβαῖνον ἀπὸ τοῦ πατρὸς τῶν φώτων,	Q 1	7.11 εἰ οὖν ὑμεῖς πονηροὶ ὄντες οἴδατε δόματα ἀγαθὰ διδόναι τοῖς τέκνοις ὑμῶν, πόσῳ μᾶλλον ὁ πατὴρ ὑμῶν ὁ ἐν τοῖς οὐρανοῖς δώσει ἀγαθὰ τοῖς αἰτοῦσιν αὐτόν.	11.13 εἰ οὖν ὑμεῖς πονηροὶ ὑπάρχοντες οἴδατε δόματα ἀγαθὰ διδόναι τοῖς τέκνοις ὑμῶν, πόσῳ μᾶλλον ὁ πατὴρ ὁ ἐξ οὐρανοῦ δώσει πνεῦμα ἅγιον τοῖς αἰτοῦσιν αὐτόν.	
1.20 ὀργὴ γὰρ ἀνδρὸς δικαιοσύνην θεοῦ οὐκ ἐργάζεται.	M 3	5.22 πᾶς ὁ ὀργιζόμενος τῷ ἀδελφῷ αὐτοῦ ἔνοχος ἔσται τῇ κρίσει·		
	M(Q) 3	6.33 ζητεῖτε...τὴν βασιλείαν τοῦ θεοῦ καὶ τὴν δικαιοσύνην αὐτοῦ,		
1.21 δέξασθε τὸν ἔμφυτον λόγον τὸν δυνάμενον σῶσαι τὰς ψυχὰς ὑμῶν.	Mk 3	16.25 ὃς γὰρ ἐὰν θέλῃ τὴν ψυχὴν αὐτοῦ σῶσαι, ἀπολέσει αὐτήν· ὃς δ' ἂν ἀπολέσῃ τὴν ψυχὴν αὐτοῦ ἔνεκεν ἐμοῦ, εὑρήσει αὐτήν.	9.24 ὃς γὰρ ἐὰν θέλῃ τὴν ψυχὴν αὐτοῦ σῶσαι, ἀπολέσει αὐτήν· ὃς δ' ἂν ἀπολέσῃ τὴν ψυχὴν αὐτοῦ ἔνεκεν ἐμοῦ, οὗτος σώσει αὐτήν.	8.35 ὃς γὰρ ἐὰν θέλῃ τὴν ψυχὴν αὐτοῦ σῶσαι, ἀπολέσει αὐτήν· ὃς δ' ἂν ἀπολέσει τὴν ψυχὴν αὐτοῦ ἔνεκεν ἐμοῦ καὶ τοῦ εὐαγγελίου, σώσει αὐτήν.
	L(Mk) 2		8.13 ...οἳ ὅταν ἀκούσωσιν μετὰ χαρᾶς δέχονται τὸν λόγον...	

James		Matthew	Mark	Luke
1.22 γίνεσθε δὲ ποιηταὶ λόγου, καὶ μὴ ἀκροαταὶ μόνον παραλογιζόμενοι ἑαυτούς…	Q 1	7.24-27 πᾶς οὖν ὅστις ἀκούει μου τοὺς λόγους τούτους καὶ ποιεῖ αὐτούς, ὁμοιωθήσεται ἀνδρὶ φρονίμῳ…		6.46-49 τί δέ με καλεῖτε, Κύριε κύριε, καὶ οὐ ποιεῖτε ἃ λέγω; πᾶς ὁ ἐρχόμενος πρός με καὶ ἀκούον μου τῶν λόγων καὶ ποιῶν αὐτούς, ὑποδείξω ὑμῖν τίνι ἐστὶν ὅμοιος…
1.25 ὁ δὲ παρακύψας εἰς νόμον τέλειον τὸν τῆς ἐλευθερίας καὶ παραμείνας, οὐκ ἀκροατὴς ἐπιλησμονῆς γενόμενος ἀλλὰ ποιητὴς ἔργου, οὗτος μακάριος ἐν τῇ ποιήσει αὐτοῦ ἔσται.	M 3	5.17 μὴ νομίσητε ὅτι ἦλθον καταλῦσαι τὸν νόμον ἢ τοὺς προφήτας· οὐκ ἦλθον καταλῦσαι ἀλλὰ πληρῶσαι.		
1.26-27 εἴ τις δοκεῖ θρησκὸς εἶναι, μὴ χαλιναγωγῶν γλῶσσαν αὐτοῦ ἀλλὰ ἀπατῶν καρδίαν αὐτοῦ, τούτου μάταιος ἡ θρησκεία. θρησκεία καθαρὰ καὶ ἀμίαντος παρὰ τῷ θεῷ καὶ πατρὶ αὕτη ἐστίν…	M(Q) 3	7.21 οὐ πᾶς ὁ λέγων μοι, Κύριε κύριε, εἰσελεύσεται εἰς τὴν βασιλείαν τῶν οὐρανῶν, ἀλλ' ὁ ποιῶν τὸ θέλημα τοῦ πατρός μου τοῦ ἐν τοῖς οὐρανοῖς.		

James		Matthew	Luke	Mark
1.27 ἐπισκέπτεσθαι ὀρφανοὺς καὶ χήρας ἐν τῇ θλίψει αὐτῶν...	M 3	25.36 ...ἠσθένησα καὶ ἐπεσκέψασθέ με...		
	Mk 3		20.47 ...οἳ κατεσθίουσιν τὰς οἰκίας τῶν χηρῶν...	12.40 ...οἳ κατεσθίοντες τὰς οἰκίας τῶν χηρῶν...
2.4 οὐ διεκρίθητε ἐν ἑαυτοῖς καὶ ἐγένεσθε κριταὶ διαλογισμῶν πονηρῶν...	Mk 3	15.19 ἐκ γὰρ τῆς καρδίας ἐξέρχονται διαλογισμοὶ πονηροί		7.21, 23 ἔσωθεν γὰρ ἐκ τῆς καρδίας τῶν ἀνθρώπων οἱ διαλογισμοὶ οἱ κακοί...πάντα ταῦτα τὰ πονηρὰ ἔσωθεν ἐκπορεύεται...
2.5 οὐχ ὁ θεὸς ἐξελέξατο τοὺς πτωχοὺς τῷ κόσμῳ πλουσίους ἐν πίστει καὶ κληρονόμους τῆς βασιλείας ἧς ἐπηγγείλατο τοῖς ἀγαπῶσιν αὐτόν;	Q 1	5.3, 5 μακάριοι οἱ πτωχοὶ τῷ πνεύματι, ὅτι αὐτῶν ἐστιν ἡ βασιλεία τῶν οὐρανῶν... μακάριοι οἱ πραεῖς, ὅτι αὐτοὶ κληρονομήσουσιν τὴν γῆν.	6.20 μακάριοι οἱ πτωχοί, ὅτι ὑμετέρα ἐστὶν ἡ βασιλεία τοῦ θεοῦ.	
	Q 2	11.5 ...πτωχοὶ εὐαγγελίζονται...	7.22 ...πτωχοὶ εὐαγγελίζονται...	

James		Matthew	Luke	Mark
	M 2	25.34 δεῦτε οἱ εὐλογη-μένοι τοῦ πατρός μου, κληρονομήσατε τὴν ἡτοιμασ-μένην ὑμῖν βασιλείαν...		
2.8 εἰ μέντοι νόμον τελεῖτε βασιλικὸν κατὰ τὴν γραφήν, Ἀγαπήσεις τὸν πλησίον σου ὡς σεαυτόν, καλῶς ποιεῖτε·	Mk 3	22.37-39 Ἀγαπήσεις κύριον τὸν θεόν σου ἐν ὅλῃ τῇ καρδίᾳ σου καὶ ἐν ὅλῃ τῇ ψυχῇ σου καὶ ἐν ὅλῃ τῇ διανοίᾳ σου. αὕτη ἐστὶν ἡ μεγάλη καὶ πρώτη ἐντολή. δευτέρα δὲ ὁμοία αὐτῇ, Ἀγαπήσεις τὸν πλησίον σου ὡς σεαυτόν.	10.27 Ἀγαπήσεις κύριον τὸν θεόν σου ἐξ ὅλης καρδίας σου καὶ ἐν ὅλῃ τῇ ψυχῇ σου καὶ ἐν ὅλῃ τῇ ἰσχύϊ σου καὶ ἐν ὅλῃ τῇ διανοίᾳ σου, καὶ τὸν πλησίον σου ὡς σεαυτόν.	12.29-31 ...πρώτη ἐστίν, Ἄκουε, Ἰσραήλ, κύριος ὁ θεὸς ἡμῶν κύριος εἷς ἐστιν, καὶ ἀγαπήσεις κύριον τὸν θεόν σου ἐξ ὅλης τῆς καρδίας σου καὶ ἐξ ὅλης τῆς ψυχῆς σου καὶ ἐξ ὅλης τῆς διανοίας σου καὶ ἐξ ὅλης τῆς ἰσχύος σου. δευτέρα αὕτη, Ἀγαπήσεις τὸν πλησίον σου ὡς σεαυτόν.
2.10 ὅστις γὰρ ὅλον τὸν νόμον τηρήσῃ, πταίσῃ δὲ ἐν ἑνί, γέγονεν πάντων ἔνοχος.	Q 2	5.18 ἕως ἂν παρέλθῃ ὁ οὐρανὸς καὶ ἡ γῆ, ἰῶτα ἓν ἢ μία κεραία οὐ μὴ παρέλθῃ ἀπὸ τοῦ νόμου, ἕως ἂν πάντα γένηται.	16.17 εὐκοπώτερον δέ ἐστιν τὸν οὐρανὸν καὶ τὴν γῆν παρελθεῖν ἢ τοῦ νόμου μίαν κεραίαν πεσεῖν.	

James		Matthew	Luke	Mark
2.11 ὁ γὰρ εἰπών, Μὴ μοιχεύσῃς, εἶπεν καί, Μὴ φονεύσῃς...	M 3	5.21, 27 Οὐ φονεύσεις... Οὐ μοιχεύσεις...		10.19 Μὴ φονεύσῃς, Μὴ μοιχεύσῃς...
	Mk 3	19.18 Οὐ φονεύσεις, Οὐ μοιχεύσεις...	18.20 Μὴ μοιχεύσῃς, Μὴ φονεύσῃς...	
2.13 ἡ γὰρ κρίσις ἀνέλεος τῷ μὴ ποιήσαντι ἔλεος· κατακαυχᾶται ἔλεος κρίσεως.	M(Q) 1	5.7 μακάριοι οἱ ἐλεήμονες, ὅτι αὐτοὶ ἐλεηθήσονται.		
	M 3	23.23 ...ἀφήκατε τὰ βαρύτερα τοῦ νόμου, τὴν κρίσιν καὶ τὸ ἔλεος καὶ τὴν πίστιν		
	L(Q) 2		6.36 γίνεσθε οἰκτίρμονες καθὼς καὶ ὁ πατὴρ ὑμῶν οἰκτίρμων ἐστίν.	
	Mk 3	6.14-15 Ἐὰν γὰρ ἀφῆτε τοῖς ἀνθρώποις τὰ παραπτώματα αὐτῶν, ἀφήσει καὶ ὑμῖν ὁ πατὴρ ὑμῶν ὁ οὐράνιος... cf. 18.21-35		11.25 ἀφίετε εἴ τι ἔχετε κατά τινος, ἵνα καὶ ὁ πατὴρ ὑμῶν ὁ ἐν τοῖς οὐρανοῖς ἀφῇ ὑμῖν τὰ παραπτώματα ὑμῶν.

James		Matthew	Luke	Mark
	L 3		1.72 ...ποιῆσαι ἔλεος μετὰ τῶν πατέρων ἡμῶν…	
2.14-26	Q 3	7.21-23 parable of the two builders.	6.46-49 parable of the two builders.	
	Q 3	25.31-46 parable of the great judgment.		
2.15-16 ἐὰν ἀδελφὸς ἢ ἀδελφὴ γυμνοὶ ὑπάρχωσιν καὶ λειπόμενοι τῆς ἐφημέρου τροφῆς, εἴπῃ δέ τις αὐτοῖς ἐξ ὑμῶν, Ὑπάγετε ἐν εἰρήνῃ, θερμαίνεσθε καὶ χορτάζεσθε, μὴ δῶτε δὲ αὐτοῖς τὰ ἐπιτήδεια τοῦ σώματος, τί τὸ ὄφελος;	M 2	25.35-36 ...ἐπείνασα γὰρ καὶ ἐδώκατέ μοι φαγεῖν, ἐδίψησα καὶ ἐποτίσατέ με, ξένος ἤμην καὶ συνηγάγετέ με, γυμνὸς καὶ περιεβάλετέ με...		
	L 2		3.11 Ὁ ἔχων δύο χιτῶνας μεταδότω τῷ μὴ ἔχοντι, καὶ ὁ ἔχων βρώματα ὁμοίως ποιείτω.	
	Q 3	6.11 ...τὸν ἄρτον ἡμῶν τὸν ἐπιούσιον δὸς ἡμῖν σήμερον…	11.3 ...τὸν ἄρτον ἡμῶν τὸν ἐπιούσιον δίδου ἡμῖν τὸ καθ᾽ ἡμέραν…	

James		Matthew	Luke	Mark
2.15 ἐὰν ἀδελφὸς ἢ ἀδελφὴ γυμνοὶ ὑπάρχωσιν καὶ λειπόμενοι τῆς ἐφημέρου τροφῆς...	Q 2	6.25 μὴ μεριμνᾶτε τῇ ψυχῇ ὑμῶν τί φάγητε ἢ τί πίητε, μηδὲ τῷ σώματι ὑμῶν τί ἐνδύσησθε.	12.22 μὴ μεριμνᾶτε τῇ ψυχῇ τί φάγητε, μηδὲ τῷ σώματι τί ἐνδύσησθε.	
2.16 ...Ὑπάγετε ἐν εἰρήνῃ...	Mk 3			5.34 ...ὕπαγε εἰς εἰρήνην...
2.19 σὺ πιστεύεις ὅτι εἷς ἐστιν ὁ θεός; καλῶς ποιεῖς...	Mk 2	19.17 ...εἷς ἐστιν ὁ ἀγαθός...	18.19 ...οὐδεὶς ἀγαθὸς εἰ μὴ εἷς ὁ θεός...	10.18 ...οὐδεὶς ἀγαθὸς εἰ μὴ εἷς ὁ θεός...
	Mk 1			12.29-30 ...Κύριος ὁ Θεὸς ἡμῶν Κύριος εἷς ἐστιν...
3.1 ...ὅτι μεῖζον κρίμα λημψόμεθα.	M(Mk) 1	12.36-37 πᾶν ῥῆμα ἀργὸν ὃ λαλήσουσιν οἱ ἄνθρωποι ἀποδώσουσιν περὶ αὐτοῦ λόγον ἐν ἡμέρᾳ κρίσεως· ἐκ γὰρ τῶν λόγων σου δικαιωθήσῃ, καὶ ἐκ τῶν λόγων σου καταδικασθήσῃ.		
3.2 πολλὰ γὰρ πταίομεν ἅπαντες· εἴ τις ἐν λόγῳ οὐ πταίει, οὗτος τέλειος ἀνήρ.	Mk 3		20.47 ...οὗτοι λήμψονται περισσότερον κρίμα.	12.40 ...οὗτοι λήμψονται περισσότερον κρίμα.

James		Matthew	Luke	Mark
3.9 ἐν αὐτῇ εὐλογοῦμεν τὸν κύριον καὶ πατέρα…	Q 3	11.25 Πάτερ, κύριε τοῦ οὐρανοῦ καὶ τῆς γῆς…	10.21 Πάτερ, κύριε τοῦ οὐρανοῦ καὶ τῆς γῆς…	
3.10 ἐκ τοῦ αὐτοῦ στόμ- ατος ἐξέρχεται εὐλογία καὶ κατάρα.	M(Mk) 3	15.11 …τὸ ἐκπορευόμενον ἐκ τοῦ στόματος, τοῦτο κοινοῖ τὸν ἄνθρωπον.		
	Q 2	12.34-35 ἐκ γὰρ τοῦ περισσεύματος τῆς καρδίας τὸ στόμα λαλεῖ. ὁ ἀγαθὸς ἄνθρωπος ἐκ τοῦ ἀγαθοῦ θησαυροῦ ἐκβάλλει ἀγαθά, καὶ ὁ πονηρὸς ἄνθρωπος ἐκ τοῦ πονηροῦ θησαυροῦ ἐκβάλλει πονηρά.	6.45 ὁ ἀγαθὸς ἄνθρωπος ἐκ τοῦ ἀγαθοῦ θησαυροῦ τῆς καρδίας προφέρει τὸ ἀγαθόν, καὶ ὁ πονηρὸς ἐκ τοῦ πονηροῦ προφέρει τὸ πονηρόν· ἐκ γὰρ περισσεύματος καρδίας λαλεῖ τὸ στόμα αὐτοῦ.	

James		Matthew	Luke	Mark
3.12 μὴ δύναται, ἀδελφοί μου, συκῆ ἐλαίας ποιῆσαι ἢ ἄμπελος σῦκα;	Q 2	7.16 ἀπὸ τῶν καρπῶν αὐτῶν ἐπιγνώσεσθε αὐτούς. μήτι συλλέγουσιν ἀπὸ ἀκανθῶν σταφυλὰς ἢ ἀπὸ τριβόλων σῦκα... 12.33 ἢ ποιήσατε τὸ δένδρον καλὸν καὶ τὸν καρπὸν αὐτοῦ καλόν, ἢ ποιήσατε τὸ δένδρον σαπρὸν καὶ τὸν καρπὸν αὐτοῦ σαπρόν· ἐκ γὰρ τοῦ καρποῦ τὸ δένδρον γινώσκεται.	6.43-44 οὐ γάρ ἐστιν δένδρον καλὸν ποιοῦν καρπὸν σαπρόν, οὐδὲ πάλιν δένδρον σαπρὸν ποιοῦν καρπὸν καλόν. ἕκαστον γὰρ δένδρον ἐκ τοῦ ἰδίου καρποῦ γινώσκεται· οὐ γὰρ ἐξ ἀκανθῶν συλλέγουσιν σῦκα, οὐδὲ ἐκ βάτου σταφυλὴν τρυγῶσιν.	
3.13-17	M(Q) 3	11.25, 29 ἔκρυψας ταῦτα ἀπὸ σοφῶν καὶ συνετῶν, καὶ ἀπεκάλυψας αὐτὰ νηπίοις... ἄρατε τὸν ζυγόν μου ἐφ᾽ ὑμᾶς καὶ μάθετε ἀπ᾽ ἐμοῦ, ὅτι πραΰς εἰμι καὶ ταπεινὸς τῇ καρδίᾳ, καὶ εὑρήσετε ἀνάπαυσιν ταῖς ψυχαῖς ὑμῶν.		

James	Matthew	Luke	Mark
3.13 Τίς σοφὸς καὶ ἐπιστήμων ἐν ὑμῖν; δειξάτω ἐκ τῆς καλῆς ἀναστροφῆς τὰ ἔργα αὐτοῦ ἐν πραΰτητι σοφίας.	Q 2 11.19 ἐδικαιώθη ἡ σοφία ἀπὸ τῶν ἔργων αὐτῆς.	7.35 ἐδικαιώθη ἡ σοφία ἀπὸ πάντων τῶν τέκνων αὐτῆς.	
3.18 καρπὸς δὲ δικαιοσύνης ἐν εἰρήνῃ σπείρεται τοῖς ποιοῦσιν εἰρήνην.	M(Q) 2 5.9 μακάριοι οἱ εἰρηνοποιοί, ὅτι αὐτοὶ υἱοὶ Θεοῦ κληθήσονται.		
4.2-3 ἐπιθυμεῖτε, καὶ οὐκ ἔχετε…οὐκ ἔχετε διὰ τὸ μὴ αἰτεῖσθαι ὑμᾶς· αἰτεῖτε καὶ οὐ λαμβάνετε, διότι κακῶς αἰτεῖσθε.	Q 1 7.7 Αἰτεῖτε, καὶ δοθήσεται ὑμῖν	11.9 αἰτεῖτε, καὶ δοθήσεται ὑμῖν.	
4.4 μοιχαλίδες, οὐκ οἴδατε ὅτι ἡ φιλία τοῦ κόσμου ἔχθρα τοῦ Θεοῦ ἐστιν; ὃς ἐὰν οὖν βουληθῇ φίλος εἶναι τοῦ κόσμου, ἐχθρὸς τοῦ Θεοῦ καθίσταται.	M(Mk) 3 12.39 γενεὰ πονηρὰ καὶ μοιχαλίς cf. 16.4 Mk 3		8.38 …ἐν τῇ γενεᾷ ταύτῃ τῇ μοιχαλίδι…

James		Matthew	Luke	Mark
	Q 2	6.24 οὐδεὶς δύναται δυσὶ κυρίοις δουλεύειν· ἢ γὰρ τὸν ἕνα μισήσει καὶ τὸν ἕτερον ἀγαπήσει...	16.13 οὐδεὶς οἰκέτης δύναται δυσὶ κυρίοις δουλεύειν· ἢ γὰρ τὸν ἕνα μισήσει καὶ τὸν ἕτερον ἀγαπήσει...	
	M(Q) 3	5.8 μακάριοι οἱ καθαροὶ τῇ καρδίᾳ, ὅτι αὐτοὶ τὸν θεὸν ὄψονται.		
4.8 καθαρίσατε χεῖρας, ἁμαρτωλοί, καὶ ἁγνίσατε καρδίας, δίψυχοι.	L(Q) 1		6.21, 25 μακάριοι οἱ κλαίοντες νῦν, ὅτι γελάσετε ...οὐαί, οἱ γελῶντες νῦν, ὅτι πενθήσετε καὶ κλαύσετε.	
4.9 ταλαιπωρήσατε καὶ πενθήσατε καὶ κλαύσατε· ὁ γέλως ὑμῶν εἰς πένθος μετατραπήτω καὶ ἡ χαρὰ εἰς κατήφειαν.	M(Q) 2	5.4 μακάριοι οἱ πενθοῦντες, ὅτι αὐτοὶ παρακληθήσονται.		
4.10 ταπεινώθητε ἐνώπιον κυρίου, καὶ ὑψώσει ὑμᾶς.	Q 1	23.12 ὅστις δὲ ὑψώσει ἑαυτὸν ταπεινωθήσεται, καὶ ὅστις ταπεινώσει ἑαυτὸν ὑψωθήσεται. cf. 18.4	14.11 πᾶς ὁ ὑψῶν ἑαυτὸν ταπεινωθήσεται, καὶ ὁ ταπεινῶν ἑαυτὸν ὑψωθήσεται cf. 22.26; 18.14	

James		Matthew	Luke	Mark
4.11 μὴ καταλαλεῖτε ἀλλήλων, ἀδελφοί. ὁ κατα-λαλῶν ἀδελφοῦ ἢ κρίνων τὸν ἀδελφὸν αὐτοῦ καταλαλεῖ νόμου καὶ κρίνει νόμον·	Q 1	7.1 μὴ κρίνετε, ἵνα μὴ κριθῆτε·	6.37 μὴ κρίνετε, καὶ οὐ μὴ κριθῆτε· καὶ μὴ καταδικάζετε, καὶ οὐ μὴ καταδικασθῆτε.	
4.12 εἷς ἐστιν ὁ νομοθέτης καὶ κριτής, ὁ δυνάμενος σῶσαι καὶ ἀπολέσαι· σὺ δὲ τίς εἶ, ὁ κρίνων τὸν πλησίον;	M(Q) 2	10.28 φοβεῖσθε δὲ μᾶλλον τὸν δυνάμενον καὶ ψυχὴν καὶ σῶμα ἀπολέσαι ἐν γεέννῃ.		
4.13-17	M(Q) 2	6.34 μὴ οὖν μεριμνήσητε εἰς τὴν αὔριον...		
4.17 εἰδότι οὖν καλὸν ποιεῖν καὶ μὴ ποιοῦντι, ἁμαρτία αὐτῷ ἐστιν.	L 3		12.47 ἐκεῖνος δὲ ὁ δοῦλος ὁ γνοὺς τὸ θέλημα τοῦ κυρίου αὐτοῦ καὶ μὴ ἑτοιμάσας... δαρήσεται πολλάς·	

James	Matthew	Luke	Mark
5.1 Ἄγε νῦν οἱ πλούσιοι, κλαύσατε ὀλολύζοντες ἐπὶ ταῖς ταλαιπωρίαις ὑμῶν ταῖς ἐπερχομέναις.	L(Q) 1	6.24-25 πλὴν οὐαὶ ὑμῖν τοῖς πλουσίοις, ὅτι ἀπέχετε τὴν παράκλησιν ὑμῶν. οὐαὶ ὑμῖν, οἱ ἐμπεπλησμένοι νῦν, ὅτι πεινάσετε. οὐαί, οἱ γελῶντες νῦν, ὅτι πενθήσετε καὶ κλαύσετε.	
5.2-3 ὁ πλοῦτος ὑμῶν σέσηπεν, καὶ τὰ ἱμάτια ὑμῶν σητόβρωτα γέγονεν, ὁ χρυσὸς ὑμῶν καὶ ὁ ἄργυρος κατίωται, καὶ ὁ ἰὸς αὐτῶν εἰς μαρτύριον ὑμῖν ἔσται καὶ φάγεται τὰς σάρκας ὑμῶν ὡς πῦρ. ἐθησαυρίσατε ἐν ἐσχάταις ἡμέραις.	Q 1 6.19-20 μὴ θησαυρίζετε ὑμῖν θησαυροὺς ἐπὶ τῆς γῆς, ὅπου σὴς καὶ βρῶσις ἀφανίζει, καὶ ὅπου κλέπται διορύσσουσιν καὶ κλέπτουσιν· θησαυρίζετε δὲ ὑμῖν θησαυροὺς ἐν οὐρανῷ, ὅπου οὔτε σὴς οὔτε βρῶσις ἀφανίζει,	12.33 ποιήσατε ἑαυτοῖς βαλλάντια μὴ παλαιούμενα, θησαυρὸν ἀνέκλειπτον ἐν τοῖς οὐρανοῖς, ὅπου κλέπτης οὐκ ἐγγίζει οὐδὲ σὴς διαφθείρει·	
5.5 ἐτρυφήσατε ἐπὶ τῆς γῆς καὶ ἐσπαταλήσατε, ἐθρέψατε τὰς καρδίας ὑμῶν.	L 3	16.19 ἄνθρωπος δέ τις ἦν πλούσιος, καὶ ἐνεδιδύσκετο πορφύραν καὶ βύσσον εὐφραινόμενος καθ’ ἡμέραν λαμπρῶς…	

James		Matthew	Luke	Mark
5.6 …κατεδικάσατε, ἐφονεύσατε τὸν δίκαιον	L(Q) 3		6.37 μὴ καταδικάζετε, καὶ οὐ μὴ καταδικασθῆτε.	
5.7 ἰδοὺ ὁ γεωργὸς ἐκδέχεται τὸν τίμιον καρπὸν τῆς γῆς, μακροθυμῶν ἐπ᾽ αὐτῷ ἕως λάβῃ πρόϊμον καὶ ὄψιμον.	Mk 3			4.26-29 *parable of the growth of the seed.*
5.8 …ὅτι ἡ παρουσία τοῦ κυρίου ἤγγικεν.	M(Mk) 2	24.3 τί τὸ σημεῖον τῆς σῆς παρουσίας;…		
	M(Q) 2	24.27, 37, 39 …οὕτως ἔσται ἡ παρουσία τοῦ υἱοῦ τοῦ ἀνθρώπου.		
5.9 μὴ στενάζετε, ἀδελφοί, κατ᾽ ἀλλήλων ἵνα μὴ κριθῆτε· ἰδοὺ ὁ κριτὴς πρὸ τῶν θυρῶν ἕστηκεν.	M 2	5.22 …πᾶς ὁ ὀργιζόμενος τῷ ἀδελφῷ αὐτοῦ ἔνοχος ἔσται τῇ κρίσει		
	Q 2	7.1 μὴ κρίνετε, ἵνα μὴ κριθῆτε.	6.37 μὴ κρίνετε, καὶ οὐ μὴ κριθῆτε.	

James		Matthew	Luke	Mark
	Mk 1	24.33 …γινώσκετε ὅτι ἐγγύς ἐστιν ἐπὶ θύραις.		13.29 …γινώσκετε ὅτι ἐγγύς ἐστιν ἐπὶ θύραις.
5.10 ὑπόδειγμα λάβετε, ἀδελφοί, τῆς κακοπαθίας καὶ τῆς μακροθυμίας τοὺς προφήτας οἳ ἐλάλησαν ἐν τῷ ὀνόματι κυρίου.	Q 2	5.12 χαίρετε καὶ ἀγαλλιᾶσθε, ὅτι ὁ μισθὸς ὑμῶν πολὺς ἐν τοῖς οὐρανοῖς· οὕτως γὰρ ἐδίωξαν τοὺς προφήτας τοὺς πρὸ ὑμῶν.	6.23 χάρητε ἐν ἐκείνῃ τῇ ἡμέρᾳ καὶ σκιρτήσατε· ἰδοὺ γὰρ ὁ μισθὸς ὑμῶν πολὺς ἐν τῷ οὐρανῷ· κατὰ τὰ αὐτὰ γὰρ ἐποίουν τοῖς προφήταις οἱ πατέρες αὐτῶν.	
5.11 ἰδοὺ μακαρίζομεν τοὺς ὑπομείναντας· τὴν ὑπομονὴν Ἰὼβ ἠκούσατε, καὶ τὸ τέλος κυρίου εἴδετε, ὅτι πολύσπλαγχνός ἐστιν ὁ κύριος καὶ οἰκτίρμων.	Mk 2	10.22 …ὁ δὲ ὑπομείνας εἰς τέλος, οὗτος σωθήσεται. cf. 24.13	21.19 …ἐν τῇ ὑπομονῇ ὑμῶν κτήσασθε τὰς ψυχὰς ὑμῶν.	13.13 …ὁ δὲ ὑπομείνας εἰς τέλος, οὗτος σωθήσεται.

James	Matthew	Luke	Mark
5.12 μὴ ὀμνύετε, μήτε τὸν οὐρανὸν μήτε τὴν γῆν μήτε ἄλλον τινὰ ὅρκον· ἤτω δὲ ὑμῶν τὸ Ναὶ ναὶ καὶ τὸ Οὒ οὔ, ἵνα μὴ ὑπὸ κρίσιν πέσητε.	M 1		
	5.34-37 μὴ ὀμόσαι ὅλως· μήτε ἐν τῷ οὐρανῷ, ὅτι θρόνος ἐστὶν τοῦ θεοῦ· μήτε ἐν τῇ γῇ, ὅτι ὑποπόδιόν ἐστιν τῶν ποδῶν αὐτοῦ· μήτε εἰς Ἱεροσόλυμα, ὅτι πόλις ἐστὶν τοῦ μεγάλου βασιλέως· μήτε ἐν τῇ κεφαλῇ σου ὀμόσῃς, ὅτι οὐ δύνασαι μίαν τρίχα λευκὴν ποιῆσαι ἢ μέλαιναν. ἔστω δὲ ὁ λόγος ὑμῶν, Ναὶ ναί, οὒ οὔ.		
5.13-16	Mk 1		
	21.22 καὶ πάντα ὅσα ἂν αἰτήσητε ἐν τῇ προσευχῇ πιστεύοντες λήμψεσθε.		11.24-25 προσεύχεσθε καὶ αἰτεῖσθε, πιστεύετε ὅτι ἐλάβετε, καὶ ἔσται ὑμῖν. καὶ ὅταν στήκετε προσευχόμενοι, ἀφίετε εἴ τι ἔχετε κατά τινος, ἵνα καὶ ὁ πατὴρ ὑμῶν ὁ ἐν τοῖς οὐρανοῖς ἀφῇ ὑμῖν τὰ παραπτώματα ὑμῶν.
5.14 ἀλείψαντες αὐτὸν ἐλαίῳ ἐν τῷ ὀνόματι τοῦ κυρίου.	Mk 3		6.13 …ἤλειφον ἐλαίῳ πολλοὺς ἀρρώστους καὶ ἐθεράπευον.

James		Matthew	Luke	Mark
5.16 ἐξομολογεῖσθε οὖν ἀλλήλοις τὰς ἁμαρτίας...	Mk 3	3.6 ...ἐξομολογούμενοι τὰς ἁμαρτίας αὐτῶν.		1.5 ...ἐξομολογούμενοι τὰς ἁμαρτίας αὐτῶν.
5.17 Ἠλίας ἄνθρωπος ἦν ὁμοιοπαθὴς ἡμῖν, καὶ προσευχῇ προσηύξατο τοῦ μὴ βρέξαι, καὶ οὐκ ἔβρεξεν ἐπὶ τῆς γῆς ἐνιαυτοὺς τρεῖς καὶ μῆνας ἕξ.	L 3		4.25 ...ἐν ταῖς ἡμέραις Ἠλίου ἐν τῷ Ἰσραήλ, ὅτε ἐκλείσθη ὁ οὐρανὸς ἐπὶ ἔτη τρία καὶ μῆνας ἕξ...	
5.19-20 ἀδελφοί μου, ἐάν τις ἐν ὑμῖν πλανηθῇ ἀπὸ τῆς ἀληθείας καὶ ἐπιστρέψῃ τις αὐτόν, γινωσκέτω ὅτι ὁ ἐπιστρέψας ἁμαρτωλὸν ἐκ πλάνης ὁδοῦ αὐτοῦ σώσει ψυχὴν αὐτοῦ ἐκ θανάτου καὶ καλύψει πλῆθος ἁμαρτιῶν.	Q 2	18.15 ἐὰν δὲ ἁμαρτήσῃ εἰς σὲ ὁ ἀδελφός σου, ὕπαγε ἔλεγξον αὐτὸν μεταξὺ σοῦ καὶ αὐτοῦ μόνου. ἐάν σου ἀκούσῃ, ἐκέρδησας τὸν ἀδελφόν σου...	17.3 ἐὰν ἁμάρτῃ ὁ ἀδελφός σου, ἐπιτίμησον αὐτῷ, καὶ ἐὰν μετανοήσῃ ἄφες αὐτῷ.	

Chapter 3

THE PRESENTATION OF THE ADDRESSEES

3.1 *Introduction*

Every text represents a process of communication between the author of the text and those to whom it is addressed. The previous chapter examined a number of aspects of self-presentation of the author of the Epistle of James and his relation to authoritative socioreligious traditions of his environment. The task of this chapter is to examine the reverse side of the communication process, that is, the addressees. The interpreter, however, does not have such direct access to the addressees as to the author. The author's self-presentation in the text can be analysed; the addressees, on the other hand, are accessible, not by self-presentation, but according as they are depicted by the author in the text. It is always possible that the perception of the addressees implied by the author may be quite different to how the addressees would have presented themselves.

In an examination of the implied addressees of the Epistle of James, there are two ways of extracting relevant information. First, the direct designations which the author applies to the addressees comprise a crucial indication of his perception of them.[1] Second, following the characterisation of the addressees which emerges through this naming process, specific emphases which appear particularly important within what the author has to say to the addressees can be analysed to reveal

---

1. On the significance of titles and names as social 'labels', both positive and negative, see B.J. Malina and J.H. Neyrey, *Calling Jesus Names: The Social Value of Labels in Matthew* (Sonoma, CA: Polebridge Press, 1988), pp. 35-42: 'While positive labeling carries with it the force of celebrity standing, negative labeling bears the force of stigma. When carried out publicly or at times even secretly, such labeling can carry with it an institutional sanctioning of overwhelming proportions: positively by granting symbolic reward potential, negatively by granting symbolic devastation potential, both of deep and enduring quality' (p. 38).

further details of what the author sees as key issues concerning the addressees. Thus, this chapter will look first at the significance of how the addressees are directly named in the text, and then analyse, as a test-case, a specific instance of what appears as a particularly strong concern of the author regarding his addressees, set against the general context of the culture of the early Christian movement.

3.2 Naming the Addressees

There are several important direct designations used by the author in relation to the addressees: first, the address, 'to the twelve tribes in the diaspora' (ταῖς δώδεκα φυλαῖς ταῖς ἐν τῇ διασπορᾷ), in the opening letter-greeting (1.1), second, the vocative 'brothers' (ἀδελφοί), used a total of 15 times in the epistle, and third, the figurative reproach 'adul-teresses' (μοιχαλίδες, 4.4), which is followed by two more negative designations, 'sinners' and 'double-minded' (ἁμαρτωλοί, δίψυχοι, 4.8). Of other instances in the text where direct designations are used, the address 'empty person' in 2.20 functions as a rhetorical device addressed to an imaginary individual opponent, and the two summons, 'Come now, you who say...' (4.13), and 'Come now, you rich...' (5.1), should also be seen as rhetorical in effect, rather than intended to func-tion as literal designations of some or all of the addressees.[2]

3.2.1 'The Twelve Tribes in the Diaspora'
As the introductory disclosure of the identity of the addressees, this verse obviously is of great importance for the view of the addressees throughout the whole epistle. Unfortunately, the precise reference of the 'twelve tribes' has proved difficult to determine satisfactorily.

One possibility for the interpretation of the phrase is a literal, ethnic and geographical meaning. In this case, 'twelve tribes' (δώδεκα φυλαί) would refer to the twelve tribes of Israel, that is, to the Jewish people. 'In the Diaspora' (ἐν τῇ διασπορᾷ) would, in turn, designate those Jews resident outside of their traditional Palestinian homeland. Thus, the epistle could be seen to be written to Jews, not necessarily exclusively to Christian Jews, dwelling outside Palestine.[3] A second possibility is

---

2.   See below, §6.3.1.

3.   For this view, see particularly, Mayor, *James*, pp. cxxxiv-cxliii, 29-30; Schlatter, *Jakobus*, pp. 89-96; A.S. Geyser, 'The Letter of James and the Social Condition of his Addressees', *Neot* 9 (1975), pp. 25-33.

that the designation should be read symbolically, in which case 'twelve tribes' denotes the Christian movement as the 'true Israel', who have responded positively to the message of Jesus as God's messiah. For such, whether Jewish or gentile, their true abode is in heaven, and thus their earthly life represents a 'diaspora'.[4]

A variation on this symbolic reading is that proposed by Cargal, who suggests that 'diaspora' is intended to correspond to the idea of wandering from the truth expressed in the closing verses of the epistle (5.19-20); the addressees are in exile because they have strayed from the truth. The use of 'diaspora' as a figurative designation for living erroneously would, however, be unusual,[5] and the suggestion seems to stem principally from the necessity, for Cargal's structural semiotic methodology, of having a close correlation of this kind between the opening and closing verses.[6]

Of the likely interpretative possibilities, a figurative view of twelve tribes is preferable. The Jewish Diaspora in the first century CE was numerically very large, and was spread throughout a very wide area.[7] It seems unlikely that this short text would have been composed for circulation to such a wide audience, encompassing large populations of Jews in Babylon, Egypt and other areas of north Africa, Asia Minor, Greece,

---

4.   See Dibelius, *James*, pp. 66-67; Ropes, *James*, pp. 118-27; Frankemölle, *Jakobus*, pp. 54-57; Vouga, *Jacques*, p. 37. This is also stressed by L. Simon, *Une éthique de la sagesse* (Geneva: Editions Labor et Fides, 1961), pp. 13-15, who parallels the usage with, in particular, Jeremiah's letter to the Diaspora (Jer. 29). E. Tamez, *The Scandalous Message of James: Faith without Works Is Dead* (New York: Crossroad, 1990), pp. 23-24, draws attention to the implication of religious and social marginalisation involved in the Diaspora designation.

5.   K.L. Schmidt, 'διασπορά', *TDNT*, II, pp. 98-104, notes that the word occurs very rarely outside Jewish and Christian texts. In the LXX, it functions as 'a technical term for the dispersion of the Jews among the Gentiles' (p. 99).

6.   T.B. Cargal, *Restoring the Diaspora: Discourse Structure and Purpose in the Epistle of James* (SBLDS, 144; Atlanta, GA: Scholars Press, 1993), pp. 45-49. Cargal's suggestion that 'diaspora' indicates wandering from the truth contrasts with the view of the Diaspora propounded, for instance, by Jer. 24, in which God's favour is directed towards those who have been exiled, and disfavour towards those who have remained in the land.

7.   M. Stern, 'The Jewish Diaspora', *CRINT* 1.1, pp. 117-83, notes the difficulty in establishing accurate figures, but concludes that the Diaspora Jewish population 'considerably exceeded the number of Jews living in the homeland' (p. 122). Philo, *Leg. Gai.* 281-82, and Acts 2.9-11 both describe the Diaspora as stretching through Mesopotamia, north Africa, Asia Minor and Europe.

the Mediterranean islands and Italy.[8] Moreover, the fact that the text can be seen to have its setting in specific circumstances, as will be argued below, makes doubtful its relevance, if not, in fact, its comprehensibility at anything beyond a superficial level, to such a wide-ranging and diverse group of possible addressees.

One of the key functions of Jewish letters of religious contents addressed to those living in the Diaspora was to enhance and strengthen the sense of unity of the people.[9] The address to the twelve tribes in the Diaspora can be seen as such an affirmation of unity, binding together the author and the whole, dispersed, chosen people of God. The author's status as 'slave of God and of the Lord Jesus Christ' (1.1a) may function here to assert his authority, as the representative of God and of Jesus, to make this kind of wide-ranging address.

The importance of the term is the fact that it is rooted in the ancient tradition of the promises to the patriarchs and the special status of their descendants as the chosen people of God. As such, it expresses the aspiration of the restoration of God's chosen people, the twelve dispersed tribes. The likelihood of this figurative interpretation is strengthened by the symbolic value of the figure of the twelve tribes in other Jewish texts in contexts of hope for the restoration of God's people.[10]

As early as the prophet Ezekiel, the vision of a reconstituted twelve-tribe entity provided a powerful image for God's restoration of the defeated and dispersed people of Israel/Judah (Ezek. 47.13–48.35; cf. 45.8). Sir. 36.10 prays that God will gather all the tribes of Jacob, and give them their inheritance as in the beginning, again indicating the idea of the restoration of Israel symbolised through the reconstitution of the dispersed tribes. A similar sentiment is found in *Pss. Sol.* 17. This psalm speaks of the sanctification of the tribes, the redistribution of the land and restoration of Jerusalem to the original state of holiness in the

---

8.   A more limited understanding of ἐν τῇ διασπορᾷ, such as that of Mussner, *Jakobusbrief*, pp. 11-12, who sees the designation as probably confined to the Syrian region, is already a move away from a strictly literal interpretation.

9.   See I. Taatz, *Frühjüdische Briefe* (NTOA, 16; Göttingen: Vandenhoeck & Ruprecht, 1991), pp. 102-104.

10.   See C. Maurer, 'φυλή', *TDNT*, IX, pp. 245-50 (248); S. Freyne, *The Twelve: Disciples and Apostles* (London: Sheed & Ward, 1968), pp. 27-32; R. Horsley, *Jesus and the Spiral of Violence* (San Francisco: Harper & Row, 1987), pp. 199-201; E.P. Sanders, *Jesus and Judaism* (London: SCM Press, 1985), pp. 95-98; Penner, *James*, pp. 181-83; Jackson-McCabe, 'Letter', pp. 510-15.

reign of God's appointed Christ (χριστός, *Pss. Sol.* 17.26-34). The motif is also found in apocalyptic literature. *4 Ezra* 13.39, 46-48 speaks of the regathering of the exiled ten tribes in the last days. The letter of Baruch to the nine and a half tribes in *2 Bar.* 78–86 speaks of the captivity of the twelve tribes (*2 Bar.* 78.4), and the reassembling of those who are dispersed (*2 Bar.* 78.7).[11]

The Qumran texts also make use of the language of the twelve tribes in this restorationist sense. In the *Temple Scroll*, the gates of the court-yards will be named after the twelve tribes; offerings and sacrifices will be made according to the twelve tribes (11QT 18; 23-24; 39). The future king will be guarded by 12,000 warriors, and will be accompanied by 12 princes, 12 priests and 12 levites (11QT 57). The *War Scroll* speaks of the perpetual ministry of 12 levites, one for each tribe (1QM 2.2-3). The names of the twelve tribes are to be inscribed on the banners of the army (1QM 3.14) and on the shield of the Prince of the congregation (1QM 5.1). Other texts, while not explicitly mentioning twelve tribes, clearly suggest the anticipation of a restored Israel along these lines: 'When the glory of Judah shall arise, the simple of Ephraim…shall abandon those who lead them astray and shall join Israel' (4Q169 3).

The reconstitution of the twelve tribes as a symbol of God's restoration of God's people is also clearly expressed in early Christian literature. Rev. 7.4-8 depicts the preservation of 12,000 from each of the tribes, whose names are inscribed on the gates of the new Jerusalem (Rev. 21.12-13). Jesus' appointment of the twelve in the gospel narratives surely also represents a symbolic figure for the restoration of God's people.[12] In Acts 26.6-7, Paul speaks of his Christian faith in terms of the hopes of the twelve tribes (τὸ δωδεκάφυλον) in the promises of God. As Sanders comments:

> The expectation of the reassembly of Israel was so widespread, and the memory of the twelve tribes remained so acute, that *'twelve' would necessarily mean 'restoration'*.[13]

In the light of the widespread figurative use of the idea of the twelve

---

11. On this passage, see particularly Taatz, *Briefe*, pp. 66-69. The letter of 2 Macc. 1.10–2.18 also ends with the hope that God will gather his people together from everywhere under heaven (2 Macc. 2.17-18).

12. See Horsley, *Spiral of Violence*, pp. 199-208; Sanders, *Jesus and Judaism*, pp. 98-106.

13. Sanders, *Jesus and Judaism*, p. 98 (his emphasis).

tribes as a symbol for restoration, it seems overwhelmingly likely that such a use is also the case in Jas 1.1. It has been noted already that the Epistle of James affirms fundamental presuppositions of the Jewish world-view, and also that it is closely identified with traditions associated with Jesus as the authoritative interpretation of this Jewish perspective. Thus, the addressees symbolically designated by the twelve tribes can best be seen as those sharing a Jewish world-view, and, in particular, those sharing the conviction of the authority of the interpretation of this view associated with Jesus and his movement.[14] The occurence of the name 'Lord Jesus Christ' in the first line of 1.1 supports the view that the author expects recognition by the addressees of the authority of Jesus. The fact that the twelve tribes are depicted as being in the Diaspora fits the strong sense of eschatological expectation present elsewhere in the epistle (e.g. 5.7-9). That the addressees are designated the twelve tribes (a figure of restoration) in the Diaspora (from whence they will be gathered) can thus itself be seen to carry strong overtones of the expected imminent fulfilment and consummation of God's promises to Israel. Despite the apparently wide-ranging address, the author may well have had in mind quite a small circle of addressees, who in turn would probably have been able to appreciate the symbolism of the designation 'the twelve tribes in the Diaspora'.

In seeing the addressees in this way, however, several important considerations must be noted. First, this does not necessarily imply that the text is addressed either exclusively to ethnic Jews, or exclusively to Christians as the inheritors of the true tradition of Israel. These alternatives assume a clear drawing of boundaries between Christians and Jews which did not exist until well after the time of writing of the New Testament texts.[15] Second, seeing the addressees as 'Jewish Christians' in this sense does not mean that they should be seen as a distinct and well-defined dissident group which stood over against 'mainstream'

---

14. Cf. Baasland, 'Literarische Form', p. 3676.

15. On the plural nature of Judaism at this time, see Boccaccini, *Middle Judaism*: 'A plurality of groups, movements and traditions of thought coexisted in a dialectical relationship which was sometimes polemic but never disengaged. This complex and pluralistic period, however, has a clear, distinct and unitary personality. The multiple and divergent answers offered by the different groups come from the same urgent questions... Christianity is unique, precisely as unique as Rabbinism. In both cases, uniqueness consists of a peculiar mixture of traditional elements and fresh developments, that is, in the creation of a system capable of giving new sense to the same unrejected heritage' (pp. 14, 17).

Judaism. Rather, such a group would have been part of the dynamic plurality of 'Judaisms' whose divergent interpretations of the same socioreligious heritage coexisted and competed with each other in the late second Temple period. On occasions, such plurality could lead to tensions or hostility, but this was not necessarily always the case.[16] Third, in this context, the communication between the author and addressees of the epistle would be an example of the ongoing articulation and clarification of the implications of adherence to the movement which recognised the authority of Jesus. As such, the epistle would be part of the gradual process of self-definition on the part of the emergent early Christian movement. At times, such self-definition took place at the expense of the vilification of others,[17] but this does not have to have been the case in every instance. Fourth, this view does not presuppose a uniform standpoint on the part of all those who could be seen as adherents of such a 'Jewish Christian' group. Rather, a spectrum should be envisaged, ranging from the strongly committed to the wavering. What they have in common is that they all are familiar with the message of the early Christian movement and sympathetic—to varying degrees—with it.

3.2.2 'Brothers'

The plural vocative 'brothers' (ἀδελφοί) is used 15 times in the epistle, 4 times on its own (4.11; 5.7, 9, 10), 8 times as 'my brothers' (ἀδελφοί μου, 1.2; 2.1, 14; 3.1, 10, 12; 5.12, 19) and 3 times as 'my beloved brothers' (ἀδελφοί μου ἀγαπητοί, 1.16, 19; 2.5).[18] It is significant that the term expresses equality of relationship (cf. Mt. 23.8), an aspect which distinguishes the Epistle of James noticeably from the hierarchic forms of address typical of traditional Jewish exhortation (son [בֵּן, בַּר, υἱός], Prov. 1.8, 10; Sir. 7.3; Prov. 31.2 [LXX 24.70]; child [τέκνον], Sir. 2.1 etc.). Unlike Paul, and the author of 1 John, who also use

---

16. A good example of the fluid and dynamic relationships between different Jewish groups is given by the different attitude to the Pharisees offered by the same early Christian author in Lk. 11.37-44 and in Acts 23.6-10.

17. See S. Freyne, 'Vilifying the Other and Defining the Self: Matthew's and John's Anti-Judaism in Focus', in J. Neusner and E.S. Frerichs (eds.), *'To See Ourselves as Others See Us': Jews, Christians, Others in Antiquity* (Chico, CA: Scholars Press, 1985), pp. 117-44.

18. Gruson (ed.), *Jacques*, p. 27, suggests that the occurrences of this strongest form of the direct address, ἀδελφοί, point towards deep tension, rather than tenderness, in the author's relation to the addressees.

father–child language to undergird their authority (e.g. 1 Cor. 4.14-17; 1 Thess. 2.11; 1 Jn 2.1, 18), the author of the Epistle of James uses only the more egalitarian 'brothers' in relation to the addressees, although he clearly expects the acknowledgement of his authority, even among equals.[19]

The use of fraternity as an expression of co-belonging to the people of God was already familiar in Jewish writings,[20] and occurs frequently in early Christian writings, as an address both to fellow-Jews[21] and to fellow-Christians.[22] As such, this address marks out the addressees as members of a fictive kin group of which the author is also a member.[23] This group would be presupposed to share the ties of loyalty, mutual commitment and support which bonded the members of a physical family.[24]

3.2.3 *Adulteresses, Sinners, Double-minded*

The use of the feminine plural vocative 'adulteresses' (μοιχαλίδες) appears at first glance a little strange, but on closer examination again discloses the assumption of a shared appreciation of the Jewish religious language and heritage, and also the possible influence of early Christian tradition.

This address, as part of a sharp reproach sequence, is drawn from the image of Israel as a shameless adulterous wife in relation to her God,

19. Cf. 3.1; in this verse, the author, while claiming the authoritative role of teacher, still addresses the recipients as brothers, and apparently accepts, although reluctantly, that they also may fulfil the role of teacher.

20. Schlatter, *Jakobus*, pp. 96-97; Ropes, *James*, pp. 131-32; H. von Soden, 'ἀδελφός', *TDNT*, I, pp. 144-46.

21. E.g. Acts 2.29, 37; 3.17; 7.2; 13.15, 26, 38 etc.

22. E.g. Acts 1.16; 6.3; Rom. 1.13; 7.4; 8.12; 1 Cor. 1.10-11; 2.1; 3.1; 4.6; 2 Cor. 1.8; Heb. 3.1, 12; 10.19; 13.22; 1 Jn 3.13.

23. On 'brothers' as a fictive kin group, cf. Malina and Neyrey, *Names*, p. 16. On the significance of the language of kinship as applied to non-blood relationships in general, see J. Pitt-Rivers, 'Pseudo-Kinship', in *International Encyclopedia of the Social Sciences*, VIII (ed. D. Sills; London: MacMillan, 1979), pp. 408-13. On fictive kinship in early Christianity, cf. B.J. Malina, 'Early Christian Groups', in P.F. Esler (ed.), *Modelling Early Christianity: Social-scientific Studies of the New Testament in its Context* (London: Routledge, 1995), pp. 96-113 (108-110).

24. On the central role of kinship and family in the ancient Mediterranean world, see K.C. Hanson and D.E. Oakman, *Palestine in the Time of Jesus* (Minneapolis: Fortress Press, 1980), pp. 19-60; K.C. Hanson, 'Kinship', in Rohrbaugh (ed.), *The Social Sciences*, pp. 62-79.

which is found particularly in traditional prophetic hortatory literature, especially the prophet Hosea.[25] The metaphor depicts God's people as disobedient to God's order, expressed in the covenant relationship between God and Israel. They dishonour God through their unfaithful behaviour.[26] This idea is brought to expression in the rest of 4.4, in the contrast between God and the world: 'Don't you know that friendship with the world is enmity with God?' It is also worth noting that, in the synoptic gospels, those who do not accept the authority of Jesus' proclamation are several times characterised as an 'adulterous generation' (γενεὰ μοιχαλίς, Mt. 12.39; 16.4; Mk 8.38). It is possible that proximity between the Jesus traditions and the author of the Epistle of James have influenced the choice of imagery in this verse. Here, as in the gospels, the image is used in the censure of those whom the author sees as not accepting as appropriate the authoritative interpretation, deriving from Jesus, of how the world is to be viewed. This connection with the gospels, however, cannot be asserted with certainty. It is clear, nevertheless, that the use of the word derives from the assumption of a shared awareness of the Jewish religious heritage, and in this light, depicts the addressees as inconstant in their fulfilment of their responsibility in relation to God.

The two further direct designations which occur several verses later, 'sinners' and 'double minded' (ἁμαρτωλοί, δίψυχοι 4.8), likewise depict the addressees in a negative light, and can be seen as developing the negative portrayal forcefully expressed in 4.4 through the use of 'adulteresses'. As sinners, they are accused of having breached the

---

25. E.g. Hos. 1–3; 4.13-14; Ezek. 16.32, 38; 23.37, 43; Jer. 3.8-9. Mal. 3.5 is particularly noteworthy, containing the explicit accusations of swearing falsely (cf. Jas 5.12), withholding the wages of labourers (cf. Jas 5.4), and oppressing (καταδυναστεύω, cf. Jas 2.6) widows and orphans (cf. Jas 1.27).

26. Cf. Ropes, *James*, p. 260; Mayor, *James*, p. 139; Mussner, *Jakobusbrief*, p. 180; Dibelius, *James*, pp. 219-20. J.J. Schmitt, ' "You Adulteresses!" The Image in James 4.4', *NovT* 28 (1986), pp. 327-37, argues, on the grounds that Israel is a masculine noun, that the above-mentioned passages do not contain an image of Israel as God's adulterous wife. This, however, is mistaken; when such figurative language is being employed, there is no reason why a female quality cannot be applied to a male subject. Schmitt seeks to derive the usage in Jas 4.4 from LXX Prov. 24.55 (30.20), but when his rejection of the traditional prophetic usage is seen to be unnecessary, there is no need to relate the background of Jas 4.4 exclusively to this or any other single LXX occurence.

standards of God's order,[27] thus falling short of what is expected of them as God's chosen people. They are thus separated from God and outside of his eschatological order, threatened with death (cf. 1.15; 5.20). The word δίψυχος, which occurs for the first time in any existing Greek text in the Epistle of James,[28] depicts the addressees as being 'double-minded', leading lives which are divided, instead of being whole in commitment to God (cf. 1.6-8).

3.2.4 *Summary*

The most significant direct appellations used by the author for the addressees share, in particular, a common derivation from the Jewish tradition in which the early Christian movement was rooted. Each suggests an important aspect of how the author wishes to present those to whom the text is addressed. 'The twelve tribes in the Diaspora' implies the chosenness and unity of God's people and, in the link with the author as 'slave of God and of the Lord Jesus Christ' in the first part of 1.1, probably should also be seen as asserting the decisive importance of Jesus and the movement associated with him in this context of the special status of God's people. The use of this appellation is also very likely to have been influenced by the sense of eschatological restoration and the fulfilment of God's promises to Israel in the early Christian movement. The address, ἀδελφοί, suggests the fraternity and sense of common identity of both the Jewish people and of the early

---

27.   On the use of ἁμαρτωλός to describe the ungodly in Jewish and early Christian tradition, see K.H. Rengstorf, 'ἁμαρτωλός', *TDNT*, I, pp. 317-33. A thorough analysis of the identity of the 'sinners' in the gospel traditions is offered by Sanders, *Jesus and Judaism*, pp. 174-211. Sanders sees the term as a designation for 'those who sinned wilfully...and did not repent' (p. 177).

28.   Although this is the first preserved occurrence of the word, there are noteworthy precedents in other Jewish writings for the use of the doubleness of a part of the body as an image for instability, untrustworthiness and a divided attitude, especially towards God (e.g. 'double-tongued' [δίγλωσσος, Sir. 5.9]; 'double-faced' [διπρόσωπος, *T. Ash.* 2.5; 3.1-2; 4.1-3]; cf. also δύο γλῶσσαι [*T. Benj.* 6.5]; ἐν καρδίᾳ καὶ ἐν καρδίᾳ ἐλάλησαν [LXX Ps. 11.3 (בלב ולב ידברו)]). Various views on the background of the term δίψυχος in Jas 1.8 and 4.8 are presented by O.J.F. Seitz, 'The Relationship of the Shepherd of Hermas to the Epistle of James', *JBL* 63 (1944), pp. 131-40; *idem*, 'Antecedents and Significance of the Term ΔΙΨΥΧΟΣ', *JBL* 66 (1947), pp. 211-19; *idem*, 'Afterthoughts on the Term "Dipsychos"', *NTS* 4 (1957), pp. 327-34; S.S.C. Marshall, 'Δίψυχος: A Local Term?', *SE* 6 (TU 112) (1973), pp. 348-51; S.E. Porter, 'Is *dypsuchos* (James 1.8, 4.8) a "Christian" Word?', *Bib* 71 (1990), pp. 469-98.

Christians. Third, the address 'adulteresses' again draws on the idea of the special relation to God, but this time in a negative evaluation of the addressees as failing to behave in accordance with the demands of this relation. This negative dimension is further underlined by the use of 'sinners' and 'double-minded' in 4.8. Thus, from the examination of these three terms, it appears that the author assumes that the addressees share the fundamental presupposition of the Jewish view of the order of the universe. He apparently also assumes that they share an appreciation of the decisive nature of the particular interpretation of this view associated with Jesus. He also sees them, however, as inconsistent in their discharge of the practical consequences of this worldview.

This apparent discrepancy between the world-view of the author and the socioreligious situation of the addressees should now be analysed in detail. This will be undertaken in the following subsection, through the examination, as a test case, of one of the most strongly expressed instances of inconsistency between the author's expectations and the behaviour of the addressees.

3.3 *Inconsistency between the Socioreligious Worldview of the Author and the Addressees: The Marginal and God's Kingdom*

It is clear that the author sees inconsistency between the shared world-view, which he presupposes as authoritative, and the behaviour of the addressees. A plausible explanation for this situation is that this inconsistency is to be located in their respective evaluation of the significance of the interpretation of the Jewish world-view by Jesus and his movement. That is, for the author, this reinterpretation is a deviant, but coherent, meaningful and authoritative version of the Jewish symbolic universe. This deviant symbolic universe does not (yet/any longer) provide a framework for the addressees similarly to be able to integrate their lives coherently in the world, although they are assumed to be familiar with its contours and sympathetic towards it. This thesis is borne out by the following examination of one of the key points of inconsistency in the addressees' realization of the author's expectations, expressed in 2.5-6.

One of the most striking concerns of the author of the Epistle of James, which he appears to feel the addressees should share, but do not adequately do so, is the affirmation of the honourable status within God's order of the universe of the socially marginal. This is most strongly expressed in 2.5: 'Has God not chosen the poor by the world's standards, rich in faith and inheritors of the kingdom which he promised to those who love him?' (οὐχ ὁ θεὸς ἐξελέξατο τοὺς πτωχοὺς τῷ κόσμῳ πλουσίους ἐν πίστει καὶ κληρονόμους τῆς βασιλείας ἧς ἐπηγγείλατο τοῖς ἀγαπῶσιν αὐτόν;). The failure of the addressees to act in correspondence to this is stated in the following verse: 'But you have dishonoured the poor' (ὑμεῖς δὲ ἠτιμάσατε τὸν πτωχόν). The contrast outlined in these verses is worthy of note for a number of reasons. First, it expresses a very clear case of the failure of the addressees to correspond to the author's expectations of them. Second, the use of the imperative 'Listen!' and the direct address in its longest form, 'my beloved brothers', draws particular attention within the rhetoric of the text to the following statement. Third, this case is formulated in terms of the central cultural values of the ancient Mediterranean world, in the language of honour and dishonour.[29] The assertion of the honourable status of the poor (πτωχόι), however, raises the question of their identity within the social world of early Christianity.

3.3.1 *The Identity of the Poor*
Malina has drawn attention to the significant difference in terms of normative cultural values between the term πτωχός (poor) in the ancient Mediterranean world and the idea of poverty in twentieth-century Western society. πτωχός is not principally an economic term, but rather denotes one who, due to unfortunate circumstances, has experienced a devaluation of his inherited status within the structures of kinship and politics, consequently having to exist precariously, in destitution or near-destitution, on the margins of society:

> the 'poor' rank among those who cannot maintain their inherited status due to circumstances that befall them and their family, such as debt, being in a foreign land, sickness, death (widow), or some personal physical accident. Consequently, from the viewpoint of the vast majority of people, the poor would not be a permanent social class but a sort of revolving class of people who unfortunately cannot maintain their inherited status.[30]

29. On honourable status as the key standard of social value in the ancient Mediterranean world, see Malina, *New Testament World*, pp. 28-62; H. Moxnes, 'Honor and Shame', in Rohrbaugh (ed.), *The Social Sciences*, pp. 19-40.

30. B.J. Malina, 'Wealth and Poverty in the New Testament and its World', *Int* 41 (1987), pp. 354-67 (356). Similarly, 'rich' (πλούσιος) was not simply an

As such the πτωχός is to be distinguished from the πένης, which meant poor in the sense of a person of few means who had to labour cease-lessly to maintain a living, but was not destitute as the πτωχός was.[31] Within the New Testament texts, πτωχός frequently occurs alongside other terms designating this kind of social dislocation: those who hunger, thirst and mourn (Mt. 5.3-6//Lk. 6.20-21), the blind, the deaf, the lame and the skin-diseased (Mt. 11.5//Lk. 7.22), the widowed (Mk 12.43//Lk. 21.3), the wretched, the blind and the naked (Rev. 3.17). In a society where the vast majority of people were poor (in the sense of πένης) in any case, it is not surprising that there is considerable evidence for the socially marginal πτωχός as a widespread social phenomenon.[32]

3.3.2 *Marginality and the Jesus Movement*

There is also consistent evidence within the gospel traditions that socially marginal people (πτωχοί) were of considerable importance in the ministry of Jesus: they are described as favoured, because God's kingdom is theirs (Lk. 6.20; Mt. 5.3); to them Jesus announces the good news (Lk. 7.22; Mt. 11.5),[33] which is characteristic of his public activity. Theissen has drawn attention to the radical, socially marginal nature of the first followers of Jesus, in their pursuit of a lifestyle

economic term in the present-day sense: 'Rich meant powerful due to greed, avarice and exploitation, while poor meant weak due to inability to maintain one's inherited social station. Consequently, the opposite of rich would not necessarily be the economically poor. In the perception of people in peasant society, the majority of people are neither poor nor rich, rather all are equal in that each has a status to maintain in some honorable way' (p. 357). Cf. also E. Tamez, *Bible of the Oppressed* (Maryknoll, NY: Orbis Books, 1982), pp. 66-74. E. Bammel, 'πτωχός', *TDNT*, VI, pp. 888-915 (888), points out that the sense of 'wrongfully impoverished or dispossessed' is fundamental to the main Hebrew equivalent of πτωχός, עָנִי. From this, in turn, derives the strong conviction, particularly in the legal and prophetic texts, that God is the protector of the poor.

31. Cf. the distinction between the πένης and the πτωχός presented by Aristophanes, *Plut.* 552-54. See further Tamez, *James*, pp. 24-25.

32. See L. Schottroff and W. Stegemann, *Jesus and the Hope of the Poor* (Maryknoll, NY: Orbis Books, 1986), pp. 6-17; cf. G. Theissen, '"We have left everything..." (Mark 10.28)', in Theissen, *Social Reality*, pp. 60-93 (66-86).

33. See further Schottroff and Stegemann, *Hope*, pp. 17-32; also P. Hoffmann, 'Die Basileia-Verkündigung Jesu und die Option für die Armen', in P. Hoffmann, *Studien zur Frühgeschichte der Jesus-Bewegung* (Stuttgart: Katholisches Bibelwerk, 1994), pp. 41-72 (44-47).

characterized by typical features of the πτωχοί: without possessions
(Mt. 10.9-10; Mk 6.8-9; Lk. 9.3; 10.4), of devalued status in the kinship
system (Mt. 10.21, 34-37; Mk 13.12; Lk. 12.52-53), homeless (Lk.
9.58; Mt. 8.20), publicly despised and rejected (Mt. 10.22-23).[34]

Theissen's well-known thesis asserts that the early Jesus movement,
following Jesus' own lifestyle, represents an ethical radicalism of
itinerants on the fringes of normal life, renouncing possessions, family
and home.[35] The adoption of this kind of vagabond behaviour by Jesus
and his followers, according to Theissen, was made feasible by the
existence of settled groups of sympathisers within local communities,
who received, sustained and supported the activity of the itinerants.[36]
Their relationship to each other was inherently based upon their mutual
positive, though different, response to and relationship with the central
figure of the movement, especially as characterized by the title 'Son of
Man' in the synoptic gospels.[37] Theissen summarizes his thesis as
follows:

> The internal structure of the Jesus movement was determined by the
> interaction of three roles: the wandering charismatics, their sympathisers
> in the local communities, and the bearer of revelation. There was a
> complementary relationship between the wandering charismatics and the
> local communities: wandering charismatics were the decisive spiritual
> authorities in the local communities, and local communities were the
> indispensable social and material basis for the wandering charismatics.
> Both owed their existence and legitimation to their relationship to the
> transcendent bearer of revelation.[38]

Theissen appears to see their response to the call of the charismatic
figure of Jesus as the decisive impetus in taking on this radical
existence.[39] Such emphasis on call and response, however, could easily

---

34.   See G. Theissen, 'The Wandering Radicals', in Theissen, *Social Reality*,
pp. 33-59.
35.   Theissen, 'Wandering Radicals', p. 40; see further G. Theissen, *Sociology
of Early Palestinian Christianity* (Philadelphia: Fortress Press, 1978 [*The First
Followers of Jesus* (London: SCM Press, 1978)]), pp. 8-16.
36.   Theissen, *Sociology*, pp. 17-23.
37.   Theissen, *Sociology*, pp. 24-30; cf. M. Hengel, *The Charismatic Leader
and his Followers* (Edinburgh: T. & T. Clark, 1981), pp. 61-63.
38.   Theissen, *Sociology*, p. 7.
39.   Theissen, *Sociology*, p. 8; cf. Hengel, *Charismatic Leader*, pp. 61-73. The
appropriateness of the use of the Weberian type of charismatic leadership in relation
to the early Christian movement is questioned by B.J. Malina, 'Jesus as Charismatic

lead to a one-sided focus on the ideational dimensions of adherence to the early Christian movement. On the contrary, the existence of itinerant radicalism in early Christianity should not be seen as unrelated to underlying insecure socioeconomic circumstances and the extensive phenomenon of social uprooting.[40] Rather than seeing the movement as based primarily on an *ideal* of ethical radicalism, the social conditions in which such a lifestyle was viable, even preferable for those who undertook such activity, should be regarded as having fundamental importance. As Stegemann points out in his review of Theissen's work:

> they reflect not an ascetical ethos, but the radicality of a life situation in which poverty, hunger, and violence are the dominant factors. The Q prophets encounter the radical suffering of the majority of the Palestinian population with their own radical trust in God.[41]

Leader?', *BTB* 14 (1984), pp. 55-62 (reprinted in B.J. Malina, *Social World*, pp. 123-42), who favours 'reputational' over 'charismatic', this term being more fitting for the social dynamics involved than the individualist, isolated, inspired charismatic leader. The helpfulness of the term 'wandering', translating the German *wander-* could also be questioned, as the English word has strong connotations of aimlessness, which are not appropriate to the early Christian movement.

40.   Theissen, *Sociology*, pp. 39-45; 'We Have Left Everything...', pp. 86-93: 'It was the people who had declined into poverty [cf. πτωχός], rather than the people born into poverty [cf. πένης], who set out to pass their lives beyond the boundaries of normal life, or even to seek for ways of renewing society' (p. 88, parantheses added). Cf. Schottroff and Stegemann, *Hope*, pp. 39-51.

41.   W. Stegemann, 'Vagabond Radicalism in Early Christianity', in W. Schottroff and W. Stegemann (eds.), *God of the Lowly: Socio-historical Interpretations of the Bible* (Maryknoll, NY: Orbis Books, 1984), pp. 148-68 (164); cf. also Schottroff and Stegemann, *Hope*, pp. 48-49. A much more trenchant critique of Theissen, *Sociology*, is provided by R. Horsley, *Sociology and the Jesus Movement* (New York: Crossroad, 1989), particularly pp. 30-64. Horsley rejects the use of functionalist social theory as a conservatively biased, utopian schematization whose categorizations obfuscate rather than clarify the position of the Jesus movement within Palestinian society, being inattentive to historical change and the importance of social conflict (pp. 30-41). This methodological criticism is later refuted by Theissen, in a clarification of his 'expanded functionalist' approach (Theissen, 'Sociological Theories', pp. 254-56). Horsley also rejects the thesis of itinerant radicalism in early Palestinian Christianity, arguing that 'there is little or no evidence for this reconstruction' (p. 43). Much of his review of Theissen's use of the biblical evidence is, however, unconvincing, proceeding by assertion as much as by close argument. For example, he states that texts such as Mt. 8.18-22 are 'problematic for [Theissen's] purposes', as they 'were surely addressed to a broader audience than a few dozen wandering charismatics' (p. 44). The assertion, however,

In this perspective, the Jesus movement offered an interpretation of social reality within a cosmological framework which gave a positive evaluation of the devalued status of the socially marginal poor (πτωχοί). Those of low social standing are those to whom God, the ultimate authority, ascribes honourable status within a universal framework, a vision of eschatological reversal in which the first are last and the last first (Mt. 19.30, cf. 20.16; Lk. 13.30; Mk 10.31), and in which those who exalt themselves will be humbled and those who become servile will be exalted (Lk. 14.11, cf. 22.26; 18.14; Mt. 23.12; 18.4; 20.26-27; Mk 9.35; 10.43-44).[42] It was thus possible for a socially marginal lifestyle, with loss of home, family and possessions, which was normally a signal of the loss of honourable standing and the inability to maintain one's social status, to be taken on board positively by the followers of Jesus. Such a lifestyle implied utter dependence on God (Mt. 6.25-34//Lk. 12.22-31; cf. Mt. 7.7-11//Lk. 11.9-13). This sense of complete reliance on God's provision is probably also expressed in the conviction of the effectiveness of faithful prayer (Mt. 17.20; 21.21-22; Mk 11.23-24) and in the petition for daily provision of the prayer of Jesus (Mt. 6.11, cf. Lk. 11.3). In practical terms, this entailed dependence on those sympathisers who would meet their needs (Lk. 10.5-8; cf. 9.4; Mk 6.10; Mt. 10.11) and who themselves would receive eschatological blessing in return (Lk. 10.8-9; Mt. 10.40-42; 25.31-40).[43] Nevertheless, it is likely that they could not always rely on acceptance and adequate support (Mt. 5.10-12; 10.22-23; Lk. 6.22-23).[44]

is unsubstantiated, and raises several questions: how is he sure that these sayings were addressed to a broader audience? Even if they were addressed to a broader audience, does this prevent them reflecting a more radical tendency, typified by the itinerant, socially marginal 'ministry' of Jesus, and (possibly) also typical of (some) of his followers? Horsley's stress on the importance of social and economic structures and divisions in the reconstruction of the Jesus movement and its role in Palestinian society is useful, as is his view of the Jesus movement as aiming towards a revitalization of local Jewish communities. Revitalization, however, does not need to exclude automatically a role for itinerant radicals within this 'mission'.

42.   See Schottroff and Stegemann, *Hope*, pp. 17-32; cf. also P. Hoffmann, 'Herrschaftsverzicht: Befreite und befreiende Menschlichkeit', in Hoffmann, *Studien*, pp. 139-70.

43.   See Theissen, 'Wandering Radicals', pp. 47-49.

44.   See Theissen, 'Wandering Radicals', pp. 49-51.

3.3.3 *The Marginal in the Epistle of James: Analysis of 2.1-13*

This perspective on the relation of Jesus and his movement to the social realities of their environment has considerable potential for illuminating the question of the marginal in the Epistle of James.[45]

Since Dibelius, it has been common to depict the presentation of the status of the poor in the Epistle of James as part of the Jewish religious tradition of 'the piety of the poor',[46] which gives primacy to a theological interpretation of the idea of poverty. In such a view, idealized poverty need not bear any close relation to actual social circumstances: 'The pious thought of themselves as the poor because *poverty had become a religious concept*'.[47]

There is, of course, a heritage of affirming God's concern for the poor in Jewish tradition, which no doubt did inform the concerns of the Jesus movement. This kind of idealizing interpretation of texts, however, which removes them from the sphere of concrete physical human experience, constitutes unwarranted reductionism:

> Our habit of depriving the biblical texts of their concretion and spiritualizing them must be noticed and amended. When poverty is mentioned in the text, we must not read 'poverty'—poverty in a merely symbolic sense.[48]

The analysis, outlined above, of the social environment of the Jesus movement offers the possibility of a plausible interpretation, in terms of

---

45. Theissen's depiction of the relations between itinerant charismatics and settled communities is also drawn upon by S.J. Patterson, *The Gospel of Thomas and Jesus* (Sonoma, CA: Polebridge Press, 1993), pp. 178-88, in the interpretation of the Epistle of James, which he uses in support of his linking of the Gospel of Thomas with the itinerant charismatic groups in early Christianity. There seems, however, to be a fundamental inconsistency between his attempt to relate the text to tensions between different groups in early Christianity and his opening acceptance of Dibelius's position that 'the fact that it is not really an epistle at all, but a paraenetical collection fitted with a catholicizing epistolary introduction (1.1) excludes any discussion of its specific social-historical setting' (p. 179).

46. See Dibelius, *James*, pp. 39-45. Cf. Mussner, *Jakobusbrief*, pp. 76-84.

47. Dibelius, *James*, p. 40 (his emphasis).

48. L. Schottroff, Preface to Schottroff and Stegemann, *Hope*, p. vi; cf. Tamez, *James*, pp. 28, 44-45. L.E. Keck, 'The Poor among the Saints in the New Testament', *ZNW* 56 (1965), pp. 100-29, and 'The Poor among the Saints in Jewish Christianity and Qumran', *ZNW* 57 (1966), pp. 54-78, argues strongly against the idea that the early Palestinian Jewish Christian movement referred to itself as 'the Poor', in such a 'religious' sense of 'poor'.

concrete social realities, of the concerns of the epistle. The precise nuance of the key verse: 'Has God not chosen the poor by the world's standards, rich in faith and inheritors of the kingdom which he promised to those who love him?' (οὐχ ὁ θεὸς ἐξελέξατο τοὺς πτωχοὺς τῷ κόσμῳ πλουσίους ἐν πίστει καὶ κληρονόμους τῆς βασιλείας ἧς ἐπηγγείλατο τοῖς ἀγαπῶσιν αὐτόν; 2.5), will now be examined, and then set in its wider context within the text of the epistle (2.1-13).[49]

3.3.3.1 *The Poor in James 2.5*. In this verse, those chosen by God are designated by three conjoined terms: they are 'poor by the world's standards' (πτωχοὶ τῷ κόσμῳ), 'rich in faith' (πλούσιοι ἐν πίστει), and inheritors of the kingdom which he promised to those who love him (κληρονόμοι τῆς βασιλείας ἧς ἐπηγγείλατο τοῖς ἀγαπῶσιν αὐτόν).

As noted above, the word used here, πτωχός, means someone of devalued social means and status, someone in destitute or near-destitute circumstances, who has failed to maintain his standing in society and has fallen to a marginal position in the social order. The qualifying dative case of the noun κόσμος, 'world', bears out the acceptablity of this concrete interpretation of πτωχός. The word occurs four other times in the text: 1.27; 3.6; and 4.4 (twice). In each of these cases, κόσμος stands in contrast to God's order of the universe.[50] In 1.27, it is contrasted with 'pure and undefiled religion'; in 3.6, it is characterized by unrighteousness, the opposite of God's order; and in 4.4, it is presented in direct hostility to God: 'Friendship with the world is enmity with God'. The term κόσμος can thus be seen to represent the order of the world in which the socially marginal poor (πτωχοί) are the dishon-

49. Practically all interpreters (even Dibelius, *James*, pp. 124-48), read Jas 2.1-13 as a unified subsection. D.F. Watson, 'James 2 in the Light of Greco-Roman Schemes of Argumentation', *NTS* 39 (1993), pp. 94-121, sees 2.1-26 as a single rhetorical unit, subdivided into two related parts, 2.1-13, 14-26.

50. Cf. L.T. Johnson, 'Friendship with the World/Friendship with God: A Study of Discipleship in James', in F. Segovia (ed.), *Discipleship in the New Testament* (Philadelphia: Fortress Press, 1985), pp. 166-83: 'it represents a measure of reality, or a system of meaning, which can be contrasted to that of God' (p. 173). The contrast between faithful commitment to God and 'secular existence' is seen as the unifying theme of the whole text by K. Weiss, 'Motiv und Ziel der Frömmigkeit des Jakobusbriefes', *Theologische Versuche* 7 (1976), pp. 107-14. Cf. also P. Hartin, 'The Poor in the Epistle of James and the Gospel of Thomas', *Hervormde Teologiese Studies* 53 (1997), pp. 146-62, who compares the hostility to the world found in these two texts.

ourable and the despised, and which does not recognize the eschatological reversal of the kingdom of God, where the first will be last and the last first.

Central to the significance of 'rich in faith' is the meaning of 'faith' (πίστις), which should not be taken in the modern sense of 'belief' or 'credence', but which had a much more social relational sense in the ancient world:

> the words 'faith', 'have faith', and 'believe' refer to the social glue that binds one person to another, that is, the social, externally manifested, emotional behaviour of loyalty, commitment, and solidarity.[51]

Thus, 'rich in faith' can be seen to refer to the extent of loyalty and commitment to God which marks those who are 'poor by the world's standards'. This depiction is strongly suggestive of the sense of absolute dependence upon God which was characteristic of the socially marginal followers of Jesus.[52] That these are the ones who are to inherit the kingdom promised to those who love God strengthens this suggestion.[53]

Moreover, the closeness in phraseology of this verse, linking the poor (πτωχοί) with the kingdom (βασιλεία), to the saying of Jesus in Lk. 6.20 ('Blessed are you poor, for yours is the kingdom of God' [μακάριοι οἱ πτωχοί, ὅτι ὑμετέρα ἐστὶν ἡ βασιλεία τοῦ θεοῦ]; cf. Mt. 5.3, 5), further argues in favour of seeing Jas 2.5 in the context of the role of social marginality in the Jesus movement. The kingdom in this verse is surely the same kingdom as that announced by Jesus in the synoptic gospels. Just as the socially marginal poor (πτωχοί) in the gospels are promised the kingdom, so also the author of the Epistle of James points out that they have been chosen by God as the inheritors of God's kingdom. Thus, it seems appropriate, initially at any rate, to see this verse as referring to concrete social circumstances, typical of the marginal lifestyle of the radical itinerant followers of Jesus.

51. B.J. Malina and R.L. Rohrbaugh, *Social-Science Commentary on the Synoptic Gospels* (Minneapolis: Fortress Press, 1992), p. 131, cf. pp. 252-53. See also B.J. Malina, 'Faith/Faithfulness', in Malina and Pilch (eds.), *Biblical Social Values*, pp. 67-70.

52. Cf. Tamez, *James*, p. 46.

53. Especially when ἀγαπάω is read in a non-individualistic, non-introspective sense appropriate to the first-century Mediterranean world, signifying devotion or attachment within one's social group, or to a significant person. See B.J. Malina, 'Love', in Malina and Pilch (eds.), *Biblical Social Values*, pp. 110-14.

Moreover, the direct address to the addressees in 2.6a: 'But you have dishonoured the poor person' (ὑμεῖς δὲ ἠτιμάσατε τὸν πτωχόν), indicates that they constitute a different group from the 'poor by the world's standards' of 2.5. The fact that the author reproves the addressees for not treating these poor (πτωχοί) appropriately indicates that he expects other behaviour from them. This suggests that those who are directly addressed in the epistle are viewed by the author as 'sympathisers' in Theissen's framework. That is, the author expects that they will receive and support the socially marginal followers of Jesus, whose lifestyle entails dependence on God's provision, through such sympathisers, of their needs. This interpretation must now be tested in the verse's wider context within the text.

3.3.3.2 *The Wider Context of James 2.5; 2.1-7.* Within the text of the epistle, 2.5 falls in the subsection of the text 2.1-13. This section begins with the injunction: 'Do not hold commitment to our Lord Jesus Christ of glory in ways which show favouritism' (μὴ ἐν προσωπολημψίαις ἔχετε τὴν πίστιν τοῦ κυρίου ἡμῶν Ἰησοῦ χριστοῦ τῆς δόξης). This prohibition of partiality or bias for those who hold commitment or loyalty (πίστις) to the authority-figure of Jesus[54] implies the accusation that such incompatible behaviour exists. The injunction is illustrated by an example, narrated in the subjunctive (2.2-4).

According to Dibelius,[55] the Epistle of James represents situationless paraenetic literature; depiction of real-life circumstances, such as this appears to be, cannot be accepted as such. Rather, it constitutes a stylized and flagrantly portrayed example 'in quite unrealistic terms'.[56] It has already been asserted that this insistence on the impossibility of discerning historical circumstances behind the text in relation to the Epistle of James is mistaken;[57] moreover, it will be argued below that the circumstances described are anything but 'quite unrealistic'. Rather than a stylized and exaggerated example of partiality without any necessary relation to reality, it is far more probable that the depiction is

54. On the significance of the designation κύριος ἡμῶν Ἰησοῦς χριστός τῆς δόξης see above, §2.3.2.1.
55. Dibelius, *James*, pp. 128-32; cf. Patterson, *Thomas*, p. 181; Mussner, *Jakobusbrief*, pp. 116-17.
56. Dibelius, *James*, p. 129.
57. See above, §1.1.2.

typical of the actual experience of those involved, and thus immediately accessible and meaningful to them.[58]

In examining these verses the question of the nature of the assembly (συναγωγή) immediately presents itself. The Greek word may refer to the building for assembly or the actual gathering of people. The difference between these is not significant as, even if the primary referent is intended to be the building,[59] it is presupposed that it is housing a gathering of people on the occasion in question.

The word συναγωγή is used frequently to refer to Jewish assembly,[60] being used in the LXX as the principal equivalent of עֵדָה, assembly, gathering, and also used quite regularly for קָהֵל, congregation, although ἐκκλησία is the more usual translation for this word. συναγωγή is also the usual term in the early Christian texts for reference to the Jewish assembly, usually for worship or instruction, but is less frequently used to denote a distinctly Christian gathering (Ignatius, *Pol.* 4.2; Hermas, *Man.* 11.9). It is not necessary, however, to make a sharp differentiation as to whether this assembly should be seen as either Jewish or Christian. Such a differentiation would presuppose a much more definitive split between Christians and Jews than is likely for the period of writing of the New Testament texts. The identity of early Christians as Jews means that a Jewish gathering could consist of a significant number of sympathizers towards the Jesus movement, and an early Christian gathering could consist entirely of Jews.[61] A 'Jewish Christian' gathering of this kind seems most likely here. Theissen states concerning the

58. Cf. Maynard-Reid, *Poverty*, pp. 52-53; Tamez, *James*, pp. 15-16; Frankemölle, *Jakobus*, p. 387; Laws, *James*, p. 98: 'it must presumably bear some relation to his readers' experience'.

59. Hort, *James*, p. 49; most interpreters favour seeing συναγωγή as referring to the gathering of those present. In his discussion of the nature of the synagogue in the first century CE, H.C. Kee concludes that the term, in this period, is used predominantly to refer to an assembly of people, rather than to a specific building or institution. See H.C. Kee, 'Defining the First Century Synagogue: Problems and Progress', *NTS* 41 (1995), pp. 481-500.

60. See Ropes, *James*, pp. 188-89; Dibelius, *James*, pp. 132-34; Mayor, *James*, pp. 82-83; Hort, *James*, pp. 48-49; Laws, *James*, pp. 99-101. Mayor, and Schlatter, *Jakobus*, pp. 165-66, favour seeing a predominantly Christian assembly, on the basis of the Christian reference in 2.1, and the qualifying ὑμῶν in 2.2.

61. Cf. E. Schweizer, *Church Order in the New Testament* (London: SCM Press, 1961), pp. 20-25, 46-47, who stresses that Jesus and the members of the early Christian movement did not conceive of themselves as separate from Israel.

settled sympathizers: 'These groups remained wholly within the
framework of Judaism and had no intention of founding a new
'church'''.[62]

A further consideration, as to whether the assembly refers to a
gathering for worship or to a judicial asssembly, is largely connected to
the question of the identity of the two incomers, the person with gold
rings (ἀνὴρ χρυσοδακτύλιος) and the poor person (πτωχός), as the
argument that this is a depiction of a judicial meeting is based upon the
treatment of these two figures. There are two principal solutions: either
they are both members of the community, coming to attend a judicial
assembly, or they are both outsiders, coming into a gathering for
worship.

The traditional view has been that the two are not usual members of
the assembly, as they do not seem to be recognized, and they are treated
on the grounds of their appearance, rather than on previous familiarity
within the group.[63] More recently it has been argued, largely following
the influential essay of Ward,[64] that this is a judicial assembly, before
which two members of the community are coming for judgment.[65]
Ward cites several examples from rabbinic literature of a judicial
setting, in which the scene described bears resemblances to the situation
depicted in 2.2-3. In one instance, a richly-dressed man is instructed
either to dress like his poorly-dressed fellow-litigant, or to dress him as
he himself is dressed, and in the second, in a dispute between a rabbinic

62. Theissen, *Sociology*, p. 17.
63. E.g. Ropes, *James*, pp. 189-91; Mayor, *James*, p. 83; Burchard, 'Gemeinde',
p. 323; Hoppe, *Jakobusbrief*, p. 52.
64. R.B. Ward. 'Partiality in the Assembly, Jas 2.2-4', *HTR* 62 (1969), pp. 87-
97; cf. R.P. Martin, *James*, p. 61; Laws, *James*, p. 101 (tentatively); Maynard-Reid,
Poverty, pp. 55-58; Patterson, *Thomas*, pp. 181-82; Davids, *James*, pp. 107-10; M.
Ahrens, *Der Realitäten Widerschein: Reich und Arm im Jakobusbrief* (Berlin:
Alektor Verlag, 1995), pp. 113-15. R.W. Wall, *Community of the Wise* (Valley
Forge, PA: Trinity Press International, 1997), pp. 103-105, 111-13, sees a judicial
assembly with the richly dressed man as an insider, but the poorly dressed man as a
member of the community.
65. Frankemölle, *Jakobus*, pp. 387-89, asserts that both are members of the
community; the nature of the assembly is undefined. He describes the view that the
rich in the Epistle of James are to be seen as outsiders as 'pure speculation' (p. 387),
but fails to take adequately into account the fact that the πλούσιοι are always
negatively depicted, and are never described as ἀδελφοί. Cf. also Frankemölle,
Jakobus, pp. 251-59.

scholar and an uneducated person, if the rabbi is allowed to sit, the uneducated person should also be offered this unusual privilege for legal litigants.[66]

Although the parallels drawn by Ward are suggestive, there are still a number of weaknesses. It is not clear that the man with gold rings and the poor person are in fact regular members of the community; Ward's suggestion that the use of the description 'a man with gold rings wearing fine clothes', rather than the elsewhere negatively viewed 'rich person' (πλούσιος, 1.9-10; 2.6-7; 5.1-6), indicates a member of the community is not convincing.[67] Also, the questionable extent to which parallels can be drawn from Talmudic examples to explain the circumstances of the second half of the first century CE—a time span during which Judaism underwent considerable transition—makes it difficult to draw secure conclusions from such parallels. Although Mt. 18.15-17 and 1 Cor. 6.1-6 suggest that there were procedures within local Christian groups for the discipline of members or adjudication in disputes between members, there is little evidence from early Christian texts of the holding of elaborate judicial gatherings of the kind portrayed in the rabbinic examples.

If the thesis that a judicial gathering of early Christians is represented here is held to be unlikely, it is, nevertheless, still necessary to show that the alternative, that is, that both the man with gold rings and the socially marginal poor person are outsiders, offers a more satisfactory explanation. Thus, it is necessary to show why two such outsiders should be entering the assembly.

It is was suggested above that the scene depicts a gathering of which at least a sizeable proportion are supposed by the author to be Jewish Christians, sympathetic towards the ministry of the socially marginal followers of Jesus, who are 'poor by the world's standards' (πτωχοί τῷ κόσμῳ) In this case, such an unsympathetic reception as is depicted here for the poor person (πτωχός) would give concern to an author who

---

66. *b. Šebu.* 31a, 31b. See Ward, *Partiality*, pp. 89-95.

67. Ward, *Partiality*, p. 96-97. If the purpose of the example is to show wrongly biased judgment, on the basis of the outward appearance of the two incomers, then the description 'a man with gold rings wearing fine clothes' serves to highlight this wrong criterion for judgment, rather than to suggest that the person so described is not one of the rich πλούσιοι. Further, the contrast between the socially marginal poor (πτωχός) and the rich (πλούσιος) in the following verses (2.5-7) suggests that a contrast between these categories is also in question in 2.2-3.

affirms the conviction that such itinerant radicals are specially honoured by God as the inheritors of the eschatological kingdom.[68] As an itinerant, he would be embracing a socially marginal lifestyle, and also would not be a regular member of a local assembly. If he fulfilled the stipulations of Mt. 10.9-10 on travel without possessions, he could well be clad in shabby clothing, as depicted here.

It is also necessary to explain why a socially well-placed stranger should enter such a gathering. It is doubtful that well-to-do outsiders in the first century simply strayed into this kind of assembly out of curiosity. The nature of the social system in the first century, however, offers a plausible background to such an occurence. The principal means of the distribution of resources, which were perceived as limited in availability,[69] was a patron–client system of relationships. Patron–client relationships involved alliances on a vertical level, between partners of different social standing.[70] Patronage is described as:

> An enduring bond between two persons of unequal social and economic status which implies and is maintained by periodic exchange of goods and services, and also has social and affective dimensions.[71]

Patrons make needed goods or services, which are not available within the world of one's equals, available to a client. They likewise receive 'in return labour, produce, political support and social prestige'[72] from their clients:

68.   Patterson, 'Didache 11–13', pp. 324-28, and *Thomas*, pp. 172-78, sees the *Didache* as reflecting similar tensions between the radical itinerants and the settled groups on which they were dependent for support.

69.   On the perception of all resources as limited, see Malina, *New Testament World*, pp. 90-99; Hanson and Oakman, *Palestine*, pp. 111-12; H. Moxnes, *The Economy of the Kingdom* (Philadelphia: Fortress Press, 1988), pp. 76-83; R.L. Rohrbaugh, 'A Peasant Reading of the Parable of the Talents/Pounds', *BTB* 23 (1993), pp. 32-39 (33-35).

70.   In relation to the New Testament world, see Moxnes, *Economy*, pp. 36-47; J.H. Elliott, 'Patronage and Clientage', in Rohrbaugh, *The Social Sciences*, pp. 144-56; B.J. Malina, 'Patron and Client: The Analogy behind Synoptic Theology', in Malina, *Social World*, pp. 143-48.

71.   P. Garnsey and G. Woolf, 'Patronage of the Rural Poor in the Roman World', in A. Wallace-Hadrill (ed.), *Patronage in Ancient Society* (London: Routledge, 1989), pp. 153-70 (154).

72.   P. Garnsey, *Famine and Food Supply in the Graeco-Roman World* (Cambridge: Cambridge University Press, 1988), p. 58.

> Where a patronage system exists, it functions as the primary means of allocating such strategic resources. From the patron's viewpoint, clients are also one such strategic resource.[73]

For a person of higher standing, to act as patron was a necessary element in one's socially evaluated image as honourable. This need on the part of the patron facilitated the need of the client to gain access to certain resources, which were only available through the use of a patron.

The role of well-placed outsiders, who acted as patrons towards local Jewish communities, is mentioned several times in the New Testament (e.g., Lk. 7.4-5; Acts 10.2). Competition for clients was not an uncommon feature of the struggle to maintain one's status in the world of Roman Palestine.[74] Thus, it should not be surprising to see a scene depicted which appears to show a socially well-placed (prospective) patron, who is attempting to gain the support of clients in the local community,[75] entering such a gathering and being warmly received by those present, who would benefit from access to the additional resources, which such a patron would have controlled.[76]

73. T. Johnson and C. Dandeker, 'Patronage: Relation and System', in Wallace-Hadrill (ed.), *Patronage*, pp. 219-42 (233).

74. Malina and Rohrbaugh, *Commentary*, p. 75: 'As the Roman style of patronage spread to provinces such as Syria (Palestine), its formal and hereditary character changed. The newly-rich, seeking to aggrandize family position in a community, competed to add dependents... Clients competed for patrons just as patrons competed for clients in an often desperate struggle to gain economic or political advantage'. R. Saller, *Personal Patronage under the Early Empire* (Cambridge: Cambridge University Press, 1982), pp. 145-94, in his discussion of patronage in north Africa, notes that there is much less source material for patronage in the provinces, especially in relation to the lower classes. Such sources as do exist, however, consistently point to the pervasive presence of the patronage system.

75. B. Reicke, *The Epistles of James, Peter and Jude* (New York: Doubleday, 1964), p. 27, suggests that the man in fine clothes is a Roman of senatorial rank, who is seeking support for election to office, in which case, this verse depicts the wearing of a *toga candida*. In view, however, of the pervasiveness of the patron–client system in the eastern provinces of the Roman empire, as well as in Rome, where the system of exchange originated, such a precise location is unnecessary, apart from the consideration that Reicke's setting of the epistle in Rome is also unlikely.

76. It might appear that the saying of Jesus concerning the scribes and/or Pharisees (Mt. 23.6; Mk 12.39; Lk. 11.43; 20.46), who love the best seats in

According to this interpretation of the situation described in 2.2-3, the author portrays the different responses of a local community, which he feels should be sympathetic towards the radical itinerant prophets of the early Christian movement, to two incoming strangers. The socially marginal poor person (πτωχός), who is most likely to be seen as one of these itinerant adherents of the early Jesus movement, is given a dishonouring reception. His special status and authority as an inheritor of God's kingdom is not respected. On the other hand, a well-to-do prospective patron is treated with honour, as fits his standing in the social system. The contrast receives particularly strong ironic rhetorical effect in the context of the exhortation of 2.1: partiality is incompatible with commitment to Jesus, who as 'our Lord Jesus Christ of glory' is accorded particularly honourable standing, yet the addressees are accused of showing partiality in a manner which dishonours the very ones who perpetuate Jesus' lifestyle and proclamation, and who have been chosen by God as heirs of the kingdom. If this scene is read as taking place in a religious gathering, it depicts an all the more doleful discrepancy in outlook between the author, who is more sympathetic towards the socially marginal itinerants (πτωχοί), and the addressees, as depicted in 2.2-3. Rather than being dependent on God's provision, as typical of the radical trust of the followers of Jesus, the addressees prefer to seek security in the political benefits of a well-to-do patron.

The message and behaviour of these radical itinerant followers of Jesus also offers a plausible context for the interpretation of 2.4: 'Have you not discriminated among yourselves, and become judges with evil thoughts?' Schottroff draws attention to the practice of love of enemies

synagogues, suggests an alternative to this interpretation of Jas 2.2-3. The target of the author's criticism here, however, is preferential treatment towards a well-to-do individual. There is no indication that the man with gold rings and fine clothing is a teacher of a rival understanding of Judaism. Rather, the problem, in the author's view, is that he receives a place of honour on the grounds that he is rich. If this individual were a teacher representing another Jewish movement, it is highly surprising that this would not be mentioned. Penner, *James*, pp. 272-76, tentatively suggests in his conclusion that 'rich' in the Epistle of James may be a stylised codeword for Jews opposed to the emergent Christian movement. He offers little argument in support of his suggestion, apart from general comments about tensions between early Christians and other Jews in Matthew, John and the Pauline corpus, which have no real bearing on the possibility that 'rich' here represents rival Jews. Further, this suggestion depends on an unnecessary downplaying of the literal meaning of 'rich'.

and the proclamation of judgment, in the face of hostility, by these people.[77] This announcement of judgment constitutes a warning to repent, in the light of the coming of God's kingdom:

> the proclamation of judgement is not to be mistaken for a curse, but must, rather, be understood as dictated by the positive goal of salvation for all Israel. Its aim is not to deliver the addressees to their unhappy destiny, much less to call down divine punishment.[78]

In doing so, the radical itinerant early Christians thereby continued Jesus' message of the good news of the kingdom, in their actions and words, even to those who continued to reject both the message and its bearers. The judgment which is announced is God's judgment: they themselves are forbidden from judging others (Mt. 7.1; cf. Lk. 6.37). This motif of judgment as the prerogative of God alone occurs elsewhere in the Epistle of James in 4.11-12; the human renunciation of judgment is probably also reflected in 2.12-13. Those of the assembly depicted in 2.2-3, however, have usurped God's place of judgment by their actions in discriminating against the itinerant prophet, and in putting their trust in a human patron, rather than in God. Hence the strong reproach addressed to them in 2.4.

The assertion of the honourable status within God's universal order of those 'poor by the standards of the world' (πτωχοί τῷ κόσμῳ), whom the addressees are accused of dishonouring, already examined above, follows in 2.5-6a.[79] The phrasing of this affirmation in a question indicates that the author clearly expects the addressees' assent to this position.

This is followed by a contrasting depiction of the rich (πλούσιοι), again phrased in two rhetorical questions, in vv. 6b-7. The first question ('Is it not the rich who oppress you, and is it not they who drag you into court?') focuses on the position of the rich in relation to the addressees, while the second ('Is it not they who blaspheme the good name which was invoked over you?') views their position in relation to God. Neither portrays them in a positive light. As noted above, 'rich' (πλούσιος), like 'poor' (πτωχός), was more than simply an economic term in the ancient Mediterranean world.[80] πλούσιος meant rich, having access to a

77. See Schottroff and Stegemann, *Hope*, pp. 57-66.
78. Schottroff and Stegemann, *Hope*, p. 63.
79. See above, §3.3.3.1.
80. See above, n. 30.

more than average extent of material resources, but access to such a measure of the limited and scarce resources often implied that others had to do without, were deprived and exploited in order for the rich selfishly to accumulate their extra share. As well as meaning economically well-to-do, πλούσιος also often meant greedy and exploitative.[81]

Such economically self-advanced persons would find themselves in a position where they could act as a patron within the patron–client system of social organization, an activity which was necessary for a person of material means who wanted to claim any kind of honourable status. Consequently, it is quite plausible to identify the man with gold rings and fine clothing of 2.2 as a representative of the rich of 2.6-7.[82] Thus 2.6b can be seen to point out the inherent nature of the control of resources possessed by the rich: they have access to their resources only by the exploitation and oppression of others. There is no reason to see the verb 'oppress' (καταδυναστεύω) as referring to deliberate persecution of early Christians as such. Rather, the phrase depicts the widespread socio-economic reality of the time.[83] This verb is also used in the LXX with reference to the oppression of the socially lowly placed, such as the socially marginal πτωχοί (so explicitly in Amos 8.4; Ezek. 18.12; 22.29; cf. Ezek. 22.7; Mic. 2.2; Mal. 3.5; Wis. 2.10, etc.).

The oppression of the populace by greedy self-advancement on the part of the rich fits entirely with the second accusation against them: 'Is it not they who drag you into court?' The likely reference here is to the calling to account of at times unpayable debts owed by ordinary people (poor in the sense of πένης) to socially higher-placed persons.[84] A

81. See Malina, 'Wealth', pp. 363-66. Such a view of the accumulation of wealth is frequently attested in ancient literature; see, e.g., Plutarch, *On the Love of Wealth*; Aristophanes, *Plut.* 193-97, 353-55, 754-56.

82. The word χρυσοδακτύλιος occurs for the first time here, and seems to indicate the wearing of a gold ring (or rings) as a sign of affluence. See Mayor, *James*, p. 83.

83. On the oppression of the poor, see, e.g., D.J. Smit, 'Show No Partiality... (James 2.1-13)', *Journal of Theology for South Africa* 70 (1990), pp. 59-68 (63-64).

84. Cf. Ropes, *James*, pp. 195-96; Maynard-Reid, *Poverty*, pp. 63-64; Tamez, *James*, pp. 28-29. On the growing levels of indebtedness in Palestine under the early empire, see D.E. Oakman, *Jesus and the Economic Questions of his Day* (Queenston, Ontario: Edwin Mellen Press, 1986), pp. 72-77; also Horsley, *Sociology*, pp. 88-90.

number of situations parallel to this are depicted in the parables in the synoptic gospels (Mt. 18.23-34; Lk. 7.41-42). Again, it is very unlikely to represent the juridical persecution of Christians, for instance, by the wealthy Sadducees.[85] Thus, far from being appropriate figures to turn to for security, the rich are those who endanger the finely balanced security of the peasant economy by exploitation, even to the point of the possible legal exaction of unaffordable payments.

Having pointed out the oppressive and exploitative relation of the rich to the addressees, the following rhetorical question concerns their status in relation to God: 'Is it not they who blaspheme the good name which was invoked over you?' In general Greek usage, βλασφημέω meant to speak abusively, but in Jewish Greek writings it is almost always used to designate speaking abusively of God or dishonouring God.[86] This religious implication is clearly intended in 2.7, where the object of the blasphemy is 'the good name which was invoked over you' (τὸ καλὸν ὄνομα τὸ ἐπικληθὲν ἐφ᾽ ὑμᾶς).

The way in which the precise nature of this blasphemy is to be interpreted depends somewhat upon whether 'the good name' is seen to refer simply to God or, in a more specifically Christian sense, to the name of Jesus. The occurrence of this phrase is most likely influenced by the frequent use of the passive of the verb 'invoke' (ἐπικαλέομαι), with ἐπί and a name, in the LXX, as a designation of possession, especially in relation to God, equivalent to the niphal of the verb קרא.[87] Many interpreters favour seeing this as a reference to the invocation of the name of Jesus/Christ over the Christian at baptism.[88] As the phrase

---

85. Cf. Mayor, *James*, p. 87. Davids admits that 'one cannot determine whether the Christians are exploited as poor or as Christians', but his suggestion that 'certainly the disfavour people earned as Christians would do nothing to hinder their being hauled into court on trumped-up charges' (Davids, *James*, p. 113) gives too much precedence to theological considerations at the expense of awareness of social circumstances.

86. See H.W. Beyer, 'βλασφημέω', *TDNT*, I, pp. 621-25.

87. Amos 9.12; Isa. 43.7; Jer. 7.10-11, 14, 30; 2 Sam. 6.2; 2 Chron. 6.33; 7.14 etc.

88. Davids, *James*, pp. 113-14; Mayor, *James*, pp. 88-89; Mussner, *Jakobusbrief*, pp. 122-23; 'Christologie', p. 113; Dibelius, *James*, pp. 140-41; Laws, *James*, pp. 105-106; Hoppe, *Jakobus*, p. 58; Vouga, *Jacques*, p. 77. Ropes, *James*, pp. 196-97, sees reference to the name of Christ, but not necessarily to baptism. R.P. Martin, *James*, pp. 66-67, appears to prevaricate: 'God is the one whose name

draws on a common septuagintal idiom for the relation to God of God's people, however, it seems more likely that 'the good name' which is blasphemed is the name of God, to whom the addressees belong.[89] The circumlocutory expression 'the good name' would then also be explained by the traditional ineffability of the divine name. Even if there is an allusion to baptism as a symbolic ritual within the early Christian movement,[90] this does not imply the establishment of a Christian movement separate from its Jewish identity.[91] Davids's assertion that 'for Christians the name of Jesus was substituted for that of Yahweh, or Yahweh translated as κύριος was simply transferred to Jesus' is not nearly nuanced enough to depict satisfactorily the complex and often controversial development of Christology in the early Christian movement.[92]

Of course, it is true that to dishonour God would also imply dishonouring Jesus as God's specially appointed one, and that to dishonour Jesus likewise cast disrespect on God. In any case, it is clear that the rich who blaspheme are seriously out of place within God's order of the universe. There is a number of ways in which they may dishonour God: either by overt disparagement, or by their greed and oppressive actions

is invoked over Christians… The name blasphemed by the rich is (probably) either Jesus or the Christian's own title to faith'.

89.   Frankemölle, *Jakobus*, pp. 396-98, cautions against a quick identification of this phrase as a reference to baptism, or to the name of Jesus, although he also considers that this remains possible; cf. also Burchard, 'Stellen', pp. 363-64.

90.   Acts suggests the practice of baptism ἐπὶ (ἐν) τῷ ὀνόματι Ἰησοῦ Χριστοῦ (Acts 2.38; 10.48; cf. Mt. 28.19; *Did.* 7.1, 3) from an early date; however, the practice of baptism as a sign of repentance within the early Jesus movement is more likely to have indicated the restoration of relationship with God, whose appointed one Jesus was, rather than the initiation of relationship to Jesus himself. In Rom. 6.3-4, Paul appears to understand baptism as a sharing of some kind in the death and resurrection of Jesus; how widespread his views were, and whether they were identical with those of the early Palestinian followers of Jesus, is difficult to discern. E. Lohse, 'Taufe und Rechtfertigung bei Paulus', *Kerygma und Dogma* 11 (1965), pp. 305-24, argues for the influence of Hellenistic mystery religions on Pauline baptismal ideas. The influence of such Hellenistic religions on Paul is denied by A.J.M. Wedderburn, 'The Soteriology of the Mysteries and Pauline Baptismal Theology', *NovT* 29 (1987), pp. 53-72.

91.   Theissen notes the greater importance of baptism as a sign of conversion among the settled sympathizers, who remained within the traditional framework of Judaism, than among the itinerant radicals: *Sociology*, p. 21.

92.   Davids, *James*, p. 113; cf. Dibelius, *James*, p. 141.

which contravene God's order. In any case, to look for security to those who are so negatively situated in relation to God, the supreme ascriber of honourable status, rather than embracing the radical dependence on God typified by the socially marginal poor (πτωχοί) who are the heirs of God's kingdom, would obviously be ultimately disastrous for the addressees.[93]

Thus, to review what has been argued so far concerning the significance of the ascription of honourable status to the socially marginal poor by God in 2.5, within the context of the surrounding verses, the addressees are instructed against showing discrimination, which is incompatible with loyalty and commitment to Jesus Christ. What this implicit accusation entails is elaborated in the following narrative example: deference to the well-to-do, who may be in a position to offer material benefits, and dishonouring of the marginal. The identity and status of those so dishonoured is clarified in v. 5. This verse suggests they should be seen as socially marginal figures, whose special status in relation to God was proclaimed by Jesus, and whose marginal existence was given a radically positive interpretation in terms of depencence on God within the early Christian movement. The addressees, however, have not respected this view of ultimate reality. The contrast between the socially marginal poor and the rich is further stressed in vv. 6b-7. So far in the subsection, 2.1-13, the emphasis has been on presenting a negative evaluation of the addressees' attitudes towards the socially marginal poor and the rich; vv. 8-13 shift the stress towards a positive concluding exhortation in vv. 12-13.

3.3.3.3 *The Wider Context of James 2.5; 2.8-13.* The authority of the command to love one's neighbour is asserted by 2.8: 'If indeed you fulfil the kingly law, according to the scripture, "You shall love your neighbour as yourself", you are doing well'. This command contrasts with the kind of biased behaviour already shown in the previous verses. One of the key questions here is the precise sense of the 'kingly law' (νόμος βασιλικός). The juxtaposition of this expression with the citation from Lev. 19.18 is interesting in that it parallels the word νόμος,

---

93. J.S. Kloppenborg, 'Status und Wohltätigkeit bei Paulus und Jakobus', in R. Hoppe and U. Busse (eds.), *Von Jesus zu Christus* (Berlin: de Gruyter, 1998), pp. 127-54, notes the critique of patronage implied in the Epistle of James, but does not observe that dependence on the rich as patrons is contrasted with dependence on God, the supreme patron (pp. 150-54).

'law', with a single command. Usually νόμος is used for the entirety of the law's commands, indicating God's order for God's people, rather than for a single command, for which ἐντολή, 'commandment', would be more usual.[94] Some interpreters take this reference to mean a particularly significant command among others.[95] Others argue that the phrase should not be seen as designating the love command itself, but rather the authoritative order of which it is a part.[96] Others see the unusual apposition of νόμος with one command (Lev. 19.18) as equating the substance of the law with the love command.[97] This can then be seen as analogous to Jesus' double love command as the encapsulation of the law in the synoptic gospels (Mt. 22.39; Mk 12.31; Lk. 10.27; cf. also Rom. 13.8-10).

The view that the love command is being referred to by the designation 'kingly law' (νόμος βασιλικός) is preferable. This interpretation makes much better sense of the word sequence in the sentence. If the love command is simply one command among others, it is much more difficult to understand why this particular command is cited following the reference to the 'kingly law'. Indeed, it is possible that awareness of the linking in early Christianity of Lev. 19.18 with Deut. 6.4-5, the

94.   Thus, for instance, ἐντολή is used in relation to the double love command in Mk 12.28 and Mt. 22.36.

95.   Mussner, *Jakobusbrief*, p. 124.

96.   Ropes, *James*, pp. 198-99; Dibelius, *James*, pp. 142-43; C. Burchard, 'Nächstenliebegebot, Dekalog und Gesetz in Jak 2.8-11', in E. Blum, C. Macholz and E. Stegemann (eds.), *Die hebräische Bibel und ihre zweifache Nachgeschichte* (Festschrift Rolf Rendtorff; Neukirchen–Vluyn: Neukirchener Verlag, 1990), pp. 517-33 (524-29); O.J.F. Seitz, 'James and the Law', *SE* 2 (TU 87) (1963), pp. 472-86 (475, 484).

97.   Cf. particularly Hoppe, *Hintergrund*, pp. 88-90; also Schlatter, *Jakobus*, pp. 174-75; Tamez, *James*, pp. 62-63; Mayor, *James*, pp. 90-91; J. Zmijewski, 'Christliche "Vollkommenheit": Erwägungen zur Theologie des Jakobusbriefes', *SNTU* 5, Series A (1980), pp. 50-78 (74). According to P. Sigal, 'The Halakhah of James', in D.Y. Hadidian (ed.), *Intergerini Parietis Septum* (Festschrift Markus Barth; PTMS, 33; Pittsburgh, PA: Pickwick Press, 1981), pp. 337-53 (346), Lev. 19.18 is seen by the author of the epistle as 'the "royal" or "supreme" norm of religion'. M. Ludwig, *Wort als Gesetz: Eine Untersuchung zum Verständnis von 'Wort' und 'Gesetz' in israelitisch-frühjüdischen und neutestamentlichen Schriften. Gleichzeitig ein Beitrag zur Theologie des Jakobusbriefes* (Frankfurt am Main: Peter Lang, Europäischer Verlag der Wissenschaften, 1994), pp. 171-72, identifies the νόμος with the love command, but asserts that it is unlikely that the author of the Epistle of James thereby wished to stress its importance for Christians.

beginning of the *Shema,* which includes the command to love God (Mk 12.29-31; cf. Mt. 22.37-39; Lk. 10.27), has influenced this unusual expression.[98] Just a few lines prior to the citation of Lev. 19.18, the author refers to the eschatological reward of those who love God (Jas 2.5). In this case, it constitutes an allusion to the itinerant prophets and preachers of the Jesus movement, who fulfil the command to love God. The same phrase, however, is used in connection with the reward which the addressees themselves would receive for endurance in loyalty to God in 1.12. Both the citation of Lev. 19.18 and the allusion to the *Shema* in Jas 2.19[99] are followed by the same comment, 'you are doing well' (καλῶς ποιεῖς/ποιεῖτε), and key expressions from both these verses are later combined in 4.12 (εἷς ἐστιν [cf. 2.19] and πλησίον [cf. 2.8]).

Further, in the context of the early Christian movement, the idea of the kingdom (βασιλεία) of God was a particularly central idiom. Thus, the use of the adjective 'kingly' (βασιλικός), deriving from the same root as βασιλεία, can scarcely have been used without carrying some connotation of the kingdom proclaimed by Jesus.[100] This is all the more likely in view of the fact that the kingdom has been mentioned explicitly just a few lines earlier (2.5).

The frequency of occurrence of the love command of Lev. 19.18 in early Christian writings (Mt. 5.43; 19.19; 22.39; Mk 12.31, 33; Lk. 10.27; Rom. 13.9; Gal. 5.14; *Did.* 1.2) suggests that it was considered to be of particular importance within early Christian circles. As such it must have been seen as a key command not just among the radical, socially marginal followers of Jesus, but also among those sympathetic to his proclamation of the kingdom, such as the scribe depicted by

98. See further Hutchinson Edgar, 'The Use of the Love-Command'.

99. Cf. See Frankemölle, *Jakobus,* pp. 402-405; Tamez, *James,* p. 41; Hoppe, *Hintergrund,* p. 89. Hoppe's view, that such a prioritizing of the love command(s) was unthinkable in a non-Christian Jewish setting (cf. A. Nissen, *Gott und der Nächste im antiken Judentum: Untersuchungen zum Doppelgebot der Liebe* [Tübingen: J.C.B. Mohr (Paul Siebeck), 1974], pp. 219-44) is not necessarily accurate; see K. Berger, *Die Gesetzesauslegung Jesu: Ihr historischer Hintergrund im Judentum und im Alten Testament* (WMANT, 40; Neukirchen–Vluyn: Neukirchener Verlag, 1972), pp. 38-55. K. Berger, *Gesetzesauslegung,* pp. 56-257, provides a detailed analysis of the developing interpretation of the two commands and their combination in the synoptic gospels.

100. Cf. Davids, *James,* p. 114; Laws, *James,* p. 110; Frankemölle, *Jakobus,* p. 402; Karrer, 'Christus der Herr', p. 174.

Mk 12.28-34, who is told by Jesus, 'You are not far from the kingdom of God'. Thus, if, as suggested, the Epistle of James was addressed to sympathizers who were acting less sympathetically than the author desired, the citation of Lev. 19.18 formed a particularly suitable basis for appeal by the author. Moreover, the command to love one's neighbour is closely related to the foregoing theme of discrimination against the socially marginal (πτωχός) Christians in Jas 2.5. The Greek word πλησίον (translating the Hebrew רֵעַ) meant another person within one's community group. In a strongly group-oriented and non-individualistic ancient Mediterranean social context, one would normally be bound by strong ties of group-belonging to such a person. As such, the love command comprises an injunction towards commitment and attachment to one's significant social group.[101] For those sympathetic to the Jesus movement, an early Christian itinerant prophet should have been seen as a 'neighbour', and given honourable treatment. If the addressees fulfil this command, then they do indeed do well. On the other hand, if they show partiality,[102] such as already depicted, then they do not accord with God's order, typified by the love command. Rather, they commit sin and are convicted as transgressors, out of order.

The expression, 'the whole law' (ὅλος ὁ νόμος), and the citation of two commands from the Decalogue in the following verses do not provide an argument against seeing the equation of Lev. 19.18 with the 'kingly law' as the expression of the essence of God's order for God's people. Rather, murder and adultery, like partiality in Jas 2.9, can be seen as breaches of the definitive love command, which itself embraces the whole law.[103] To fulfil the whole law, expressed through the love

101. Burchard, 'Nächstenliebegebot', pp. 525-26, argues that if both the socially marginal poor person and the man with gold rings in 2.2-3 are not members of the group, then they do not fall within the range of the command to love one's neighbour, and therefore it is not directly connected with the sin of partiality. Even if both were outsiders, however, if the implications of Lev. 19.18 drawn out by both Mt. 5.43-46 and Lk. 10.29-37 are in any way typical of early Christianity, then his argument is still questionable.

102. 2.9 may be an allusion to Lev. 19.15, 'You shall not show partiality to the poor or yield deference to the powerful' rather than directly to Lev. 19.18, but it is not necessary to see the connection between the love command and the issue of biased attitudes as dependent on the link in Lev. 19, as L.T. Johnson, 'The Use of Leviticus 19 in the Letter of James', *JBL* 101 (1982), pp. 391-401 (393), argues.

103. Cf. D.C. Allison, Jr, 'Mark 12.28-31 and the Decalogue', in C.A. Evans and W.R. Stegner (eds.), *The Gospels and the Scriptures of Israel* (JSNTSup, 104;

command, but still to stumble in one thing, that is, in one thing not to fulfil the love command, obviously renders one guilty of breaching the law in its entirety.[104] When the law is essentially expressed through this one command, then it is either kept or broken; there can be no further relativizing of less important stipulations, when there is one definitive principle. All other stipulations have already been relativized, inasmuch as the love command contains the measure of the law in its entirety. This does not mean, of course, that other commands, such as the two decalogue commands cited in 2.11, are invalidated. Rather, they are now to be seen from the perspective of the love command.[105]

The discomfort shown by some interpreters[106] that this view indulges legalism and casuistry of details is unnecessary. This perspective is quite in keeping with the fundamental view that the world, including the world of human affairs, is ordered by God, and thus holy. This divine character of the standard for the ordering of human activity is expressed explicitly by the attribution of these commands to God as their giver in 2.11.

There is no reason to see the citation of these two commands from the Decalogue as anything other than an example which will be easily

Sheffield: Sheffield Academic Press, 1994), pp. 270-78 (274): 'Jas 2.8-13...refers to Lev. 19.18 as the "royal law" and then cites the prohibitions of adultery and murder as instances of that law'.

104. The basic principle is that God's order is whole; to transgress in any way means to put oneself out of harmony within this whole. This idea is not unique to the Epistle of James. Elsewhere in the early Christian texts, a similar sentiment is expressed by Paul in Gal. 5.3, and in the gospels in Mt. 5.17-20; 23.23; Lk. 16.17. It is found in other Greek Jewish writings (e.g. *T. Ash.* 2; LXX Deut. 27.26; 4 Macc. 5.20), in a variety of rabbinic texts (see Davids, *James*, p. 116; Dibelius, *James*, p. 144; Mayor, *James*, pp. 92-93; Schlatter, *Jakobus*, pp. 177-78; Vouga, *Jacques*, p. 80), and also has parallels in Stoic thought (see M.O. Boyle, 'The Stoic Paradox of James 2.10', *NTS* 31 [1985], pp. 611-17).

105. Whether or not the author considered this to include such regulations as those on circumcision, clean and unclean foods, and so on, which were contentious in at least some early Christian groups, is impossible to tell from the references in the text; there is simply no mention of these issues. If the letter was composed with sympathizers towards the ministry of Jesus within local Jewish communities in mind, then there would be no need for these matters to be controversial, although, in this case, it would also not give any information on the attitude of the author towards the redefinition of these regulations in situations where they were disputed.

106. See, e.g., Dibelius, *James*, p. 145; Adamson, *James*, pp. 116-17, who speaks of 'the ruthless legalism of all passages like this'.

appreciated, drawing, as it does, on one of the centrepieces of the Torah.[107] That is, the words, 'If you do not commit adultery, but you do commit murder, you have become a transgressor of the law', should not be seen to imply that the author is accusing the addressees of having committed murder, in either a literal sense,[108] or in allusion to Jesus' deepening of the murder prohibition in Mt. 5.21-22.[109]

The conviction of those who breach God's order as transgressors (παραβάτης, Jas 2.9, 11), raises the question of the status of these transgressors before God's ultimate judgement. This question is taken up in v. 12 and turned to a positive exhortation: 'So speak and so act as those who are going to be judged by the law of freedom'.[110] Eschatological themes, including judgment, occur frequently within the epistle (e.g. 3.1; 4.11-12; 5.9, 12). This reflects their importance for the author's perspective, and is in keeping with the concerns of the early Christian movement.[111] Here in 2.12, the standard of judgment by which one's place in or outside God's order is to be established is designated as the 'law of freedom' (νόμος ἐλευθερίας). This law of freedom is clearly an echo of the phrase 'perfect law of freedom' (εἰς νόμον τέλειον τὸν τῆς ἐλευθερίας), used in 1.25. In the context of the developing discussion within 2.1-13 this is surely to be identified with the 'kingly law' (νόμος βασιλικός) in 2.8. God's law, expressing God's eschatological order, by which right human conduct is to be measured, is thus to be seen as fundamentally expressed in the command to love one's neighbour.[112]

It is worth noting that 'law' (νόμος) in the Epistle of James occurs in contexts which are marked by an eschatologically oriented early

107. It is impossible to tell if the order of occurence of the two prohibitions is of any significance. The usual order of both the Hebrew and LXX texts is the reverse of this, although adultery does precede murder in codex B of LXX Deut. 5.17-18. This is also the order used in Lk. 18.20, by contrast with Mt. 19.18, which follows both the usual LXX order and negative future construction, οὐ φονεύσεις, οὐ μοιχεύσεις. This may suggest awareness of a minority textual tradition, or may simply be a coincidental loose quotation. Mk 10.19 has μὴ φονεύσῃς, μὴ μοιχεύσῃς; Rom. 13.9 has οὐ μοιχεύσεις, οὐ φονεύσεις.

108. Cf. R.P. Martin, *James*, p. 70.

109. Cf. Reicke, *James*, p. 29.

110. This exhortation also prefigures key themes of the following two subsections: right human action in 2.14-26, and right human speech in 3.1-12.

111. See also above, §3.3.3.2, on Jas 2.4.

112. See Hoppe, *Hintergrund*, p. 89; Frankemölle, *Jakobus*, pp. 412, 414.

Christian perspective. In 2.8, it is associated with the kingdom theme, which thus should be seen to permeate the following usages of the word in 2.9-12, including the designation 'law of freedom' in 2.12. In the light of the identification of this law with the love command in 2.8-12, it seems likely that the author is also thinking in these terms in the use of the almost identical phrase 'perfect law of freedom' in 1.25, although this was not made explicit in 1.25. Further, in 4.11-12, law (νόμος) is used in association with the idea of the divine prerogative, and human renunciation, of judgment (cf. Mt. 7.1; Lk. 6.37; and above on 2.4). In any case, it seems relatively clear that, on the one hand, the author of the epistle grounds the authority of his view of the order of the world in the traditional Jewish authority of law as God's order. On the other hand, he also relates the definition of this law to the authoritative traditions deriving from Jesus' ministry and from the movement which continued after his crucifixion. Thus, law (νόμος) in the Epistle of James should be seen to refer to the early Christian interpretation of the Jewish order of the universe, essentially expressed through the love command.[113]

That this standard for judgment, the law of freedom, is to be seen in accordance with a Jewish perception of the world, strongly influenced by early Christianity, is borne out by the following verse, the concluding verse of the subsection: 'For judgment is without mercy for the person who does not act with mercy; mercy triumphs over judgment'. The importance of mercy (ἔλεος) as an honourable quality, for which the subject in return receives mercy from God is mentioned several times in the synoptic gospels (Mt. 5.7; 6.12, 14; 18.21-35; Mk 11.25; Lk. 11.4; 6.36).[114] The showing of mercy in an ancient Mediterranean context can be seen as the restitution to honourable status of one who has lost such standing through a breach of social relations, or the treatment as honourable of one who has lost status through personal

113. See Hutchinson Edgar, 'The Use of the Love-Command'. Cf. Frankemölle, *Jakobus*, pp. 354-57; R. Bauckham, 'The Old Testament in the New Testament: James, 1 and 2 Peter, Jude', in D.A. Carson and H.G.M. Williamson (eds.), *It is Written: Scripture Citing Scripture* (Festschrift Barnabas Lindars; Cambridge: Cambridge University Press, 1988), pp. 303-17 (308-309).

114. The importance of mercy in the early Christianity obviously has its roots in the idea of God's steadfast love/mercy towards Israel (חסד, usually translated as ἔλεος in the LXX [e.g. Exod. 20.6; 34.6-7; Deut. 5.10; cf. also Hos. 6.6, cited in Mt. 9.13; 12.7]).

misfortune.[115] Not to show mercy implied passing judgment on the other person, which as already noted, is the prerogative of God, not of humans, and which in turn brought God's judgment on the one who so behaved (Mt. 7.1-2; Lk. 6.37-38).

Moreover, the concluding aphorism, κατακαυχᾶται ἔλεος κρίσεως, gives expression to a key characteristic of the early Christian view of the universe. This is the sharp prioritizing of God's mercy over God's judgment, and the location of the possibility of human salvation in radical dependence on God's mercy (cf. the parables in Mt. 20.1-16 and Lk. 18.9-14). This constituted a reinterpretation of the usual balance between forgiveness and condemnation in God's judgment of the people of the world, weighed according to the measure of their behaviour.[116] Thus, for example, Sirach set out the equal measure of God's mercy and his wrath: 'For mercy and wrath belong to the Lord; he is mighty to forgive, and he pours out wrath. As great as his mercy, so great is also his reproof; he judges a man according to his deeds' (Sir. 16.11-12).

This stress on God's mercy does not mean that human conduct becomes irrelevant for the evaluation of human status in relation to God. Corresponding to the stress on God's mercy as supreme, mercy becomes the prerequisite for human behaviour in harmony within God's order. In this early Christian perspective, judgment is renounced and left to God, in whose righteous action mercy triumphs over judgment; correspondingly, righteous human action is to do mercy.

In the kind of situational context suggested for the interpretation of the epistle, the addressees can be seen to have acted without showing mercy, thus putting themselves under judgment (v. 13a), by their discriminating attitude towards the socially marginal itinerant radicals of the early Christian movement (vv. 2-3). They have judged such people according to their devalued social standing, rather than showing mercy by treating them honourably. The socially marginal prophet is radically dependent on God's mercy; the addressees are thus warned to

---

115. Cf. Malina and Rohrbaugh, *Commentary*, pp. 63-64, on forgiveness. B.J. Malina, 'Gratitude', in Malina and Pilch (eds.), *Biblical Social Values*, pp. 86-88, notes the social sense of acts of mercy as deeds of favour shown by a superior to an inferior. In the song of Mary in Lk. 1.46-55, God is praised for his mercy, characterized by the exaltation of the lowly, including the filling of the hungry.

116. See Boccaccini, *Middle Judaism*, pp. 214-20.

act accordingly in showing mercy, in correspondence with the standard of God's order and God's judgment (2.12-13).

3.3.3.4 *Summary*. At this point, it is appropriate to summarize what has emerged from the examination of the apparent discrepancy in attitude between the author and the addressees with regard to the status of the socially marginal. This was particularly expressed in the strong statement of 2.5-6a. The foregoing analysis has viewed these verses within the textual context of 2.1-13, set against the background of the social dynamics of early Christianity and the world-view of the Jesus movement.

1. The emphasis on the special status of the marginal and oppressed fits entirely with the positive evaluation of social marginality within God's order of things, as proclaimed by Jesus' announcement of good news to the poor (2.5).
2. The dependence of socially marginal prophetic figures, who perpetuated Jesus' lifestyle and proclamation, upon the material support of settled 'sympathizers' within local communities provides a plausible context of situation for the discrepancy in attitude apparent between the author and addressees on the status of the socially marginal. The author affirms the early Christian view of their special status; the depiction of the addressees' conduct suggests that they have behaved less sympathetically towards such itinerant prophets than the author expects. Rather, they have preferred more materially tangible means of security to the radical dependence on God typical of the more socially marginal followers of Jesus. In this context, the author warns the addressees away from the rich, pointing out their real nature as exploiting oppressors who are opposed to God's order. This also serves rhetorically to urge the addressees to identify with God's standards and with the socially marginal (πτωχοί), who are chosen by God (2.1-7).
3. The author draws on authoritative Jewish socioreligious tradition, the view of the order of the universe represented by God's law (νόμος). In particular, he brings out the early Christian perspective on this order, to admonish the addressees for their conduct, and to warn them towards appropriate behaviour in correspondence to God's mercy, facing judgment in accordance with the standards of God's order (2.8-13).

3.4 *Conclusion*

The two principal parts of this chapter have examined a number of aspects of the depiction of the addressees by the author of the Epistle of James. The findings can be summarized briefly as follows:

1. Analysis of the names used by the author to depict the addressees established firmly the rootedness in Jewish tradition of the assumptions which the author expects the addressees to share. It can be accepted that this was a reasonably accurate expectation, otherwise these statements would have been incomprehensible. This analysis also suggested the particular influence of the authoritative traditions associated with Jesus and his movement on the interpretation of these shared assumptions of Jewish background about the nature of the world. The names (especially 'twelve tribes in the Diaspora') used by the author for the addressees drew on the eschatological hopes of God's restoration of the chosen people. The addressees were thus presenting as belonging to that restoration, and consequently expected to share the values associated with it. Other names used for the addressees (especially 'adulteresses', 'sinners' and 'double-minded') suggested inconsistency between the views held by the author and the behaviour of the addressees.

2. Examination of the key inconsistency in view between author and addressees, namely, the status of the socially marginal, provided a context within the social environment of the early Christian movement in which the findings of (1) above can be plausibly located. Particular attention in this analysis was paid to the expression of this issue in 2.5-6a, set in the wider context of 2.1-13. According to this suggested location, the Epistle of James is addressed to a group or groups sympathetic towards the early Christian movement, within the fundamental Jewish framework in which the movement emerged. These addressees, however, have a less convinced appreciation of the conclusive authority of the reinterpretation of the traditional Jewish world-view put forward by Jesus and his movement, than that held by the author. They compromise dependence on God by a favourable attitude to earthly benefactors, and

neglect those who do show the radical dependence on God affirmed by the author in 2.5. The exigencies of day-to-day existence may well lie behind this situation. While positively disposed to the message of Jesus and his followers, such people may simply have found the demands of radical dependence on God's provision impractical in everyday life.

3. Although tension between the socially marginal, radical strand in early Christianity and local communities provides a clear indication of the likely background of the epistle, the text as such does not constitute an overt defence of the rights of these radicals. Obviously the author is strongly sympathetic towards them, and disapproves of the way the addressees have dishonourably treated them. The focus of this passage, however, is on the addressees' standing in relation to God. Thus, 2.1 opens with reference to their commitment (πίστις) in relation to Jesus, God's specially appointed and vindicated authority figure. Likewise, 2.8-13 stresses the need for their conduct to correspond to the standards of God's eschatological world order, apparently strongly influenced by the early Christian world-view, with particular stress on the love command and the prioritizing of God's mercy.

The author does not call explicitly for proper treatment of the marginal radicals (although this concern is clearly implied), rather, the presentation of the socially marginal early Christian prophets (πτωχοί) in this passage serves two key argumentative functions, directed towards the addressees. First, it provides a contrast between the addressees' present attitudes towards such figures and what their attitudes should be, if they were in harmony with the standards of God's eschatological order. Second, by drawing attention to those whose lives are radically dependent on God's mercy and providence, the author provides a contrast with the addressees' own wavering dependence upon God. Their wavering dependence upon God is also shown by their favourable disposition towards the patronage of the rich, who are exposed as God's enemies. In these ways, the author highlights the shortcomings of their commitment to God.

Thus, the author's key concerns, highlighted by the strongly expressed contrast of 2.5-6a can be seen to relate essentially to the addressees' relationship to God: in particular, exhortation towards unwavering commitment to God, the supreme authority and ascriber of honourable status within the ultimately real, eschatological order of things. The avoidance of the material benefits available from earthly patrons, who, however, represent opposition to God's order, is a subsidiary component of this concern that the addressees remain undivided in their dependence on God. This insight will be explored in greater detail through the rest of the text of the epistle in the following chapters.

Chapter 4

READING THE TEXT: JAMES 1.2-18

4.1 *Introduction*

The previous chapter found that a key element in the implied relationship between the author and addressees was the degree of inconsistency between the addressees' conduct and the author's expectations of them. Analysis of the striking instance of such inconsistency expressed in 2.5, within the textual context of 2.1-13, suggested that the social location of such concerns could be found in tensions between radical, socially marginal members of the Jesus movement, who perpetuated his lifestyle and proclamation, and local communities (or a local community), whom the author reproves for failing to receive such figures with respect and honour. This implied that the addressees were considered by the author to have been sympathetic to the message of the Jesus movement, but that their continued adherence to the values and social implications of the movement, and recognition of the authority of its interpretation of the Jewish world-view, now stood in question. In this light, the key concern of the text emerged as exhortation to show unwavering commitment towards God, in accordance with the standards of God's eschatological world order proclaimed by the early Christian movement, resisting the enticements of worldly patrons.

Two particular aspects of this hortatory goal should be pointed out. The first aspect focuses on the depiction of the addressees' shortcomings and on direct exhortation to firm reliance upon God. The second aspect focuses on the reverse side of this relationship, the depiction of God's supreme status, authority and beneficence. The rejection of those who oppose God and compete with God for the allegiance of the addressees is entailed in this second aspect.

If this preliminary view of the epistle's social location and strategy is accurate, it must be discernible throughout the text as a whole, and should also be reflected in the text's rhetorical development. Thus, the

138 Has God not Chosen the Poor?

138   *Has God not Chosen the Poor?*

task of this chapter is to investigate further the helpfulness, or otherwise, of the insights gleaned from the analysis of 2.1-13.

The opening passage of any text is of particular importance, as it is
here that the material with which the text is concerned is introduced,
shaping the hearers'/readers' initial impressions and expectations, and
to a large extent setting the tone for the entire text. Thus, the first step in
a further analysis of the epistle, after identifying the opening section of
the text, will be to examine this section, 1.2-18, in detail. Particular
attention will be paid to indications of the importance of the two
aspects of the exhortation to the addressees towards commitment to
God highlighted above: depiction of the addressees' shortcomings and
admonition towards loyalty, and depiction of God as the supreme and
benevolent authority.

Jas 1.2-18, after the letter-greeting (1.1), has been analysed as a unity
by a number of scholars;[1] others variously see a new section beginning
in v. 12, v. 13, v. 9 and v. 12, or v. 19b.[2] The key considerations in such
analyses tend to be the relation of vv. 9-11 to the preceding and following verses, and whether v. 12 ends the opening section, begins a new
section, or recapitulates certain themes already raised earlier in the
section.

A clear recapitulation of the language and motifs of vv. 2-8 occurs in
v. 12, with the repetition of the words/cognates 'endurance' (ὑπομονή,
vv. 3-4), 'testing' (πειρασμός, v. 2), 'proven' (δόκιμος, cf. δοκίμιον, v.
3),[3] 'will receive' (λήμψεται, v. 7). Some have suggested that while the
reference to enduring testing in v. 12 echoes v. 2, it differs from the use
of the verb 'test' (πειράζομαι) in vv. 13-14. In the former case,
πειρασμός is seen to refer to external 'trials', in the latter, to internal

1.   Dibelius, *James*, pp. 69-107 ('this unity is nevertheless only superficial',
p. 69); Mussner, *Jakobusbrief*, pp. 62-97; a little more enthusiastic about its unity
are Hoppe, *Jakobusbrief*, pp. 19-42; Frankemölle, *Jakobus*, pp. 133-320; Baasland,
'Literarische Form', pp. 3655-59; Schlatter, *Jakobus*, pp. 98-139; L. Thurén, 'Risky
Rhetoric in James', *NovT* 37 (1995), pp. 262-84 (269-73).

2.   Verse 12, Francis, 'Form', p. 118; Penner, *James*, pp. 144-46; F. O Fearghail,
'On the Literary Structure of the Letter of James', *Proceedings of the Irish Biblical
Association* 19 (1996), pp. 73-76; v. 13, Wuellner, 'Jakobusbrief', p. 42; von Lips,
Traditionen, p. 412; v. 9, v. 12, Laws, *James*, pp. 62, 66; v.19b, R.P. Martin, *James*,
p. 44.

3.   τὸ δόκιμον, the neuter adjective used as a substantive, does occur in place
of τὸ δόκιμιον in v. 3 in a small number of Greek miniscules, but δοκίμιον is
easily the best attested and most reliable option.

'temptations';[4] thus it has been argued that v. 12 should be seen as a summarizing beatitude at the end of 1.2-12, with a new section beginning in v. 13, attached to the preceding verse by means of the superficial catchword link. The problem with this view is that it presupposes that an explicit differentiation of meaning in translation ('trials'/'temptations') also applies to the Greek text. The use of the same root-word, even when developing slightly different shades of meaning, should rather be seen as the discussion of various aspects of the same issue. Thus, it is preferable to see v. 12 and vv. 13-15 as related, substantively as well as formally, and thus part of the same subsection.

The apparently disjointed relation of vv. 9-11 to the rest of the section can also best be resolved by reading these verses as part of a larger subsection. The subdivisions of 1.2-18 on either side of vv. 9-11 both begin with positive evaluations of human circumstances, which in themselves would not be automatically positive: 'Consider it all joy when you encounter testing' (v. 2); 'Blessed is the man who endures testing' (v. 12). Likewise, the injunction, 'Let the lowly brother claim honour in his exaltation' (v. 9), advocates the evaluation in a positive light of a condition (ταπείνωσις) not normally viewed favourably.[5] This contrast with the transitory nature of the apparently high status of the rich marks the exaltation of the lowly as ultimately more secure. Thus, vv. 9-11 in fact can be seen to fit well within the context of the internal development of 1.2-18. Jas 1.2-8 speaks of the full (final/ultimate) effect of patient endurance in testing as being perfect and complete; v. 12 speaks of ultimately receiving the crown of life; between these, v. 9 speaks of the ultimate and actual exaltation of the lowly brother. This does not mean that the testings are to be explicitly identified as oppression by the rich (although this is possible, cf. 2.6); the principal function of the rich in vv. 9-11 is the contrast between their status and that of the lowly brother.

4. See Ropes, *James*, pp. 150, 153-54; Dibelius, *James*, pp. 71, 88, 90; Wuellner, 'Jakobusbrief', p. 42.
5. Cf. Hort, *James*, p. 14; Maynard-Reid, *Poverty*, pp. 38-39.

4.2 *The Opening Section, 1.2-18*

4.2.1 *Analysis of the Text: 1.2-8*

In the opening sentence, the addressees, named as 'my brothers', are exhorted to rejoice in the midst of testing (πειρασμοί). This word is usually translated by terms like 'trials', 'testing', 'temptation', and designates difficult circumstances, without necessarily giving precise content to those adverse circumstances. Some interpreters have taken πειρασμοί to refer specifically to the persecution of Christians,[6] others see a more general reference to the everyday difficulties of life for ordinary people in the ancient world.[7] As there is little indication of a situation of systematic persecution of Christians as such within the epistle, this explanation must be considered unlikely. Further, the generalized phrasing of 'whenever you encounter various tests' (ὅταν πειρασμοῖς περιπέσητε ποικίλοις), using ὅταν with the subjunctive of the verb περιπίπτω, and the adjective ποικίλος, 'various/diverse', seems to indicate that specific acts of hostility against the faithful are not in question here.

The reason for joy amidst testing is that 'the proven quality of your faith produces endurance' (τὸ δοκίμιον ὑμῶν τῆς πίστεως κατεργάζεται ὑπομονήν). πίστις, as noted above, in the ancient Mediterranean world had a much stronger social connotation, and less of a sense of individual belief than today, referring principally to the bonds of social loyalty and commitment.[8] The noun δοκίμιον, a substantivized neuter form of the adjective δοκίμιος, is rare in the New Testament, occurring only here and in 1 Pet. 1.7,[9] where it seems to mean the genuineness or trustworthiness of something which has been successfully tested. Most scholars deny that this word carries the same sense in Jas 1.3, preferring to see it as a near-equivalent of πειρασμός, with the sense of 'testing' or 'means of testing'.[10] The main reason for

---

6.   Davids, *James*, p. 67; R.P. Martin, *James*, pp. 14-15. Dibelius, *James*, pp. 71-72, sees an allusion to persecution, as an attempt to 'revive again the heroic sentiment' of the past, but the reference is not to any concrete social circumstances.

7.   Laws, *James*, pp. 51-52; Hoppe, *Jakobusbrief*, p. 20; *idem, Hintergrund*, p. 21; Ropes, *James*, p. 133.

8.   See above, Chapter 3 n. 51.

9.   It occurs four times in the LXX: 1 Chron. 29.4; Ps. 11.7; Prov. 27.21; Zech. 1.13.

10.   Dibelius, *James*, pp. 72-73; Davids, *James*, p. 68; Laws, *James*, p. 52;

this is that, unlike 1 Pet. 1.7, Jas 1.3 is not seen to be set in an overtly eschatological context. The sense of 'genuineness proved in testing', however, fits just as well in the context of 1.3, and, particularly in view of the otherwise similar phraseology of this verse and 1 Pet. 1.7, is to be preferred here also.[11] Moreover, the present context does contain resonances of the eschatological tone which elsewhere is made strongly explicit in the epistle. 'Joy' (χαρά) occurs frequently in eschatological contexts in early Christian and Greek Jewish literature,[12] and 'faith' (πίστις), 'testing' (πειρασμός), 'endurance' (ὑπομονή) and 'work' (ἔργον) all occur later in the epistle with clear eschatological connotations.[13]

This genuineness of commitment to God amidst testing produces ὑπομονή, patient endurance. This word carries an active sense of perseverance,[14] the consequences of which are drawn out in 1.4: 'Let endurance have its complete effect, so that you may be complete and

Mussner, *Jakobusbrief*, p. 65; Hoppe, *Hintergrund*, pp. 23-24; P.J. Hartin, 'The Call to Be Perfect through Suffering (James 1.2-4): The Concept of Perfection in the Epistle of James and the Sermon on the Mount', *Bib* 77 (1996), pp. 477-92 (477-78).

11. This interpretation also clarifies the position of ὑμῶν in the sentence, as it can now be read without difficulty in relation to δοκίμιον, rather than with πίστις, following the author's usual practice of placing the genitive pronoun after the noun.

12. E.g. Isa. 55.12; 66.10; Zech. 8.19; *T. Levi* 17.2; *T. Jud.* 25.4, 5; *T. Ash.* 6.6; *1 En.* 103.3; 104.12; Lk. 10.17, cf. 10.20; 15.7; 1 Thess. 2.19-20; Heb. 12.2; 1 Pet. 1.8.

13. πίστις, 2.14-26; ὑπομονή, 5.11; cf. ὑπομένω (1.12; 5.11); ἔργον, 2.14-26. In this context, τέλειος (1.4) can also easily be seen to have eschatological overtones (cf. the cognate words τέλος [5.11] and τελειόω [2.22]). Cf. Mussner, *Jakobusbrief*, pp. 65-67.

14. It is used of Abraham's (*Jub.* 17.18; 19.8) and of Joseph's (*T. Jos.* 2.7) demeanour under trying circumstances, and is characteristic of the heroic martyrs of *4 Maccabees* and of Job (cf. Jas 5.11). This exhortation can be seen to draw on the widespread tradition of the testing of loyalty to God in difficult circumstances (πειρασμοί); e.g. Gen. 22.1; Exod. 15.25; 16.4; Deut. 8.2, 16; 2 Chron. 32.31; Job 1–2; Jdt. 8.25-27; Wis. 3.4-6; Sir. 2.1-18; 15.11-20; 27.5, 7; 31.8-11; *Jub.* 17, 18, 19.3, 8; *T. Jos.* 2.7; *T. Reub.* 5.3-5; 1 Pet. 1.6-7; 4.12-14; Mt. 5.1-2; Heb. 10.32-36. Although the statistics provided by Frankemölle on the occurrence of the same words or concepts in Sir. 2.1-18 as in the opening verses of the Epistle of James confirm the widespread combination of these themes, the parallels do not prove, as he argues, that the author consciously chose the material for these verses from this passage in Sirach. See Frankemölle, *Jakobus*, pp. 190-96; also Frankemölle, 'Thema'.

whole, lacking in nothing'. Dibelius argues that 'complete effect' (ἔργον τέλειον) should be seen in correspondence to τέλειοι in the following phrase, referring to the addressees: '*You* are that perfect work'.[15] It is preferable, however, to understand ἔργον to refer to the consequences of endurance and faithfulness in terms of concrete actions in the lives of the addressees.[16]

It is significant that this is described as 'complete' (τέλειον), and results in being 'complete and whole, lacking in nothing' (τέλειοι καὶ ὁλόκληροι ἐν μηδενὶ λειπόμενοι). The early Christian use of this term has its background in the LXX use of τέλειος to translate תמים and שלם meaning complete in dedication and obedience to God, thus in full harmony with God's order.[17] תמים also occurs frequently in the Qumran scrolls as a designation of excellence before God.[18] When read in conjunction with the use of the word in Matthew and in the *Didache*, both of which have strong associations with the Jesus movement, the word τέλειος offers a striking link to concerns with uncompromising and undivided commitment to God. In Mt. 5.48, the command, 'Therefore you shall be perfect (τέλειοι), as your heavenly father is perfect (τέλειος)',[19] comes at the end of the amplification of the love of neighbour command (Lev. 19.18) to include love of enemies (Mt. 5.43-47), a command typically effected by the marginal disciples of the Jesus movement,[20] and coming at the climax of the reinterpretation and radicalization by Jesus of the traditional precepts of God's law (Mt.

15. Dibelius, *James*, p. 74 (his emphasis); cf. Davids, *James*, p. 69; Hartin, 'Call', pp. 479-80.

16. It may be argued that the plural (ἔργα, cf. 2.14, 17-18, 20-22, 24-26; 3.13) would fit this sense better than the singular form (ἔργον) used in this verse, but the author does use singular forms with a generalizing or collective sense elsewhere in the epistle (e.g. 1.9, 12; 2.6; 5.6). Cf. R. Heiligenthal, *Werke als Zeichen* (Tübingen: J.C.B. Mohr [Paul Siebeck], 1983), pp. 28-29, who also sees such an active sense for ἔργον in this verse. His assertion, that the author has substituted this term for ἀγάπη in an already common Christian concatenation, beginning with πίστις and ending in ἀγάπη, is difficult to substantiate.

17. See G. Delling, 'τέλειος', *TDNT*, VIII, pp. 67-78; also Davids, *James*, pp. 69-70; R.P. Martin, *James*, p. 16; Hoppe, *Hintergrund*, pp. 27-29.

18. See Delling, 'τέλειος', p. 73; Davids, *James*, p. 70; Hoppe, *Hintergrund*, p. 28.

19. The Lukan version of this saying (Lk. 6.36), uses 'merciful' (οἰκτίρμων) in the place of τέλειος in Mt. 5.48, which is also a key idea in early Christianity, cf. Jas 5.11, and closely related to ἔλεος (Jas 2.13, see above, §3.3.3.3).

20. See Schottroff and Stegemann, *Hope*, pp. 57-66.

5.21-48). In Mt. 19.21, links with the sense of radical dependence upon God's provision and obedience to his demands are even more explicit, as Jesus tells the young man with many possessions:[21] 'If you want to be perfect/complete (τέλειος), go and sell your belongings and give to the poor, and you will have treasure in heaven, and come and follow me'.[22] In the *Didache*, the following exhortation occurs at the end of the teaching of the 'Two Ways': 'If you are able to bear the whole yoke of the Lord, you will be perfect/complete (τέλειος), but if you are not able, do what you can' (*Did.* 6.2). Here, the impression is that those who embrace the whole of the radical proclamation of the Jesus movement, spelt out in the 'way of life' (*Did.* 1.2–4.14), are particularly approved as τέλειος.[23]

Undivided commitment to God, entailing dependence upon God and obedience to the demands of God's order, as authoritatively interpreted by Jesus and his movement is thus the core sense of 'perfect' (τέλειος) in Matthew and the *Didache*. This sense fits well with the context of Jas 1.4. Genuine faith-commitment to God and patient endurance, in adverse circumstances, enables full correspondence to the demands of God's eschatological order, by whose standards the addressees could then be accounted perfect and lacking in nothing.[24] 'Whole' (ὁλόκληροι) and 'lacking in nothing' (ἐν μηδενὶ λειπόμενοι), paralleled with 'complete' (τέλειοι) in 1.4, express the same basic idea,

21. ἔχων κτήματα πολλά (Mt. 19.22; Mk 10.22); only Luke refers to him explicitly as 'rich' (πλούσιος) (Lk. 18.23).

22. Here, the Matthean redactor substitutes εἰ θέλεις τέλειος εἶναι for the Markan 'you are missing one thing' (ἕν σε ὑστερεῖ, Mk 10.21). The Lukan redactor at this point also modifies the Markan text to read 'you still lack one thing' (ἔτι ἕν σοι λείπει, Lk. 18.22), which is also interesting in the context of Jas 1.2-5, in view of the use of the verb λείπω in 1.4-5.

23. Cf. K. Niederwimmer, *Die Didache* (Göttingen: Vandenhoeck & Ruprecht, 1989), pp. 155-56.

24. This also fits well with the other uses of τέλειος in the epistle. The word appears to be a favourite term of the author, occurring 5 times out of a total of 19 uses in the whole of the New Testament: as well as twice in 1.4, it also occurs in 1.17, where it refers to God's giving (πᾶν δώρημα τέλειον), to which right human action should of course correspond; in 1.25, it refers to God's order for right human behaviour (νόμος τέλειος) and in 3.2 it refers to human behaviour completely in harmony with God's order (τέλειος ἀνήρ). Frankemölle, *Jakobus*, pp. 495-99, stresses the link between τέλειος and the idea of wholeness and undividedness in correspondence to God's undividedness; the term's significance is also stressed by Zmijewski, 'Vollkommenheit'.

indicating completeness, wholeness, without deficiency.[25]

The verb 'lack' (λείπω) is taken up in the opening line of 1.5, which continues this theme of wholeness/deficiency, not as an abstract theological discussion, but in a firm relation to the concrete realities of life for the members of the Jesus movement: 'If any of you lacks wisdom, let him ask God, who gives generously and ungrudgingly to all, and it will be given to him'. As discussed earlier, wisdom (σοφία) was a key term in Jewish self-understanding, used with a variety of nuances, basically referring to the sense of the world as ordered by God, and right human behaviour in correspondence to this.[26] Thus, a lack of wisdom in this context can be seen to refer to a lack of appreciation of the authoritative order of God, proclaimed by Jesus, in which the poor and lowly are honoured in God's kingdom, with its call to radical love and mercy.[27] In practical terms, to lack wisdom would also mean not behaving in accordance with this understanding. That such wisdom is the gift of God is no surprise, and draws on the long Jewish tradition of wisdom as coming from God.[28] It is worth noting, however, that for the author of the epistle, wisdom is revealed by God to those who seek it from God (cf. Wis. 7.7; 8.21), rather than, for instance, being inherent in the Torah (cf. Sir. 24).

The lack of wisdom is to be remedied by prayer to God. The instruction, 'Let him ask...and it will be given to him' (αἰτείτω...καὶ δοθήσεται αὐτῷ), bears a noticeable resemblance to the saying of Jesus in Mt. 7.7//Lk. 11.9: 'Ask and it will be given to you' (αἰτεῖτε καὶ δοθήσεται ὑμῖν).[29] Here, however, the basic idea is considerably

25. The importance of this theme in the epistle is particularly developed by Elliott, 'Epistle of James', pp. 75-80.

26. See above, §2.3.1.

27. J.A. Kirk, 'The Meaning of Wisdom in James', *NTS* 16 (1969), pp. 24-38, argues that this term in the Epistle of James is used with a similar sense to the way in which the term 'Holy Spirit' is used elsewhere in early Christian writings (cf. Davids, *James*, pp. 51-56). Neither 1.5 nor 3.13-17, however, give unequivocal support to the view that wisdom is actively hypostasized in this manner in the epistle.

28. See Hoppe, *Hintergrund*, pp. 32-40; Davids, *James*, pp. 71-72; R.P. Martin, *James*, pp. 17-18; Frankemölle, *Jakobus*, pp. 212-15, who admits the contrast between Sir. 4.17 and the sentiments of Jas 1.5, but still maintains that this passage draws its theme from Sirach.

29. Radical and unwavering faith in God's provision of the requests of those who ask in wholehearted commitment is a striking feature of the Jesus movement of

expanded through the introduction of God as the one who gives: 'God, who gives generously and ungrudgingly' (παρὰ τοῦ διδόντος θεοῦ πᾶσιν ἁπλῶς καὶ μὴ ὀνειδίζοντος). This expansion serves a number of important rhetorical functions. First, it lays a marked stress on God's nature as *one who gives*. Second, this giving by God is characterized as undivided and ungrudging, and thus clearly to be relied upon. Third, God's reliable and unstinting giving contrasts sharply with the divided and doubting human behaviour[30] portrayed in the following verses (1.6-8). Such a negatively portrayed disposition towards God, clearly lacking in the necessary enduring commitment, is obviously out of order, and cannot expect God's giving to correspond to its vacillations (v. 7). Rather, the correct disposition towards God is to ask 'in faith, doubting nothing'. The importance of faith (πίστις) as confident and loyal commitment to God has already been mentioned in relation to v. 3; such faithful commitment constitutes the appropriate attitude towards a generous and benevolent divine patron.

A further possible contrast between divine and human activity may be implied in these verses. God is characterized as the one who gives generously and ungrudgingly to all; righteous human behaviour should correspond to the characteristics of divine action.[31] If the epistle entails

the synoptic gospels, typified by the assurance of Mt. 7.7//Lk. 11.9, and also clearly depicted in the lesson drawn from the withered fig tree (Mk 11.22-24; Mt. 21.21-22). These parallel passages also have noticeable verbal contacts with Jas 1.5-8, thus: ἐὰν ἔχητε **πίστιν** καὶ **μὴ διακριθῆτε**...καὶ πάντα ὅσα ἂν **αἰτήσητε** ἐν τῇ προσευχῇ **πιστεύοντες λήμψεσθε** (Mt. 21.21-22). The portrayal of the effectiveness of faithful prayer in 1.5-8, and later in 5.13-18, shows no sign of compromise away from the dramatic confidence in God of the early movement towards a less radical standpoint; cf. W. Rebell, *Alles ist möglich dem, der glaubt: Glaubensvollmacht im frühen Christentum* (Munich: Kaiser Verlag, 1989), pp. 96-98, 102.

30. The fundamental importance of this undesirable lack of correspondence between divine and human behaviour is particularly stressed by G. Schille, 'Wider die Gespaltenheit des Glaubens', *Theologische Versuche* 9 (1977), pp. 71-89, and also by H. Frankemölle, 'Gespalten oder ganz?', in H.U. von Brachel and N. Mette (eds.), *Kommunikation und Solidarität* (Freiburg: Edition Exodus, 1985), pp, 160-78. The importance of integrity and undividedness, both at an individual and a communal level, is likewise emphasised by Tamez, *James*, esp. Chapter 4; cf. E. Tamez, 'Elemente der Bibel, die den Weg der christlichen Gemeinde erhellen: Eine hermeneutische Übung anhand des Jakobusbriefes', *EvT* 51 (1991), pp. 92-100.

31. Tamez, *James*, pp. 58-62, draws attention to the contrast between human duplicity and God as the model of integrity in these verses. In the *Testaments of the Twelve Patriarchs*, ἁπλῶς (here translated as 'generously') and ἁπλότης is

implicit admonition to wavering 'sympathisers' towards radical itinerant followers of Jesus, there would be a contrast between the generous
benevolence of God, on whom these marginal disciples depend, and the
failure of the addressees to act accordingly in their treatment of the
itinerants, as suggested by the discussion of 2.1-13 in the previous
chapter.[32] Wavering commitment to God manifests itself in wavering
commitment to those specially chosen by God (cf. Jas 2.5-6).

It is already apparent that the two key themes highlighted as a result
of the investigations in the previous chapter are also very much present
in the opening verses of the text. On the one hand, the theme of exhortation to the addressees to unwavering commitment to God dominates
these verses. They are told to rejoice in the difficult circumstances of
testing, with test-worthy faith, patient endurance, and complete
identification with God's order. They are urged to be wholehearted in
their dependence upon God. They are warned against divided loyalty to
God, doubt-ridden faith, instability and doublemindedness which contrasts with God's own activity and the demands of his eschatological
world order. On the other hand, God is depicted clearly as the supreme
authority and benefactor, who gives generously to those who ask in
loyal commitment.

4.2.2 *Analysis of the Text: 1.9-11*
It was noted earlier that negative depiction of the rich (πλούσιοι) can
be seen to be rooted in the perception of the rich as opposed to God's
order. They oppose God both through their exploitative conduct and
through their function as rivals to God for the allegiance of the
addressees, to whom they could offer material benefits through the
exchange-mechanism of a patron–client relationship.[33] The fact that
such a negative depiction of the rich (1.9-11) follows the opening
exhortation to undivided commitment to God, and the depiction of God

frequently associated with human behaviour in correspondence to God's order, e.g.
T. Iss. 7.6-7; contrast the duplicity of Beliar, e.g. *T. Benj.* 6.7. Cf. J. Amstutz,
'*ΑΠΛΟΤΗΣ: Eine begriffsgeschichtliche Studie zum jüdisch-christlichen Griechisch*
(Bonn: Peter Hamstein Verlag, 1968), pp. 64-85.

32. Support for this possibility comes from *Did.* 4.3-4, where exhortation
against divisions (οὐ ποιήσεις σχίσμα), partiality (οὐ λήμψη πρόσωπον, cf. Jas 2.1,
9) and double-mindedness (οὐ διψύχησεις, cf. Jas 1.8) is followed immediately
by exhortation to giving without complaining and sharing with one's brother (*Did.*
4.5-8).

33. See above, §3.3.3.2.

as the supreme benefactor (1.2-8) strengthens the sense that this is indeed a key concern for the author.

Verses 9-11 echo the intent of the instruction of 1.2 to rejoice amidst difficult circumstances, through an exhortation to awareness of the contrast between ultimate status within God's order of things and standing within the present order of the world: 'Let the lowly (ταπεινός) brother claim honour in his exaltation, but the rich in his humiliation (ταπεινώσει), because like a flowering plant he will pass away'.

On the whole, scholars have interpreted this passage under the heading 'poor/rich' or 'poverty/wealth'. Understood in terms of the cultural anthropology of the ancient Mediterranean world,[34] however, poverty and wealth are not necessarily the opposites which they comprise in industrial or post-industrial societies today, where economic considerations are a key influence in evaluating social status. In the ancient world, rich persons who acquired personal possessions beyond their legitimate share of limited resources through the exploitation of others could be seen as just as dishonourable as social marginal beggars, who, through whatever cause, had lost their inherited standing in society (πτωχοί). Thus, it should not immediately be assumed that the Epistle of James represents concerns with the themes of poverty and wealth in their modern sense as economically evaluated opposites.

That 1.9-11 should not immediately be taken in this sense is borne out by the particular nuance of the adjective 'lowly/humble' (ταπεινός), which is contrasted with 'rich' (πλούσιος) in these verses. The principal meaning of ταπεινός is not socio-economically poor; rather the word means humble, of lowly standing, in a servile or subservient position.[35] In general, a humble or servile position would imply a lack of material resources on the part of such a person, but lack of possessions is not the decisive feature of the term as an indicator of social standing. This sense of humble status predominates in the LXX use of the term,[36] where it is also used of submission to God (Isa. 25.6; Zeph. 3.12; Prov. 16.19), and the lowly are promised God's help and comfort (Isa. 49.13; 54.10-11; Ezek. 17.24; 21.31; Job 5.11; 12.21; Prov. 3.34 [cited in Jas 4.6]; LXX Ps. 101.18; Sir. 10.15; 35.17-19).

---

34. See above, §3.3.1.
35. See W. Grundmann, 'ταπεινός, κτλ.', *TDNT*, VIII, pp. 1-26; cf. also R.P. Martin, *James*, p. 25.
36. See Grundmann, 'ταπεινός', pp. 6, 9-10.

The lowly person of Jas 1.9 is a 'brother' (ἀδελφός), understood by the author as a member of God's chosen twelve tribes and presumed to share his basic viewpoints, in spite of the apparent inconsistencies between what the author expects and the behaviour of the addressees. Thus, the lowly brother is told that his status as ταπεινός is one which, contrary to appearances, is ground for boasting. Whether the term should be seen to mean 'subservience to God' or 'subservient in society' is not immediately clear, but the two nuances are not mutually exclusive. Viewed socially, ταπεινός could designate the lowly status of much of the ordinary population of the ancient world, and therefore there is no difficulty in accepting this sense.[37] The occasion for claiming honour, however, 'in his exaltation', draws on the Jewish tradition of God's favour towards the lowly, which received particularly strong expression within the Jesus movement (Mt. 23.12//Lk. 14.11; 18.14; cf. also Mt 18.4; Lk. 22.26; Mk 10.15//Mt. 19.14//Lk. 18.16-17).

The rich person (πλούσιος, 1.10) is not explicitly described as a 'brother', and in view of the overwhelmingly negative depiction of the rich elsewhere in the epistle (2.6-7; 5.1-6) should not be seen as a member of the group addressed as brothers.[38] In contrast to the lowly brother, he is ironically told to boast in his lowliness and humble status; his present exploitative power is utterly transitory and will perish,[39] like withered plants under the heat of the sun.[40] It is not simply the possessions of the rich which are transitory, rather the rich person him-

---

37. Cf. Tamez, *James*, p. 42; Wall, *Community*, pp. 55-56; Maynard-Reid, *Poverty*, pp. 40-41.

38. See Dibelius, *James*, pp. 87-88; Davids, *James*, pp. 76-77; R.P. Martin, *James*, pp. 25-26; Maynard-Reid, *Poverty*, pp. 41-44, although Laws, *James*, pp. 62-63; Mussner, *Jakobusbrief*, p. 74; J. Soucek, 'Zu den Problemen des Jakobusbriefes', *EvT* 18 (1958), pp. 460-68, and Frankemölle, *Jakobus*, p. 243, argue that ὁ πλούσιος should be read in parallel to ὁ ταπεινός, also qualifying ὁ ἀδελφός. While this is grammatically possible, it is unlikely in view of the author's overwhelmingly negative use of πλούσιος.

39. It is interesting to note that the verb ἀπόλλυμι, used in 1.11, occurs again in 4.12 in a strongly eschatological context, and is frequently used with this eschatological sense in the synoptic gospels, e.g. Mk 8.35; Mt. 10.28, 39; also Jude 5.

40. On the imagery of this verse, see particularly P. von Gemünden, *Vegetationsmetaphorik im neuen Testament und seiner Umwelt* (NTOA, 18; Göttingen: Vandenhoeck & Ruprecht, 1993), pp. 305-306. The possible significance of the language of Isa. 40.1-8 for the eschatological imagery of these verses is explored by Penner, *James*, pp. 204-208.

self is so depicted: 'Like a flowering plant he will pass away...so also the rich person (πλούσιος) will wither away in the midst of his pursuits'.

Frankemölle argues that because considerably more space is dedicated to depicting the transitory nature of the rich, this indicates that the author's priority here is admonition of rich members of the addressed community.[41] This view, however, overlooks the rhetorical effect of such a depiction of a third party in the communication between author and addressees. First, by providing a counter-instance to the circumstances of the lowly brother, it highlights all the more the fact of their own exaltation. Second, it warns the addressees away from a positive disposition towards those who are destined to perish. Third, it stresses the ultimately real nature of God's eschatological order, by contrast with the transitoriness of the present order of the world. Fourth, by showing the downfall of the rich it offers comfort to those whose present circumstances are influenced by their exploitative behaviour. The woes against the wicked rich in the 'epistle' of *1 En.* 91–107 can be seen to constitute a similar rhetorical denunciation,[42] and possibly also the woes against the rich in Lk. 6.24-25.

It is significant that ταπεινός is used to qualify 'brother' here, referring to ordinary lowly situated people, and the use of this word indicates that the addressees are to be found among such people. For them, the attractiveness of the patronage of the rich, rather than appreciation of their status as defended, comforted and ultimately exalted by God, is not to be underestimated. In this context, the author encourages them to view their lowly status positively in the light of the ultimate reversal of status within God's order, a central theme of the good news announced by Jesus.

41. Frankemölle, *Jakobus*, p. 241. Cf. the excursus, 'Die soziale Situation der Adressaten', pp. 251-59. It is difficult to understand why he believes that Sir. 11.14 (good things and bad, life and death, poverty and wealth are from the Lord), provides a better key to understanding the author's attitude towards the wealthy and the poor (p. 257) than the synoptic gospel traditions (p. 243), in view of the epistle's clear links with the traditions of the sayings of Jesus; the location, in terms of time, space and social circumstances of the epistle must surely be closer to that behind the synoptic traditions than to Sirach.

42. P.J. Hartin, '"Who Is Wise and Understanding among You?" (James 3.13): An Analysis of Wisdom, Eschatology and Apocalypticism in the Epistle of James', *SBLSP* 33 (1996), pp. 483-503, provides a comparison of the 'epistle' of Enoch with the Epistle of James, pp. 495-98.

4.2.3 *Analysis of the Text: 1.12-15*

This second exhortation to the addressees to view their situation positively, in the light of the eschatological realities of God's kingdom (Jas 1.9-11), is followed by a third positive evaluation of difficult circumstances in 1.12, which takes up again the idea of enduring testing from the opening exhortation (1.2-8), expressed here in the form of a beatitude.[43]

In this verse, the eschatological motivation hinted at in the opening exhortation, and implied in the status-reversal motif of 1.9-11, is made fully explicit. The eschatological blessing promised to those who endure difficult circumstances in devotion to God[44] contrasts sharply with the withering of the rich in the previous verse. This promise of God's ultimate favour for those approved through their enduring dedication serves to reinforce further the author's appeal to the addressees to remain loyal to God and to God's people. Not only is God the benefactor who gives ungrudgingly to those who ask (1.5), God is also the supreme authority who rewards those who remain loyally committed with honourable status within the ultimately real eschatological world order.

The theme of testing (πειρασμοί) is expanded within the framework of the divine-human relationship in the following verses. The development of a further nuance in 1.13-15, the origin of such testing, does not mean, as Dibelius argued, that these verses are unconnected to the pre-

43. The expression of this assurance is strongly marked by common usage of both traditional Jewish and early Christian traditions. The formulation μακάριος ἀνήρ occurs frequently in the LXX, especially in the Psalms (e.g. Pss. 1.1; 31.1; 33.9; 39.5; 83.6; 111.1; cf. Prov. 8.32, 34; Isa. 56.2; Job 5.17; Sir. 14.1, 20), and also is used often in the synoptic sayings of Jesus, most notably in the beatitudes of Mt. 5.3-11//Lk. 6.20-22 (cf. also Mt. 13.16; 16.17; Lk. 10.23; 14.14-15; 23.29, often with reference to those who faithfully fulfil what is required of them, thus Mt. 11.6; 24.46; Lk. 1.45; 7.23; 11.27-28; 12.37-38, 43). Likewise, the image of a crown (στέφανος) to signify eschatological reward is common in both Jewish and early Christian texts (e.g. Wis. 5.15-16; *T. Levi* 8.2, 9; *T. Benj.* 4.1; 4 Macc. 17.15; Zech. 6.14; 1 Pet. 5.4; 2 Tim. 4.8; Rev. 2.10).

44. As in the interpretation of the same phrase in 2.5 (τοῖς ἀγαπῶσιν αὐτόν), in the context of the non-individualistic nature of ancient Mediterranean social relations, ἀγαπάω should be read with more of a sense of social devotion, than of the individual-emotional affection associated with the usual translation 'love' today. See above, Chapter 3 n. 53.

vious verse, and with 1.2, linked only by an external catchword.[45] Rather, it approaches the other possibility of human response to testing, that of failure to endure, and also continues the theme of God's giving from v. 12.

In 1.13, the author warns that no one in such trying circumstances should blame God for his difficulties, or infer the reproach that God is tempting him towards sin (failure to endure). A close parallel to this occurs in Sir. 15.11-12: 'Do not say, "Because of the Lord I left the right way"; for he will not do what he hates. Do not say, "It was he who led me astray"; for he has no need of a sinful man'.[46] The statement of 1.13 may appear to conflict with the petition of the prayer of Jesus in Mt. 6.13//Lk. 11.4;[47] Laws comments on this verse:

> It is not clear if James would deny God any role in the process of trial; he could hardly ignore Old Testament references to God's testing of, for instance, Abraham, to whom he refers in 2.21... James's concern is simply to deny that God has any interest in man a state of sin as the outcome of trial, so that [God] might be seen as tempter.[48]

On the other hand, there is also a tradition in Jewish thought which distances God from the action of testing the faithful. Thus, 1 Chron. 21.1 amends 1 Sam. 24.1 to attribute David's census to the activity of Satan; likewise, in *Jub.* 17.15-18, the testing of Abraham's faith is initiated by Mastema (*Jub.* 17.16, by contrast with Gen. 22.1), who is put to shame at the end of the account (18.12).[49] The Job story also

45. Dibelius, *James*, pp. 71, 90.

46. μὴ εἴπῃς ὅτι Διὰ κύριον ἀπέστην· ἃ γὰρ ἐμίσησεν, οὐ ποιήσει. μὴ εἴπῃς ὅτι Ἀυτός με ἐπλάνησεν· οὐ γὰρ χρείαν ἔχει ἀνδρὸς ἁμαρτολοῦ. See Frankemölle, *Jakobus*, pp. 278-79. Again, his argument that the author of the Epistle of James is actually drawing his thought from this passage in Sirach is difficult to substantiate.

47. A.D. Jacobson, *The First Gospel: An Introduction to Q* (Sonoma, CA: Polebridge Press, 1992), p. 159, comments that the instruction of Jas 1.13 indicates that questions over the possibility of temptation and/or an evil outcome to temptation originating from God could arise, and notes that this possibility is also denied shortly afterwards in the reconstructed Q text (Lk. 11.11-13//Mt. 7.9-11): 'Since Q 11.11-13 denies that God can give anything evil, it may have functioned as an exposition of the Lord's Prayer, exposition which takes up a dualistic position attested elsewhere'.

48. Laws, *James*, p. 70.

49. The possibility that the author of the Epistle of James may have been familiar with *Jubilees'* interpretation of the story of Abraham's testing through the

demonstrates the removal of testing from God, and its attribution to Satan. Later in the Epistle of James, the devil (ὁ διαβόλος) is explicitly identified as the adversary of God (Jas 4.7; cf. 3.6, 15);[50] it is surely significant that there is also a firm Jewish tradition which links the evil desire (ἐπιθυμία, Jas 1.14-15; 4.2) with the activity of God's adversary, especially as represented by the figure of Beliar in the *Testaments of the Twelve Patriarchs*.[51] When the opening section, 1.2-18, is viewed as having an introductory function, it is not surprising that the link with the cosmic adversary, the διαβόλος, as the source of evil is only made explicit later in the text.[52]

The intent of these verses is clear: it is to assert from the outset that God's action is not ambivalent, and to remove any possibility of linking God with evil, or blaming God for negatively evaluated circumstances in life,[53] and given added emphasis by the use of the emphatic pronoun αὐτός at the end of v. 13. This is the letter's second assertion of the unambiguity of God's dealings with humankind; already in 1.5 it was

sacrifice of Isaac is strengthened by the similar attribution of the title 'friend of God' in *Jub.*19.9 and in Jas 2.23.

50. It is worth noting, against Frankemölle's thesis of the epistle's dependence on Sirach, that this kind of mythological dualism contrasts sharply with Sirach's resistance to such apocalyptically inclined ideas, cf. Sir. 21.27: 'When an ungodly person curses Satan, he curses his own soul'. According to Sir. 4.17, testing (πειρασμοί) is the work of God's wisdom, as instruction for her children.

51. E.g. *T. Reub.* 2.4; 4.7-9; 6.3-4; *T. Ash.* 3.2; 6.4-5; *T. Jos.* 7.4, 8. Cf. Boccaccini, *Middle Judaism*, pp. 222-23, who notes the similarity of the Epistle of James to Sirach, but particularly to the *Testaments*, in relation to the awareness of the ambivalence of human nature as the origin of the possibility of evil. The term ἐπιθυμία was also viewed negatively in Stoic thought, and, under the influence of Stoic ideas, ἐπιθυμία is condemned by Philo, e.g. *Dec.* 142; *Spec. Leg.* 4.79-91.

52. J. Marcus, 'The Evil Inclination in the Epistle of James', *CBQ* 44 (1982), pp. 606-21, interprets these verses as a reference to the 'evil inclination' (יצר הרע) of rabbinic literature; cf. Davids, *James*, p. 83; Mussner, *Jakobusbrief*, p. 88. Others, however, see this as anachronistic, arguing that there is no clear evidence of such a developed concept of the evil and good inclinations in humankind as early as the early Christian period: so Frankemölle, *Jakobus*, pp. 286-87.

53. This basic statement of the author's understanding of God is not changed whether the phrase ὁ γὰρ θεὸς ἀπείραστός ἐστιν κακῶν is understood to mean 'for God cannot be tempted by evil' (R.P. Martin, *James*, pp. 33-34; cf. Laws, *James*, pp. 70-71; Dibelius, *James*, p. 92) or 'for God ought not to be tested by evil people' (P.H. Davids, 'The Meaning of ἀπείραστος in Jas 1.13', *NTS* 24 [1978], pp. 386-92; cf. *idem, James*, pp. 82-83).

stated that God is the one who gives generously and ungrudgingly to those who ask in faithful commitment. In 1.13, the further point is stressed that God is the source only of good. God is not only the supreme authority and benefactor, but is also the *unambiguously good* authority and benefactor. Like 1.5, these verses (1.13-15) are set in a contrast between the positive, reliable action of God and the negative, unstable action of humans. The ultimate negative outcome of this human disposition is death, expressed climactically in the ironic birth-imagery of the catena in 1.15, by contrast with obedient loyalty and devotion to God, which brings the reward of the crown of life (1.12).

4.2.4 *Analysis of the Text: 1.16-18*

The command, 'Do not be deceived, my beloved brothers', in v. 16 marks a transition in the text. As the content is clearly a development of that which has gone before, it should, however, be seen as a minor transition,[54] introducing the conclusion of the section 1.2-18, and emphasizing the importance of what is expressed in these final two verses of the subsection.

The contrast between human and divine, in the context of the fundamental assertion of God's goodness, is of particular importance within a world-view where the standard for right human conduct is correspondence to God's order. After the rhetorical warning, 'do not be deceived', and the long form of the direct address, 'my beloved brothers', both of which serve to highlight the significance of what is under discussion in these verses, this depiction of the unambiguous goodness of God is continued, with its most explicit expression, in v. 17: 'Everything good which is given, and every perfect gift is from above, coming down from the father of the lights, with whom there is no seasonal change or variation'.

Here it is stated quite plainly that what comes from God (cf. 1.5) is fundamentally and exclusively good (cf. 1.13-15).[55] The phrase 'father of the lights' ($\pi\alpha\tau\dot{\eta}\rho$ $\tau\hat{\omega}\nu$ $\phi\dot{\omega}\tau\omega\nu$) is clearly a reference to creation, probably, in particular, to the creation of the heavenly luminaries (Gen. 1.14-18). This allusion to the creation story reinforces the conviction of the goodness of all that comes from God, in view of the repeated

---

54. Cf. Baasland, 'Literarische Form', p. 3655.

55. Gruson (ed.), *Jacques*, pp. 24-25, rightly notes that God is here presented in the role of patron in relation to those dependent on him.

affirmations of the goodness of God's creation in Genesis 1.[56]

The immutability of God's character, shown by God's creation and God's exclusive giving of good is expressed by the phrase (literally) 'with whom there is no change or shadow of turning'. Precisely what the author had in mind with the use of this term is difficult to establish.[57] The phrase appears to draw further on the astronomical image of the father of the lights. The word παραλλαγή can mean change or variation, and is used as a technical astronomical term to denote the varying length of the day according to the elevation of the sun. Likewise τροπή, in addition to the general sense of 'turning', is used technically to refer to the sun's solstices.[58] ἀποσκίασμα seems to refer to a shadow, or the act of casting a shadow,[59] possibly alluding to the eclipse of the sun and moon. All three terms can thus be seen to refer to mutation or change of some kind among the heavenly bodies, although the textual variants render the precise determination of the intended meaning virtually impossible. The basic intent, however, seems clear: to assert the fundamental unchangeability and reliability of God as the source of all good, more reliable and constant than even the sun and moon.[60]

The final verse of this opening section states the basis of the relation-

56. Similar phrases, designating God as father in relation to creation occur in a wide variety of Jewish texts, e.g. Job 38.28; *T. Abr.* 7.6; Philo, *Ebr.* 81. Further references are provided by Mussner, *Jakobusbrief*, p. 91; Davids, *James*, pp. 86-87; Vouga, *Jacques*, p. 57.

57. παραλλαγή and τροπή occur only here in the New Testament, while this is the first known use of the word ἀποσκίασμα. The number of textual variants for this phrase further complicates the clarification of the precise referent of παραλλαγὴ ἢ τροπῆς ἀποσκίασμα. In particular, the reading παραλλαγὴ ἢ τροπῆς ἀποσκιάσματος has strong attestation (א*, B). Cf. Mussner, *Jakobusbrief*, pp. 91-92; Dibelius, *James*, pp. 100-103; Davids, *James*, pp. 87-88; R.P. Martin, *James*, pp. 38-39; Laws, *James*, pp. 73-74; Vouga, *Jacques*, p. 57; Mayor, *James*, pp. 60-62; Ropes, *James*, pp. 162-65.

58. See particularly Mayor, *James*, pp. 60-61.

59. Mayor, *James*, pp. 60-61; Ropes, *James*, p. 165.

60. D. Verseput, 'James 1.17 and the Jewish Morning Prayers', *NovT* 39 (1997), pp. 177-91, argues that the reference to the heavenly luminaries in this verse may reflect the expression of the benedictions which shaped the morning recitation of the *Shema*, thus linking the assertion of God's identity as the unchanging source of good with Israel's identity as God's covenant people. This suggestion is particularly interesting in view of other echoes of the language of the *Shema* in Jas 2.19, 4.12 and 5.7.

ship between the addressees and God, drawing on the creation motif of the previous verse, and also taking up the birth metaphor of 1.15. The principal difficulty in this verse is the identity of that to which God gives birth: 'a kind of firstfruits of his creatures' (ἀπαρχή τις τῶν αὐτοῦ κτισμάτων).[61] The main alternatives are either that this phrase refers to humankind as the firstfruits[62] of creation in general,[63] or to the early Christian movement as the firstfruits of humankind.[64] Elliott-Binns argues, favouring the first option, that κτίσμα would not be used of humankind, and thus must refer to creation in general. He also asserts, however, the importance of the continuity between humankind and other creatures,[65] in which case there is no difficulty in seeing this as a reference to the early Christian movement as the eschatological firstfruits of the consummate, eschatological creation, not simply the firstfruits of humankind.[66] Such a reading accords well with the strong eschatological tone of the epistle. Further, the use of the first person plural pronoun ἡμᾶς, designating a group of which the author and addressees are part, is probably to be seen to have a more specific sense than simply humankind in general.

In this case, the 'word of truth' (λόγος ἀληθείας) must have some connotation of the particularities of the early Christian movement, which distinguished them as 'firstfruits'. Some have seen this reference to birth through the word of truth as a reference to baptism and

61. The use of female imagery in relation to God has precedents in the LXX (e.g., Num. 11.12; Deut. 32.18; Pss. 22.9; 90.2, etc.), and does not suggest an anti-gnostic polemic in the Epistle of James, as H. Schammberger, *Die Einheitlichkeit des Jakobusbriefes im antignostischen Kampf* (Gotha: Klotz Verlag, 1936), pp. 58-63, argued.

62. Although the LXX does not use ἀπαρχή exclusively in relation to the offering of firstfruits (see L.E. Elliott-Binns, 'James 1.18: Creation or Redemption?', *NTS* 3 [1958], pp. 148-61 [152-53]; cf. G. Delling, 'ἀπαρχή', *TDNT*, I, pp. 484-86 [485]), it is generally agreed that this is its sense in this verse.

63. Hort, *James*, pp. 31-32; Elliott-Binns, 'James 1.18'; Laws, *James*, pp. 75-78 (tentatively).

64. Dibelius, *James*, pp. 103-107; Davids, *James*, pp. 88-90; R.P. Martin, *James*, pp. 40-41; Ropes, *James*, pp. 166-67; Mayor, *James*, pp. 62-64; Mussner, *Jakobusbrief*, pp. 92-97; Hoppe, *Jakobusbrief*, p. 41; Vouga, *Jacques*, pp. 58-59. Ludwig, *Wort*, pp. 157-59, sees the phrase as a depiction of the Jewish people's special status, through the gift of the law.

65. Elliott-Binns, 'James 1.18', pp. 153, 155.

66. See also Davids, *James*, p. 89.

baptismal catechesis.[67] This is not impossible, but it seems more likely that it refers to the proclamation of Jesus, which in its interpretation of the Jewish world-view can be seen as the 'word of truth' which sets out the truth of God's order of the universe.[68] It is in this sense that λόγος can best be seen to be taken up again and equated with the 'perfect law of freedom' in 1.21-25.[69] The occurrence of this reference at the end of the opening section of the text, drawing attention to Jesus' authoritative interpretation of the Jewish understanding of the world, in the context of God's fundamental and undivided goodness, and God's relationship to the addressees (and author), is particularly important, but scarcely surprising. These closing verses, 1.17-18, thus function to assert both God's unchanging goodness, and the authority of Jesus' proclamation, over against any doubts which the addressees may have had about either.

4.3 *Conclusion*

Having analysed in detail the whole of the opening section 1.2-18, the degree to which a particular concern with exhortation to unwavering commitment to God is reflected in these verses is striking. Moreover, the two aspects of this concern noted earlier, namely, direct admonition of the addressees and presentation of God's supremacy, both run very clearly through the whole section. Thus, to summarize:

1.   This opening section of the text introduces the key theme of endurance and loyalty to God, directly exhorting the addressees to joy in the face of trying circumstances, in which they are to rely confidently and unhesitatingly upon God's provision (1.2-8), particularly in view of the reversal of present status (1.9-11) entailed in God's eschatological world

67. Mussner, *Jakobusbrief*, pp. 95-96; see also F. Mussner, 'Die Tauflehre des Jakobusbriefes', in B. Kleinheyer and H. auf der Maur (eds.), *Zeichen des Glaubens* (Festschrift B. Fischer; Freiburg: Herder, 1972), pp. 61-67 (62-64); Popkes, *Adressaten*, pp. 147-48; G. Braumann, 'Der theologische Hintergrund des Jakobusbriefes', *TZ* 18 (1962), pp. 401-410 (405-406).

68. Davids, *James*, pp. 89-90; Dibelius, *James*, p. 105. Frankemölle, *Jakobus*, p. 30, and R.P. Martin, *James*, p. 40, consider reference to either possible; the two are, of course, not mutually exclusive.

69. A lengthy tradition-historical analysis of the Jewish background of the terms λόγος and νόμος is provided by Ludwig, *Wort*, pp. 28-88.

order, in which their faithful endurance will be rewarded (1.12). On the other hand, they are warned that doubting or dividedness in loyalty to God means that they will receive nothing (1.6-8); following their own desires, rather than faithful obedience to the demands of God's order, results in death (1.13-15).

2.   God is clearly and distinctively presented in the role of supreme authority and benevolent patron. God gives ungrudgingly and undividedly to those who ask in commitment to God (1.5). He rewards those who loyally endure testingly with honour in God's eschatological order (1.12). God is the source only of good (1.13); from God come all good things (1.17). In this, God is unambiguously constant and reliable (1.17). Moreover, God stands in a special relationship to the addressees, who form the eschatological first-fruits of God's creation, through the revelation of God's eschatological world-order in the proclamation of Jesus and his followers (1.18); a right understanding of God's order is revealed by God to those who ask in faith (1.5).

3.   Negative portrayal of the rich, later depicted as those who oppose God's order, and rival God for the allegiance of the addressees, is also introduced in these verses (1.9-11), stressing the transitoriness of the present status of the rich in the light of the eschatological realities of God's order.

In view of the introductory function of this section, the importance of these issues in this passage indicates that they are of basic significance for the whole text. A further step will be to investigate how these issues are developed throughout the whole of the subsequent text. In this respect, it is important not just to trace the *presence* of these themes in the text, but also to view their presentation in the light of the text's rhetorical development and the unfolding of its literary and argumentative structure. Thus, the analysis will continue the sequential examination of how the related themes of the need for unwavering commitment to God by the addressees and the depiction of God's status are sequentially unfolded in the epistle.

Chapter 5

READING THE TEXT: JAMES 1.19–3.18

5.1 *Introduction*

As in 1.2-18, several themes which are further developed later in the text are prefigured in 1.19-27. In particular, these verses raise issues which recur in the three immediately following sections, 2.1-13, 2.14-26 and 3.1-12. Thus, the theme of law (νόμος) can be seen again in 2.1-13, where 2.8 and 2.12 clearly echo the expression of 1.25. A further aspect of the theme of the 'doer of work' (ποιητὴς ἔργου) is developed in the discussion of 'works' (ἔργα) in 2.14-26 (cf. also 'righteousness' (δικαιοσύνη) and cognate words in 1.20 and in 2.23-25). Concern with the socially marginal (1.27) occurs again in 2.1-6 and 2.15-16. The phrase, 'not bridling his tongue' (μὴ χαλιναγωγῶν γλῶσσαν αὐτοῦ, 1.26) is plainly raised again in the deliberation on the tongue (γλῶσσα) in 3.1-12, which repeats the unusual verb 'bridle' (χαλιναγωγέω, 1.26; 3.2).[1] The prefiguration of these themes in 1.19-27 is rather more substantial than the introduction of later-developed topics in 1.2-18, which are generally alluded to, rather than given an initial unfolding to the extent that significant themes of 2.1–3.12 are set forth in 1.19-27.[2]

---

1. This is the earliest recorded use of this word: see Mayor, *James*, p. 76. It also occurs in Hermas, *Man.* 12.1 and in Lucian, *Tyrannicida* 4.

2. Certain stylistic differences can also be discerned between 1.2-18 and 1.19-27. Most noticeable is the change of person in the imperatives between the sections. The section 1.2-18 begins and ends with a second person plural imperative: ἡγήσασθε (1.2) and μὴ πλανᾶσθε (1.16). In the centre of this section, however, all the imperatives are in the third person singular form, which occurs six times in 1.4-13. On the other hand, apart from ἔστω in 1.19, 1.19-27 uses the second person plural form. This difference can be seen to be grounded in a change of function between the two passages: the exhortations in 1.2-18 are given a more general form of expression, as more broadly oriented fundamental issues, which form a basic introductory layer on which the more specific later admonitions are built. This suggestion is borne out by the differences in content between 1.2-18 and 1.19-27; as

In view of the fact that both 1.2-18 and 1.19-27 can be seen to have slightly different introductory functions in terms of prefiguring issues which are raised again later in the text, the Aristotelian guidelines for the exordium and the prothesis of a speech are particularly interesting.[3] Aristotle considered that there were only two essential components of any speech, the prothesis or statement of the case (πρόθεσις), and the proof (πίστις): 'a speech has two parts... The first of these parts is the statement of the case, the second is the proof'.[4] At most, an exordium (προοίμιον) and an epilogue (ἐπίλογος) could also be added: 'the necessary parts of a speech are the statement of the case and the proof. These divisions are appropriate to every speech and at the most the parts are four in number—exordium, statement, proof, epilogue'.[5] The function of the exordium is to open the speech, 'paving the way for what follows'.[6] It should make the hearers well disposed, or arouse their

seen above, 1.2-18 deals with the more general issues of positive evaluation of adverse or ambiguous circumstances, under the surety of God's positive nature and relation to creation, while 1.19-27 deals with more concrete action and conduct.

3. It must be remembered that rhetorical guidelines such as these provided instructions for oratory, rather than for written texts, and therefore a certain amount of caution should be maintained in the use of these theoretical guidelines in the interpretation of written texts, especially when these texts are not necessarily to be identified as written speeches. Cf. S.E. Porter, 'The Theoretical Justification for the Application of Rhetorical Categories to Pauline Literature', in S.E. Porter and T.H. Olbricht (eds.), *Rhetoric in the New Testament* (JSNTSup, 90; Sheffield: Sheffield Academic Press, 1993), pp. 100-22; also (in same volume) J.T. Reed, 'Using Rhetorical Categories to Interpret Paul's Letters: A Question of Genre', pp. 292-324, and C.J. Classen, 'St. Paul's Epistles and Ancient Greek and Roman Rhetoric', pp. 264-91, who lists four possible sources for rhetorical elements in New Testament texts: 'from rhetorical theory (and its deliberate application), from a successful imitation of written or spoken practice, from unconscious borrowing from the practice of others, or from a natural gift for effective speaking or writing' (p. 269). On the other hand, the ancient world was much more a world of orality than of textuality, and it is reasonable to believe that written forms of text will bear some similarity to the primarily oral forms prescribed by the handbooks. Further, while a text like the Epistle of James is unlikely to represent a speech written down for a public display of oratory, it is likely that this text was written down for reading in public, as the frequent plural address suggests a plural audience, rather circulation among a number of individual readers.

4. Aristotle, *Rhet.* 3.13.1-2.

5. Aristotle, *Rhet.* 3.13.4.

6. Aristotle, *Rhet.* 3.14.1.

indignation, according to the desired effect.[7] The epilogue can play several functions, including that of recapitualation (ἀναμνήσις).[8]

The exhortations to positive evaluation of circumstances, which mark 1.2-18 ('consider it all joy', 1.2; 'let the lowly brother boast', 1.9; 'blessed is the man who endures testing', 1.12, etc.) would fit well with the function of the exordium to render the hearers well disposed; likewise, the general introduction of themes and the establishment of certain basic considerations which implicitly underlie the following sections can be seen as 'paving the way for what follows'. The function of 1.19-27 to introduce more concretely the topics of, in particular, 2.1–3.12, corresponds well with the role of the prothesis as the statement of the subject of the case, which is taken up for demonstration in the subsequent proof.[9]

Verses 2.1–3.12, consequently, can be seen as the proof, of the subject(s) raised in the prothesis (1.19-27). Baasland suggests that the proof can be divided into an accusatory *confutatio* (3.12–5.6) and a milder *confirmatio* (2.1–3.10a), but that any more detailed rhetorical construction of the whole cannot be established.[10] This opinion has a certain amount of plausibility; certainly chs. 2 and 3 are milder in tone than chs. 4 and 5. In view of the caution, which, as already mentioned, must be exercised in using the features of oratorical rhetoric to analyse a text which does not directly represent a speech of the type for which these rhetorical categories were formulated, the presupposition that the text must be seen to conform precisely to rhetorical rules can be questioned. There are few possible parallels among Greek texts to the apparent development of the argumentation of the proof in what Baasland describes as the *confutatio*. In Graeco-Roman rhetoric, the purpose of a *confirmatio* section was to present and corroborate one's own arguments; this is not irreconcilable with the development of 2.1–3.12. The *confutatio*, however, served for the refutation of opposing arguments, which is much less compatible with what is effected in 3.13–5.6.[11] Thus, it seems reasonable to doubt that the whole of 2.1–5.6

---

7.   Aristotle, *Rhet.* 3.14.7.

8.   Aristotle, *Rhet.* 3.19.1.

9.   That 1.2-18 forms the προοίμιον and 1.19-27 forms the πρόθεσις has also been suggested by Baasland, 'Literarische Form', p. 3655, and by Thurén, 'Rhetoric', pp. 269-73, 277-78.

10.   Baasland, 'Literarische Form', p. 3656.

11.   *Rhetorica ad Herennium* 1.3.4: 'Confirmatio est nostrorum argumentorum

is actually constructed in strict conformity to the conventions of oratorical rhetoric. The clearest usage of Greek patterns of argumentation
occurs in the sections 2.1-13, 2.14-26 and 3.1-12,[12] which, as noted
above, deal with the themes prefigured most specifically in 1.19-27.

It is worth noting here the points of contact between 3.13-18 and
other sections of the text. Although it is the shortest subsection of the
body of the text, it contains strong verbal and thematic connections
with almost all sections of the epistle, and especially with the opening
sections of ch. 1.[13] In fact, it is plausible to see 3.13-18 as giving a
summary statement of what has been developed in the previous chapters. In this respect, 3.13-18 can be seen to function as a sort of
epilogue to 1.2–3.12, closing off the proof with a short, recapitulating
statement, epitomized in the question and answer of 3.13. This suggestion, of course, is not possible if one sees the whole text as conforming
strictly to the rhetorical rules for speech-composition, but, as has been
stated already, this should not be taken as a necessary presupposition.
Obviously, however, 3.13-18 is not an epilogue as such for the entire
text, as several substantial sections still follow. To some extent, the
strong contrast expressed in 3.15 prefigures the strident warnings and
contrasts found in both 4.1-10 and 4.11–5.11, and so the section can
also be seen to provide a transition from 2.1–3.12 to the following
passages.[14]

The relative infrequency of imperatives giving direct instruction to
the addressees in these subsections points towards the more discursive
nature of this part of the epistle.[15] Two imperatives occur in the

expositio cum adseveratione. Confutatio est contrariorum locorum dissolutio.'

12. See Watson, 'James 2', and 'The Rhetoric of James 3.1-12 and a Classical
Pattern of Argumentation', *NovT* 35 (1993), pp. 48-64.

13. Thus, σοφός (3.13)/σοφία (3.13, 15, 17) takes up the term σοφία from 1.5;
compare also ἔργον (3.13; 1.4, 25; 2.14, 17-18, 20-26), πραΰτης (3.13; 1.21);
δικαιοσύνη (3.18; 1.20; 2.23); ἀλήθεια (3.14; 1.18; 5.19); ἀγαθός (3.17; 1.17);
ἄνωθεν (3.15, 17; 1.17); καρδία (3.14; 1.26; 4.8; 5.5, 8); ἀκαταστασία (3.16;
ἀκατάστατος 1.8; 3.8). The opening question, τίς σοφός...ἐν ὑμῖν, is very close in
expression to 1.5, εἰ δέ τις ὑμῶν λείπεται σοφίας.

14. Cf. Baasland, 'Literarische Form', pp. 3658-59.

15. Excluding 2.3, 16, 18; 4.13; 5.1, 4 which are not taken to be directed to the
addressee-body as a whole, there are three times as many imperatives in the rest of
the text (55 verses) as in the whole of 1.19–3.18 (53 verses). There are 8 imperatives in 1.2-18, 4 in 1.19-27, 4 in 2.1-13, none in 2.14-26, 1 in 3.1-12, 3 in 3.13-18,
10 in 4.1-10, 9 in 4.11–5.11 and 9 in 5.12-20.

transitional appeal of 1.19-20, with two more in the next two verses, laying down the basic theme of rejection of a disposition opposed to God, and active acceptance of the demands of God's eschatological order. The imperatives which occur in 2.1–3.12 do so at strategic points: in 2.1 and 3.1, at the opening of these two subsections, in 2.5, giving rhetorical emphasis, and in 2.12, at the close of the first of these parallel sections, in an exhortation pointing forward to the following two sections, whose themes are concerned principally with right action and speech, as expressed in this verse. These sections seem to be concerned more with the demonstration of the addressees' shortcomings, than with explicit admonition, although obviously this is implied. The two positive admonitions towards conduct in harmony with God's standards in 1.21 and 3.13 can be seen as an *inclusio*, framing the discussion of the addressees' failure to live according to God's order. This *inclusio* is underlined verbally by the use of the phrase ἐν πραΰτητι in both commands.

Following the findings of the analysis of 1.2-18 in the previous chapter, indicating the significance of the twin themes of exhortation to unwavering loyalty to God, and the presentation of God as supreme authority figure and patron, the development of these key issues in each of the sections of the text forms the focus of the exegesis of these sections.

5.2 Demonstration of the Addressees' Shortcomings: 1.19–3.18

5.2.1 Introduction: 1.19-27

The command of v. 19 is rhythmically tightly structured, with three cola of seven syllables each, and a shorter final colon of five syllables. This fine compositional ability is evidence of the rhetorical skill of the author, and also draws attention to the important rhetorical function of this verse. Viewed rhetorically, this verse constitutes an appeal to the addressees by the author to hear out what he has to say, to continue listening to the rest of the text, and not to break off after the introduction of 1.2-18, conceivably as an angry response (ὀργή) to the unwelcome intervention of the author in a situation of tension. This is a particularly opportune moment for such an appeal, coming at the end of the opening section, and at the outset of the more specific and concretely identified criticisms and exhortations of the addressees' conduct which are introduced in this section, 1.19-27. It also shows the author's awareness of the sensitivity of the situation he is addressing, and of the possibility that what he has to say in this context may not be met with unambiguous approval on the part of the addressees. This appeal is strengthened by the author's linking of his exhortation to the idea of God's righteousness (δικαιοσύνη θεοῦ), fundamental to the view of the world as ordered by God, and of appropriate conduct in correspondence to this order.

Several examples from Greek speeches illustrate this sort of appeal to one's audience. In Josephus' *The Jewish War,* when Agrippa addresses the Jerusalem crowd, attempting to dissuade them from revolt, he requests that he be given a quiet hearing, even by those who are displeased by what he has to say.[16] Likewise, Dio Chrysostom, in his speech to the Nicomedians on concord with Nicaea, ends his exordium with an appeal that the audience should hear him out with patience, and not reproach him for his presumption in addressing them.[17] He goes on to punctuate the prothesis with a similar request, that they listen without becoming angry until they have heard what he has to say.[18] Both of these speeches are addressed to an audience which may perceive the orator as making a presumptuous intervention in their affairs; it is plausible to suggest that the author of the Epistle of James may likewise have feared that his text would be received as an unwelcome intervention in the addressees' affairs, hence this appeal that they listen to what he has to say without speaking and without becoming angry.

This significant rhetorical strategy, underlined formally by the tightly balanced structure of the verse, makes unnecessary the suggestion that the author is here citing an unknown proverb or quotation.[19] That careful speech is a common theme in Jewish and Graeco-Roman moral

---

16. Josephus, *War* 2.347: 'If my remarks are not to the liking of any of my audience, pray let him not create a disturbance' (θορυβήσῃ δέ μοι μηδείς, ἐὰν μὴ τὰ πρὸς ἡδονὴν ἀκούῃ).

17. Dio Chrysostom, *Discourse* 38.4-5.

18. Dio Chrysostom, *Discourse* 38.6-7: 'Don't raise an outcry when I make a fresh start but bear with me... Hear me out and don't get angry before I state my reasons' (μὴ θορυβήσητε δὲ ἀρχομένῳ πάλιν, ἀλλ' ὑπομείνατε...ἀκούσατε δὲ καὶ μὴ χαλεπήνητε μηδέπω, πρὶν ἂν εἴπω τὰς αἰτίας). The verb χαλεπαίνω, 'become angry', does not occur in the New Testament, but, in the next line, Dio uses ὀργίζομαι, a cognate of ὀργή (Jas 1.19-20), in likening his audience to a sick man who should not become angry with a physician who prescribes a cure.

19. Davids, *James*, pp. 91-92; cf. Dibelius, *James*, pp. 111-12.

literature[20] also in no way lessens the rhetorical effect of 1.19 as addressed, in context, to the hearers of the text.[21] It is, of course, also the case that the verse can be seen to carry a more general applicability, through the grounding of this specific appeal in the idea of God's righteousness; this, however, should not be allowed to overshadow its important rhetorical contextual function.

Exhortation to submission and obedience to God and the standards of God's order occurs immediately in the strongly worded exhortation of 1.21. This urges the addressees to abandon behaviour which the author evaluates negatively, and, by contrast with this negative conduct: 'in humility receive the implanted word which is able to save your souls'. Precisely what is denoted by 'all filth and abundance of wickedness' (πᾶσα ῥυπαρία καὶ περισσεία κακίας) is not elaborated at this point;[22] this receives plenty of expansion in the following chapters (cf. 2.1, 2-4, 6, 9, 14-16; 3.2, 9-10, 14; 4.1-4, 11). The theme of God as giver is also present here, although not explicitly mentioned, as it is surely from God that the saving 'implanted word' is to be received.

This 'implanted word' (ἔμφυτος λόγος) can be seen to retrace the motif of the 'word of truth' (λόγος ἀληθείας) in 1.18.[23] The implications of receiving this word, as well as indications of its content are developed in vv. 22-25. The word must be done (1.22), and is equated with the 'perfect law of freedom' (νόμος τέλειος τῆς ἐλευθερίας, 1.25), through the parallel use of 'doers' (ποιηταί) and 'hearers'

20. See Davids, *James*, p. 92; Dibelius, *James*, pp. 109-110; Laws, *James*, p. 80; Frankemölle, *Jakobus*, p. 326; Vouga, *Jacques*, p. 61; L.T. Johnson, 'Taciturnity and True Religion: James 1.26-27', in D.L. Balch, E. Ferguson and W.A. Meeks (eds.), *Greeks, Romans and Christians* (Minneapolis: Fortress Press, 1990), pp. 329-39 (331-36).

21. Frankemölle, *Jakobus*, p. 326, notes that the combination of elements in this verse does not occur prior to the Epistle of James, in spite of parallels with single elements.

22. The phrase forms a general designation for wrong conduct, and does not, as Davids suggests, constitute a 'vice-catalogue' (*James*, p. 93). Nor is it necessary to see the phrase as referring only to speech, 'vulgar and malicious talk' (Laws, *James*, p. 81; cf. R.P. Martin, *James*, p. 48).

23. This ἔμφυτος λόγος cannot be understood in terms of the innate λόγος of Stoic thought, as such a λόγος could not be received appropriately. Laws, *James*, p. 84, suggests that the author has probably adopted 'a philosophical tag as a form of expression, without intending to import its full technical meaning, even if he were conscious of it'. It is not necessary, however, to envisage this kind of borrowing, in order to understand the verse.

(ἀκροαταί) in relation to both the word (1.22-23) and the perfect law of freedom (1.25). As argued in relation to the similar use of 'law of freedom' in 2.12,[24] this qualified use of 'law' should be seen to refer to Jesus' authoritative interpretation of the Jewish view of the world as ordered by God, summed up in the love-command.[25] Thus, the exhortations, 'receive the implanted word' (1.21) and 'become doers of the word' (1.22)[26] urge the addressees to accept as authoritative, and correspondingly act upon, the proclamation of Jesus.[27] The ultimate authority of this word is asserted eschatologically at the end of the v. 21: it is 'able to save your souls'. The continued injunction of 1.22b, 'and not merely hearers', indicates that the addressees can be considered to have heard this word already and to be familiar with it. In this case, the frequent allusions to the traditions of the sayings of Jesus in the epistle will have made sense to them.

These verses, 1.21-25, within the compositional structure of the whole text, introduce the motif of appropriate human action in response to God's order, which is later taken up in 2.14-26, and discussed in the context of the claim of faithful commitment to God (πίστις, already introduced as one of the text's key terms in 1.3), and the bestowal of ultimate approval within God's order (σῴζω, 1.21; 2.14). These verses also have a certain correspondence to 2.1-13, as the recurrence of the phrase 'law of freedom' (νόμος ἐλευθερίας, 2.12) indicates.

24. See above, §3.3.3.3. Cf. also the argument that the λόγος ἀληθείας should be linked to the proclamation of Jesus in §4.2.4 above.
25. So also Davids, *James*, pp. 99-100; Dibelius, *James*, p. 119; Vouga, *Jacques*, p. 65; Mussner, *Jakobusbrief*, p. 107; Schlatter, *Jakobus*, pp. 150-53; Zmijewski, 'Vollkommenheit', p. 74; Frankemölle, *Jakobus*, pp. 351, 357; H. Frankemölle, 'Gesetz im Jakobusbrief', in K. Kertelge (ed.), *Das Gesetz im Neuen Testament* (Freiburg: Herder, 1986), pp. 175-221 (204-205). Allusion to the love-command is noted by Sigal, 'Halakhah', pp. 340-41.
26. λόγος is frequently used in the synoptic gospels in relation to the proclamation of Jesus, especially by Luke, for example, Mk 2.2; 4.14-20; Mt. 13.19-23; Lk. 8.11-15 (note especially 8.13, οἳ ὅταν ἀκούσωσιν μετὰ χαρᾶς δέχονται τὸν λόγον, followed by reference to the failure of faith [πίστις] in a time of testing [πειρασμός, cf. Jas 1.2]); Lk. 4.32, 36; 5.1; 11.28. Cf. also the plural form in Mt. 7.24//Lk. 6.47, in the context of hearing and doing.
27. So also Davids, *James*, p. 95; R.P. Martin, *James*, pp. 48-49; Mussner, *Jakobusbrief*, p. 102, though as Frankemölle, *Jakobus*, p. 330, notes, it is not necessary to see this as a reference to baptism or to baptismal catechesis, as Mussner (*Jakobusbrief*), pp. 101-102, Braumann ('Hintergrund'), p. 405, and Vouga (*Jacques*), p. 63, suggest.

The prefiguration of the concerns of the following sections is further fulfilled in 1.26-27. The theme of appropriate human speech, developed in 3.1-12, is set out in 1.26. That this is intended to prefigure 3.1-12 is clear from the recurrence of the unusual verb 'bridle' (χαλιναγωγέω), as a metaphor in 3.2-3. Concern for orphans and widows raises the traditional Jewish topos of God's concern for the socially marginal,[28] elaborated in relation to the socially marginal (πτωχοί) within the Jesus movement in the immediately following section, 2.1-13. This concern should, of course, also be seen to reflect the real situation of the addressees, rather than simply being the raising of a traditional motif. The phrase 'keep himself uncorrupted by the world' (ἄσπιλον ἑαυτὸν τηρεῖν ἀπὸ τοῦ κόσμου) again prefigures the expression of 2.1-13, where the 'poor by the world's standards' (πτωχοὶ τῷ κόσμῳ, 2.5) are those favoured by God. Likewise, the connection of 'world' (κόσμος) and the verb 'corrupt' (σπιλόω) with 'tongue' (γλῶσσα) in 3.6 can be seen to pick up the language of this verse. This reference to keeping oneself unpolluted from the world can also be seen to point forward to 4.1-10, where the order of the world is contrasted starkly with God's order (4.4).

As noted, the substance of these issues as the author relates them to the addressees—right speech, rejection of the values of the present world order, a right attitude towards the socially marginal, a right understanding of God's order, the 'law of freedom' revealed through Jesus, God's chosen one, and the need for actions in accordance with this—receives more detailed exposition in the three parallel sections 2.1–3.12. Before looking more closely at these sections, it is worth noting that the principal concerns of the three following subsections, which are foreshadowed by the section 1.19-27, show a remarkable degree of correspondence to the 'three-zone personality' typical of the ancient Mediterranean world, as described by Malina and Rohrbaugh:

28. Widows and orphans fell into the same kind of social categorization as the socially marginal poor (πτωχοί), as, through the death of the husband and father, their existence was endangered through the loss of their material support base. Concern for widows and orphans, as typical of the socially marginal, of which they formed a particularly helpless instance, occurs very frequently in the Jewish Scriptures, e.g. Deut. 10.18; 14.28; 16.11, 14; 24.17-21; 26.12-13; 27.19; Pss. 10.14, 18; 68.5; 94.6; 146.9; Prov. 23.10; Isa. 1.17; Jer. 5.28; Ezek. 22.7; Zech. 7.10; Sir. 4.10; 32(35).17. Care for widows within the early Christian movement in Palestine is reflected in Acts 6.1.

(1) The zone of emotion-fused thought includes will, intellect, judgment, personality and feeling all rolled together... (2) The zone of self-expressive speech includes communication, particularly of that which is self-revealing... (3) The zone of purposeful interaction is the one of external behaviour or interaction with the environment.[29]

This model provides a framework for understanding the perception of the make-up of the human being in a non-introspective, non-individualistic cultural context:

> The way human beings are perceived as fitting into their rightful place in their environments, physical and social, and acting in a way that is typically human, is by means of their inmost reactions (eyes-heart) as expressed in language (mouth-ears) and/or outwardly realized in activity (hands-feet), or both.[30]

The subsection of the epistle 2.1-13 can be seen to be concerned primarily with the attitudes and judgments of the addressees (zone 1), while 2.14-26 is concerned principally with the addressees' actions (zone 3) and 3.1-12 deals with the theme of the addressees' speech (zone 2).[31] This observation is all the more interesting in the light of the author's reprimands of the dividedness of the addressees and his exhortations to wholeness and undividedness in their commitment to God: this demand for complete and unwavering commitment is underlined by an exposition of the need for such wholeness and integrity in each of the three constitutive 'zones of personality' in turn in these three subsections.

5.2.2 Shortcomings in Attitude and Judgment: 2.1-13

The section 2.1-13 has already been analysed in detail in Chapter 3. The section begins by demonstrating the shortcomings of the addressees' attitudes and judgments in relation to the standards of God's eschatological order. This is done by showing that commitment to Jesus, God's specially appointed and honoured one, is incompatible with the kind of conduct in relation to the rich and the socially marginal

---

29. Malina and Rohrbaugh, *Commentary*, p. 56; cf. pp. 226-27, 356. A detailed outline of this three-zone understanding of the human is provided by Malina, *New Testament World*, pp. 73-81.

30. Malina, *New Testament World*, p. 74.

31. The end of the first of these subsections, 2.1-13, leads into the themes of the following two sections, with the exhortation concerning right actions and speech in 2.12.

poor typified by the example of 2.2-3. The consequences of this example are drawn out in 2.4-7, where the real status of the πτωχοί, who are dependent on God and honoured by God, and the πλούσιοι, who live in opposition to God, is made clear. In 2.8-13, the addressees are urged to live in accordance with the standards of God's order of the universe, the 'kingly law' (2.8). As human attitudes and judgments are publicly expressed in speech and in action, so the closing verses of this section also urge speech and deeds in harmony with God's order (2.12-13), thus also providing a transition to the following two subsections, which spell out in detail the shortcomings of the addressees' actions (2.14-26) and of their speech (3.1-12).

5.2.3 *Shortcomings in Action: 2.14-26*
A narrated example, similar to that in 2.2-3, is used at the start of 2.14-26,[32] which opens in 2.14 with two abrupt rhetorical questions, and the direct address to the addressees, frequently employed by the author at the start of a new subsection. The motif of eschatological judgment, with which the previous section closed (2.12-13), is taken up again by the reference to 'save' (σῶσαι) in the second of these questions. In the context of the literary development of the text, an allusion to the necessity of accepting and putting into effect the proclamation of Jesus can be detected in these words, picking up the reference to the 'implanted word which is able to save (σῶσαι) your souls' in 1.21.

The first question demands to know what use it is, to claim to have commitment (πίστις),[33] without having actions. πίστις, in the non-individualistic context of the ancient Mediterranean world, in the sense

32. As in the case of 2.2-3, Dibelius argued that the situation depicted here constitutes a purely hypothetical portrayal, which should not be understood to bear any necessary relation to the social circumstances of the addressees, see Dibelius, *James*, pp. 128-30, 152-53; Mussner, *Jakobusbrief*, p. 132. As in this earlier instance, this scepticism is unwarranted (see above, §3.3.3.2); rather, the author depicts a situation which is seen as typically relevant to the addressees' experience, and therefore immediately accessible to them. As Davids, *James*, p. 101, comments: 'The description, then is stylized, although one should not doubt that such examples of extreme lack existed in the early church, as in most marginal societies'.

33. Either to God, which in the author's view, should imply equivalent commitment to Jesus as God's appointed one (cf. 1.1), or specifically to Jesus (cf. 2.1), which, conversely, implies commitment to God who has specially approved him. In a non-individualistic context, the claim of loyalty to God would further imply showing solidarity with those specially favoured by God (cf. 2.5).

of 'the social, externally manifested, emotional behaviour of loyalty, commitment and solidarity'[34] implies far more than intellectual assent or the claim to belief, and also more than the claim to commitment: 'If anyone says he has faith...' (ἐὰν πίστιν λέγῃ τις ἔχειν...). That the answer to the author's questions is negative is plain not just from their rhetorical formulation, but also from the cultural context. Thus, this verse calls seriously into question the genuineness of the addressees' commitment, much more explicitly than in either 1.2-8 or 2.1-13.

In v. 15, a brother or sister, thus a member of the same group to which the author sees both himself and the addressees belonging, is depicted in destitute circumstances. γυμνοὶ ὑπάρχωσιν depicts a much more dramatic lack of clothing than 'ill-clad', literally, it means naked.[35] Not only does the brother or sister lack adequate (or virtually any) clothing, she or he also 'lacking daily food' (λειπόμενοι τῆς ἐφημέρου τροφῆς). The response among the addressees to such a situation, as depicted, does not reflect the solidarity with a member of one's group which the author clearly expects. Rather, the destitute person is dismissed, but not given any material support necessary to alleviate his/her circumstances.

The brother or sister depicted in these verses clearly fits the social description of the socially marginal poor (πτωχός, 2.2, 5). Moreover, if there were grounds to suppose that the term πτωχός (τῷ κόσμῳ) in 2.2, 5 refers to the itinerant radicals of the Jesus movement, there are also indications in 2.15-16 that such a link is plausible.[36] If such socially marginal disciples did fulfil the instruction of Mk 6.9//Mt. 10.10//Lk. 9.3 to travel without a second tunic, in view of the hardships of such a

34. Malina and Rohrbaugh, *Commentary*, p. 131; cf. above, Chapter 3 n. 51.

35. If the expression is to be understood as hyberbolic, then it may refer to the lack of outer clothing, so Davids, *James*, p. 121; Laws, *James*, p. 120; R.P. Martin, *James*, p. 84; Mayor, *James*, p. 97; Vouga, *Jacques*, p. 86.

36. Jas 2.15-17 is also seen to refer to the itinerant radicals by Patterson, *Thomas*, pp. 183-84. The occurrence of the parallel male and female terms ἀδελφὸς ἢ ἀδελφή may reflect the active role of women among the radical itinerants of the Jesus movement; arguments for such an active role are presented by L. Schottroff, 'Itinerant Prophetesses: A Feminist Analysis of the Sayings Source Q', in R.A. Piper (ed.), *The Gospel behind the Gospels: Current Studies on Q* (Leiden: E.J. Brill, 1995), pp. 347-60. A. Batten, 'More Queries for Q: Women and Christian Origins', *BTB* 24 (1994), pp. 44-51, while according a slightly more limited role to itinerancy in early Christianity (p. 47) than does Schottroff, also argues for an active role for women among the Q tradents.

lifestyle it is easy to imagine how they could become virtually naked; if they travelled without food or money (Mk 6.8//Mt. 10.9-10//Lk. 9.3; cf. Lk. 10.4-7), it is equally understandable that they could be lacking food on a daily basis. Far from being a hypothetical description, exaggerated to shock as an illustration in an abstract theological discourse, Jas 2.15-16 can be seen as an uncomfortably real depiction of the extreme hardship faced by the itinerant followers of Jesus.

The dismissal, 'Go in peace' (ὑπάγετε ἐν εἰρήνῃ) may also reflect the practices of the itinerant radicals: according to Mt. 10.12-13//Lk. 10.5-6, announcement of a peace-greeting was part of their proclamation. Jas 2.15 may reflect a response in kind to this peace-greeting,[37] either in the house of a supposed sympathizer, or in the assembly (cf. 2.2-3), but constituting a non-reception of the bearer of the greeting, who is told to go away (cf. Mk 6.11//Mt. 10.13-14//Lk. 9.5; 10.10-11). The response, 'Go in peace, be warmed and be filled', does not indicate outright hostility, but, as the following line shows, it does show a failure to supply much-needed material support, for which the marginal itinerants were radically dependent on God, and which in practical terms was met by local groups who also responded favourably to the proclamation of Jesus.[38]

The obvious conclusion, for the author, from this failure, is drawn in Jas 2.17, recapitulating the expression of 2.14. Claimed commitment (to God, to Jesus as God's appointed one, and, implicitly, to God's people) (cf. 1.1; 2.1 [2.5-6]), which does not have corresponding actions, on its own is dead. Thus, this example, like that of 2.2-3, functions to demonstrate shortcoming on the part of the addressees, in this case, the deficiency of the addressees' actions, in relation to their claim of loyalty to God.

This theme is amplified in the following verses. The most satisfying attempt to determine the extent of the rhetorical interlocution in 2.18[39] is that of H. Neitzel, who argues that 'you have faith' (σὺ πίστιν ἔχεις) constitutes a question, expressing doubts about the author's own faith,

37. On the other hand, this may be a reflection of the use of εἰρήνη as a parting greeting, as the equivalent of the Hebrew שׁלום; cf. Judg. 18.6; 1 Sam. 1.17; 20.42; 29.7; 2 Sam. 15.9; Jdt. 8.35; Mk 5.34; Lk. 7.50; Acts 16.36.

38. See above, §3.3.2.

39. In addition to the commentaries, see also the discussion of C.E. Donker, 'Der Verfasser des Jakobusbriefes und sein Gegner: Zur Probleme des Einwandes in Jak 2.18-19', *ZNW* 72 (1981), pp. 227-40.

to which the author responds: 'I also have actions: show me your faith without actions, and I will show you my faith by my actions' (κἀγὼ ἔργα ἔχω· δεῖξόν μοι τὴν πίστιν σου χωρὶς τῶν ἔργων, κἀγώ σοι δείξω ἐκ τῶν ἔργων μου τὴν πίστιν).[40] This fits easily into the context: the author has called the faith of the addressees sharply into question; this is countered by calling the author's own faith into question. The response to such doubts about the authenticity of the author's commitment to God is swift: it is demonstrable from the author's actions. On the other hand, anyone questioning the author's faith and behaving in a manner lacking in solidarity towards God and God's chosen people (2.15-16) faces the challenge of showing the genuineness of his/her own claim to commitment (2.14).

This is carried further in 2.19: the addressees' claim to commitment to the one God is good in itself, but if this commitment is nothing more than giving credence to the oneness of God, to which even the demons assent,[41] then it is still questionable. Again in this verse, the author shows that his concerns are rooted firmly in the Jewish monotheistic tradition, with this echo of the words of the *Shema* (Deut. 6.4).[42] This allusion is significant in the context of the discussion, as Deut. 6.5 continues: 'You shall love the Lord your God with your whole heart and with your whole soul and with your whole might' (cf. Jas 1.12; 2.5). In their failure to receive those favoured by God (2.5), the addressees can be seen to fail to demonstrate the complete devotion to God expected by the *Shema*.[43] The intention of the allusion is not so much 'to point

40. H. Neitzel, 'Eine alte crux interpretum im Jakobusbrief 2.18', *ZNW* 73 (1982), pp. 286-93. This suggestion is also accepted in the recent commentaries by Frankemölle, *Jakobus*, p. 439; Hoppe, *Jakobusbrief*, p. 64; F. Schnider, *Der Jakobusbrief* (Regensburg: Friedrich Pustet, 1987), pp. 70-71. The doubled κἀγώ in the first and third lines of this response adds rhetorical intensity to this reply; on the use of κἀγώ to open a speech, see Neitzel, 'Jakobusbrief 2.18', pp. 290-91.

41. On the Jewish tradition of the terror of the demons before God, see Davids, *James*, pp. 125-26; Dibelius, *James*, p. 160; Laws, *James*, pp. 127-28; Mussner, *Jakobusbrief*, p. 139; Frankemölle, *Jakobus*, pp. 446-47.

42. On the significance of this allusion, see also above, §2.3.1.

43. The argument of Popkes, *Adressaten*, pp. 64-66; 76-77, that this verse suggests that the addressees are Gentile 'God-fearers', on the grounds that they are the only group whose belief could be summed up by the statement σὺ πιστεύεις ὅτι εἷς ἐστιν ὁ θεός, is unlikely, as it assumes unnecessarily that the author is here giving a full portrayal of the faith of the addressees. Likewise, the suggestion that a monotheistic confession is all that the author understands by πίστις (K. Haacker,

out its inadequacy by itself',[44] as to draw attention to its full consequences.

A further rhetorical question restates the conviction of the ineffec-
tiveness of faith (πίστις) without actions (ἔργα) in 2.20,[45] forming a
transition to 2.21, where the theme is further developed, again drawing
on the Jewish tradition of the special position of God's chosen people.
The patriarch Abraham was of fundamental importance for Jewish
people's self-understanding as the people of God.[46] It is hardly surprising that the author draws on a long Jewish tradition in his use of the
Abraham example, all the more so as this fits exactly with his concerns:

'Glaube', *TRE*, XIII, pp. 275-365 [299], followed by F.E. Wieser, *Die Abrahamvorstellungen im Neuen Testament* [Frankfurt am Main: Peter Lang, 1987], p. 87;
cf. also M. Lautenschlager, 'Der Gegenstand des Glaubens im Jakobusbrief', *ZTK*
87 [1990], pp. 163-84; A. Lindemann, *Paulus im ältesten Christentum* [Tübingen:
J.C.B. Mohr (Paul Siebeck), 1987], pp. 240-52; H. Hübner, *Biblische Theologie des
Neuen Testaments* II [Göttingen: Vandenhoeck & Ruprecht, 1993], pp. 380-86),
which is in itself without saving effect (cf. 2.14, 17, 24, 26) is entirely incompatible
with the use of πίστις in the rest of the epistle, as such an interpretation scarcely
makes sense in the contexts of 1.3, 6; 2.1; 5.15. See D. Verseput, 'Reworking the
Puzzle of Faith and Works in James 2.14-26', *NTS* 43 (1997), pp. 97-115 (97-98),
who notes the positive connotation of faith in 2.5, and C. Burchard, 'Zu Jakobus
2.14-26', *ZNW* 71 (1980), pp. 27-45 (38-39), who notes that already in 2.1, the faith
of both the author and addressees appears as more than a bare monotheistic
confession. Rather, in its context, the allusion to the *Shema* serves to remind the
addressees of the wider implications of the claim of commitment to God, in the
context of the special relationship to God of God's people (cf. 1.1, 12; 2.5), within
the framework of God's ordering of the universe (cf. 1.16-18, 21).

44. R.P. Martin, *James*, p. 89.

45. The view of Dibelius, *James*, pp. 177-79, and others, that Jewish tradition
thought of πίστις as a 'work' (ἔργον) among other works, and therefore that the use
of these terms in the Epistle of James presupposes the Pauline redefinition of πίστις
as separate from ἔργα, is inaccurate, as it is drawn entirely from later texts (rabbinic
texts and *4 Ezra*), which may well be downplaying faith in reaction to its importance in early Christianity. This view is not supported by earlier Jewish texts, and is
refuted by Wieser, *Abrahamvorstellungen*, pp. 164-65.

46. That he is introduced as 'Abraham our father' strengthens the suggestion
that the addressees are (at least predominantly) Jewish, as there is no indication of
the kind of theological allegorizing of descent from Abraham used by Paul in Gal. 3
and Rom. 4. Dibelius, *James*, p. 161, argues that *1 Clem.* 31.2 shows that Gentile
Christians could also designate Abraham as father, and thus no inferences can be
made about the epistle's background. *1 Clem.* 31.2, however, shows clear signs of
being influenced by the Pauline figurative use of Abraham as father.

Abraham was understood as the one who, above all, was found to be faithful (πιστός) towards God in testing (cf. Jas 1.2–4.12).[47] This is expressed in Sir. 44.20 and in 1 Macc. 2.52, which cites Gen. 15.6 in this context (cf. Jas 2.24), and which is also concerned with exhortation towards unflinching loyalty to God.[48] That the author is here drawing on this interpretative tradition is also suggested by the plural 'by actions' (ἐξ ἔργων), although only one instance is cited, the binding/ sacrifice of Isaac, which was commonly seen as Abraham's greatest moment of testing.[49] Thus, the willingness to sacrifice Isaac should not be seen alone as the deed by which Abraham was made righteous,[50] but rather as the climax of Abraham's demonstration of his commitment (πίστις) towards God.[51]

This commitment to God, manifested through its ongoing co-working with his actions (v. 22),[52] shows, by the citation of Gen. 15.6 (v. 23) and

47. Cf. von Lips, *Traditionen*, p. 426; Frankemölle, *Jakobus*, pp. 450-52.

48. The use of the singular ἐν πειρασμῷ in both these passages does not suggest that the authors are thinking of one single test of Abraham's loyalty to God, as opposed to ongoing testing; cf. the similar generic use of πειρασμός in Jas 1.12. Also worthy of note is *Jub.* 19.8-9, which speaks of Abraham being found faithful under trial and being designated the friend of the Lord. Analyses of this Jewish tradition are found in the excursus of Wieser, *Abrahamvorstellungen*, pp. 164-79; Dibelius, *James*, pp. 168-74.

49. E.g. Philo, *Abr.* 167; Josephus, *Ant.* 1.223, 1.223-34; *m. Ab.* 5.4. See further Davids, *James*, p. 127; Dibelius, *James*, pp. 168-69; Frankemölle, *Jakobus*, p. 452; J.S. Siker, *Disinheriting the Jews: Abraham in Early Christian Controversy* (Louisville: Westminster/John Knox Press, 1991), p. 99.

50. As Frankemölle, *Jakobus*, p. 449, points out, the participial construction of 2.21 need not be seen to introduce a *causal* subordinate clause.

51. R.B. Ward, 'The Works of Abraham: James 2.14-26', *HTR* 61 (1968), pp. 283-90, has suggested, based largely on stories in the rabbinic traditions, that the actions in question are his deeds of hospitality (Gen. 18), on the basis of which he was declared righteous, and the sacrifice of Isaac was averted. This would parallel the hospitality of Rahab (Jas 2.25), and would fit with the depiction of inhospitality in 2.15-16, and the demand for deeds of mercy in 2.12-13. This possibility is attractive, in view of the links it provides to the context; however, due to the difficulty of establishing the currency of later rabbinic haggada at the time of writing of the early Christian texts of the New Testament, it cannot be accepted with confidence. Ward's views are followed by Davids, *James*, p. 127, and Patterson, *Thomas*, p. 184, but rejected by Laws, *James*, pp. 134-35.

52. As Hoppe comments, this verse expresses the central point of the example, expressing the inseparability of πίστις and ἔργα. The correlation of πίστις and ἔργα is emphasized verbally by the use of the word συν-εργεῖν, while the

the designation 'friend of God' (v. 24), Abraham's status as one in harmony with God's order and approved by God. Abraham's commitment to God co-worked in his actions; through these actions, his faith was brought to perfection/completion (ἐτελειώθη).[53] Gen. 15.6 thus constitutes a summary statement of Abraham's commitment to God,[54] which continually co-worked with his actions, even to the point of willingness to sacrifice Isaac in obedience to God.[55]

The direct address to the addressees as a whole is resumed in v. 24, drawing the general conclusion from the Abraham example: 'You see that a person is made righteous by actions, and not by faith alone' (ὁρᾶτε ὅτι ἐξ ἔργων δικαιοῦται ἄνθρωπος καὶ οὐκ ἐκ πίστεως μόνον). It is through their actions that people are found to be in harmony with God's order; commitment to God, taken alone and not demonstrated by corresponding actions of loyalty can be nothing more than a claim to commitment (cf. 2.14), and therefore ineffective for the evaluation of one's status.[56] The possibility of works without faith is

continual co-working of πίστις and ἔργα is stressed by the use of the imperfect συνήργει in 1.22. πίστις is in no way presented as subordinate to ἔργα. See particularly: Hoppe, *Hintergrund*, p. 115; Frankemölle, *Jakobus*, p. 456. In fact, the stress is on the role of πίστις, which is used in the nominative case, as the subject of both halves of the verse: so also Hoppe, *Hintergrund*, p. 115.

53. The expression of 2.22 recalls that of 1.2-4, where already the sequence (πειρασμοί)–πίστις–(ὑπομονή)–ἔργον–τέλειος was introduced. Abraham's actions are understood in the context of his faithfulness towards God, which reaches its goal through his actions in the midst of testing.

54. The very widely attested traditional background of this use of the example of Abraham renders unlikely the suggestion that the author has here deliberately inverted the chronological order of Gen. 15//Gen. 22, in order to subordinate Abraham's faith to his works, in reaction to Pauline teaching. The similar citation of Gen. 15.6 in 1 Macc. 2.52 cannot be seen as anti-Pauline, nor can the comment at the end of the narration of the trials of Abraham in *Jub.* 19.9: 'he was found faithful (cf. πίστις/πιστεύειν), and he was recorded as a friend of the Lord (cf. φίλος θεοῦ, Jas 2.23) in the heavenly tablets' (translation by O.S. Wintermute, in *OTP*, II, p. 92).

55. ἐπληρώθη should be seen in this light, and not as an indication that the sacrifice of Isaac fulfilled the prophetic words of Gen. 15.6, as suggested by Mayor, *James*, p. 104; Ropes, *James*, p. 221.

56. It is important to note that the author does not speak of 'works of the law' (ἔργα νόμου) in this context, the phrase which Paul uses in attempting to counter any perception on the part of Gentile converts to Christianity that the adoption of the Jewish law has salvific effect (Gal. 2.16; cf. Gal. 3.2, 5, 10; Rom. 3.20, 28). While there is a similarity in vocabulary between Jas 2.24 and such verses as Gal.

never raised.[57] It is already clear from 1.2-4, 2.18, 22 that actions are seen as inseparable from faithful commitment, thus the phrase 'not by faith alone' (οὐκ ἐκ πίστεως μόνον) does not represent a downplaying of the importance of faith.[58]

2.16 or Rom. 3.28, the referent in each case is clearly different. (Cf. Burchard, 'Jakobus 2.14-26', p. 43 n. 77. He himself believes that the author of the epistle was aware of the Pauline formulation, but was not engaged in an attack on Paul's teaching [pp. 43-44].) If the author of the Epistle of James had been attempting to attack Pauline teaching in this passage, it is very difficult to understand why he did not make it apparent here that the actions (ἔργα) to which he refers are the Pauline 'works of the law' (ἔργα νόμου). In any event, the two use the term νόμος in a quite different manner, and only the over-hasty importing of Pauline nuances into the Epistle of James, rather than taking the use of νόμος in this text in its own context, obscures this. What Paul means by law has been extensively discussed (see, e.g., E.P. Sanders, *Paul, the Law and the Jewish People* [London: SCM Press, 1985]); regardless of the precise nuance attributed to Paul's usage, this is distinctly not the same as what the author of the Epistle of James means. As has been argued above, νόμος in the Epistle of James draws on the traditional Jewish understanding of the law as God's order for the conduct of his people, but this is modified under an early Christian perspective which sees the proclamation of Jesus as the definitive interpretation of God's order, and which sees the law as encapsulated in the love command. Further, as Baasland, 'Jakobusbrief', pp. 129-33, demonstrates, the apparent contradiction between Jas 2.24 and Rom. 3.28 is inherent in the epistle to the Romans itself, in the contrasting views expressed in Rom. 2 and Rom. 3.

57. The view of R. Walker, 'Allein aus Werken: Zur Auslegung von Jakobus 2.14-26', *ZTK* 61 (1965), pp. 155-92, that the Epistle of James argues for justification by works alone, in which faith plays no part, depends on the unsatisfactory presumption that rejection of 'faith without works' (πίστις χωρὶς ἔργων) means the endorsement of 'works without faith' (ἔργα χωρὶς πίστεως). On the contrary, the whole point is the inseparablility of πίστις and ἔργα, not the downplaying of one or the other.

58. As the above analysis has attempted to show, the discussion in this passage can be understood clearly against the background of the consistent parallels in a wide variety of Jewish texts. The many verbal connections between this text and the Pauline corpus, and the use of similar traditions, though—scarcely surprisingly—employed in different ways in different rhetorical contexts, reflects the common Jewish heritage of both authors. The careful and detailed analyses of Baasland, 'Jakobusbrief', pp. 127-33, L.T. Johnson, *James*, pp. 58-65 and Boccaccini, *Middle Judaism*, pp. 220-28, demonstrate how each author, read independently within the shared context of the theological diversity of contemporary Jewish (including early Christian) thought and tradition, presents a clear and coherent, although different, argument. The conclusion that the author of the Epistle of James is engaging in anti- (post-/misunderstood-)Pauline polemic does not logically follow from the

A further example from Israel's past, that of Rahab (Josh. 2),[59] follows in v. 25, paralleled with the first example in vv. 21-23 through the introductory 'likewise'. Rahab's claim to commitment (πίστις) towards God is expressed in the narrative of the conquest of Jericho in Josh. 2.8-11; her corresponding actions in receiving and sending out the messengers confirm the genuineness of her faith.[60] Another illustration, in the form of a simile drawn from physical human existence, is used to draw the subsection to a close in 2.26, summarizing the basic point which has been developed throughout the subsection.

Like the preceding subsection, 2.14-26 can be seen to focus on demonstrating the shortcomings of the addressees, this time in their failure to show through their actions the genuineness of their claim of loyalty to God.[61]

observation that both authors use similar words and traditions in different ways. Cf. also K. Berger, 'Die implizite Gegner: Zur Methode des Erschliessens von "Gegnern" in neutestamentlichen Texten', in Lührmann and Strecker (eds.), *Kirche*, pp. 373-400 (378); K. Berger, *Theologiegeschichte des Urchristentums* (Tübingen: Francke Verlag, 1994), pp. 165-73. Without any clear indication that the author of the Epistle of James is alluding to Paul's teaching, and given that the argument in Jas 2.18-26 can be understood perfectly well in context without reference to Paul, it is preferable to read the argument here, including its use of the figure of Abraham, as independent of Paul.

59. On the use of Rahab in early Christian and in rabbinic literature, see A.T. Hanson, 'Rahab the Harlot in Early Christian Theology', *JSNT* 1 (1978), pp. 53-60. On prostitution and the social perception of prostitutes in the ancient world, see J. Massynbaerde Ford, 'Prostitution in the Ancient Mediterranean World', *BTB* 23 (1993), pp. 128-34.

60. Her faith is not explicitly mentioned in 2.25, but is surely presupposed as part of a familiar story, in which it is known to be authentic commitment to God, more than a mere claim (cf. Heb. 11.31). That this is a specific example of one who showed hospitality to the messengers of God's people is hardly accidental in view of the accusation of inhospitality raised against the addressees in 2.15-16 (cf. 2.2-3; 2.5-6). If the brother or sister of 2.15 is seen as an itinerant follower of Jesus, rather than just a poor member of a local community, then the parallel with receiving guests, giving them food and shelter, and sending them safely away again is even stronger. It is possible that a deliberate parallel with the brother or sister of 2.15 is intended in the use of both a male (Abraham) and a female (Rahab) illustration from Scripture in 2.21-25.

61. It seems likely, in view of the importance of πίστις in these verses, that a connection should also be made to ἡ πίστις τοῦ κυρίου ἡμῶν Ἰησοῦ Χριστοῦ τῆς δόξης in 2.1, which can then be seen to set the whole of the central section of the letter (2.1–5.11) under this 'Christian' claim. For the author at any rate, the claim of

5.2.4 *Shortcomings in Speech: 3.1-12*

The section 3.1-12, as frequently in the Epistle of James, opens with an imperative, and direct address to the hearers: 'Not many should become teachers, my brothers, knowing that we are all the more liable for judgment'. This injunction suggests that the author sees problems with many becoming teachers, or laying claim to teaching authority among the addressees,[62] although it is not necessary to go so far as to assert that 'the church was evidently plagued by teachers who were insincere and were afflicting false doctrine upon unsuspecting listeners'.[63] Thus, many interpreters see the command as a warning against the self-seeking pursuit of positions of high status within the community.[64] It is also possible, however, to see this injunction as rooted in tensions between itinerant radicals, who perpetuated the proclamation of Jesus among local communities, and representatives of those communities,[65] similar to the tensions suggested by 2.2-3, 15-16.

Theissen points out that the itinerant radicals functioned as authorities within the groups of sympathizers who supported them.[66] Thus, the aspiration to the role of teacher among the addressees can be seen as a tendency to take over this authoritative position and appropriate it within the local group. As such, this would constitute a curtailing of the

---

commitment to God implies commitment to Jesus as his appointed and exalted one (1.1; 2.1; cf. 1.18, 21).

62. On the role of the teacher (διδάσκαλος) in early Christianity, and on the role of the author of the epistle as a teacher, see above, §2.2.2.

63. R.P. Martin, *James*, p. 108. J. Wanke, 'Die urchristlichen Lehrer nach dem Zeugnis des Jakobusbriefes', in J. Ernst, R. Schnackenburg and J. Wanke (eds.), *Die Kirche des Anfangs* (Festschrift H. Schürmann; Freiburg: Herder, 1978), pp. 489-511 (492), suggests representatives of a possibly gnosticizing heresy who may have made use of the catchword 'perfection'; while Zimmermann, *Lehrer*, pp. 201-208, argues that Jas 3.1 represents the dissolution of the office of teacher, which through faulty teaching and disputes has lost its authoritative standing.

64. See Davids, *James*, p. 136; Laws, *James*, p. 141: Mussner, *Jakobusbrief*, p. 159; Hoppe, *Jakobusbrief*, p. 76. E. Trocmé, 'Les églises pauliniennes vues du dehors', *SE* 2 (TU 87) (1964), pp. 660-69, has suggested that this passage counters disorderly tendencies in the post-Pauline churches, analogous to 1 Cor. 14 and the Pastoral Epistles. This view is followed by Popkes, *Adressaten*, pp. 34-35, 98-100. As Laws, *James*, p. 141, notes, there is no warrant within the Epistle of James for making this connection, particularly when 2.14-26 need not be seen as an anti-Pauline statement.

65. As Patterson, *Thomas*, pp. 185-86, also observes.

66. Theissen, *Sociology*, pp. 19-21.

itinerant radicals' authority, if not a rejection of their right to function in this way. This would, of course, fit well with the dishonourable reception, and with the failure to give material support, already depicted in 2.2-3 and 2.15-16.[67] As is frequently the case in the Epistle of James, this injunction is given eschatological grounding, 'knowing that we are all the more liable for judgment'.[68]

This is followed in 3.2 by an assertion of general fallibility, linked specifically to failures in speech.[69] The connection between teaching and speech is obvious; it is through speech that teaching is performed.[70]

---

67. Jas 3.2 may contain a further allusion to the authority of the marginal radicals of the Jesus movement, and their right to be received honourably as teachers. In the light of the significance of the word τέλειος (perfect/complete) in Matthew and the *Didache*, designating one who fulfils the demands of God's order, as proclaimed by Jesus (cf. above, §4.2.1), it is possible to see τέλειος in 3.2 as an allusion to the radical obedience and dependence on God which was characteristic of the marginal itinerants. In view of the ascetic nature of their lifestyle (cf. 2.2, 15), without material security, these people could be described particularly well as 'able to bridle even the whole body' (δυνατὸς χαλιναγωγῆσαι καὶ ὅλον τὸ σῶμα). The qualification of this designation, 'if anyone does not go wrong in speech' (εἴ τις ἐν λόγῳ οὐ πταίει), could be seen as an allusion to the itinerant follower of Jesus, radically obedient to God, who also does not fall short in speech, and thus is particularly fit to fulfil the authoritative role of the teacher. There is no reason to suppose that 'body' (σῶμα) is used figuratively here to designate the church, in the sense in which the word is used by Paul in Rom. 12.4-5; 1 Cor. 12.12-27, as Reicke, *James*, p. 37; R.P. Martin, *James*, p. 110; J.M. Reese, 'The Exegete as Sage: Hearing the Message of James', *BTB* 12 (1982), pp. 82-86 (83), suggest.

68. The threat of severe judgment for those who exert influence over others occurs a number of times in several synoptic gospel traditions, perhaps most notably in Jesus' criticism of the scribes, whose coming judgment is expressed similarly, 'they will receive all the greater punishment' (οὗτοι λήμψονται περισσότερον κρίμα, Mk 12.40//Lk. 20.47; cf. Mt. 23.1-36); cf. also Mt. 5.19; Mk 9.42//Mt. 18.6-7//Lk. 17.1-2.

69. A wide range of texts from the ancient world which mention the theme of speech has been assembled by W.R. Baker, *Personal Speech-Ethics in the Epistle of James* (WUNT NS, 68; Tübingen: J.C.B. Mohr [Paul Siebeck], 1995), pp. 23-83; cf. also pp. 105-22 for materials relating to the negative potential of speech.

70. When 3.1 is seen to be directed against the restriction of the authoritative teaching role of the itinerant radicals among local early Christian sympathizer-groups, the apparent disjunction—pointed out, for example, by Davids, *James*, p. 135; Dibelius, *James*, pp. 182, 184, between 3.1, traditionally seen as addressed to teachers, and 3.2-12, which appear to have a more general audience—disappears, as both 3.1 and 3.2-12 can be seen to be directed to the addressees as a whole.

Moreover, the development of the theme of appropriate speech at this point enables the author to complete his exhortation that the addressees should correspond to God's order in all areas of human activity, understood in the ancient Mediterranean world as a composite of thoughts, judgments and attitudes, purposeful actions, and self-expressive speech.[71]

The use of the images in 3.3-5a in other texts is generally positive. Thus, in these verses they can be seen as a positive, or at least neutral, depiction of the tongue's power, rather than reading the depiction of the tongue's negative potential in 3.6-12 back into these verses.[72] First, the tongue's power is expressed figuratively, then the negative potential of this power. The image of the power of fire (3.5b) provides the transition to this negative depiction.[73] A further illustration of the tongue's capacities is given in 3.7-8a, which form a skilfully structured contrast between the taming of lesser creatures by humankind and the untamable nature of the tongue.[74] This taming is clearly an allusion to the Genesis creation story, where the creatures, according to their four classes—beasts, birds, reptiles and fish—are placed under human governance (Gen. 1.26-28). The disharmony of the tongue with God's created order is effectively expressed through the two asyndeta of Jas 3.8b, whose abruptness contrasts with the flowing and balanced construction of vv. 7-8a. The tongue's instability, as an 'unstable evil' (ἀκατάστατον κακόν) recalls the instability of the double-minded man (1.8), who is

71. See above, nn. 29-30 to this chapter. The theme of human attitudes and judgments is predominant in 2.1-13, while the focus in 2.14-26 is on human actions; that the passage 3.1-12 now develops the theme of self-expressive human speech accords entirely with the author's concern for human stability and wholeness in commitment to God, and in harmony with God's order.

72. So also Frankemölle, *Jakobus*, p. 494.

73. This contrast is strengthened stylistically by the use of the imperative, ἰδού, to introduce this new image. The contrast with the 'perfect man' of 3.2 is brought out by the repetition of 'the whole body' (ὅλον τὸ σῶμα) in v. 6.

74. These verses are particularly rich in rhetorical figures, e.g., alliteration, πᾶσα–φύσις–πετεινῶν, ἑρπετῶν–ἐναλίων, δαμάζεται–δεδάμασται, οὐδεὶς–δαμάσαι–δύναται; homoioteleuton, θηρίων–πετεινῶν–ἑρπετῶν–ἐναλίων, etc. φύσις θηρίων is balanced against φύσις ἀνθρωπίνη at the beginning and end of v. 7, while δαμάζεται καὶ δεδάμασται stands parallel to οὐδεὶς δαμάσαι δύναται; the insignificance of the tongue, by comparison with the whole range of creatures tamed by humans, sets its uncontrollability in all the stronger contrast. On the rhetorically effective composition of these verses, see also Frankemölle, *Jakobus*, p. 510.

'unstable in all his ways' (ἀκατάστατος ἐν πάσαις ταῖς ὁδοῖς αὐτοῦ), and it is to the tongue as expressive of such human unwholeness that the author draws attention in the following verses.[75]

God, as Lord and father, is blessed, while other humans, who are created 'according to the likeness of God' (καθ'ὁμοίωσιν θεοῦ, cf. Gen. 1.26), are cursed.[76] In a cultural context where human action should correspond to divine action, it is highly significant that in Gen. 1.28, God's speech blesses humankind. Human speech, by contrast, is divided and unwhole. It blesses God, and curses those in God's image, who themselves have been blessed by God. That this should not happen is the unsurprising evaluation of the situation in Jas 3.10b.

The section is concluded by three further short metaphors drawn from the natural world,[77] showing the necessity of consistency, similar to the way in which a short metaphor ended the previous section in 2.26. These images, drawn from the impossibility of such doubleness in the natural world, stress again the need for undividedness in the addressees' speech. Equally well, these metaphors can apply to the need for undividedness in their attitudes and actions, coming at the end of the three more discursive sections, 2.1–3.12.

Just as 2.1-13 and 2.14-26 highlight serious shortcomings in the addressees' attitudes and actions in relation to the standards of God's

75. The problem of the duplicity of the tongue is witnessed in many other Jewish texts, e.g. LXX Ps. 61.5; Sir. 5.13; *T. Benj.* 6.5; 1QS 10.21-24. Frankemölle, *Jakobus*, pp. 514-15, fails to show why, as he asserts, Jas 3.9-10 should be dependent on Sirach, rather than being part of a widely attested Jewish tradition, although he admits the contrast between Sir. 4.5-6 (cursing as a righteous action) and Jas 3.9-10.

76. Whether the curse against fellow-humans is here intended generally or is seen by the author as related to specific circumstances, known to, and recognizable by the addressees, is not clear. Cursing in the ancient world signified exclusion from a social group. It is not impossible that this may refer to the non-reception by the addressees of the socially marginal itinerant teachers of the Jesus movement, who are specially favoured by God (cf. 2.5), particularly if blessing God is to be seen in the context of the community assembly (cf. 2.2-3, 15-16). Davids, *James*, p. 146; R.P. Martin, *James*, p. 118; Vouga, *Jacques*, p. 101, all agree that εὐλογία indicates a liturgical reference.

77. As with the previous images employed by the author, these metaphors are common in ancient texts; cf. Dibelius, *James*, pp. 203-205. On the tree/fruit image, see particularly von Gemünden, *Vegetationsmetaphorik*, pp. 141-51, 268-69. A similar image is found in Mt. 7.15-18; 12.33-37; Lk. 6.43-45, also linked to the theme of speech.

order, so 3.1-12 provides a powerful demonstration of the deficiency of
their speech. In the context of the anthropology of the ancient
Mediterranean world, which, as noted above,[78] saw the human as composed of zones of emotion-fused thought, self-expressive speech and
purposeful interaction, these three subsections together combine to
show the addressees as thoroughly divided and deficient in their commitment to God.

5.2.5 *Epilogue and Transition: 3.13-18*

The section 3.13-18 is again tightly structured, centring on the contrast
between 'the wisdom which comes down from above' (ἡ σοφία ἄνωθεν
κατερχομένη) and its opposite, focused in the central verse of the section, 3.15. As already noted, this section plays a pivotal role within the
construction of the text, showing strong verbal-semantic links with the
introductory sections, 1.2-18 and 1.19-27, with the demonstration of the
addressees' unwholeness in attitude, action and speech in 2.1–3.12, and
with the following exhortations in the rest of the epistle. As such, it
gives a summary of the exhortations already elaborated, while also
functioning as a transition to the harsher call to repentance and eschatological warnings which follow.

The section takes up again the key Jewish religious term, wisdom,
(σοφός/σοφία), used already in 1.5. As observed above, wisdom carries
different nuances for different authors in different contexts, but basically refers to the sense of the world as ordered by God, and right
human conduct in correspondence to this. In view of the questionable
nature of the addressees' commitment to God, and of their divided and
unstable conduct, the author poses the telling question: who among
them has a correct appreciation of God's order of the universe, including the order for right human conduct? The answer is implied in the
following imperative: such a person must demonstrate this through
appropriate conduct. This command clearly alludes, through its verbal
links, to what has been set out already in the text.[79] By stressing that

78. See above, nn. 29-30 to this chapter.

79. For instance, cf. 2.14-26 (especially 2.18) for the terms δείκνυμι–ἔργα; 1.4-5
for ἔργον–σοφία; 1.21 for πραΰτης. Likewise, the phrase 'the wisdom which comes
down from above' (ἡ σοφία ἄνωθεν κατερχομένη, 3.15), contains obvious allusions
to the introductory section 1.2-18. In 1.5, the addressees were told that anyone
lacking wisdom should seek it from God, who gives ungrudgingly; in 1.17-18,

wisdom is from above, the author highlights again the fact that a proper understanding of God's order is revealed by God to those loyal to God.

By contrast, what is out of harmony with God's order is marked by ζῆλος and ἐριθεία (3.14, 16), which depict jealousy, rivalry and disharmony, thus once again, division and unwholeness.[80] The contrast in disposition reaches the climax of its expression in 3.15: 'This is not the wisdom which comes from above, but is earthly, human, demonic'. It is not clear if the author actually has two conceptions of wisdom in mind, or if he is depicting the true wisdom from above, and non-wisdom (οὐκ ἔστιν αὕτη ἡ σοφία ἄνωθεν) which stands in contrast to this God-given wisdom.[81]

Divided and unwholesome attitudes, actions and speech are not characteristic of God's wisdom, rather they are 'earthly, human, demonic' (ἐπίγειος, ψυχική, δαιμονιώδης). The sequence of these adjectives is significant, for they form a climax, narrowing down the true origins of such non-wisdom. It is ἐπίγειος, a neutral word, meaning 'earthly', but here clearly standing in contrast to 'from above' (ἄνωθεν), and thus taking on a more negative nuance. It is also ψυχική, a term which has proved difficult to interpret.[82] The cognate noun ψυχή (soul/life) is used positively in 1.21 and in 5.20 to refer to human life. When the adjective ψυχικός is read simply as 'human', it fits well with the depiction of the

it was asserted that every good gift is from above (ἄνωθεν), coming down from the unchanging God.

80. The word ἀκαταστασία (3.16) probably contains an allusion to its cognate adjective, ἀκατάστατος, in 1.8 and 3.8, reflecting the instability and disharmony which is characteristic of non-correspondence to God's order. It is also possible that in the alliterative phrase πᾶν φαῦλον πρᾶγμα, a contrast is being made with πᾶσα δόσις ἀγαθὴ καὶ πᾶν δώρημα τέλειον, which in 1.17 are described as ἄνωθεν, and already linked to 3.13-18 through the repetition of ἄνωθεν in 3.15, 17.

81. See Davids, *James*, p. 152, who also notes that what those depicted in these verses possess is never actually named as σοφία.

82. Dibelius, *James*, pp. 211-12, suggests that this is a borrowed Gnostic term, but used in a non-technical sense. Similarly, Mussner, *Jakobusbrief*, pp. 171-72, sees the term as the dualistic opposite of 'spiritual' (πνευματικός), though, unlike the Gnostics, understood ethically rather than metaphysically; cf. the Pauline usage in 1 Cor. 2.14; 15.44-46; also Jude 19. That the author is thinking here in terms of a three-tier σῶμα–ψυχή–πνεῦμα person (as Frankemölle, *Jakobus*, pp. 540-41, believes; cf. 1 Thess. 5.23) is, however, not evident. B.A. Pearson, *The Pneumatikos-Psychikos Terminology* (Missoula, MT: Scholars Press, 1973), asserts that the author of the Epistle of James has read 1 Corinthians and is dependent on Pauline terminology, but this cannot be substantiated.

internal instability of the human in 1.14-15. Moreover, it thus forms an appropriate middle term in the three-part sequence, which comes to a peak in pointing out of the basic source of such negative qualities: they are demonic (δαιμονιώδης), inspired by the cosmic forces in conflict with God's order (cf. 3.6; 4.7).[83] Thus, the addressees are presented with a stark alternative in terms of the choice between identifying themselves with God, and God's universal order, or in opposition to God, with the demonic powers.

The positive side of the contrast, listing the qualities of God's wisdom, is developed in 3.17. These stand in clear contrast to 'every vile deed' (πᾶν φαῦλον πρᾶγμα) in the previous verse, and reflect undivided wholeness, in correspondence to God's wholeness and the wholeness of God's order. The section is then brought to an end by the epigrammatic concluding verse.[84] Hoppe, referring to the eschatological nuance of the word-group δικαιο- in the Epistle of James, argues that the 'fruit of righteousness' (καρπὸς δικαιοσύνης) should be seen in an eschatological setting, rather than in a general ethical context.[85] That this section should end with a note of eschatological assurance is in keeping with the frequent use of either eschatological threat or assurance in other subsections of the text.[86]

5.3 Conclusion

1. Following the close analysis of the text of 1.19–3.18, it can be concluded that these sections of the epistle serve principally to demonstrate the unwholeness of the addressees' lives in relation to what is expected of those claiming commitment to God and to God's appointed one, Jesus. The pervasive nature of the addressees' failure to live up to the

83. Boccaccini, *Middle Judaism*, pp. 222-23, notes the similarity of the sense of human instability in the Epistle of James to that of the *Testaments of the Twelve Patriarchs*, where it is attributed to Beliar.
84. Such short concluding sentences are also used in 2.13, 26 and 4.17, so there is no need to see this as an isolated saying attached by means of a catchword link, as Dibelius argues, *James*, pp. 214-15.
85. Hoppe, *Hintergrund*, pp. 67-70; followed by Frankemölle, *Jakobus*, p. 558.
86. The promise of reward to 'those who make peace' (τοῖς ποιοῦσιν εἰρήνην) is reminiscent of the pronouncement of favour towards the εἰρηνοποιοί in Mt. 5.9; this may reflect the practical outworking of the radicalization of the love command in early Christianity.

standards of God's eschatological order is given all the more emphasis by the fact that the three sections of 2.1–3.12 in turn expose the addressees' deficiency in each of the three constitutive 'zones of personality' typical of the perception of the human in the ancient Mediterranean world: attitudes and judgements in 2.1-13, actions in 2.14-26 and speech in 3.1-12. This is demonstrated through reference to instances reflecting their own reproachable conduct at the start of each section, in 2.2-3, 2.15-16 and 3.1. Argument from Scripture is used to back this up in 2.8-11 (the love command), 2.19, 21-25 (the *Shema;* the examples of Abraham and Rahab) and 3.7-9 (creation).

These central sections are preceded by 1.19-27, which, as well as pointing forward to the elaboration of these concerns, opens with basic exhortation to be rid of such pervasive wrong conduct, and to accept God's saving word. Similarly, 3.13-18 sets out the contrast between the wisdom which God reveals to those loyal to God and divided unstable human conduct, while urging the addressees to live according to God's wisdom.

2. It is scarcely insignificant that the three instances of typically deficient conduct referred to in 2.2-3, 2.15-16 and 3.1 can all be seen to be rooted in tensions between the radical, socially marginal members of the Jesus movement and a local group (or groups), whose support for these itinerant prophets and teachers is apparently being withdrawn. It indicates that the epistle's location can be seen within the area of activity of these groups, but the fact that the influence and position of these radical followers of Jesus is obviously waning suggests a later, rather than an early setting. In fact, while the author is obviously concerned by the addressees' treatment of them, the focus is firmly on the addressees' behaviour, rather than on directly defending the rights of the itinerants. As noted earlier in relation to 2.1-13, the principal roles of the itinerant radicals within the text are to help expose the contrast between the addressees' conduct and the standards of God's eschatological order, and to contrast their wavering commitment to God with the radical dependence of the itinerants.

By comparison with the focus on the shortcomings of the addressees, there is not so much stress on the overt depiction of God's status as supreme authority and benevolent patron. God's position as the one who grants ultimate honour within the eschatological kingdom is strongly asserted in 2.5, while God's gift of the saving 'implanted

word' to those prepared to receive it is stated in 1.21. The allusion to
Deut. 6.4 in Jas 2.19 emphasizes God's oneness and supremacy, drawing on a central tenet of Jewish faith, which continues with exhortation
to undivided love of God (Deut. 6.5). As in Jas 1.17, God's authority as
creator is alluded to in 3.9.

Chapter 6

READING THE TEXT: JAMES 4.1–5.20

6.1 *Introduction*

This chapter will continue detailed reading of the text of the Epistle of James undertaken in the previous two chapters through the remainder of the epistle. The final two chapters of the epistle can be divided for the purposes of closer analysis into a number of subsections: call to repentance in 4.1-10, eschatological warning and encouragement in 4.11–5.11, and the letter-closing section in 5.12-20.

Although some have argued that the section beginning with 3.13 continues as far as 4.6[1] or 4.10,[2] and others have included 4.11-12 with 4.1-10,[3] the first ten verses of James 4 can best be seen as a carefully structured formal and thematic unity in their own right.

Jas 4.1 opens abruptly with two rhetorical questions. The repetition of the interrogative 'from where' (πόθεν) adds intensity to this opening, as does a third homoioteleuton at the start of the second question, οὐκ ἐντεῦθεν. The rhetorical effect is heightened by alliteration (πόθεν πόλεμοι καὶ πόθεν μάχαι). Likewise, 'among your members' (ἐν τοῖς μέλεσιν ὑμῶν) parallels 'among you' (ἐν ὑμῖν) at the end of each

---

1. Baasland, 'Literarische Form', pp. 3657-58; 'Jakobusbrief', p. 122.

2. L.T. Johnson, 'James 3.13–4.10 and the ΤΟΠΟΣ ΠΕΡΙ ΦΘΟΝΟΥ', *NovT* 25 (1983), pp. 326-47. Baasland and Johnson see the two rhetorical questions in 3.13 and 4.1 as formally linked through the final 'among you' (ἐν ὑμῖν), and draw attention to the further thematic link between 'jealousy' (ζῆλος, 3.14, 16) and the cognate verb ζηλόω in 4.2. Certainly, ἐν ὑμῖν can be seen as a link, but a minor, rather than a major, one. Likewise ζῆλος/ζηλόω, while providing a verbal connection, is not the thematic focus of either 3.13-18 or 4.1-10.

3. Ropes, *James*, pp. 252-75; Hoppe, *Jakobusbrief*, pp. 88-96; Mussner, *Jakobusbrief*, pp. 175-89; Frankemölle, *Jakobus*, pp. 571-628; Wuellner, 'Jakobusbrief', pp. 52-53. The principal reason for viewing vv. 11-12 along with vv. 1-10 seems to be the argument that 4.13–5.6 forms a unit, thus if 4.11-12 are not to be left suspended *in vacuo* between 4.1-10 and 4.13–5.6, then they must be combined with the preceding verses.

question. The abrupt style continues in vv. 2-3 with a series of short, mostly second person plural statements, alternating, either singly or in pairs, between positive and negative. The vocative, 'adulteresses' (v. 4), stands out in sharp contrast to the previous address as 'my (beloved) brothers'. The subsequent rhetorical question (v. 4a) and its amplification (v. 4b) set out the stark cosmological opposition between friendship with the world/enmity with God and their implied reverse, friendship with God, followed by two more short rhetorical questions.[4]

Verse 6 introduces a contrast with the previously depicted human conduct, in the form of the action of God, expanded by the following citation of LXX Prov. 3.34. This verse forms a structural linchpin for the whole passage, 4.1-10: the first line of the quotation 'God opposes the arrogant' looks back to the enemies of God, who stand over against God at the climax of vv. 1-4, while the second line of the quotation 'but to the lowly (ταπεινοῖς) he gives grace' anticipates the following verses, which culminate in the command: 'Humble yourselves (ταπεινώθητε) before the Lord and he will exalt you'. Verses 7-10 comprise a contrasting stylistic parallel to the accusatory statements of 4.2-3.[5] The behaviour directed by these verses signifies a reversal of that depicted in the first half of this section. The abrupt tone of the whole passage, expressed in rhetorical questions and accusations in 4.1-5, and in imperatives in 4.7-10, gives an underlying stylistic unity.

By contrast with the abrupt questions, accusations, imperatives and harsh address of 4.1-10, a new subsection is introduced in 4.11 by the gentler and more usual 'brothers' (ἀδελφοί). Most interpreters see 4.13–5.6 as one section, or as two parallel sections, followed by 5.7-20 as a general conclusion containing final admonitions, some of which recapitulate earlier material.[6] On the surface, there is a certain unity

---

4.   Following the illuminating suggestion for the interpretation of 4.5 put forward by S.S. Laws, 'Does Scripture Speak in Vain? A Reconsideration of James 4.5', *NTS* 20 (1974), pp. 210-15; also Laws, *James*, pp. 174-79.

5.   In comparison with the 11 second person plural present indicative verbs used in vv. 2-3, vv. 7-10 contains 9 second person plural (and 1 third person singular) aorist imperatives, 3 of which are followed by καί and a third person singular future indicative verb, specifying the consequence of the fulfilment of the preceding commands (7b, 8b, 10b). Thus, the contrast between the reproach at the beginning of the section and the call to repentance at its end is underlined stylistically by changes in tense and mood.

6.   Exceptions are Elliott, 'James', p. 72, who sees 4.13–5.11 as one unit, and Laws, *James*, pp. 194-218, who takes 5.1-11 as a single subsection.

between 4.13-17 and 5.1-6, with the parallel address, 'Come now...' (ἄγε νῦν, 4.13; 5.1). To treat them without further ado as a unit (or as two parallel units), however, leaves these verses somewhat disconnected within the whole text: 'a group of sayings against worldly-minded merchants and rich people'.[7] Further, it misses the fact that they are part of a larger, carefully constructed unit, within which they function as a significant part of its formal and thematic development.

The section begins with a warning, set in the context of divine judgment. This judgment motif hangs over the entire section, coming to a climax in 5.1-6, and being relieved for those who endure patiently in the final verse (5.11), with the assurance that the Lord is compassionate and merciful. The severity increases from the usual address 'brothers' in 4.11, to reach a peak in the downright denunciation of the rich in 5.1-6. The focus of attention in 4.11–5.11 is directed towards the climax of judgment, expressed in the rhetorical question affirming God's inevitable action in 5.6, 'Does he not resist you?' (οὐκ ἀντιτάσσεται ὑμῖν;)[8] and the corresponding switch in 5.7 to exhortation to the brothers to wait patiently in the light of the eschatological climax: 'Be patient... until the coming of the Lord'. Eschatologically grounded warning and admonition are thus at the heart of this whole passage, though in 5.7-11 the eschatological threat is lightened, and the tone is more one of encouragement for the addressees.

The final verses, 5.12-20, contain a number of similarities to the typical closing formulas used in Greek epistolography.[9] The absence of the most common form, ἔρρωσθε, does not necessarily mean that the document lacks an epistolary close. The term 'above all' (πρὸ πάντων, 5.12) is frequently found in Greek letters, usually with a health-wish or prayer. In this verse, the words do not introduce a health-wish typical of Greek papyrus letters, but as this wish is frequently expressed by petition to the gods, or to a particular divinity, such as Sarapis, an exact correspondence could not be expected. It is, nevertheless, significant that 5.13-18 is concerned with the health and well-being of the recipi-

7. Dibelius, *James*, p. 230.

8. It is scarcely by chance that this is reminiscent of the pivotal position of 4.6 (ὁ θεὸς ὑπερηφάνοις ἀντιτάσσεται, ταπεινοῖς δὲ δίδωσιν χάριν) in the previous section, 4.1-10.

9. See also Francis, 'Form', p. 125; Vouga, *Jacques*, p. 139. On the other hand, O Fearghail, 'Literary Structure', argues against the interpretation of these elements in the Epistle of James as epistolary features.

ents, in association with prayer. It is not, in this case, the sender's prayer for the health of the addressees, but exhortation to them to pray. This includes prayer for one another, with a statement of assurance of the power of effective prayer to restore health, linked to the confession and forgiveness of sin. Such an injunction to prayer is not unheard of in Hellenistic letters,[10] but it is unlikely that the author of the Epistle of James is adopting an actual formula in this passage. It is more probable that he has drawn on the convention of including a health-wish/prayer in the closing section of the letter, but has shaped the precise expression according to both the cosmological presuppositions and the actual circumstances of the early Christian movement.

However, between the phrase 'above all' at the start of 5.12 and the prayer exhortation in 5.13-18 comes the prohibition of oaths. At first glance, the whole of 5.12 seems to form a self-contained unity, without a clear connection to either what precedes or follows.[11] If this were the case, it would weaken the argument that 'above all' is connected as an epistolary closing formula with the health-prayer concerns of 5.13-18. Oath formulas, however, were also a common feature of the close of letters. Thus, when reference to oaths appears alongside two other features which are associated with epistolary conclusion—the formula 'above all' and a health-prayer statement—it is plausible to suggest that the occurrence of the injunction, 'Do not swear', at this point in the text, also draws on epistolary convention, but, in adapting this convention to a cosmology in which oaths were forbidden, substitutes a prohibition of oaths for a concluding oath formula.

If 5.12-18 can be seen to form an adapted epistolary conclusion, it is necessary to see how the final two verses, 5.19-20, fit into such a conclusion. Warnings either to avoid or correct those who stray from the truth are found at the end of a number of other early Christian letter-texts;[12] similar exhortations occur in several letters of the philosophical

10. See Berger, 'Gattungen', p. 1360.

11. Dibelius, *James*, p. 248, argues that there is not any connection; Ropes, *James*, p. 300, suggests that 'Do not swear' parallels 'Do not complain' in 5.9, the first referring to other people, the second to God; Mussner, *Jakobusbrief*, pp. 211-12, uses the theme of judgment to connect 5.12 with the surrounding verses; G.H. Rendall, *The Epistle of James and Judaic Christianity* (Cambridge: Cambridge University Press, 1927), p. 68 n. 1, suggests that 5.12 is a misplaced gloss on 3.9-10.

12. Rom. 16.17-18; 2 Thess. 3.14-15; Tit. 3.9-11; 1 Jn 5.16-17; 2 Pet. 3.17; Jude 22.

schools.[13] This can still scarcely be considered a common characteristic even of community-oriented, rather than purely private, letters; nevertheless, it can be seen as an appropriate final remark in a text strongly concerned with exhortation to unity and wholeness. At the same time, a short thematic recapitulation of one of the text's major concerns can also be seen to parallel the function of the epilogue in Greek rhetoric.[14]

The sharp accusations and exhortation to submit to God in 4.1-10 contrast with the more discursive demonstration of the addressees' failures in the previous sections. This represents a further development in the text's rhetoric, building on these earlier sections and stressing strongly the key themes noted earlier: exhortation to undivided commitment to God and assertion of God's benevolent nature and authoritative status. Likewise, the strong eschatological urgency of the further warnings and admonitions of 4.11–5.11 play a distinctive role within the text, and also give considerable importance to these themes; this is similarly the case in the letter-closing section, 5.12-20. The task of this chapter is to examine in detail each of these in turn, paying attention to the presentation of these themes, and to the role played by each section within the text's development.

6.2 Call to Repentance: 4.1-10

6.2.1 Analysis of the Text
The section 4.1-10 begins abruptly with a strong symbolization of the divisions and instability of the addressees, expressed through the language of war, strife and violence in 4.1. This language should be seen as figurative, a rhetorically overstated expression of dividedness, rather than a reference to actual deeds of military violence, presupposing an anti-'Zealot' background.[15] The source of such divisions among the

13. Berger, 'Gattungen', p. 1349, cites the pythagorean letter of Lysis to Hipparchos, as well as examples from the cynic epistles of Krates and Diogenes.
14. Aristotle, *Rhet.* 3.19.1.
15. Schlatter, *Jakobus*, pp. 240-41; R.P. Martin, *James*, pp. 144-45; M.J. Townsend, 'James 4.1-4: A Warning against Zealotry?', *ExpTim* 87 (1976), pp. 211-13, see these as referring to Zealot activity. On the other hand, Frankemölle, *Jakobus*, p. 573; Davids, *James*, p. 156; Dibelius, *James*, p. 216; Laws, *James*, pp. 168-69; Mayor, *James*, p. 133; Mussner, *Jakobusbrief*, p. 176, Vouga, *Jacques*, p. 112, see them as figurative references. See Davids, *James*, p. 156, for a list of Jewish parallels to such figurative use of war-imagery. Military imagery is used by Paul in Rom. 13.12; 2 Cor. 10.4; cf. Eph. 6.11-17. It is, of course, quite possible that the

addressees is 'from your passions which wage war among your members' (ἐκ τῶν ἡδονῶν ὑμῶν τῶν στρατευομένων ἐν τοῖς μέλεσιν ὑμῶν).[16] Some commentators understand 'among your members' to refer to internal personal dividedness and unwholeness, like the similar use of μέλος to mean 'part of the body' in Jas 3.5.[17] Others see this as a reference to members of the community, synonymous with 'among you' (ἐν ὑμῖν).[18] This interpretation fits much better with the group-oriented, non-introspective nature of social life in the ancient near East. This kind of division can be seen as a typical instance of the human instability and dividedness which contrasts with God's oneness and unchangingness.

This instability and dividedness is developed further by the sequence of abrupt accusations in 4.2-3. 'You desire' (ἐπιθυμεῖτε), like 'passions' (ἡδοναί, v. 1), suggests a self-interested orientation, in contrast to a right disposition which shows loyalty to God and to God's people. Such desires, however, are not fulfilled. This striving for selfish goals and not obtaining the desired outcome is reiterated in the following lines.[19]

violent activity of groups like the Zealots provides a well-known and close-to-home background from which such imagery could be drawn, without requiring that the passage is directly aimed against any specific group.

16. ἡδονή is closely associated with ἐπιθυμία, the term which was used in 1.14-15 to denote the human origins of testing, sin and death. This connection is confirmed by the use of the verb ἐπιθυμεῖτε in 4.2. Although ἡδονή can mean pleasure in a neutral sense, among the early Christian texts it generally refers to pleasures and desires which conflict with God's order and distract the human from wholehearted obedience to God; e.g. Lk. 8.14. Cf. G. Stählin, 'ἡδονή', *TDNT*, II, pp. 909-26. Similarly, ἡδονή is associated with Beliar in *T. Dan* 5.1-2 and *T. Benj.* 6.1-3.

17. Davids, *James*, p. 157. He is, however, probably incorrect in seeing this as a reference to the 'evil inclination' (הרע יצר) of rabbinic writings, which cannot clearly be established as a current and well-defined concept for the early Christian period.

18. R.P. Martin, *James*, p. 145; Vouga, *Jacques*, p. 112. Ropes, *James*, p. 253, sees a clash of the internally rooted desires of several different people, thus combining something of both views.

19. As well as giving strong rhetorical expression to the nature of divided conduct, it is possible that an allusion to 2.11 exists in 4.2b; this is strengthened by the use of the vocative, adulteresses, in 4.4. In 2.11, it was pointed out that someone who does not commit adultery, but who does murder, is guilty of transgressing God's law. Here, in 4.2, 4, the addressees are accused of both transgressions.

The use of the verbs 'ask' and 'receive' at once recalls 1.5-8, where those lacking wisdom were told to ask God; such a request must be made in undoubting commitment to God, as those who are unstable in commitment will not receive anything. Thus, in seeking their own satisfaction, rather than demonstrating loyalty to God and to their 'brothers', the addressees are not likely to receive; they either do not ask (4.2), or they ask with an inappropriate disposition (4.3).

In view of the highly rhetorical nature of this passage, it need not be assumed that the addressees were particularly reproachable, self-seeking and factious people. Rather, it may well be that the author is expressing disapproval of competitive efforts to consolidate (personal/ group) material security, within the finely balanced social exchange structures of the ancient world. In this respect, a favourable disposition towards a rich, exploitative (potential) patron, such as seems to be depicted in 2.2-3, may serve as a concrete example of seeking the fulfilment of their own desires, rather than showing appropriate dependence on God. Thus, the tensions and lack of solidarity for which the addressees are reproached may well be rooted in the security-oriented competition for patronage, status and access to resources, rather than in an inherently evil disposition on the part of the addressees, although it is presented in this light by the author. For the author, God's ultimate favour is promised to the marginal and the lowly, who are dependent on God's provision for them (2.5; cf. 1.9); they are honoured in the eschatological role reversal of God's kingdom, while those who enjoy material security and well-being (cf. the use of ἡδονή in Lk. 8.14) will pass away (1.9-11; 4.13–5.6).

The following verses accord well with this suggestion. The vocative, 'adulteresses', at the start of 4.4, as noted above, draws on the traditional use of adultery as an image for unfaithfulness towards God,[20] and pronounces a sharp conviction of the dishonourable status of the addressees in their lack of dependence on God, the ultimate guarantor of honourable status (cf. 1.12; 2.5), and their lack of solidarity with God's people, including with one another. κόσμος, 'world', for the author of the epistle, is always a negative designation,[21] referring to the present order of the world, in which the lowly and marginal are held in dishonour, in which the rich exploit to their own advantage, and are then welcomed as patrons whose sponsorship can give greater material

20. See above, §3.2.3.
21. See above, §3.3.3.1.

security. As such, κόσμος is the opposite of God's order. Thus, 'friendship with the world' (φιλία τοῦ κόσμου) can be seen to refer to engagement within this current world-order, which involves behaviour out of harmony with God's ultimate order, and which is actively hostile towards God (ἔχθρα τοῦ θεοῦ).[22] It is not possible to have commitment towards God, unless this is effected through appropriate dependence upon God and obedience to God. Those who affirm a world-order which dishonours those chosen by God (cf. 2.5-7) cannot expect to be counted as 'friends of God' (cf. 2.23).

This is followed by two further rhetorical questions in 4.5.[23] Most interpreters take the phrase ἡ γραφὴ λέγει as the introductory formula for a quotation, 'the Scripture says', apparently quoting from an unknown text,[24] considered to be 'Scripture' by the author, but eventually excluded from the canon and now lost. Others suggest that this is a summary statement about the traditional idea of God's jealous possessiveness for God's people (e.g. Exod. 20.5).[25] As Laws points out, however, it is highly unlikely that this verse, either as a citation or as a summary reference, depicts God's possessiveness for God's people, for which ζῆλος is always used, never φθόνος, which always carries the negative sense of envy as a human vice.[26] Thus, πνεῦμα must refer to the human spirit, breathed into the human by God at creation; this fits with the other use of πνεῦμα in the epistle in 2.26. In this case, 4.5b reads better as a question than as a statement that God

---

22. A similar stark contrast is found in Mt. 6.24//Lk. 6.13. In the Matthean version, this is followed by exhortation to depend on God for one's needs.

23. Following the interpretation of Laws, 'Scripture'; cf. Laws, *James*, p. 167, who translates: 'Or do you think that scripture speaks to us to no effect? Does the spirit he made to dwell in us long enviously?'

24. Davids, *James*, p. 162; Dibelius, *James*, pp. 222-23; Mussner, *Jakobusbrief*, pp. 183-84; Ropes, *James*, p. 262, although he also mentions the possibility that an unknown Greek translation of the Hebrew Scriptures may have contained this line; Frankemölle, *Jakobus*, p. 603; J. Michl, 'Der Spruch Jakobusbrief 4.5', in J. Blinzer, O. Kuss and F. Mussner (eds.) *Neutestamentliche Aufsätze* (Festschrift J. Schmid; Regensburg: Pustet Verlag, 1963), pp. 167-74. Schlatter, *Jakobus*, pp. 247-48 suggests the citation of Christian prophecy.

25. R.P. Martin, *James*, p. 148; Vouga, *Jacques*, p. 116; L.J. Prockter, 'James 4.6: Midrash on Noah', *NTS* 35 (1989), pp. 625-27, suggests a midrash on the story of Noah; as there is little evidence in the Epistle of James of the kind of rabbinic exegesis which he invokes here, the suggestion is to be considered unlikely.

26. Laws, 'Scripture', pp. 212-13.

created humankind with a spirit inclined towards vice, which would contradict the author's conviction that God is the source only of good (1.13-18).[27]

Verse 6 takes up the theme of God's faithful giving, by contrast with the wrong asking and not receiving of the addressees depicted in the previous verses (cf. 1.5-8). The adjective μείζονα 'all the more' emphasizes the true nature of God's giving: 'He gives all the more grace' (cf. 1.5, 17). This is followed by the citation of the LXX text of Prov. 3.34: 'God opposes the arrogant, but to the lowly he gives grace'. The arrogant can be seen as representatives of those who do not acknowledge their dependence on God, and live according to the order of the world as enemies of God. By contrast, God gives grace (χάρις) to the lowly (ταπεινοί), who are dependent on God.[28] This recalls the assurance of the eschatological exaltation of the lowly in Jas 1.9, and reinforces the importance of a proper, positive evaluation of lowly status among the addressees, as dependent upon God and provided for by God.[29] This verse thus provides a transition from the negative depiction of the divisive striving for self-dependence, in contrast with God's order, in 4.1-5, concluding with the first line of the quotation, to the positive evaluation of the acknowledgement of the real status of the lowly before God in 4.7-10, introduced by the second line of the quoted verse.

The contrast between God's order and its opposite (cf. 4.4) is drawn on in 4.7, in the form of a double exhortation towards acknowledgement of God's ultimate authority and status, and a corresponding denial

27. This still does not solve the problem of the source of the apparent citation. It may come from an unknown text, though Laws's argument that it alludes to a scriptural statement of the human's rightful longing (ἐπιποθέω) towards God, such as LXX Ps. 83.3, or possibly LXX Ps. 40.2, is also plausible (Laws, 'Scripture', pp. 214-15). It is also possible that, as a rhetorical question, it asserts Scripture's general authority, prior to the quotation of Prov. 3.34, without necessitating that Jas 4.5b must be directly related to this invocation of scriptural authority.

28. Malina, 'Patron and Client', pp. 171-73, draws attention to the use of χάρις, 'grace', and related words in the context of patron–client relationships.

29. Mussner, *Jakobusbrief*, p. 184, suggests that χάρις refers to eschatological exaltation, but it may also have the more immediate sense of God's giving to those who are unwaveringly dependent upon him, even amidst testing (1.2-6, 17). The exhortation of 1.9 is thus given an ongoing and present grounding; the lowly are reminded that God provides for them; thus, they do not need to engage in jealous striving according to the standards of the world, as depicted in 4.1-5.

of that of God's cosmic adversary.[30] The ultimately inferior status of the devil is shown by the fact that when resisted he will flee.[31] The exhortation to self-orientation towards God is continued in 4.8, with the assurance of God's faithfulness in response.[32]

It is worth noting that in these verses the author invokes activity in all three zones of human personality: purposeful interaction, symbolized by the hands, emotion-fused thought, symbolized by the heart, and self-expressive speech, symbolized by the mouth (here, weeping).[33] This emphasizes the completeness of the necessary turning towards God, involving the whole person.[34] The first vocative, 'sinners', indicates the addressees' standing as out of harmony with God's order of the universe (cf. 1.15), while the second, 'double-minded', takes up the expression of their instability and dividedness in commitment towards God used in 1.8.[35] The motif of the eschatological reversal of status within God's order is strongly present in the three injunctions to self-abasement which follow in 4.9, paralleled by the command that laughter be turned to mourning and joy to gloom.[36] Current status and pursuit of status within the old order is to be rejected by the addressees, leaving themselves in a lowly standing (ταπεινώθητε), without status,[37]

---

30. This cosmic dualism (cf. 3.6, 15; 4.4) is not found in Sirach, thus these verses cannot be seen to depend on the 'dualism of decision' of Sirach, as Frankemölle, *Jakobus*, p. 609, believes.

31. This idea is found already in Jewish thought, particularly in the *Testaments of the Twelve Patriarchs*, e.g. *T. Dan* 5.1; *T. Naph.* 8.4; *T. Sim.* 3.5; *T. Iss.* 7.7.

32. The phrasing of this command probably draws on the cultic image of drawing near to God (e.g. Exod. 19.22; 24.2; Deut. 16.16), as well as the language of prophetic exhortations to repentance (e.g. Hos. 12.6-7; Zech. 1.3; Mal. 3.7). The strong reminiscence of the prophetic language of threat and repentance in Jas 4.7-10 is noted by L.T. Johnson, 'Friendship', p. 179. The cultic metaphor is continued by the two exhortations to purity in 4.8b.

33. See above, Chapter 5 nn. 29-30.

34. The negative depiction of 4.1-5 also embraced all three personality-zones: thoughts (ἐπιθυμεῖτε), actions (μάχεσθε καὶ πολεμεῖτε) and speech (κακῶς αἰτεῖσθε).

35. On these two terms see above, §3.2.3.

36. On laughter in Jewish writings as a sign of independence from, and disregard for, God see K.H. Rengstorf, 'γελάω', *TDNT*, I, pp. 658-62 (659-60).

37. Perdue, 'Paraenesis', pp. 252-53, is correct in linking Jas 4 with the concept of liminality developed by the anthropologist Victor Turner, which depicts the marginal, structureless state of 'in-betweenness' involved in the transition from one social role to another, when status, values and characteristics of the former role are

radically dependent upon God who will in turn exalt them in their dependence on God and submission to God's authority.[38]

6.2.2 *Summary*

Following the more discursive demonstration of the shortcomings of the addressees' attitudes and judgments, actions and speech in relation to God's standards in the previous sections, the opening verses of 4.1-10 serve to give climactic expression to the dividedness and instability of the addressees, accusing them of living according to the standards of this world (κόσμος), as enemies of God's ultimate eschatological order. The remedy is presented in 4.7-10, namely, unconditional repentance and submission to God. Here, the key themes highlighted earlier are very clearly in evidence. The necessity of unwavering commitment to God underlies the reproachful portrayal of the addressees as divided and compromised in their loyalty to God, through willingness to identify with the standards of the world. This need for absolute commitment to God is strongly presented in the exhortation to repentance and submission to God in 4.7-10.

Likewise, the presentation of God in these verses corresponds to the earlier portrayal of God as supreme patron. God's generous giving to those whom God favours is stressed again in 4.6. God's supreme authority is emphasized by contrast with the real powerlessness of the devil in 4.7. Again, in 4.10, God is depicted as the one who bestows honour on those who submit loyally to God's authority.

Within the overall development of the text, this passage plays a central role. The author has already demonstrated at length that in all areas of life—attitudes, actions and speech—the addressees fail to show the undivided loyalty to God which was laid down in the epistle's opening section. This failure in commitment to God is now starkly exposed as enmity towards God, and the addressees are emphatically urged to

---

laid aside, in order for new values, status and characteristics to be undertaken. Perdue's further conjectures on the relationship of liminality, paraenesis and the social setting of the Epistle of James are more doubtful: see above, §1.4.1.

38.   Here, again, is a close resonance of the saying of Jesus in Mt. 18.4; 23.12//Lk. 14.11; 18.14. Cf. also the song of Mary in Lk. 2.52; similar language in terms of status reversal is used in the beatitude–woe sequence of Lk. 6.21b, 25b: 'Blessed are you who weep now, because you will laugh ... Woe to you who laugh now, because you will mourn and weep' (μακάριοι οἱ κλαίοντες νῦν, ὅτι γελάσετε...οὐαί, οἱ γελῶντες νῦν, ὅτι πενθήσετε καὶ κλαύσετε).

reject such self-identification with God's opponents, and to submit themselves wholly to God's benevolent authority.

6.3 *Eschatological Warning and Encouragement: 4.11–5.11*

6.3.1 *Analysis of the Text*
As outlined above, 4.11–5.11 comprises a series of three eschatologically grounded warnings, rising in intensity (4.11–5.6), followed by three further eschatologically based exhortations, each introduced by the address, 'Brothers' (5.7-11).

In 4.11-12, the author takes up again the theme of solidarity and oneness among God's people, with the command not to speak ill of, or dishonour through speech, a fellow-member of God's people (ἀδελφος). Implicit in the verb καταλαλέω 'speak against/ slander' is the passing of judgment[39] on the brother who is the object of the slander. As already noted, the conviction that judgment was the prerogative of God alone was a distinctive feature of the proclamation of Jesus and his followers (cf. Mt. 7.1//Lk. 6.37).[40] To pass judgment, including dishonouring speech, implies usurping God's prerogative and the dishonouring of God's order, expressed by God's law (νόμος).[41]

The oneness and supreme authority of God is invoked in response to such usurping of God's role. Anyone who engages in such conduct loses all standing in comparison with the ultimate power of the one God, lawgiver and judge, able to save and destroy.[42] The phrase 'there

---

39.   Frankemölle, *Jakobus*, p. 622, suggests that this judgment is to be understood concretely, in connection with 2.6, as a reference to legal action by rich Christians against fellow-members of the community. This, however, is unlikely, as it is improbable that the rich are to be seen as among the actual addressees of the epistle, in view of their overwhelmingly negative portrayal by the author.

40.   See above, §3.3.3.2, on 2.4.

41.   νόμος here, as elsewhere in the epistle, is understood to refer to the early Christian radicalization, expressed in the love command, of the Jewish demands of God's order. See above, §3.3.3.3, on 2.8-13.

42.   A similar reference to God's power to destroy occurs in Mt. 10.28 (cf. Lk. 12.4-7), though the context is somewhat different to that of Jas 4.12. In 4.12, for the first time in the text, an assertion about God's nature contains a threat in relation to the addressees, rather than the previous emphasis on God as the giver of all that is good. This can be understood as a rhetorical development: having made the choice between God and the world clear in the previous subsection, the threat of destruction if they continue to fail to identify themselves with God and God's order is made all the more plain.

is one lawgiver and judge' (εἷς ἐστιν ὁ νομοθέτης καὶ κριτής) is probably an allusion to the statement of God's oneness in 2.19, and, like that
verse, to the *Shema* (Deut. 6.4-9), with its fundamental expression of
God's oneness and of appropriate human conduct in complete commitment to God. Likewise, the use of 'neighbour' (πλησίον) at the end of
4.12 is most likely a deliberate allusion to the encompassing precept of
God's order, the love command of Lev. 19.18, cited as the 'kingly law'
in 2.8.[43]

The second part of the subsection begins in 4.13 with the rhetorical
summons, 'Come now', and the depiction of those summoned. These
are not small local traders but large-scale merchants,[44] for whose trade
the use of the verb ἐμπορεύεσθαι is appropriate; they have at their
disposal sufficient resources to travel around the trading cities of the
Hellenistic world, to stay in a city for a long period, in order to do
business and make profit.

It is debated whether these people are to be seen among the addressees
themselves,[45] or whether this paragraph is a rhetorical apostrophe
addressed to another group.[46] Several considerations favour the second
option. Through the parallel use of 'Come now' (ἄγε νῦν) in 4.13 and
5.1, it is clear that these groups are linked, and, as already indicated, it
is unlikely, in view of the consistently negative portrayal of the rich
(πλούσιοι, 1.10-11; 2.6-7; 5.1-6), that they should be included among
the 'brothers'.[47] As Laws notes,[48] the addressees are specifically called

43. The combination of Deut. 6.4 and Lev. 19.18 in Mk 12.29-31; cf. Lk.
10.27; Mt. 22.37-39 is worth noting here. It is possible, as already noted, that the
author is also making an allusion in this verse to the combination of these verses in
the early Christian tradition, see further Hutchinson Edgar, 'The Use of the Love-
Command'.

44. Contrary to Frankemölle, *Jakobus*, p. 637, who claims that such large-scale
activities were also possible for small business people. An outline of the possibilities and activities of such merchants, with particular attention to Syria-Palestine, is
provided by Maynard-Reid, *Poverty*, pp. 71-77.

45. Davids, *James*, pp. 171-72; Frankemölle, *Jakobus*, p. 631; Hoppe,
Jakobusbrief, p. 97; Burchard, 'Gemeinde', p. 327; Sato, 'Jakobusbrief', pp. 59-60.

46. Dibelius, *James*, p. 231; Laws, *James*, pp. 189-90; Mussner, *Jakobusbrief*,
p. 189. R.P. Martin, *James*, p. 165, and Ropes, *James*, p. 276, leave the question
open.

47. Davids's suggestion that the address, οἱ λέγοντες, means that they should
be seen as distinct from the πλούσιοι as members of the community, is not substantiated, and ignores the link created by the double use of ἄγε νῦν.

48. Laws, *James*, p. 190.

'brothers' in 4.11-12, and again in 5.7, 9, 10, whereas in 4.13 and 5.1 this designation is avoided. The style of both 4.13-17 and 5.1-6, resembling a prophetic address, also suggests that it is unnecessary to see those addressed in these verses among the actual hearers of the epistle; there are frequent examples of prophetic speeches addressed to those who could not have heard them.[49] Moreover, although they are not named as 'rich' (πλούσιοι), the depiction of their activity suggests that they fall into this category,[50] especially the last of the four verbs used to describe their plans: κερδήσομεν, 'we will make profit', suggests the greedy desire to accumulate more than one's share of the world's limited goods, typical of the negative perception of the rich as exploitative.[51] Thus, it is preferable not to see those directly addressed in 4.13 as included by the author among the 'brothers' who are the addressees of the letter as a whole.[52]

By contrast with such ambitious plans, the next verse points out that such people cannot even have certain knowledge about the next day. This depiction of transitoriness is addressed to the planmakers of 4.13, rather than forming a general statement of human fragility, and recalls the impermanence of the rich in 1.10-11, in contrast to the promise of lasting honour from God to the lowly who are dependent upon and commited to God (1.9; 1.12; 2.5; 4.10). A statement of the correct perspective on human conduct is given in 4.15: everything is to be seen under the authority of God. 'We will live and do this or that' stands in marked contrast to the large-scale, detailed and ambitious proposition of v. 13. The contrast returns in 4.16 to the present conduct of those depicted in v. 13. ἀλαζονεία depicts boastful arrogance, often with the

---

49. Cf. Dibelius, *James*, p. 231; Mussner, *Jakobusbrief*, p. 189.

50. B. Noack, 'Jakobus wider die Reichen', *ST* 18 (1964), pp. 10-25; Maynard-Reid, *Poverty*, p. 69, sees those depicted in 4.13 as identical with the rich of 5.1.

51. See above, Chapter 3 n. 30. Vouga's view, *Jacques*, p. 122, that the author is not criticizing commerce or profit-making shows unawareness of this negative perception of profit-making; likewise, Davids's statement that 'these are people who have shut God out of their commercial lives, although they may be pious enough in church and at home' (*James*, p. 123; cf. R.P. Martin, *James*, p. 168) reflects a twentieth-century, industrialized, individualistic world-view, rather than that of the first century Mediterranean world.

52. It is not impossible that such people may have been present in an assembly like that envisaged in 2.2-3, but, as far as the author is concerned, they are unwelcome outsiders, who are not part of the group he addresses as ἀδελφοί.

sense of a falsely grounded presumptuousness,[53] which accords well with the depiction of the real insecurity of the plans and planmakers in v. 14.[54]

Even if these verses as a whole are not addressed directly to the actual recipients of the epistle, they do have a function in relation to them, depicting the vanity of life which does not acknowledge fundamental dependence on God, but seeks its security and wellbeing from other sources, a tendency against which the author has warned the addressees already. This warning against those who accumulate earthly wellbeing is intensified and brought to an eschatological climax in the next paragraph, which opens by commanding the rich to weep, wailing over their coming misery.[55]

The real nature of the present wellbeing of the rich, and also of their exploitative acquisition and hoarding, is disclosed in the next lines where the use of the perfect tense strengthens the depiction. Their wealth is decayed, their garments are motheaten, and their gold and silver are rusted. From the perspective of the coming judgment, their exploitatively acquired and hoarded possessions are worthless.[56] The

53. See Ropes, *James*, p. 281.

54. Dibelius, *James*, p. 234, is correct in asserting that 'this verse adds nothing materially to v. 13'. The attitude of greedy and self-seeking traders is here explicitly spelt out as it would appear in a context where all goods are perceived as limited, and acquisitiveness and profit-making imply the exploitation of others, contrary to Frankemölle, *Jakobus*, p. 642, who sees 4.16 as a negative interpretation of the neutral statement of v. 13. From a limited-good perspective, however, the statement of v. 13 is not neutral in terms of the values it embodies. Wall, *Community*, pp. 214-17, 220-21, links these verses to the 'vanity' topos of Ecclesiastes.

55. There is nothing positive portrayed in the abasement of the rich, in the way in which the brothers in 1.2 are urged to rejoice amidst testing. This lack of positive possibility in the abasement of the rich speaks against their being considered among the actual addressees. There is an echo here of the language of 4.9, but it is used quite differently; the rich are not told to abase themselves before God but to weep in distress at their coming misery. This is not a call to repentance, but an announcement of judgment, strongly reminiscent of the oracles of woe of the prophets. It is significant, in view of the renunciation of judgment among the early Christian movement, that the author does not pronounce an actual judgment. This is still left to God's prerogative, implied in the closing rhetorical question, 'Does he not resist you?' (5.6).

56. The right use of resources is to employ them in social exchange relations, not to hoard them, cf. Lk. 12.33-34. See Malina, 'Wealth', p. 366. M. Mayordomo-Marín, 'Jak 5.2-3a: Zukünftiges Gericht oder gegenwärtiger Zustand?', *ZNW* 83

utter worthlessness of such wealth is emphasized all the more by the fact that silver and gold, which do not rust, are said to have been eaten away by rust.[57] Even the most valuable of earthly possessions becomes valueless before the eschatological judgment.[58] This rust will give witness to their wrong conduct in acquiring and possessing riches; this again obviously refers to the eschatological judgment.[59] The final, ironic line of 5.3 reflects the folly and falsity of the acquisition of possessions by the rich; these are the last days, and God's judgment and the final establishment of his eschatological order are imminent.

The rhetorical imperative 'See!' at the start of 5.4, heightens the dramatic portrayal, introducing an accusation of wrong conduct against rich landowners,[60] again strongly marked by the prophetic traditions.[61]

(1992), pp. 132-37, points out that 5.2-3 can be seen as a present-based accusation against the rich, reflecting their wrong action in hoarding their wealth.

57. So Ropes, *James*, pp. 284-85; Laws, *James*, pp. 198; cf. also P.J. Hartin, 'Come now, you rich, weep and wail...(James 5.1-6)', *Journal of Theology for South Africa* 84 (1993), pp. 57-63 (59-60). Frankemölle's suggestion, *Jakobus*, p. 648, that the impossibility of the rusting of gold and silver is intended to show that exploitative behaviour by rich Christians against their poorer fellow-Christians is similarly contrary to nature stretches the image unnecessarily far. This thus forms a powerful image of destruction, rather than a slightly inaccurate proverbial usage, as Dibelius, *James*, p. 236, R.P. Martin, *James*, p. 177, and Mussner, *Jakobusbrief*, p. 194, suggest.

58. The image of the accumulation of treasures is employed in Mt. 6.20, cf. Lk. 12.21, 33-34, in the exhortation to store treasures in heaven, rather than on earth (ἐπὶ τῆς γῆς, cf. Jas 5.5). The exposure of earthly treasures to destruction by moths is mentioned in both versions, while the Matthean version also mentions rust, though using a different term to Jas 5.2-3 (βρῶσις; cf. σητόβρωτα, Jas 5.2).

59. ἰός probably picks up the use of the image in 3.8, where it depicts corruption and poison. This likelihood is strengthened by the image of fire, which also occurred in association with the tongue's negative power in 3.6. In that instance, the fire was linked to the fire of Gehenna, and it is not unlikely that a similar allusion is being made here in 5.3.

60. Oakman, *Economic Questions*, pp. 37-48, describes the changing patterns of land tenure and ownership in Palestine during the Hellenistic period, concluding that land possession came to be controlled by an elite hierarchy. Cf. Maynard-Reid, *Poverty*, pp. 85-90.

61. Frankemölle, *Jakobus*, pp. 652-53, sees a criticism not of the status of the rich landowners in itself, but of their failure to show Christian solidarity. As has been argued, it is unlikely that the rich are seen by the author as Christian. There is no evidence of rich landowners having been attracted by the early Christian movement, and the author's hostile attitude to the rich renders it unlikely that criticism of

The personification of the labourers' wages adds to the rhetorical effect, reiterating the idea that their wrongly accumulated wealth bears witness against the rich. Hired labourers are mentioned frequently in the synoptic gospels,[62] and were, in socio-economic terms, among the most precariously located groups in first-century Mediterranean society, because of the insecure and irregular nature of their means of subsistence.[63] The rights of hired labourers were defended in the legal and prophetic texts;[64] thus, what the rich have done is in blatant contravention of God's order.[65] They behave in a manner firmly opposed to God, and in hostility to the socially marginal labourers,[66] who are among those specially protected by God. Thus, God's judgment awaits the rich, just as it awaited those, who, in Israel's past, flouted God's order, and were denounced by the prophets.

This charge is followed in 5.5 by the accusatory depiction of the self-indulgent luxury of the rich. As in Mt. 6.19-20, 'upon the earth' (ἐπὶ τῆς γῆς) can be seen to refer to their selfish and exploitative earthly satisfaction, in contrast to the lasting satisfaction of God's eschatological order, and to the perishing of their wealth depicted in 5.2-3.

An interpretative difficulty is posed by the identity of the 'righteous one' (δίκαιος) in 5.6. Most have seen this as a generic depiction of the

the position of the rich in itself was not intended, especially within a limited-good perception of the world's resources.

62.   E.g. Mk 1.20; Mt. 9.37-38; 10.10; 20.1, 8; Lk. 10.2, 7; 15.17, 19, 21.

63.   See J. Jeremias, *Jerusalem in the Time of Jesus* (London: SCM Press, 1969), p. 111; S. Applebaum, 'Economic life in Palestine', *CRINT* 1.2, pp. 631-700 (657); Maynard-Reid, *Poverty*, pp. 90-92; Ahrens, *Widerschein*, pp. 128-31; Malina and Rohrbaugh, *Commentary*, p. 124.

64.   E.g. Lev. 19.13; Deut. 24.14-15; Jer. 22.13; Mal. 3.5. The designation κύριος Σαβαώθ for God occurs frequently in Isaiah, though rarely in the rest of the LXX; the phrase used here 'to the ears of the Lord of Hosts' (εἰς τὰ ὦτα κυρίου Σαβαώθ) occurs in Isa. 5.9, in an oracle against those who accumulate property, thus, like the rich here, taking over others' share of God-bestowed resources.

65.   The cries of the wages and of the harvesters recall the tradition that God hears the cries of the oppressed righteous (for example, the cry of the similarly personified blood of Abel, Gen. 4.10).

66.   Frankemölle, *Jakobus*, p. 655, appears to suggest that the charges against the rich are to be understood as metaphors for the exploitative behaviour of rich Christians towards their poorer sisters and brothers. This, however, constitutes unwarranted 'spiritualizing' of the text, in order to help justify seeing the rich as Christians.

oppression by the rich of the poor, who are righteous before God,[67] although some have suggested a reference to the murder of James, the brother of the Lord,[68] or to the death of Jesus.[69] It seems most likely that the first view is correct, particularly as a generic singular is used several times in the epistle (e.g. 1.4, 9, 12; 2.5). This may be an allusion to the reference to judicial oppression by the rich in 2.6, and while it is possible that the accusation of murder may be exaggerated for rhetorical effect,[70] it may also reflect real experiences of the consequences of the oppression of the socially lowly placed and marginal by the rich.[71]

The best reading of the phrase οὐκ ἀντιτάσσεται ὑμῖν is that proposed by Alonso Schökel,[72] who argues that it forms a rhetorical question, picking up the unusual biblical word ἀντιτάσσεται from the citation of Prov. 3.34 in 4.6, and thus with God as subject. As such, it forms a fitting climax to the paragraph, reinforcing the sense of the coming judgment of God upon God's opponents: 'Does [God] not oppose you?'[73]

Although this paragraph, like 4.13-17, is not addressed directly to the intended hearers of the letter, it has a number of significant functions in relation to them within the text's rhetorical development. It brings to a

67. Davids, *James*, pp. 179-80; Dibelius, *James*, p. 239; Laws, *James*, pp. 204-206; R.P. Martin, *James*, pp. 181-82; Mayor, *James*, p. 160; Ropes, *James*, p. 291; Frankemölle, *Jakobus*, p. 658; Vouga, *Jacques*, p. 131.

68. H. Greeven in Dibelius, *James*, p. 240 n. 58.

69. A. Feuillet, 'Le sens du mot parusie dans l'Evangile de Matthieu', in D. Daube and W.D. Davies (eds.), *The Background of the New Testament and Its Eschatology* (Festschrift C.H. Dodd; Cambridge: Cambridge University Press, 1956), pp. 261-80 (274-76); Mussner, *Jakobusbrief*, p. 199, does not wish to exclude this possibility.

70. See Mussner, *Jakobusbrief*, p. 198; cf. also Davids, *James*, p. 179; Frankemölle, *Jakobus*, p. 658.

71. R.P. Martin, *James*, p. 181; cf. Laws, *James*, p. 205; Maynard-Reid, *Poverty*, p. 93.

72. L. Alonso Schökel, 'James 5.6 and 4.6', *Bib* 54 (1973), pp. 73-76.

73. This interpretation is preferable to the traditional view that the subject of ἀντιτάσσεται, read as a statement, is the 'righteous one', who does not resist, either because he cannot, or because he is waiting for God's judgment; so virtually all the major commentators, although Ropes, *James*, p. 292, favours seeing the phrase as a question, with the 'righteous one' as subject. As a question, with God as subject, however, it forms an appropriately effective conclusion to 5.1-6, and reflects the compositional correspondence between 4.6 and 5.6.

peak the strong sense of eschatological expectation which is present throughout the letter, and highlights the terrible eschatological threat to those who oppose God and live in violation of God's order. Further, it emphasizes all the more the ultimate loss of status of the rich (cf. 1.10-11) and the fundamental opposition of their conduct to God's order (cf. 2.6-7), and thus their utter unreliability as a source of patronage and security.

These two themes are taken up again in the next verses, linked by the particle 'therefore' (οὖν): the impending coming of the Lord (παρουσία τοῦ κυρίου) and, in contrast to the ultimate unreliability of the security which can be gained by aligning oneself with the rich as their clients, the reliability of God as the supreme patron. Having reached a rhetorical peak in the announcement of eschatological judgment in 5.1-6, the author now resumes the address to the 'brothers', exhorting patience in the light of these eschatological realities.[74] Moreover, there are a number of significant parallels, or rather contrasts, between the content and language of 5.1-6 and 5.7-8. The image of the farmer and his activity stands over against that of the rich in 5.4-5. Both are engaged in agricultural activities, but the rich landowners, rather than receiving a worthy harvest (v. 7), are indicted for exploitative luxury (v. 5). The rich are reproached with fattening their hearts (v. 5), while the addressees are urged to strengthen their hearts (v. 8). The rich are placed under the judgment of the Lord of Hosts (v. 4) while the addressees are exhorted to be patient until the coming of the Lord (v. 7), and are assured that the coming of the Lord is at hand (v. 8).

It is very appropriate that the author should return to this theme here at the end of the main body of the letter, having exposed the ultimately worthless nature of sources of security other than God, and having highlighted evidence of the addressees' dubious commitment to God, reflecting a lack of the endurance advocated at the start of the letter.

The rewards of patience are demonstrated by the image of the farmer,[75] who waits patiently while the crop receives the early and late

---

74.   μακροθυμέω is close in meaning to ὑπομένω, used in 1.12 to designate endurance in faithful commitment to God; that ὑπομένω/ὑπομονή occurs parallel to μακροθυμία in 5.10-11 suggests that they are used more or less synonomously.

75.   Mk 4.26-29 contains a similar narration, although there the form is that of a parable, rather than an illustration of the kind given here. On the use of this image, see particularly von Gemünden, *Vegetationsmetaphorik*, pp. 296-99.

rains,[76] and receives in the end a worthy harvest. The reference to early and late rains may also contain a further allusion to the *Shema* (cf. 2.19; 4.12), of which Deut. 11.14 was also a part, thus, appropriately in this context, drawing on the basic tradition of God's unfailing care and provision for God's people.[77] The exhortation to patience is reinforced by the command to strengthen their hearts in 5.8; the heart symbolizes the centre of the zone of emotion-fused thought,[78] thus, the addressees are urged to establish firmly their attitudes and thoughts in commitment to God.

The phrase 'the coming of the Lord' (ἡ παρουσία τοῦ κυρίου) probably refers to the coming of Jesus as God's exalted one (cf. Mt. 24.27, 37, 39).[79] The early Christian tradition of the gathering of the elect ones at the coming of the exalted eschatological Son of Man (Mk 13.26-27//Mt. 24.30; cf. Lk. 21.27-28) fits particularly well here.[80] The addressees are exhorted to hold out in faithful commitment to God and to Jesus as God's appointed one, until they will be gathered in among God's chosen ones (cf. 1.1, 2-4).

Having urged endurance in commitment to God in the face of the imminent coming of the Lord, when their enduring loyalty will be

76. The traditional reading of πρόϊμος καὶ ὄψιμος, referring to the seasonal rains in Palestine, is preferable to that of Frankemölle, *Jakobus*, p. 680, and Vouga, *Jacques*, pp. 134-35, that they depict early and late fruits, referring to καρπός in the previous line; see von Gemünden, *Vegetationsmetaphorik*, pp. 298-99. Both Vouga and Frankemölle misrepresent Davids's position when they claim that he also supports the reading of πρόϊμος καὶ ὄψιμος with καρπός; he clearly does not: see Davids, *James*, pp. 183-84.

77. This, of course, does not rule out the possibility that the author is referring to the actual climatic conditions in Palestine; cf. D.Y. Hadidian, 'Palestinian Pictures in the Epistle of James', *ExpTim* 63 (1952), pp. 227-28; an allusion both to the *Shema* and to the actual Palestinian climate is quite likely.

78. See above, Chapter 5 nn. 29-30.

79. It could also refer to God's coming (cf. κύριος in 1.7; 3.9; 4.10, 15; 5.4), but the evidence for the use of παρουσία in relation to God is sparse, and in some cases textually uncertain; for details, see Dibelius, *James*, pp. 242-43.

80. The strength of the sense of imminence is striking. It is boldly asserted that the parousia is drawn near, and the judge is at the doors; this is done without reference to signs or conditions, as is the case in Mk 13, Mt. 24 and *Did.* 16, and there is no indication of the accomodation of expectations to the delay of the parousia, as is evident in Lk. 21. The proximity of the parousia is emphasized by the use of the perfect ἤγγικεν, the form also used in the gospels to announce the arrival of the kingdom of God (Mk 1.15; cf. Mt. 3.2; 4.17; 10.7; Lk. 10.9, 11).

rewarded, the author turns in 5.9 to the dimension of loyalty to God implicit in a non-individualistic understanding of such a relationship: appropriate loyalty and solidarity among God's people. The addressees are not to groan or grumble against one another, showing a lack of the solidarity which demonstrates their commitment to God. Since the addressees' situation was described in 1.2 as characterized by various tests, such complaining is not unlikely; the base meaning of the verb στενάζω is to groan under the burden of difficult circumstances. This is reinforced by another statement of the imminence of the end, expressed in terms of the impending judgment. In view of the fact that God is described by the phrase, 'there is one lawgiver and judge' in 4.12, the judge (κριτής) of this verse must also be seen as God,[81] rather than as the coming exalted Jesus[82] depicted in the previous verses. 'At the gates' (πρὸ τῶν θυρῶν), as an image of imminence, has parallels in Mk 13.29//Mt. 24.33.[83]

The exhortation to patient endurance is reinforced in 5.10-11 with examples from Jewish tradition, culminating in the assurance of God's faithfulness in vindicating those who remain committed to God. First, the endurance of the prophets[84] in adverse circumstances (κακοπαθεία)

---

81.   So also Laws, *James*, p. 213; Frankemölle, *Jakobus*, p. 688; Burchard, 'Stellen', p. 360; *idem*, 'Jakobus 2.14-26', p. 28. This does not necessarily conflict with the presentation of the coming of the Son of Man in the synoptic gospels, characterized by the gathering of the chosen (Mk 13.26-27//Mt. 24.30-31; cf. Lk. 21.27-28). In the parable of Mt. 25.31 the Son of Man seems to be presented as judge, if he is the same figure as the king (Mt. 25.34). There is some degree of vagueness in the synoptic gospel traditions about who will judge; in Mt. 19.28//Lk. 22.30, the disciples of Jesus will sit on thrones judging the twelve tribes of Israel.

82.   Davids, *James*, p. 185; R.P. Martin, *James*, p. 192; Mussner, *Jakobusbrief*, p. 205.

83.   In these verses in the gospels, the subject is not specified, but seems to be the Son of Man; the parallel passage in Luke, which drops this image, has 'the kingdom of God is near'.

84.   Sirach's eulogy of Israel's heroes includes Samuel (46.13-20), Nathan (47.1), Elijah (48.1-12) and Elisha (48.13-14). That the prophets are not of particular importance for Sirach is suggested by the fact that only these figures from the historical books are mentioned; Isaiah also occurs in 48.22, but only in relation to the praise of Hezekiah. This consideration, plus the fact that Job only occurs in the Hebrew text of Sir. 49.9, speaks against Frankemölle's attempt to derive Jas 5.10-11 from Sir. 44–50; besides, the function of these examples is entirely different to Sir. 44–50. The existence of legends such as the apocryphal *Lives of the Prophets* shows the popularity of the prophets as heroes; cf. the allusion to the tombs of

is cited, and their loyalty and special relation to God is made explicit in
the qualifying phrase, 'who spoke in the name of the Lord'. Those who
have endured patiently, in loyalty to God, are esteemed as honourable
figures by the addressees (5.11). The clear implication is that they, too,
can expect to be ascribed honourable status for their endurance. This is
emphasized all the more by the verbal connection with the assurance of
ultimate honour, guaranteed by God to those who endure, in 1.12:
'Blessed is the man who endures testing'. This is followed by the
example of Job.[85] Although the noun 'endurance' (ὑπομονή) does not
occur in the LXX translation of Job, its use by Theodotion, Aquila and
the *Testament of Job*, as well as in Jas 5.11, shows the widespread
association of the figure of Job with this quality.[86] Job's faithfulness to
God in the midst of trials is proved, and ultimately vindicated by God.
As such, he is a particularly suitable example of the kind of endurance
already urged in Jas 1.2-4.[87]

In this context, the noun τέλος, 'end', is best seen to refer to God's
vindication of Job's loyalty (Job 42.10-17), thus serving as a further
reminder to the addressees of God's ultimate reward for those who
remain committed to God, even amid the most adverse of circumstances. Thus, although the principal reference here is the Job story,
Strobel is correct in seeing in 'the end of the Lord' (τὸ τέλος κυρίου) a
double sense, alluding also to the vindication of the addressees at the
parousia (cf. 5.7-8).[88] The assurance of God's faithfulness to those who

prophets as holy places in Mt. 23.29. The most significant parallel to the use of the
example of the prophets in Jas 5.10 is probably Mt. 5.11-12//Lk. 6.22-23, where the
suffering and public dishonour of the followers of Jesus is likened to that of the
prophets; they are told to rejoice in their sufferings (cf. Jas 1.2), and promised
eschatological reward (cf. Jas 1.12; 5.7-8, 11). The mention of the prophets of
Israel's past may thus also serve as a reminder of the honourable status, through
their loyalty to God, of the early Christian itinerant prophets, who stood in the
heritage of the great prophets of Jewish tradition.

85. The most detailed analysis of the use of this example is that of
T. Hainthaler, *'Von der Ausdauer Ijobs habt ihr gehört' (Jak 5.11): Zur Bedeutung
des Buches Ijob im Neuen Testament* (Frankfurt am Main: Peter Lang, 1988),
pp. 311-36.

86. Hainthaler, *Von der Ausdauer*, pp. 324-26, 335-36.

87. Hainthaler, *Von der Ausdauer*, pp. 318-23.

88. A. Strobel, *Untersuchungen zum eschatologischen Verzögerungsproblem*
(NovTSup, 2; Leiden: E.J. Brill, 1961), pp. 258-59; also R.P. Gordon, 'καὶ τὸ τέλος
κυρίου εἴδετε (Jas 5.11)', *JTS* 26 (1975), pp. 91-95. Endurance (ὑπομονή) is also
urged in an eschatological setting in Mk 13.13//Mt. 10.22; 24.13; (cf. Lk. 21.19),

remain loyal to God is further stressed in the final line of 5.11.[89] As noted above, the sense of the greatness of God's mercy was a particularly central concept within the early Christian movement.[90] It is thus particularly appropriate that the final line of the main body of the letter-text should emphasize the assurance of God's mercy.

6.3.2 *Summary*

The thoroughly eschatological tone of the verses 4.11–5.11 is striking. This eschatological dimension serves to give a final underlining to the exhortation to the addressees to persevere in their commitment to God (4.11-12; 5.7-11). God's supreme status is emphasized strongly in a similar way as the eschatological judge (4.12; 5.9). Likewise, God's benevolence to those dependent on God is stressed: God provides God's people's needs (5.7, cf. Deut. 11.14), and ultimately honours those who endure loyally (5.10-11). Thus, the two key themes which were particularly highlighted in the opening section of the text, and which have been seen to underlie its development, are both clearly present in this section, where they are stressed with eschatological urgency. This urgency is particularly brought out by the expectation of the imminent parousia of Jesus, God's exalted one (5.7-8).[91]

Moreover, as well as exhortation to endurance and the assurance of God's faithfulness to those loyal to him, this section contains a long vilification of the well-to-do of this world, who oppose God's righteous

---

resulting in salvation; interestingly, both Mark and Matthew also use the word τέλος in this context. Vouga, *Jacques*, p. 137, sees a reference to the death and vindication of Jesus, which, while not impossible, is unlikely, as in view of the special, authoritative role of Jesus in the Epistle of James, it is improbable that he would be referred to obliquely as one example among others. On the rejection of the view that τὸ τέλος κυρίου refers to the death of Jesus, see particularly Laws, *James*, pp. 215-16.

89.   There are strong verbal parallels with LXX Ps. 102.8-9, suggesting an allusion to this psalm in praise of God's mercy towards those who fear him. The use of τέλος in Ps. 102.9 strengthens the suggestion that τὸ τέλος κυρίου in the previous line of Jas 5.11 contains an eschatological allusion, hinting at the ultimate restoration by God of those who are faithful to him.

90.   See above, §3.3.3.3, on Jas 2.13.

91.   It is interesting to note that this passage of the Epistle of James plays a similar function to the synoptic 'apocalypse' of Mk 13: exhortation to endurance and confidence in the face of the parousia. This perhaps emphasizes the widespread importance of such an eschatologically oriented understanding of early Christian existence (cf. also 1 Thess. 5).

order (4.16; 5.4-6), but whose present status is transitory (4.14), and who are destined to perish under God's eschatological judgment (5.1-6). The passing away of the rich was already mentioned in 1.10-11, and their opposition to God was indicated in 2.6-7. In that case, it was suggested that the rich are seen as rivalling God, offering security and material benefits through patronage of the addressees, hence the depiction of them as evil, exploitative and destined to perish in the light of the eschatological order of God, the supreme authority and benevolent patron. This suggestion is borne out by the presentation here of their ultimate perishing (5.1-6), in comparison with God's provision for God's people and honouring of those loyal to God (5.7-11).

6.4 *The Letter Close: 5.12-20*

6.4.1 *Analysis of the Text*
The section identified at the start of this chapter as the letter-closing section opens in 5.12 with the epistolary closing formula, 'above all' (πρὸ πάντων), and the direct address, 'my brothers', followed not by an oath formula, as in pagan Greek letters, but, in keeping with early Christian tradition, by a prohibition of oaths, which has a close parallel in Mt. 5.34-37.[92] As oaths were permitted by the Pentateuch,[93] this is

---

92.   The Matthean form is longer, and uses the aorist, rather than the present tense. Most interpreters see the Matthean version as a later expression of a more primitive logion preserved by the Epistle of James, cf. Dibelius, *James*, pp. 250-51; Laws, *James*, p. 223; R.P. Martin, *James*, p. 199; Hoppe, *Jakobusbrief*, p. 111; Vouga, *Jacques*, p. 139. On the other hand, Ropes, *James*, p. 301, thinks Jas 5.12 is derived from the Matthean version. Davids, *James*, p. 190, argues that priority cannot be established; cf. Laws, *James*, p. 223, who also argues for their independence from each other.

93.   E.g. Exod. 20.7; 22.1-2; Lev. 19.12; Num. 30.3. Oaths by heaven or by earth were usually circumlocutions for oaths by God, as is made explicit by the Matthean form of the prohibition. As such, they invoked God's honour in defence of the truth of the statement, and thus risked bringing God's name and status into disrepute. Philo felt discomfort over such oaths and advocated the avoidance of swearing, *Dec.* 82–95; the Essenes, apart from an oath on entry to the group, also appear to have prohibited oaths, although Josephus, *War* 2.135, 139-42; (cf. 1QS 5.8-11; CD 15, 16) states that they allowed oaths in restricted situations, such as before a court. Examples of reservations about oaths in Egyptian, Greek and Roman, as well as Jewish texts are provided by W.R. Baker, '"Above All Else": Contexts of the Call for Verbal Integrity in James 5.12', *JSNT* 54 (1994), pp. 57-71;

usually seen as an example of Jesus' radical interpretation of the Jewish view of God's ordering of the world.[94] That this is not cited as a saying of Jesus does not mean that the author was not here drawing on the traditions of Jesus' sayings, as he never cites directly from such traditions, which probably did not yet exist in a fixed and authoritative form.

Two more letter-closing features are combined in 5.13-18: the health of the addressees, and prayer. These are not expressed by the usual formulas, but are combined in a way which fits the text's concern with exhortation to show steadfast commitment to God and solidarity with other group members. The verb 'suffer' (κακοπαθεῖ) in 5.13 echoes the suffering (κακοπαθία) of the prophets in v. 10: anyone who is in hardship should remain committed to God (as the prophets did), showing dependence on God in prayer (cf. 1.5-8). εὐθυμεῖ τις expresses the circumstances more positively: someone who is cheerful should sing to God. εὐθυμέω carries the sense of encouragement in a difficult situation (cf. 1.2),[95] and is thus more likely to refer to a positive outlook of confident commitment to God, than to favourable external life-circumstances.

The opening of 5.14 follows the pattern of the previous verse; the third person singular imperative, however, receives considerable expansion. Someone who is ill is to call the 'elders of the assembly' (πρεσβύτεροι τῆς ἐκκλησίας), whose identity is not immediately clear. As Frankemölle argues, the view that they should be seen as those who perform particular service,[96] rather than the holders of an institutionalized office,[97] is more appropriate to the period of composition of the text. The service which they perform, however, is that of prayer in faith. Prayer is something which all can do, and are urged to do (5.13, 16). Thus, it seems that the elders are those whose prayer is perceived as specially effective; their standing is thus derived from the experience

---

cf. Baker, *Speech-Ethics*, pp. 249-82. Baker, however, ignores the possibility that this verse may be an adapted epistolary formula.

94. Contrary to G. Dautzenberg, 'Ist das Schwurverbot Mt 5.33-37; Jak 5.12 ein Beispiel für die Torakritik Jesu?', *BZ* 25 (1981), pp. 47-66, who sees it as having originated in possibly Hellenistic, Jewish-Christian circles. Dautzenberg's opinion is followed by Frankemölle, *Jakobus*, pp. 701-702.

95. Cf. the other uses of this word group in early Christian writings, Acts 24.10; 27.22, 25, 36. See Ropes, *James*, p. 303; Davids, *James*, p. 192.

96. Frankemölle, *Jakobus*, pp. 709-10.

97. Dibelius, *James*, pp. 252-53; R.P. Martin, *James*, p. 207; Mayor, *James*, p. 169; Ropes, *James*, p. 304; Mussner, *Jakobusbrief*, p. 219.

of the effectiveness of their prayer in commitment to God, rather than effectiveness in prayer being derived from holding the title 'elder' (πρεσβύτερος).[98]

Their identity is complicated by the qualification 'of the assembly' (τῆς ἐκκλησίας). ἐκκλησία denotes an assembly, and was the usual LXX translation for the Hebrew קהל.[99] It does not seem to have taken on a religious sense in Greek-speaking Judaism, where synagogue (συναγωγή) was the usual term.[100] Mt. 16.18 and 18.17 are the only occurrences in the synoptic gospels, but it occurs frequently in Acts, designating an early Christian group, or the whole movement.[101] It is possible that the word was chosen deliberately here, as distinct from the use of συναγωγή in 2.2, to designate a local group who acknowledged the authority of the proclamation of Jesus as God's specially appointed messiah. The fact that the author uses both terms in the epistle perhaps indicates that fundamental continuity still exists between the early Christians ('sympathizers') to whom he writes and the wider Jewish environment, notwithstanding the gradual emergence of a distinct Christian identity in its own right, reflected in the use of ἐκκλησία in 5.14. In this light, the elders would refer to those within the local emergent Christian group whose commitment to God is known by the proven effectiveness of their prayers. Their coming to pray for an ill person shows the solidarity necessary among God's people.[102]

Anointing was a common practice in the ancient world,[103] and is also referred to in Mk 6.13. The participial construction shows, however, that the action of anointing was subordinate to the prayer of the elders; its importance lies in being performed in the name of the Lord. It is not clear whether 'Lord' refers to God, suggested by the parallel with 'in the name of the Lord' in Jas 5.10, or to Jesus,[104] whose access to healing power was a vital part of his proclamation, and in whose name

98. Burchard, 'Gemeinde', p. 318.
99. See K.L. Schmidt, 'ἐκκλησία', *TDNT*, III, pp. 501-36; pp. 527-29.
100. Cf. Jas 2.2. See above, §3.3.3.2.
101. E.g. Acts 5.11; 8.1, 3; 9.31; 11.22, 26; 12.1, 5; 13.1, etc. See also Laws, *James*, p. 225.
102. As Tamez, *James*, p. 58, notes (in a different context): 'Integralness, then does not occur only in the body of one member of the community, but rather in the entire community'.
103. See Ropes, *James*, pp. 305-306; Mayor, *James*, pp. 170-73.
104. So Davids, *James*, pp. 193-94; Dibelius, *James*, p. 253; R.P. Martin, *James*, p. 208; Mussner, *Jakobusbrief*, p. 221.

healings are frequently recorded in Acts.[105] As healing in his name demonstrates his role as the mediator of God's power, there is no necessary contrast between these two possibilities.[106]

The effectiveness of prayer in unwavering commitment to God is again asserted in Jas 5.15a, expressing utter confidence in the response of God,[107] the supreme patron, to prayer made in faithful commitment (ἐν πίστει).[108] This is followed in 5.15b-16 with an injunction and assurance concerning solidarity within the group. Verse 15b obviously still refers to the ill person of vv. 14-15a. The link between prayer for the restoration of health and the forgiveness of sins[109] appears problematic if read in a present-day context, but fits quite naturally within the non-individualistic, group-oriented society of the first-century Mediterranean world.[110] Sin, in such an honour-shame society, 'is a breach of interpersonal relations'.[111] It denotes a breakdown in solidarity and loyalty, whether to God or to other members of the group; one often implies the other (cf. Lk. 15.18, 21). When a right disposition of loyalty to one another and to God is shown, the author assures the addressees of God's forgiveness, releasing them from the

105. E.g. Acts 3.6; 4.30; 16.18; also Mk 9.38; Mt. 7.22; Lk. 10.17.

106. So also Frankemölle, *Jakobus*, p. 712.

107. The unshakeable confidence of the author in the effectiveness of prayer made in commitment to God is striking. Similar confidence in the power of prayer made in faith is found in in Mk 11.22-24//Mt. 21.21-22; the fact that Luke's Gospel drops this passage may reflect the problem of the ongoing failure of such bold belief to bear the expected results. Cf. Rebell, *Alles ist möglich*, pp. 98-102.

108. Vouga, *Jacques*, p. 142 (cf. Karrer, 'Christus der Herr', p. 185), is probably correct in seeing an eschatological reference in σώσει, but incorrect in seeing it as a reference to the eschatological raising of the ill person, regardless of the outcome of the illness. Rather, God's raising of the ill person shows his favourable patronage towards a member of the unified client-group, which has shown appropriate loyalty in its petition of unwavering commitment, the ultimate consequence of which is the eschatological favour implied by this verb.

109. The juxtaposition of medical and non-medical terminology, as Frankemölle, *Jakobus*, pp. 720-21, notes, displays the author's skill in composition; non-medical terms are used in relation to the physical healing (σῴζω, ἐγείρω), while a medical term is used for the restoration of relations in the forgiveness of sins (ἰάομαι).

110. On healing in group-oriented cultures, see J. Pilch, 'Understanding Healing in the Social World of Early Christianity', *BTB* 22 (1992), pp. 26-33, especially pp. 29, 31; cf. also his comments on the cultural significance of illness and healing in J. Pilch, 'Understanding Biblical Healing', *BTB* 18 (1988), pp. 60-66.

111. Malina and Rohrbaugh, *Commentary*, p. 63; cf. pp. 188, 303-304.

consequences of their breach in the relationship. Healing demonstrates God's benefaction towards the ill person; in order for this to take place, it is presupposed that any breach in the relationship must be restored.[112] God, as the benevolent supreme patron, both restores the relationship, where necessary,[113] and grants the benefit of healing power. Thus, Jas 5.16 urges acknowledgement of such breaches in relations and the seeking of restoration within the group, through confession of sins to one another, and demonstration of the necessary solidarity with one another and commitment to God, through prayer for one another.[114] The last line of 5.16 stresses again the effectiveness of the prayer of someone in harmony with God's order, reinforced in 5.17-18 by the example of Elijah's powerful prayer.[115]

The entire text is concluded by 5.19-20, which are appropriately stressed, as the final basic point, through the use of the vocative direct address. As already noted, these verses are not typical of a letter close, but can be seen to have been combined with the letter-closing section, playing a role within the whole text analogous to that of the epilogue in Greek speeches, giving a short thematic recapitulation. Throughout the text, the addressees have been urged to show complete commitment to God and dependence upon God, with corresponding loyalty and solidarity to be shown among God's people. This is within a context in

112. For parallels in the synoptic gospel traditions to the forgiveness of sins entailed in divinely brokered healing, see, e.g., Mk 2.1-12.

113. The Epistle of James does not link sin to illness as retribution in a cause and effect relationship, cf. Lk. 13.1-5; this view is most clearly expressed (and repudiated) in the Johannine tradition (e.g. Jn 9.1-3).

114. It is worth noting that the restoration of breaches in interpersonal relationships is also connected to the Markan passage on the effectiveness of faithful prayer (Mk 11.25), and to the teaching on prayer in Mt. 6.12, 14-15//Lk. 11.4; cf. also Mt. 5.23-24.

115. Elijah is described as ὁμοιοπαθὴς ἡμῖν, drawing attention to the hardships which he faced (cf. κακοπαθεία, 5.10; κακοπαθεῖ, 5.13), but in which he remained unwaveringly committed to God. His unshakeable loyalty to God and effective prayer form a strong contrast to the inconstancy of the double-minded person of 1.6-8. Throughout the epistle, the addressees have been exhorted to show this kind of unconditional loyalty towards God; cf. K. Warrington, 'The Significance of Elijah in James 5.13-18', *EvQ* 66 (1994), pp. 217-27; M. Öhler, *Elia im Neuen Testament* (BZNW, 88; Berlin: W. de Gruyter, 1997), pp. 257-66. The suggestion of R.P. Martin, *James*, pp. 200-201, 213, that the author is here attempting to present James, the brother of the Lord, as a second Elijah, in the moderation of nationalist zeal, is highly speculative.

which the author sees the addressees' commitment to God as wavering and questionable, and their lack of solidarity with one another as open to reproach. Thus, 'if anyone among you has strayed from the truth' (ἐάν τις ἐν ὑμῖν πλανηθῇ ἀπὸ τῆς ἀληθείας) is an appropriate designation for the addressees' inconstancy. That they should turn back from their error to full commitment to God has been the author's central concern. The verb 'save' (σώσει, 5.20; cf. 1.21; 2.14; 4.12; 5.15) can be seen to contain the overtone of the ultimate vindication of God's people, and the covering of many sins again depicts the restoration of breached relations.

This final statement is formulated in the third person and is thus of general applicability. It is possible that here the author is making an allusion to what he himself has attempted, that is, to turn back to harmony with God's order those who have strayed. As such, these verses constitute a final, rhetorically subtle appeal to respond positively to the epistle's warnings and exhortations.

6.4.2 *Summary*

Again in this letter-closing section, which creatively adapts typical closing forms for Greek letters, combined with an epilogue-like summary of the basic aim of the text, the fundamental concerns which have characterized the whole text are reinforced. These concerns are, in particular, exhortation to unwavering commitment to God and assurance of God's unfailing loyalty to those who are thus committed to God. Positive confidence in commitment to God in difficult circumstances is urged (cf. 1.2; 1.9; 1.12), stressing the importance of undivided prayer (cf. 1.5-8; 4.1-3). Assurance concerning the restoration of breached relationships is particularly fitting at the end of a text strongly concerned with the addressees' wavering relationship to God and lack of solidarity with God's people.

Likewise, God's status as the supreme and benevolent patron is brought out in these verses. God gives the benefit of healing powers when requested by those loyal to God, and generously grants restoration of breached interpersonal relationships. The ultimate eschatological significance of God's patronage is stressed by the use of the verb 'save' (σῴζω) in both 5.15 and 5.20.

6.5 *Conclusion*

The subsections of the letter examined in this chapter (4.1-10; 4.11–5.11; 5.12-20) represent a shift in tone from the more discursive demonstration of the addressees' shortcomings in Jas 2.1–3.18 to an urgent, eschatologically-motivated appeal to the addressees to submit themselves wholly to God's ultimate order of the universe. Sylistically this reproach and exhortation probably owes more to the literary paradigms of the Jewish scriptures, especially the prophets, than it does to the conventions of Greek rhetoric. Significantly, the key concerns of the author noted in the development of the epistle thus far can also be seen to dominate these final three subsections:

1. Direct exhortation to the addressees to show unwavering commitment to God reaches its bluntest expression in 4.7-10. The sense of endurance in loyalty to God, even in the face of trying circumstances (cf. 1.2-4), is developed in 5.7-11, with the assurance of God's reward for such behaviour. Prayer in faith will bring its due results (5.15-18).

2. This conviction of God's benevolence, as the supreme patron, to those who are faithful in commitment to God also persistantly pervades these sections of the epistle. God gives grace to the humble (4.6), and will exalt those who humble themselves (4.10). God will vindicate those who endure in obedient faithfulness (5.7-11), and will restore those in need of healing, whether physical or relational (5.14-16). On the other hand, the reverse side of God's supreme authority is also depicted starkly in the threat of judgment for those who oppose God (4.4-6; 4.11–5.6).

3. Negative portrayal of the rich as those who oppose God and who flagrantly flout the righteous requirements of God's order reaches a climax in 4.13–5.6. Standing under the threat of destruction, they are clearly not suitable patrons for the addressees. Their presents status faces reversal in the light of the coming of God's eschatological order.

James 4–5, then, can be seen to continue the author's efforts to urge the addressees to show wholehearted commitment to God, especially in accordance with the understanding of God's order proclaimed by Jesus and his movement. The significance of these concerns throughout the whole letter will be reviewed in the next chapter.

Chapter 7

CONCLUSION

7.1 *Introduction*

This concluding chapter serves a number of distinguishable, though closely related, functions. First, it sums up systematically the results of the investigation of the previous chapters. Second, it spells out the consequences of these findings for key questions in relation to the interpretation of the text, which have not, so far, been directly answered. In particular, these are the issues of the identity of the author, the date of composition of the text and the geographical location of the text's context. Third, the chapter offers a brief summary of the epistle's significance within the complex world of Jewish Christianity and the gradual development of Christian identity.

7.2 *Results of the Preceding Investigation*

7.2.1 *The Literary Composition of the Epistle*

Examined from the perspective of its literary composition, the Epistle of James displays unity of structure and a clear thematic development. This can be set out as follows:

1.1	Letter greeting.
1.2–5.11	Letter body:

      1.2-18   Introductory passage, setting the basis for all of what follows: urges unwavering commitment to God, who is the good, unchanging, supreme patron.

      1.19-27   Introduces more specific issues, especially those dealt with in 2.1–3.12.

      2.1-13   Demonstration of deficient attitudes and judgments on the part of the addressees: looking towards the rich as patrons instead of dependence on God; dishonouring of those who show appropriate dependence on God; right attitude is whole obedience to God's order, expressed in the love command.

2.14-26	Demonstration of deficient actions on the part of the addressees: failure to support those radically dependent on God for their needs; claim of commitment to God incompatible with deficient actions.
3.1-12	Demonstration of deficient speech, including the implication of the unworthiness of the addressees to usurp the authority of teachers.
3.13-18	Summary and transitional section: right disposition, in accordance with God's order, is represented by wisdom; contrast with a deficient disposition in disharmony with God's order.
4.1-10	Stark contrast between harmony with God's order and enmity with God's order, culminating in appeal to the addressees to submit completely to God's authority.
4.11–5.11	Series of warnings and exhortations, in the light of the imminent eschaton; further demonstration of the unsuitability of the rich as patrons, and final exhortation to unwavering reliance on God.
5.12-20	Letter close:
5.12	Oath formula, adapted to Christian situation.
5.13-18	Health and prayer wishes, also adapted to the situation.
5.19-20	Short recapitulation of key theme: salvation in returning to God of those who have strayed.

7.2.2 *The Self-Presentation of the Author*

The author depicts himself as 'slave of God and of the Lord Jesus Christ', setting himself under the complete authority of God, and of Jesus, God's specially appointed, vindicated and honoured one. This expression of being under the commission of God implies the invocation of divine authority behind his work, reminiscent of the prophets of Israel's past, who spoke in the name of the Lord. The author also describes himself as a teacher, a role which was closely linked with that of prophets in early Christianity. Teaching, at least sometimes, seems to have involved an itinerant vocation. As a teacher, the author draws on the Jewish religious world-view, under the clear influence of the traditions of the sayings of Jesus and the ethos of the early Christian movement, to admonish and exhort the addressees.

7.2.3 *The Presentation of the Addressees*

The addressees are introduced as 'the twelve tribes in the Diaspora', a figurative depiction, which draws attention to their chosenness, and also to their unity, as the people of God. This designation also reflects the strong sense of expectation of the eschatological restoration of God's people associated with the symbol of the twelve tribes. From the unqualified use of terms drawn from Jewish tradition—including the manner in which the addressees are directly named by the author—it is apparent that the author presupposes their familiarity with the traditions of the Jewish world-view and their acceptance of its authority. From the frequent and likewise unqualified allusion to early Christian tradition, it also seems clear that he presupposes that the addressees are familiar with these traditions, and recognise, at least to some extent, the authority of the interpretation of the Jewish world-view proclaimed by Jesus and perpetuated by those who followed him.

7.2.4 *Tensions between the Author and the Addressees*
Although the author presupposes that the addressees should recognise the authority of his standpoint, it is also apparent that they are persistently reproached for their failure (in the author's view, at any rate) to actualize wholly the implications of this world-view as a way of life. There is a gap between the author's expectations and the addressees' performance of these demands, which the author sees as indicative of wavering, unwholeness and deficient commitment to God.

7.2.5 *The Addressees' Position in Relation to the Early Christian Movement*
Concretely symptomatic of the addressees' shortcomings is their treatment of the radical itinerant members of the early Christian movement, who have been received with dishonour, refused material support and had their authority as teachers called into question. The wavering and divided commitment of the addressees contrasts with the exemplary fulfilment of the call to dependence upon God and obedience to God represented by these socially marginal adherents of the movement. A further contrast is that between the addressees' treatment of these figures and what it should be if their conduct was in correspondence to the demands of God's eschatological order. Another sign of the addressees' lack of commitment to God is their apparently positive attitude to wealthy potential patrons, whose exploitative and oppressive conduct marks them as clearly out of harmony with God's order of the universe.

7.2.6 *The Rhetorical Strategy of the Epistle*
The author seeks to tackle this situation through his letter. The key persuasive themes in this regard include:

- direct exhortation to endurance and unwavering commitment towards God;
- depiction of God as the one, supremely good, unchanging creator, orderer and judge, who is thus the only fitting patron for God's chosen people;
- demonstration of the shortcomings of the addressees' attitudes, actions and speech—that is, in all areas of life;
- sharp reproach for their failures to live in harmony with God's standards;
- appeal to turn to God and submit to God's authority;
- demonstration of the ultimate unsuitability of the rich, who can offer short-term material security, as patrons;
- assertion of the fundamental difference between God's ultimate eschatological world-order, and the present order of the world.

On the basis of these results, the question of the setting of the Epistle of James within the world of early Christianity can now be approached.

7.3 *The Setting of the Epistle of James*

7.3.1 *The Identity of the Author*
It has been established above that:

1. The author of the epistle calls himself 'James' or 'Jacob' ('Ιάκωβος).
2. He describes himself as 'slave of God and of the Lord Jesus Christ', a self-designation which implies his absolute recognition of God's, and Jesus', authority.
3. He also describes himself as a teacher, an authoritative role within early Christianity, which at times was associated with an itinerant ministry.
4. He affirms the honourable standing of the radical itinerant followers of Jesus.
5. It is of concern to him that those who have shown at least obvious sympathies towards the emergent Christian movement should be (or remain) clearcut and wholehearted in their dependence upon God and their commitment to God, in accordance with the early Christian interpretation of the Jewish view of the world.

6.   He composes stylistically good quality and rhetorically effective Greek, and adapts the letter-form to his exhortations.

The question now arises: does this information fit what we know of any particular person called James/Jacob ('Ιάκωβος) within the early Christian movement? James, son of Zebedee, one of the twelve, would have been associated with the radical itinerant followers of Jesus, but his death (Acts 12.2) during the reign of Agrippa 1 (41–44 CE) would seem to rule him out as a possible author. Of James, father of Judas (Lk. 6.16; Acts 1.13) nothing further is known. James, son of Alphaeus, was also one of the twelve, but nothing further reliable is known of him. The James who is best known to us, however, and who played the most important role within early Christianity, is James, the brother of the Lord, leader of the group in Jerusalem.[1] The possibility that the epistle was composed by another James, whose precise identity is unknown to later scholarship, but was known to the addressees of the text, cannot be ruled out, but in view of his importance James, the brother of the Lord, must be considered the most likely possible author of the text. Thus, the basic issue is whether the text should be attributed to his personal authorship, or should be seen as a pseudepigraphon, drawing upon his authority.

Although none of the main sources—Acts, Galatians, Josephus and Eusebius—can be described as objective by modern standards of historiography, the picture we have of this James from these texts is reasonably consistent.

1.   He lived in Jerusalem, and was probably the most important leader of the group of early Christians there, until his death under the high priest Ananus in 62 CE.
2.   He remained a law-observing Jew, who recognized Jesus as messiah; his piety was respected even by non-Christian Jews.
3.   Like his brother, he most likely spoke Aramaic (cf. Mk 5.41) as his everyday language.
4.   On the question of the admission of Gentiles to the movement, he seems to have taken a moderating position, according to both Paul and Acts (Gal. 2.9; Acts 15.13-21).
5.   It should also be noted that James was regarded with great honour in strands of Christianity which later came to be

---

1.   See above, §1.2.

regarded as heterodox, in particular, those more conservatively Jewish strands which rejected the authority of Paul's teaching. Thus, James was the primary witness to the resurrection in the *Gospel of the Hebrews*,[2] and the one 'for whose sake heaven and earth came into being' according to *Gospel of Thomas* 12.2.

The next step in examining the possibility that this James was the author of the epistle is to compare the findings with regard to the self-identification of the epistle's author, listed above, with what is reliably known of James, the brother of the Lord, also listed above.

1. Little inference can be drawn from the first two points noted in relation to the author's self-identification: the use of the name James ('Ιακωβός) and his acknowledgment of the supreme authority of God and of Jesus. Both of these are compatible with James, the brother of the Lord, but certainly not distinctive to him.

2. James, the brother of the Lord, is nowhere described as a teacher (διδάσκαλος), and his leadership role in Jerusalem seems to have entailed a greater degree of authority than that implied by this role.[3] This, however, is also inconclusive, as it does not preclude James from referring to himself using this term.

3. James, the brother of the Lord, does not seem to have been a member of the radical itinerant followers of Jesus during the latter's lifetime (cf. Mk 3.32-35; 6.3), and, although Eusebius describes him as an ascetic,[4] he is never clearly associated with those who perpetuated Jesus' radical ministry. He is consistently depicted as resident in Jerusalem; 'certain people from James' (τινες ἀπὸ 'Ιακώβου, Gal. 2.12) cannot be seen as evidence that he sponsored itinerant missionaries, nor does 1 Cor. 9.2 indicate that he himself was one. Nevertheless, in

---

2. Quoted by Jerome, *De vir. ill.* 2. This gospel was the one used by the Ebionites, according to Eusebius, *Eccl. Hist.* 3.25.5; 3.27.4. The role of James in the *Pseudo-Clementine Homilies* and *Recognitions* should also be noted in the context of his importance for non-Pauline Jewish Christianity.

3. On the role of the διδάσκαλος within the early Christian movement, see above, §3.2.2.

4. Eusebius, *Hist. Eccl.* 2.23.

view of his own ascetic lifestyle, and his probable understanding of the early Christian movement as God's eschatological restoration of the people of Israel, suggested by his strong affirmation of emergent Christianity's Jewish heritage, it is not unlikely that he would have been sympathetically disposed towards the radical itinerants of the early Christian movement.

4. The concern of the epistle's author for the continuation and consolidation of the commitment of those wavering in their adherence to the early Christian movement is one which James would hardly have contradicted, but he certainly would not have been alone in this respect.

5. While not in any way disparaging his abilities—it is quite likely that he did know *some* Greek in view of the widespread use of Greek in Palestine—it remains unlikely that an Aramaic-speaking Galilean, even at the end of his life, would have composed such fluent and rhetorically polished Greek, even allowing for the indications of Semitic influences in the text.[5]

6. The positive use of terms like 'law' (νόμος) by the author of the epistle, although under a strongly Christian perspective, also does not influence considerations very much. James, the brother of the Lord, certainly retained a positive understanding of the status of God's law, but evidence on the decisive issues is lacking. On the one hand, it is not clear if he would have subscribed to the encapsulation of the whole law in the love command, as represented by the epistle. On the other hand, the views of the author of the epistle on the ongoing validity of such stipulations as those to do with clean and unclean foods, or on the admission of Gentiles to the movement (concerning which we have some idea of the stance of James) are simply not mentioned.

7. While later strands of Christianity which rejected the teachings of Paul appealed to the figure of James, the brother of the Lord, as their hero, this does not help much in resolving the question of the authorship of the epistle. As the Lutheran

5. In this regard, however, the hypothesis that James was assisted by a 'secretary' who was more fluent in Greek cannot be ruled out, although this suggestion is somewhat unsatisfactory, being neither falsifiable nor verifiable.

(mis)understanding of the text has shown, it can indeed be read as an anti-Pauline text in parts; this does not mean that it was composed as a deliberately anti-Pauline text. Certainly the epistle's perspective is non-Pauline, but, as was indicated above,[6] it can be understood more satisfactorily as independent of Paul, than as anti-Pauline. Likewise, although James probably did not agree with Paul on all points, there is no evidence that he fundamentally opposed him.[7]

Unfortunately, none of these considerations offers conclusive evidence for or against the authorship of the epistle by James, the brother of the Lord. The fine quality of the epistle's Greek would seem to suggest that authorship by James is the less likely option; the fact that the concerns of the epistle do not coincide with any of the issues associated elsewhere with this James may also point in this direction. To these reservations can be added a number of reasons why he would have been an appropriate figure to whom to attribute the text pseudepigraphically, conceivably a short while after his death. First, he was an acknowledged leader in the early Christian movement, whose name thus carried significant authority. Second, if the text is addressed to wavering Jewish Christians, whom the author had expected to be 'sympathizers' towards the radical itinerants of the early movement, James' adherence to Jewish customs, and the respect in which he was held even by non-Christian Jews, would make him a particularly convincing authority to whom to appeal in this context.

Thus, it seems somwhat better to consider the epistle a pseude-pigraphical composition, appealing to the authority of James, the brother of the Lord. It must be conceded that none of the above considerations offers conclusive evidence that James could not have written the text which bears his name; it is the less probable option, but certainly not impossible by any means. What is more important for the interpretation of the epistle is not that this identity-issue can be answered with certainty, but that due attention is paid to the role and

6. See above, §5.2.3 nn. 56, 58.

7. See above, §1.5.1, on the rejection of Hengel's arguments. James's stance in relation to certain aspects of the relationship between emergent Christianity and contemporary Judaism may have lent itself to his being hailed later as the champion of those who maintained a more conservative view on such issues, but he himself seems to have attempted to avoid the kind of deep divisions which eventually led to 'Jewish Christianity' being regarded as heretical.

self-identification of the author implied within the text.

Can anything further be said about the presumed pseudepigraphical author of the text? He shows sympathy for the itinerants who continued Jesus' radical lifestyle and proclamation and calls himself a teacher, a role sometimes associated with such radicalism within early Christianity. He advocates radical dependence upon God, subordinates himself entirely to God's authority as 'slave', and utilizes a text-form which already had some links with prophetic exhortation. Does this suggest that the author should be seen as one of the itinerant early Christian teachers? This is not unlikely, but it is also possible that he was not an itinerant, as teachers do not seem always to have been itinerants.[8] Nevertheless, he certainly affirms the radical strand within the early Christian movement, although the fact that the main concern of the text is with the continued commitment of the addressees, rather than with directly defending the rights of the itinerants may suggest that the importance of these socially marginal figures is already on the wane. It also seems likely that he already knew the addressees, at least to some degree. Some familiarity with them and their situation explains his ability to make assumptions about them, for instance, the expectation that they will recognize allusions to the sayings of Jesus, and will acknowledge the authority of these sayings.

A further, although somewhat speculative, suggestion about the author's identity can be made. He writes good quality Greek, which suggests some degree of education, which in turn suggests that his background was not among the lowest social levels. He, however, unambiguously affirms the Jesus movement's proclamation of God's honouring of the socially marginal poor (πτωχοί) and the lowly (ταπεινοί), and displays marked hostility to the wealthy and powerful of this world. In view of the finely balanced and precariously competitive nature of society in this period, it is not implausible to suggest that the author was one who, in this context, had lost social standing, conceivably including his material security. This would explain the fine quality of the language, the hostility, based on personal experience of their exploitation, towards the rich, and the attraction towards the Jesus movement, which announced God's favour towards those who have lost their social position, and promised eschatological reversal when the first in this world's order shall be last and the last first.

---

8. See above, §2.2.2.

7.3.2 *The Location of the Epistle*

If the sphere of reference of the Epistle of James is wavering 'sympathizers' towards the itinerant radicals of the Jesus movement, then the text must be located within the area of their activity. Thus, it is essentially the region of Syria-Palestine which comes into question, but it is difficult to narrow the possible setting of the text to a more precise geographical location. Obviously, the author and addressees need not necessarily be located in the same place; as the author's concerns were formulated in letter form, it seems likely that he was spatially separated from the addressees.

The link with the name of James might suggest Jerusalem as the place of origin of the text. The address to the twelve tribes in the Diaspora, whose focal point of symbolic identification was Jerusalem, might also support this suggestion. Both the claim to the authority of the figure of James, however, and the consequently fitting link with the symbolic centre of the holy city can be attributed to the pseudepigraphical author, and does not mean that he actually resided in Jerusalem, or that he should be linked with the early Christian group there. A precise identification of the place of origin of the text does not seem to be possible.

As the text is composed in Greek, it appears that the addressees should be sought among the Greek-speaking, though, of course, not necessarily monolingual, Jewish population of Syria-Palestine. There is evidence for relatively widespread acquaintance with Greek;[9] thus, this consideration does not help much in geographically locating the addressees. Anywhere in the region of activity of the itinerant followers of Jesus is possible; it is also possible that more than one group may have been intended as the recipients of the text, although the opening address to the twelve tribes in the Diaspora functions principally as a figurative literary rhetorical device, rather than as an indication of the literal, geographical destination of the text.

The indications of the socio-economic background against which the

---

9. See, e.g., J.N. Sevenster, *Do You Know Greek? How Much Greek Could the First Jewish Christians Have Known?* (NovTSup, 19; Leiden: E.J. Brill, 1968); G. Mussies, 'Greek in Palestine and the Diaspora', *CRINT* 1.2, pp. 1040-64. S.E. Porter, 'Did Jesus ever Teach in Greek?', *TynBul* 44 (1993), pp. 200-35, argues that Jesus himself knew and used Greek, but to an unknown extent; nevertheless, he believes that such utterances as Mk 15.2 and Mt. 16.17-19 may well be original sayings of Jesus in Greek.

text is set, especially in the depiction of the rich in 4.13–5.6, support a Palestinian location. In 5.4, the rich are accused of withholding the wages of the labourers who harvested their estates. Large estates already existed in Palestine well before the first century CE;[10] the area of land under the control of such large holders would have been increased considerably by the confiscations and resettlements of Herod.[11] Applebaum notes the presence of both isolated individual farms and nucleated villages associated with large estates in the foothills and mountain country of Judaea and Samaria in the early Roman period;[12] Freyne sees peasant ownership of small holdings of land as the dominant form of land possession in Galilee, alongside large estates, worked by tenants, share-croppers and day-labourers.[13] This mixed pattern of land ownership, with both large estates, apparently increasing in number during the Hellenistic and Roman period, and small individual holdings may be reflected in the contrast between the exploitative rich landowners in 5.1-6 and the farmer, who is commended by the author in 5.7.[14]

As well as estate-owners in 5.1-6, large-scale merchants come in for censure in 4.13-17. This kind of trade was dominated by the Mediterranean ports;[15] a considerable amount of commerce was centred on Jerusalem, due to the city's religious and political importance, although not part of a major trade route.[16] A number of major routes did

10. Cf. Applebaum, 'Economic Life', pp. 633-36; on Galilee in particular, cf. also M. Hengel, 'Das Gleichnis von den bösen Weingärtnern (Mc 12.1-12) im Lichte der Zenonpapyri und der rabbinischen Gleichnisse', *ZNW* 59 (1968), pp. 1-39.

11. See Josephus, *Ant.* 17.305, 307. Cf. Applebaum, 'Economic Life', pp. 643, 657-58; Oakman, *Economic Questions*, pp. 47-48; S. Freyne, *Galilee from Alexander the Great to Hadrian* (Wilmington, DE: Michael Glazier, 1980), pp. 163-65.

12. Applebaum, 'Economic Life', pp. 641-44.

13. Freyne, *Galilee from Alexander*, pp. 156-70; cf. also *idem, Galilee, Jesus and the Gospels: Literary Approaches and Historical Investigations* (Dublin: Gill & Macmillan, 1988), pp. 159, 161; *idem*, 'Hellenistic/Roman Galilee', *ABD*, II, pp. 895-99; A.N. Sherwin-White, *Roman Society and Roman Law in the New Testament* (Oxford: Clarendon Press, 1963), pp. 139-42.

14. Freyne, *Galilee, Jesus and the Gospels*, p. 157, notes the inevitable conflict in norms and values between the older socioeconomic system (represented by peasant land holding and production) and the newer socioeconomic developments, particularly under the Herods.

15. See Applebaum, 'Economic Life', pp. 667-69, 679-80.

16. See Jeremias, *Jerusalem*, pp. 51-57.

pass through Palestine, particularly through Galilee, which lay in the hinterland of the coastal cities of Ptolemais and Tyre, on the east–west route from these ports.[17] The coincidence of merchants (4.13-17) and those who control large estates (5.1-6) in this region may suggest it as a likely location for the epistle. The fact that Galilee was an important grain-growing area is compatible with the description of the work of the day-labourers in 5.4 as harvesters.[18] The close links between the Epistle of James and the traditions of the sayings of Jesus may also point to Galilee as a plausible location.[19] While this can be proposed as a likely setting, it cannot, however, be established conclusively.

7.3.3 *The Date of Composition of the Epistle*
Several considerations favour seeing the text as having originated prior to the outbreak of the Jewish war in 66 CE. First, the most significant activity of the early Christian itinerant teachers in Palestine is to be located during this period. The treatment of these figures suggested by the epistle points towards a later, rather than an earlier date within this period. The dishonourable reception, refusal of material support and restriction of their authority indicate a time when the role and status of the socially marginal itinerant teachers within early Christianity was already in decline, while the local groups which had previously supported them and accepted their authoritative role were emerging with a strong enough identity to be able to dispense with the itinerants, appropriating their authority to within their own local group.[20]

17. See Freyne, 'Hellenistic/Roman Galilee', p. 897; *idem, Galilee, Jesus and the Gospels*, p. 156.
18. See Applebaum, 'Economic Life', pp. 646-47; Freyne, *Galilee, Jesus and the Gospels*, p. 160; *idem, Galilee from Alexander*, pp. 171-72.
19. This was Elliott-Binns' reason for situating the epistle in Galilee (*Galilean Christianity*, pp. 45-49). The Galilean context of the traditions of the sayings of Jesus is discussed by Freyne, *Galilee from Alexander*, pp. 374-77. J.S. Kloppenborg, 'Literary Convention, Self-evidence and the Social History of the Q People', *Semeia* 55 (1992), pp. 77-102, argues that those behind the Q collection of the sayings of Jesus (which he sees as a written text, with several redactional layers) can best be located in a region such as Galilee, among 'the lower administrative and scribal sectors' (p. 87), which, like the peasants, were adversely affected by social and economic difficulties. He suggests (p. 89) that in this context the itinerancy of the early movement may have been confined to a network of villages within a quite small geographical area.
20. The fact that tensions between the itinerant radicals and settled early

Second, the hostility of the author to the exploitative rich fits well with Josephus' accounts of oppression and self-advancement under Roman government in Palestine in the years prior to the war.[21] Josephus raises the charge that the procurator Albinus (62–64 CE) 'in his official capacity [stole] and plunder[ed] private property and burden[ed] the whole nation with extraordinary taxes'.[22] The accusation against Gessius Florus (64–66 CE) is even stronger:

> The crimes of Albinus were, for the most part, perpetrated in secret and with dissimulation; Gessius, on the contrary, ostentatiously paraded his outrages upon the nation, and, as though he had been sent as hangman of condemned criminals, abstained from no form of robbery or violence... To make gain out of individuals seemed beneath him: he stripped whole cities, ruined entire populations, and almost went the length of proclaiming throughout the country that all were at liberty to practise brigandage, on condition that he received his share of the spoils.[23]

This exploitation was scarcely an innovation on the part of these two procurators,[24] although matters at this stage reached the crisis-point which exploded in the Jewish war in 66 CE; similar charges are made by Josephus against the Herodian rulers in the course of his writings.[25] Such exploitation, of course, was not simply the work of the individual rulers; it was practised by their subordinates and collaborators, both Jewish and Roman,[26] in the struggle to maintain and enhance their

Christian 'sympathiser'-groups are treated by the author as symptomatic of the key issue of the addressees' wavering loyalty to God, rather than itself constituting the disease to be remedied, suggests that, even for an author relatively sympathetic to their cause, the local group is the more important focus of attention. That prayer for healing, a role associated with the radical itinerants (Mt. 10.8//Mk 6.13//Lk. 9.2; 10.9) is urged within the local group also appears to indicate their decline in influence, perhaps suggesting a numerical decline as well, which would necessitate prayer by emergent local leaders in such circumstances.

21. See, for example, Josephus' accounts of the last two procurators before the war, Lucceius Albinus and Gessius Florus, in *War* 2.272-79; *Ant.* 20.254-55.

22. Josephus, *War* 2.273.

23. Josephus, *War* 2.277-78.

24. See, for example, Josephus' remark about the misdeeds of Felix (52–60 CE) in *Ant.* 20.182; cf. Tacitus, *Hist.* 5.9.

25. See, e.g., Josephus, *Ant.* 17.305-308; *War* 2.85-86 (against Herod the Great); *Ant.* 20.212 (against Agrippa II); cf. *War* 2.218; *Ant.* 19.352, on the extravagance of Agrippa I.

26. The Herods were, of course, both a Jewish family and Roman rulers; on corruption among the priestly aristocracy in Jerusalem, who were also allies of the

positions in relation to one another. The widespread activities of the brigands during the decades prior to the war[27] can be seen, at least in part, as a reaction against the consequences of this situation among sections of the oppressed populace.

Third, not only is this general situation compatible with the concerns of the Epistle of James, this background may also provide a clue as to the relationship between those addressed by the author of the epistle and well-to-do patrons against whom the author warns them. It is generally held that Jesus and the movement which followed him were opposed to active perpetrations of hostility against the Romans.[28] In the period of heightened tension between significant sections of the population and those who controlled and, as noted, often exploited them, in the years just before the outbreak of the war, it would not be unreasonable for a well-to-do person, whether a Roman or a pro-Roman Jew, to look for secure support and pacific clients among the adherents of a group which did not appear to be explicitly hostile to them.

These considerations do not prove conclusively that the epistle was written during this time; they do, however, provide a plausible socio-historical background against which the text's concerns make sense. If the epistle is a pseudepigraphical work, drawing on the name of James, the brother of the Lord, who was killed in 62 CE, then the years just after his death, when his repute as a recent martyr was probably at a high point, would have been an ideal time to compose a text appealing to the authority of his name. Thus, it seems likely that the epistle was written between the death of James in Jerusalem and the outbreak of the Jewish War, that is, during the years 62–66 CE.

7.4 *The Epistle of James in the Setting of Jewish Christianity*

Some comments on the issue of continuity between emergent Christianity and wider contemporary Judaism are also appropriate. The Epistle of James represents a deeply rooted Jewish view of the world,

Romans, see Josephus, *Ant.* 20.180-81, 205-208.

27. E.g. Josephus, *Ant.* 20.124, 164-65; *War* 2.264-65.

28. See, e.g., L. Schottroff, 'Gewaltverzicht und Feindesliebe in der urchristlichen Jesustradition', in *idem, Befreiungserfahrungen: Studien zur Sozialgeschichte des Neuen Testaments* (Munich: Kaiser Verlag, 1990), pp. 12-35; G. Theissen, 'Nonviolence and Love of our Enemies', in *idem, Social Reality*, pp. 115-56.

decisively influenced by its early Christian perspective. Yet there is no indication of hostility between the Jewish Christians of the epistle and other Jews. The epistle shows the development of self-identity within the movement, but not the self-identification of the movement over against other rival groups, such as is found particularly in Matthew and in John. The roots of such tensions can certainly be seen, for instance, in the address to the twelve tribes, which suggests an understanding of the early Christian movement as the restored Israel. The crisis for identity, which could be ignited by such claims and their eventual rejection by others, is not yet visible in the relation of the Epistle of James to the Jewish heritage of emergent Christianity. By the time of writing of Matthew's Gospel, issues which were still open for the author/addressees of the Epistle of James have become battle lines.

This raises the issue of the relation of the Epistle of James to other early Christian writings, especially the synoptic gospels. The striking contacts between the epistle and, in particular, the traditions of the sayings of Jesus were set out in the appendix to Chapter 2, above. This proximity to the synoptic gospel traditions has had profound significance in the interpretation of the epistle and its setting developed in this work. On many issues, the epistle shows a very similar perspective to that in the sayings of Jesus. This is often backed up by resonances of those sayings in the text of the epistle. As such, the Epistle of James surely offers a unique insight into the vitality and authority of these traditions within the early Christian movement, at a stage in their development and transmission prior to the framing of the traditions in a fixed written form.

The findings of this work on a text which stands so close to the traditions of the sayings of Jesus would thus seem to be of particular importance in relation to Q, notwithstanding the difficulties involved in attempting to trace the precise trajectories of this relationship. Indeed, it is perhaps precisely because of these difficulties that the insights gleaned in relation to the Epistle of James could be of importance in the study of Q. In view of the variety of reconstructions of Q, and the accompanying theories of its composition, its purpose, its setting and its theological stance, comparison of these views with the findings on the Epistle of James could be very worthwhile. For instance—although here there is only room to pose the question—what sort of implications for our understanding of the circles which preserved the sayings of Jesus does the combination of sapiential and apocalyptic elements in the presentation of Jesus in the epistle, as noted above, have for debates on the presence and relation to each other of sapiential and apocalyptic elements in Q?

7.5 *Conclusion*

This work has examined the question of the setting of the Epistle of James from a perspective which is particularly informed by the view of a text as instance of meaningful communication between author/sender and readers/hearers/recipients, within a particular cultural and situational context. The application of this perspective has shown that the epistle can be seen as a coherent and finely crafted composition, urging those wavering in their loyalty to the emergent Christian movement to show wholehearted commitment to God, and to the understanding of God's order of the universe proclaimed by Jesus and the movement which followed him. Typical aspects of the text's social environment, such as the significant role played by patron–client relationships, provide important images in the expression of this message. The exploration of dimensions such as these has allowed new insights to be opened up on the setting and purpose of the text. As such, the epistle's unique contribution to our understanding of the emergence and development of early Christian thought and identity within its sociohistorical context is particularly important and worthy of far more attention than has usually been the case.

BIBLIOGRAPHY

Adamson, J.B., *The Epistle of James* (NICNT; Grand Rapids: Eerdmanns, 1976).

Ahrens, M., *Der Realitäten Widerschein: Reich und Arm im Jakobusbrief* (Berlin: Alektor Verlag, 1995).

Allison, D.C., Jr, 'Mark 12.28-31 and the Decalogue', in Evans and Stegner (eds.), *The Gospels and the Scriptures of Israel*, pp. 270-78.

Alonso Schökel, L., 'James 5.6 and 4.6', *Bib* 54 (1973), pp. 73-76.

Amstutz, J., *ΑΠΛΟΤΗΣ: Eine begriffsgeschichtliche Studie zum jüdisch-christlichen Griechisch* (Bonn: Peter Hamstein Verlag, 1968).

Applebaum, S., 'Economic Life in Palestine', *CRINT* 1.2, pp. 631-700.

Aune, D.E., *Prophecy in Early Christianity and the Ancient Mediterranean World* (Grand Rapids: Eerdmans, 1983).

Baasland, E., 'Der Jakobusbrief als neutestamentliche Weisheitsschrift', *ST* 36 (1982), pp. 119-39.

—'Literarische Form, Thematik und geschichtliche Einordnung des Jakobusbriefes', *ANRW* 2.25.5, pp. 3646-86.

Baker, W.R., ' "Above All Else": Contexts of the Call for Verbal Integrity in James 5.12', *JSNT* 54 (1994), pp. 57-71.

—*Personal Speech-Ethics in the Epistle of James* (WUNT NS, 68; Tübingen: J.C.B. Mohr [Paul Siebeck], 1995).

Balch, D.L., E. Ferguson and W.A. Meeks (eds.), *Greeks, Romans and Christians* (Minneapolis: Fortress Press, 1990).

Bammel, E., 'πτωχός', *TDNT*, VI, pp. 888-915.

Batten, A., 'More Queries for Q: Women and Christian Origins', *BTB* 24 (1994), pp. 44-51.

Bauckham, R., 'The Old Testament in the New Testament: James, 1 and 2 Peter, Jude', in Carson and Williamson (eds.), *It Is Written*, pp. 303-317.

Berger, K., *Die Gesetzesauslegung Jesu: Ihr historischer Hintergrund im Judentum und im Alten Testament* (WMANT 40; Neukirchen–Vluyn: Neukirchener Verlag, 1972).

—'Apostelbrief und apostolische Rede: Zum Formular frühchristlicher Briefe', *ZNW* 65 (1974), pp. 190-231.

—'Die implizite Gegner: Zur Methode des Erschliessens von "Gegnern" in neutestamentlichen Texten', in Lührmann and Strecker (eds.), *Kirche*, pp. 373-400.

—*Exegese des Neuen Testaments* (Heidelberg: Quelle & Meyer, 1984).

—'Hellenistische Gattungen im Neuen Testament', *ANRW* 2.25.2, pp. 1031-1378.

—*Theologiegeschichte des Urchristentums* (Tübingen: Francke Verlag, 1994).

Berger, P., *The Social Reality of Religion* (London: Faber & Faber, 1969).

Berger, P., and T. Luckmann, *The Social Construction of Reality* (Garden City, NY: Doubleday, 1967).

Betz, O., and G. Hawthorne (eds.), *Tradition and Interpretation in the New Testament* (Festschrift E. Earle Ellis; Grand Rapids: Eerdmanns, 1987).

Beyer, H.W., 'βλασφημέω', *TDNT* I, pp. 621-25.

Blinzer, J., O. Kuss and F. Mussner (eds.), *Neutestamentliche Aufsätze* (Festschrift J. Schmid; Regensburg: Pustet Verlag, 1963).

Blondel, J.-L., 'Le fondement théologique de la parénèse dans l'épître de Jacques', *RTP* 111 (1979), pp. 141-52.

Blum, E., C. Macholz, and E. Stegemann (eds.), *Die hebräische Bibel und ihre zweifache Nachgeschichte* (Festschrift Rolf Rendtorff; Neukirchen–Vluyn: Neukirchener Verlag, 1990).

Boccaccini, G., *Middle Judaism: Jewish Thought 300 BCE–200 CE* (Minneapolis: Augsburg/Fortress Press, 1991).

Boring, M.E., *Sayings of the Risen Jesus* (SNTSMS, 46; Cambridge: Cambridge University Press, 1982).

Boyle, M.O., 'The Stoic Paradox of James 2.10', *NTS* 31 (1985), pp. 611-17.

Brachel, H.U. von, and N. Mette (eds.), *Kommunikation und Solidarität* (Freiburg: Edition Exodus, 1985).

Braumann, G., 'Der theologische Hintergrund des Jakobusbriefes', *TZ* 18 (1962), pp. 401-10.

Breytenbach, C., and H. Paulsen (eds.), *Anfänge der Christologie* (Festschrift Ferdinand Hahn; Göttingen: Vandenhoeck & Ruprecht, 1991).

Bultmann, R., *Glauben und Verstehen*, I (Tübingen: J.C.B. Mohr [Paul Siebeck], 1958).

—'Die Bedeutung des geschichtlichen Jesus für die Theologie des Paulus', in Bultmann, *Glauben und Verstehen*, I, pp. 188-213.

Burchard, C., 'Zu Jakobus 2.14-26', *ZNW* 71 (1980), pp. 27-45.

—'Gemeinde in der strohernen Epistel: Mutmassungen über Jakobus', in Lührmann and Strecker (eds.), *Kirche*, pp. 315-28.

—'Nächstenliebegebot, Dekalog und Gesetz in Jak 2.8-11', in Blum, Macholz and Stegemann (eds.), *Die hebräische Bibel*, pp. 517-33.

—'Zu einigen christologischen Stellen des Jakobusbriefes', in Breytenbach and Paulsen (eds.), *Anfänge der Christologie*, pp. 353-68.

Byrskog, S., *Jesus the Only Teacher: Didactic Authority and Transmission in Ancient Israel, Ancient Judaism and the Matthean Community* (ConBNT, 24; Stockholm: Almqvist & Wiksell, 1994).

Cargal, T.B., *Restoring the Diaspora: Discourse Structure and Purpose in the Epistle of James* (SBLDS, 144; Atlanta, GA: Scholars Press, 1993).

Carson, D.A., and H.G.M. Williamson (eds.), *It Is Written: Scripture Citing Scripture* (Festschrift Barnabas Lindars; Cambridge: Cambridge University Press, 1988).

Chaine, J., *L'Epître de Saint Jacques* (Paris: Libraire Lecoffre, 1927).

Charlesworth, J.H. (ed.), *The Messiah: Developments in Earliest Judaism and Christianity* (Minneapolis: Fortress Press, 1992).

—'From Messianology to Christology: Problems and Prospects', in Charlesworth, *Messiah*, pp. 3-35.

Classen, C.J., 'St. Paul's Epistles and Ancient Greek and Roman Rhetoric', in Porter and Olbricht (eds.), *Rhetoric in the New Testament*, pp. 264-91.

Daube, D., and W.D. Davies (eds.), *The Background of the New Testament and its Eschatology* (Festschrift C.H. Dodd; Cambridge: Cambridge University Press, 1956).

Dautzenberg, G., 'Ist das Schwurverbot Mt 5.33-37; Jak 5.12 ein Beispiel für die Torakritik Jesu?', *BZ* 25 (1981), pp. 47-66.

Davids, P.H., 'The Meaning of ἀπείραστος in Jas 1.13', *NTS* 24 (1978), pp. 386-92.

—*The Epistle of James: A Commentary on the Greek Text* (NIGTC; Exeter: Paternoster Press, 1982).

—'Jesus and James', in Wenham (ed.), *The Jesus Tradition*, pp. 63-84.

—'The Epistle of James in Modern Discussion', *ANRW* 2.25.5, pp. 3621-45.

Davies, W.D., *Paul and Rabbinic Judaism* (London: SPCK, 1955).

—*The Setting of the Sermon on the Mount* (Cambridge: Cambridge University Press, 1964).

Delling, G., 'ἀπαρχή', *TDNT*, I, pp. 484-86.

—'τέλειος', *TDNT*, VIII, pp. 67-78.

Dibelius, M., *James* (rev. H. Greeven; trans. M.A. Williams; Hermeneia; Philadelphia: Fortress Press, 11th edn, 1975).

Donker, C.E., 'Der Verfasser des Jakobusbriefes und sein Gegner: Zur Probleme des Einwandes in Jak 2.18-19', *ZNW* 72 (1981), pp. 227-40.

Doty, W.G., *Letters in Primitive Christianity* (Philadelphia: Fortress Press, 1973).

Draper, J.A., 'Social Ambiguity and the Production of Text: Prophets, Teachers, Bishops and Deacons and the Development of the Jesus Tradition in the Community of the *Didache*', in Jefford (ed.), *Didache in Context*, pp. 284-312.

Dungan, D.L., *The Sayings of Jesus in the Churches of Paul* (Oxford: Basil Blackwell, 1971).

Easton, B.S., 'James', *IB*, XII, pp. 3-74.

Eckart, K.-G., 'Zur Terminologie des Jakobusbriefes', *TLZ* 89 (1964), cols. 521-26.

Edwards, R.B., 'Which Is the Best Commentary? The Epistle of James', *ExpTim* 103 (1992), pp. 263-68.

Elliott, J.H., 'Social-Scientific Criticism of the New Testament: More on Methods and Models,' *Semeia* 35 (1986), pp. 1-33.

—'The Epistle of James in Rhetorical and Social-Scientific Perspective: Holiness-Wholeness and Patterns of Replication', *BTB* 23 (1993), pp. 71-81.

—*What Is Social-Scientific Criticism?* (Minneapolis: Fortress Press, 1993).

—'Patronage and Clientage', in Rohrbaugh, *Social Sciences*, pp. 144-56.

Elliott-Binns, L.E., *Galilean Christianity* (SBT, 16; London: SCM Press, 1956).

—'James 1.18: Creation or Redemption?', *NTS* 3 (1958), pp. 148-61.

Ernst, J., R. Schnackenburg and J. Wanke (eds.), *Die Kirche des Anfangs* (Festschrift H. Schürmann; Freiburg: Herder, 1978).

Esler, P.F. (ed.), *Modelling Early Christianity: Social-Scientific Studies of the New Testament in its Context* (London: Routledge, 1995).

Evans, C.A., and W.R. Stegner (eds.), *The Gospels and the Scriptures of Israel* (JSNTSup, 104; Sheffield: Sheffield Academic Press, 1994).

Exler, F.X.J., *The Form of the Ancient Greek Letter: A Study in Greek Epistolography* (Washington: Catholic University of America, 1923).

Feuillet, A., 'Le sens du mot parusie dans l'Evangile de Matthieu', in Daube and Davies (eds.), *Background of the New Testament*, pp. 261-80.

Filson, F.V., 'The Christian Teacher in the First Century', *JBL* 60 (1941), pp. 317-28.

Fornberg, T. and D. Hellholm (eds.), *Texts and Contexts: Biblical Texts in their Textual and Situational Contexts* (Festschrift Lars Hartmann; Oslo: Scandinavian University Press, 1995).

Francis, F.O., 'The Form and Function of the Opening and Closing Paragraphs of James and 1 John', *ZNW* 61 (1970), pp. 110-26.

Frankemölle, H., 'Gespalten oder ganz?', in Brachel and Mette (eds.), *Kommunikation und Solidarität*, pp. 160-78.

—'Gesetz im Jakobusbrief', in Kertelge (ed.), *Das Gesetz im Neuen Testament*, pp. 175-221.

—'Zum Thema des Jakobusbriefes im Kontext der Rezeption von Sir 2.1-18 und 15.11-20', *BN* 48 (1989), pp. 21-49.

—*Der Brief des Jakobus* (Ökumenischer Taschenbuch Kommentar zum Neuen Testament, 17; Gütersloh: Gütersloher Verlagshaus, 1994).

Freyne, S., *The Twelve: Disciples and Apostles* (London: Sheed & Ward, 1968).

—*Galilee from Alexander the Great to Hadrian* (Wilmington, DE: Michael Glazier, 1980).

—'Vilifying the Other and Defining the Self: Matthew's and John's Anti-Judaism in Focus', in Neusner and Frerichs (eds.), *To See Ourselves*, pp. 117-44.

—*Galilee, Jesus and the Gospels: Literary Approaches and Historical Investigations* (Dublin: Gill & Macmillan, 1988).

—'Hellenistic/Roman Galilee', *ABD*, II, pp. 895-99.

Friedrich, G., 'προφήτης', *TDNT*, VI, pp. 781-861.

Furnish, V.P., *The Love Command in the New Testament* (London: SCM Press, 1973).

Garnsey, P., *Famine and Food Supply in the Graeco-Roman World* (Cambridge: Cambridge University Press, 1988).

Garnsey, P., and G. Woolf, 'Patronage of the Rural Poor in the Roman World', in Wallace-Hadrill (ed.), *Patronage*, pp. 153-70.

Gemünden, P. von, *Vegetationsmetaphorik im Neuen Testament und seiner Umwelt* (NTOA, 18; Göttingen: Vandenhoeck & Ruprecht, 1993).

Gerhardsson, B., *Memory and Manuscript: Oral Tradition and Written Transmission in Rabbinic Judaism and Early Christianity* (Uppsala: C.W.K. Gleerup, 1961).

Geyser, A.S., 'The Letter of James and the Social Condition of his Addressees', *Neot* 9 (1975), pp. 25-33.

Gordon, R.P., 'καὶ τὸ τέλος κυρίου εἴδετε (Jas 5.11)', *JTS* 26 (1975), pp. 91-95.

Grässer, E., and O. Merk (eds.), *Glaube und Eschatologie* (Festschrift W.G. Kümmel; Tübingen: J.C.B. Mohr [Paul Siebeck], 1985).

Greeven, H., 'Propheten, Lehrer, Vorsteher bei Paulus', *ZNW* 44 (1952–53), pp. 1-43.

Grundmann, W., 'ταπεινός, κτλ.', *TDNT*, VIII, pp. 1-26.

Gruson, P. (ed.), *La Lettre de Jacques: Lecture socio-linguistique* (Cahiers Evangiles, 61; Paris: Cerf, 1988).

Haacker, K., 'Glaube', *TRE*, XIII, pp. 275-365.

Hadidian, D.Y., 'Palestinian Pictures in the Epistle of James', *ExpTim* 63 (1952), pp. 227-28.

Hadidian, D.Y. (ed.), *Intergerini Parietis Septum* (Festschrift Markus Barth; PTMS, 33; Pittsburgh, PA: Pickwick Press, 1981).

Hainthaler, T., *'Von der Ausdauer Ijobs habt ihr gehört' (Jak 5.11): Zur Bedeutung des Buches Ijob im Neuen Testament* (Frankfurt am Main: Peter Lang, 1988).

Halliday, M.A.K., *Language as Social Semiotic* (London: Edward Arnold, 1978).

Halliday, M.A.K., and R. Hasan, *Language, Context and Text* (Oxford: Oxford University Press, 1989).

Hanson, A.T., 'Rahab the Harlot in Early Christian Theology', *JSNT* 1 (1978), pp. 53-60.

Hanson, K.C., 'Kinship', in Rohrbaugh (ed.), *Social Sciences*, pp. 62-79.

Hanson, K.C., and D.E. Oakman, *Palestine in the Time of Jesus* (Minneapolis: Fortress Press, 1980).

Harnack, A., 'Die Lehre der zwölf Apostel' (TU 2; 1886), pp. 94-137.

Hartin, P.J., *James and the Q sayings of Jesus* (JSNTSup, 47; Sheffield: JSOT Press, 1991).

—'Come now, you Rich, Weep and Wail... (James 5.1-6)', *Journal of Theology for South Africa* 84 (1993), pp. 57-63.

—'The Call to Be Perfect through Suffering (James 1.2-4): The Concept of Perfection in the Epistle of James and the Sermon on the Mount', *Bib* 77 (1996), pp. 477-92.

—' "Who Is Wise and Understanding among you?" (James 3.13): An Analysis of Wisdom, Eschatology and Apocalypticism in the Epistle of James' (*SBLSP* 33; 1996), pp. 483-503.

—'The Poor in the Epistle of James and the Gospel of Thomas', *Hervormde Teologiese Studies* 53 (1997), pp. 146-62

Heiligenthal, R., *Werke als Zeichen* (Tübingen: J.C.B. Mohr [Paul Siebeck], 1983).

Hengel, M., 'Das Gleichnis von den bösen Weingärtnern (Mc 12.1-12) im Lichte der Zenonpapyri und der rabbinischen Gleichnisse', *ZNW* 59 (1968), pp. 1-39.

—*Judaism and Hellenism: Studies in their Encounter in Palestine during the Early Hellenistic Period* (2 vols.; London: SCM Press, 1974).

—*The Charismatic Leader and his Followers* (Edinburgh: T. & T. Clark, 1981).

—'Jakobus der Herrenbruder—der erste Papst?', in Grässer and Merk (eds.), *Glaube und Eschatologie*, pp. 71-104.

—'Der Jakobusbrief als antipaulinische Polemik', in Betz and Hawthorne, *Tradition and Interpretation*, pp. 248-78.

Hoffmann, P., *Studien zur Frühgeschichte der Jesus-Bewegung* (Stuttgart: Katholisches Bibelwerk, 1994).

—'Herrschaftsverzicht: Befreite und befreiende Menschlichkeit', in Hoffmann, *Studien*, pp. 139-70.

—'Die Basileia-Verkündigung Jesu und die Option für die Armen', in Hoffmann, *Studien*, pp. 41-72.

Hoppe, R., *Der theologische Hintergrund des Jakobusbriefes* (FzB, 28; Würzburg: Echter Verlag, 1977).

—*Jakobusbrief* (Stuttgarter Kleiner Kommentar zum Neuen Testament, 15; Stuttgart: Katholisches Bibelwerk, 1989).

Hoppe, R., and U. Busse (eds.), *Von Jesus zu Christus* (Berlin: W. de Gruyter, 1998).

Horsley, R., *Jesus and the Spiral of Violence* (San Francisco: Harper & Row, 1987).

—*Sociology and the Jesus Movement* (New York: Crossroad, 1989).

Hort, F.J.A., *The Epistle of St. James* (London: Macmillan, 1909).

Hübner, H., *Biblische Theologie des Neuen Testaments*, II (Göttingen: Vandenhoeck & Ruprecht, 1993).

Hutchinson Edgar, D., 'The Use of the Love-Command and the Shema' in the Epistle of James', *Proceedings of the Irish Biblical Association* 23 (2000), pp. 9-22.

Jackson-McCabe, M., 'A Letter to the Twelve Tribes in the Diaspora: Wisdom and Apocalyptic Eschatology in the Letter of James' (*SBLSP* 33; 1996), pp. 504-17.

Jacobson, A.D., *The First Gospel: An Introduction to Q* (Sonoma, CA: Polebridge Press, 1992).

Jefford, C.N. (ed.), *The Didache in Context: Essays on its Text, History and Transmission* (NovTSup, 77; Leiden: E.J. Brill, 1995).

Jeremias, J., *Jerusalem in the Time of Jesus* (London: SCM Press, 1969).

Johnson, L.T., 'The Use of Leviticus 19 in the Letter of James', *JBL* 101 (1982), pp. 391-401.

—'James 3.13–4.10 and the ΤΟΠΟΣ ΠΕΡΙ ΦΘΟΝΟΥ', *NovT* 25 (1983), pp. 326-47.

—'Friendship with the World/Friendship with God: A Study of Discipleship in James', in Segovia, *Discipleship*, pp. 166-83.

—'Taciturnity and True Religion: James 1.26-27', in Balch, Ferguson and Meeks (eds.), *Greeks, Romans and Christians*, pp. 329-39.

—*The Letter of James* (AB, 37A; New York: Doubleday, 1995).

Johnson, T., and C. Dandeker, 'Patronage: Relation and System', in Wallace-Hadrill (ed.), *Patronage*, pp. 219-42.

Karrer, M., 'Christus der Herr und die Welt als Stätte der Prüfung: Zur Theologie des Jakobusbriefes', *Kerygma und Dogma* 35 (1989), pp. 166-88.

Keck, L.E., 'The Poor among the Saints in the New Testament', *ZNW* 56 (1965), pp. 100-29.

—'The Poor among the Saints in Jewish Christianity and Qumran', *ZNW* 57 (1966), pp. 54-78.

Kee, H.C., 'Defining the First Century Synagogue: Problems and Progress', *NTS* 41 (1995), pp. 481-500.

Kelber, W.H., 'Jesus and Tradition: Words in Time, Words in Space', *Semeia* 65 (1994), pp. 139-67.

Kertelge, K. (ed.), *Das Gesetz im Neuen Testament* (Freiburg: Herder, 1986).

Kirk, J. A., 'The Meaning of Wisdom in James', *NTS* 16 (1969), pp. 24-38.

Kittel, G., 'Der geschichtliche Ort des Jakobusbriefes', *ZNW* 41 (1942), pp. 71-105.

—'Der Jakobusbrief und die apostolischen Väter', *ZNW* 43 (1950), pp. 54-112.

Kleinheyer, B., and H. auf der Maur (eds.), *Zeichen des Glaubens* (Festschrift B. Fischer; Freiburg: Herder Verlag, 1972).

Kloppenborg, J.S., *The Formation of Q* (Philadelphia: Fortress Press, 1987).

—'Literary Convention, Self-Evidence and the Social History of the Q People', *Semeia* 55 (1992), pp. 77-102.

—'Status und Wohltätigkeit bei Paulus und Jakobus', in Hoppe and Busse (eds.), *Von Jesus zu Christus*, pp. 127-54.

Koester, H., 'Written Gospels or Oral Tradition?', *JBL* 113 (1994), pp. 293-97.

Koskenniemi, H., *Studien zur Idee und Phraseologie des griechischen Briefes bis 400n. Chr.* (Helsinki: Suomalaien Tiedeakatemie, 1956).

Kuhn, H.W, 'Der irdische Jesus bei Paulus', *ZTK* 67 (1970), pp. 195-320.

Kümmel, W.G., *Introduction to the New Testament* (London: SCM Press, 1966).

Lautenschlager, M., 'Der Gegenstand des Glaubens im Jakobusbrief', *ZTK* 87 (1990), pp. 163-84.

Laws, S.S., 'Does Scripture Speak in Vain? A Reconsideration of James 4.5', *NTS* 20 (1974), pp. 210-15.

—*A Commentary on the Epistle of James* (London: A. & C. Black, 1980).

Lindemann, A., *Paulus im ältesten Christentum* (Tübingen: J.C.B. Mohr [Paul Siebeck], 1987).

Lips, H. von, *Weisheitliche Traditionen im Neuen Testament* (WMANT, 64; Neukirchen–Vluyn: Neukirchener Verlag, 1990).

Llewelyn, S.R., 'The Prescript of James', *NovT* 39 (1997), pp. 385-93.

Lohse, E., 'Taufe und Rechtfertigung bei Paulus', *Kerygma und Dogma* 11 (1965), pp. 305-24.

Luck, U., 'Weisheit und Leiden: Zum Problem Paulus und Jakobus', *TLZ* 92 (1967), cols. 253-58.
—'Der Jakobusbrief und die Theologie des Paulus', *TGl* 61 (1971), pp. 161-79.
—'Die Theologie des Jakobusbriefes', *ZTK* 81 (1984), pp. 1-30.
Ludwig, M., *Wort als Gesetz: Eine Untersuchung zum Verständnis von 'Wort' und 'Gesetz' in israelitisch-frühjüdischen und neutestamentlichen Schriften. Gleichzeitig ein Beitrag zur Theologie des Jakobusbriefes* (Frankfurt am Main: Peter Lang, Europäischer Verlag der Wissenschaften, 1994).
Lührmann, D., and G. Strecker (eds.), *Kirche* (Festschrift Günther Bornkamm; Tübingen: J.C.B. Mohr [Paul Siebeck], 1980).
Malina, B.J., 'Jesus as Charismatic Leader?', *BTB* 14 (1984), pp. 55-62 (reprinted in Malina, *Social World*, pp. 123-42).
—*Christian Origins and Cultural Anthropology* (Atlanta, GA: John Knox Press, 1986).
—'Wealth and Poverty in the New Testament and its World', *Int* 41 (1987), pp. 354-67.
—'Christ and Time: Mediterranean or Swiss?', *CBQ* 51 (1989), pp. 1-31 (reprinted in Malina, *Social World*, pp. 179-214).
—'Faith/Faithfulness', in Malina and Pilch (eds.), *Biblical Social Values*, pp. 67-70.
—'Gratitude', in Malina and Pilch (eds.), *Biblical Social Values*, pp. 86-88.
—'Love', in Malina and Pilch (eds.), *Biblical Social Values*, pp. 110-14.
—*The New Testament World: Insights from Cultural Anthropology* (Louisville: Westminster/John Knox Press, 2nd edn, 1993).
—'Early Christian Groups', in Esler (ed.), *Modelling Early Christianity*, pp. 96-113.
—*The Social World of Jesus and the Gospels* (London: Routledge, 1996).
—'Patron and Client: The Analogy behind Synoptic Theology', in Malina, *Social World*, pp. 143-48
Malina, B.J., and J.H. Neyrey, *Calling Jesus Names: The Social Value of Labels in Matthew* (Sonoma, CA: Polebridge Press, 1988).
Malina, B.J., and J. Pilch (eds.), *Biblical Social Values and their Meaning* (Peabody, MA: Hendrickson, 1993).
Malina, B.J., and R.L. Rohrbaugh, *Social-Science Commentary on the Synoptic Gospels* (Minneapolis: Fortress Press, 1992).
Marcus, J., 'The Evil Inclination in the Epistle of James', *CBQ* 44 (1982), pp. 606-21.
Marshall, S.S.C., 'Δίψυχος: A Local Term?', *SE* 6 (TU 112) (1973), pp. 348-51.
Martin, D.B., *Slavery as Salvation* (New Haven: Yale University Press, 1990).
Martin, R.A., 'James', in R.A. Martin and J.H. Elliott, *James, 1 and 2 Peter, Jude* (ACNT; Minneapolis: Augsburg, 1982), pp. 7-51.
Martin, R.P., 'The Life-Setting of the Epistle of James in the Light of Jewish History', in Tuttle (ed.), *Biblical and Near Eastern Studies*, pp. 97-103.
—*James* (WBC, 48; Waco, TX: Word Books, 1988).
Massebieau, L., 'L'Épître de Jacques, est-elle l'oeuvre d'un chrétien?', *RHR* 32 (1895), pp. 241-83.
Massynbaerde Ford, J., 'Prostitution in the Ancient Mediterranean World', *BTB* 23 (1993), pp. 128-34.
Maurer, C., 'φυλή', *TDNT*, IX, pp. 245-50.
Maynard-Reid, P., *Poverty and Wealth in James* (Maryknoll, NY: Orbis Books, 1987).
Mayor, J.B., *The Epistle of St. James* (London: Macmillan, 1913).
Mayordomo-Marín, M., 'Jak 5.2-3a: Zukünftiges Gericht oder gegenwärtiger Zustand?', *ZNW* 83 (1992), pp. 132-37.

McKenzie, J.L., 'Reflections on Wisdom', *JBL* 86 (1967), pp. 1-9.

Merklein, H. (ed.), *Neues Testament und Ethik* (Freiburg: Herder, 1989).

Michl, J., 'Der Spruch Jakobusbrief 4.5', in Blinzer, Kuss and Mussner (eds.) *Neutestament-liche Aufsätze*, pp. 167-74.

Moxnes, H., *The Economy of the Kingdom* (Philadelphia: Fortress Press, 1988).

—'Honor and Shame', *BTB* 23 (1993), pp. 167-76.

—'Honor and Shame', in Rohrbaugh (ed.), *Social Sciences*, pp. 19-40.

Mussies, G., 'Greek in Palestine and the Diaspora', CRINT 1.2, pp. 1040-64.

Mussner, F., 'Direkte und indirekte Christologie im Jakobusbrief', *Catholica* 24 (1970), pp. 111-17.

—'Die Tauflehre des Jakobusbriefes', in Kleinheyer and auf der Maur (eds.), *Zeichen des Glaubens*, pp. 61-67.

—*Der Jakobusbrief* (HTKNT, 13.1; Freiburg: Herder Verlag, 5th edn, 1987).

—'Die ethische Motivation im Jakobusbrief', in Merklein (ed.), *Neues Testament und Ethik*, pp. 416-23.

Neitzel, H., 'Eine alte crux interpretum im Jakobusbrief 2.18', *ZNW* 73 (1982), pp. 286-93.

Neusner, J., and E.S. Frerichs (eds.), *'To See Ourselves as Others See Us': Jews, Christians, Others in Antiquity* (Chico, CA: Scholars Press, 1985).

Neusner, J., W.S. Green and E.S. Frerichs (eds.), *Judaisms and their Messiahs at the Turn of the Christian Era* (Cambridge: Cambridge University Press, 1987).

Niederwimmer, K., *Die Didache* (Göttingen: Vandenhoeck & Ruprecht, 1989).

Nissen, A., *Gott und der Nächste im antiken Judentum: Untersuchungen zum Doppelgebot der Liebe* (Tübingen: J.C.B. Mohr [Paul Siebeck], 1974).

Noack, B., 'Jakobus wider die Reichen', *ST* 18 (1964), pp. 10-25.

O Fearghail, F., 'On the Literary Structure of the Letter of James', *Proceedings of the Irish Biblical Association* 19 (1996), pp. 73-76.

Oakman, D.E., *Jesus and the Economic Questions of his Day* (Queenston, Ontario: Edwin Mellen Press, 1986).

Öhler, M., *Elia im Neuen Testament* (BZNW, 88; Berlin: W. de Gruyter, 1997).

Patterson, S.J., *The Gospel of Thomas and Jesus* (Sonoma, CA: Polebridge Press, 1993).

—'Didache 11–13: The Legacy of Radical Itinerancy in Early Christianity', in Jefford (ed.), *Didache in Context*, pp. 313-29.

Paulsen, H., 'Jakobusbrief', *TRE*, XVI, pp. 488-95.

Pearson, B.A., *The Pneumatikos-Psychikos Terminology* (Missoula, MT: Scholars Press, 1973).

Penner, T., *The Epistle of James and Eschatology* (JSNTSup, 121; Sheffield: Sheffield Academic Press, 1996).

Perdue, L.G., 'Paraenesis and the Epistle of James', *ZNW* 72 (1981), pp. 241-56.

—'The Social Character of Paraenesis and Paraenetic Literature', *Semeia* 50 (1990), pp. 5-39.

Perrin, N., and D.C. Duling, *The New Testament: An Introduction* (New York: Harcourt, Brace, Jovanovich, 1982).

Pilch, J., 'Understanding Biblical Healing', *BTB* 18 (1988), pp. 60-66.

—'Understanding Healing in the Social World of Early Christianity', *BTB* 22 (1992), pp. 26-33.

Piper, R.A. (ed.), *The Gospel behind the Gospels: Current Studies on Q* (Leiden: E.J. Brill, 1995).

Pitt-Rivers, J., 'Pseudo-Kinship', in *International Encyclopedia of the Social Sciences*, VIII (ed. D. Sills; London: Macmillan, 1979), pp. 408-13.

Popkes, W., *Adressaten, Situation und Form des Jakobusbriefes* (Stuttgart: Katholisches Bibelwerk, 1986).

—'James and Paraenesis, Reconsidered', in Fornberg and Hellholm (eds.), *Texts and Contexts*, pp. 535-61.

Porter, S.E., 'Is *dypsuchos* (James 1.8, 4.8) a "Christian" Word?', *Bib* 71 (1990), pp. 469-98.

—'Did Jesus Ever Teach in Greek?', *TynBul* 44 (1993), pp. 200-35.

—'The Theoretical Justification for the Application of Rhetorical Categories to Pauline Literature', in Porter and Olbricht (eds.), *Rhetoric*, pp. 100-22.

Porter, S.E., and T.H. Olbricht (eds.), *Rhetoric in the New Testament* (JSNTSup, 90; Sheffield: Sheffield Academic Press, 1993).

Pratscher, W., *Der Herrenbruder Jakobus und die Jakobustradition* (Göttingen: Vandenhoeck & Ruprecht, 1987).

—'Der Standort des Herrenbruders Jakobus im theologischen Spektrum der frühen Kirche' (SNTU [Series A] 15 [1990]), pp. 41-58.

Prockter, L.J., 'James 4.6: Midrash on Noah', *NTS* 35 (1989), pp. 625-27.

Rad, G. von, 'δόξα', *TDNT*, II, pp. 238-39.

Ramsey, A.M., *The Glory of God and the Transfiguration of Christ* (London: Longmans, Green & Co., 1949).

Rebell, W., *Alles ist möglich dem, der glaubt: Glaubensvollmacht im frühen Christentum* (Munich: Kaiser Verlag, 1989).

Reed, J.T., 'Using Rhetorical Categories to Interpret Paul's Letters: A Question of Genre', in Porter and Olbricht (eds.), *Rhetoric in the New Testament*, pp. 292-324.

Reese, J.M., 'The Exegete as Sage: Hearing the Message of James', *BTB* 12 (1982), pp. 82-86.

Reicke, B., *The Epistles of James, Peter and Jude* (New York: Doubleday, 1964).

Rendall, G.H., *The Epistle of James and Judaic Christianity* (Cambridge: Cambridge University Press, 1927).

Rengstorf, K.H., 'ἁμαρτωλός', *TDNT*, I, pp. 317-33.

—'διδάσκαλος', *TDNT*, II, pp. 148-59.

—'γελάω', *TDNT*, I, pp. 658-62.

Riesner, R., *Jesus als Lehrer: Eine Untersuchung zum Ursprung der Evangelien-Überlieferung* (WUNT NS, 7; Tübingen: J.C.B. Mohr [Paul Siebeck], 1981).

Robbins, V.K., *Jesus the Teacher* (Philadelphia: Fortress Press, 1984).

Roberts, J.J.M., 'The Old Testament's Contribution to Messianic Expectations', in Charlesworth (ed.), *Messiah*, pp. 39-51.

Rohrbaugh, R.L., 'A Peasant Reading of the Parable of the Talents/Pounds', *BTB* 23 (1993), pp. 32-39.

Rohrbaugh, R.L. (ed.), *The Social Sciences and New Testament Interpretation* (Peabody, MA: Hendrickson, 1996).

Ropes, J.H., *A Critical and Exegetical Commentary on the Epistle of James* (ICC; Edinburgh: T. & T. Clark, 1916).

Rordorf, W., 'Does the Didache Contain Jesus Tradition Independently of the Synoptic Gospels?', in Wansborough (ed.), *Jesus and the Oral Gospel Tradition*, pp. 394-423.

Saller, R., *Personal Patronage under the Early Empire* (Cambridge: Cambridge University Press, 1982).

Sanders, E.P., *Jesus and Judaism* (London: SCM Press, 1985).
—*Paul, the Law and the Jewish People* (London: SCM Press, 1985).
Sato, M., *Q und Prophetie* (WUNT NS, 29; Tübingen: J.C.B. Mohr [Paul Siebeck], 1988).
—'Wozu wurde der Jakobusbrief geschrieben?: eine mutmassliche Rekonstruktion', *Annual of the Japanese Biblical Institute* 17 (1991), pp. 55-76.
Schammberger, H., *Die Einheitlichkeit des Jakobusbriefes im antignostischen Kampf* (Gotha: Klotz Verlag, 1936).
Schiffman, L., 'Messianic Figures and Ideas in the Qumran Scrolls', in Charlesworth, *Messiah*, pp. 116-29.
Schille, G., 'Wider die Gespaltenheit des Glaubens', *Theologische Versuche* 9 (1977), pp. 71-89.
Schlatter, A., *Der Brief des Jakobus* (repr.; Stuttgart: Calwer Verlag, 1985 [1956]).
Schmidt, K.L., 'διασπορά', *TDNT*, II, pp. 98-104.
—'ἐκκλησία', *TDNT* III, pp. 501-36.
Schmitt, J.J., ' "You Adulteresses!" The Image in James 4.4', *NovT* 28 (1986), pp. 327-37.
Schnider, F., *Der Jakobusbrief* (Regensburg: Friedrich Pustet, 1987).
Schottroff, L., *Befreiungserfahrungen: Studien zur Sozialgeschichte des Neuen Testaments* (Munich: Kaiser Verlag, 1990).
—'Gewaltverzicht und Feindesliebe in der urchristlichen Jesustradition', in Schottroff, *Befreiungserfahrungen*, pp. 12-35.
—'Itinerant Prophetesses: A Feminist Analysis of the Sayings Source Q', in Piper (ed.), *Gospel behind the Gospels*, pp. 347-60.
Schottroff, L., and W. Stegemann, *Jesus and the Hope of the Poor* (Maryknoll, NY: Orbis Books, 1986).
Schottroff, W., and W. Stegemann (eds.), *God of the Lowly: Socio-historical Interpretations of the Bible* (Maryknoll, NY: Orbis Books, 1984).
Schrage, W., 'Der Jakobusbrief', in W. Schrage and H. Balz, *Die katholischen Briefe* (NTD, 10; Göttingen: Vandenhoeck & Ruprecht, 1973), pp. 5-58.
Schroeder, D., 'Paraenesis', *IDBSup*, p. 643.
Schürmann, H., *Orientierungen am Neuen Testament* (Düsseldorf: Patmos Verlag, 1978).
—'Und Lehrer', in Schürmann, *Orientierungen*, pp. 116-56.
Schweizer, E., *Church Order in the New Testament* (London: SCM Press, 1961).
Segovia, F (ed.), *Discipleship in the New Testament* (Philadelphia: Fortress Press, 1985).
Seitz, O.J.F., 'The Relationship of the Shepherd of Hermas to the Epistle of James', *JBL* 63 (1944), pp. 131-40.
—'Antecedents and Significance of the Term ΔΙΨΥΧΟΣ', *JBL* 66 (1947), pp. 211-19.
—'Afterthoughts on the Term "Dipsychos" ', *NTS* 4 (1957), pp. 327-34.
—'James and the Law', *SE* 2 (TU 87) (1963), pp. 472-86.
Sevenster, J.N., *Do You Know Greek? How Much Greek Could the First Jewish Christians Have Known?* (NovTSup, 19; Leiden: E.J. Brill, 1968).
Shepherd, M.H., 'The Epistle of James and the Gospel of Matthew', *JBL* 75 (1956), pp. 40-51.
Sherwin-White, A.N., *Roman Society and Roman Law in the New Testament* (Oxford: Clarendon Press, 1963).
Sigal, P., 'The Halakhah of James', in Hadidian (ed.), *Intergerini Parietis Septum*, pp. 337-53.
Siker, J.S., *Disinheriting the Jews: Abraham in Early Christian Controversy* (Louisville: Westminster/John Knox Press, 1991).

Simon, L., *Une éthique de la sagesse* (Geneva: Editions Labor et Fides, 1961).

Smit, D.J., 'Show No Partiality … (James 2.1-13)', *Journal of Theology for South Africa* 70 (1990), pp. 59-68.

Soden, H. von, 'ἀδελφός', *TDNT* I, pp. 144-46.

Soucek, J., 'Zu den Problemen des Jakobusbriefes', *EvT* 18 (1958), pp. 460-68.

Spitta, F., *Zur Geschichte und Literatur des Urchristentums* (Göttingen: Vandenhoeck & Ruprecht, 1896).

Stählin, G., 'ἡδονή', *TDNT*, II, pp. 909-26.

Stegemann, W., 'Vagabond Radicalism in Early Christianity', in Schottroff and Stegemann (eds.), *God of the Lowly*, pp. 148-68.

Stern, M., 'The Jewish Diaspora', *CRINT* 1.1, pp. 117-83.

Strobel, A., *Untersuchungen zum eschatologischen Verzögerungsproblem* (NovTSup, 2; Leiden: E.J. Brill, 1961).

Taatz, I., *Frühjüdische Briefe* (NTOA, 16; Göttingen: Vandenhoeck & Ruprecht, 1991).

Talmon, S., 'Waiting for the Messiah: The Spiritual Universe of the Qumran Covenanters', in Neusner, Green and Frerichs (eds.), *Messiahs*, pp. 111-38.

Tamez, E., *Bible of the Oppressed* (Maryknoll, NY: Orbis Books, 1982).

—*The Scandalous Message of James: Faith without Works Is Dead* (New York: Crossroad, 1990).

—'Elemente der Bibel, die den Weg der christlichen Gemeinde erhellen: Eine hermeneutische Übung anhand des Jakobusbriefes', *EvT* 51 (1991), pp. 92-100.

Theissen, G., *Sociology of Early Palestinian Christianity* (Philadelphia: Fortress Press, 1978 [*The First Followers of Jesus* (London: SCM Press, 1978)]).

—'Nonviolence and Love of our Enemies', in Theissen, *Social Reality*, pp. 115-56.

—'Sociological Theories of Religion and the Analysis of Early Christianity', in Theissen, *Social Reality*, pp. 231-56.

—'Some Ideas about a Sociological Theory of Early Christianity', in Theissen, *Social Reality*, pp. 257-87.

—'The Wandering Radicals', in Theissen, *Social Reality*, pp. 33-59.

—' "We have left everything…" (Mark 10.28)', in Theissen, *Social Reality*, pp. 60-93.

—*Social Reality and the Early Christians* (Edinburgh: T. & T. Clark, 1992).

Thurén, L., 'Risky Rhetoric in James', *NovT* 37 (1995), pp. 262-84.

Tollefson, K.D., 'The Epistle of James as Dialectical Discourse', *BTB* 21 (1991), pp. 62-69.

Trocmé, E., 'Les églises pauliniennes vues du dehors', *SE* 2 (TU 87) (1964), pp. 660-69.

Tuttle, G.A. (ed.), *Biblical and Near Eastern Studies* (Festschrift W.S. LaSor; Grand Rapids: Eerdmans, 1978).

Verseput, D., 'James 1.17 and the Jewish Morning Prayers', *NovT* 39 (1997), pp. 177-91.

—'Reworking the Puzzle of Faith and Works in James 2.14-26', *NTS* 43 (1997), pp. 97-115.

Vouga, F., *L'Epître de Saint Jacques* (CNT, 13a; Geneva: Labor et Fides, 1984).

Walker, R., 'Allein aus Werken: Zur Auslegung von Jakobus 2.14-26', *ZTK* 61 (1965), pp. 155-92.

Wall, R.W., *Community of the Wise* (Valley Forge, PA: Trinity Press International, 1997)

Wallace-Hadrill, A. (ed.), *Patronage in Ancient Society* (London: Routledge, 1989).

Walter, N., 'Paul and the Early Jesus-Tradition', in Wedderburn (ed.), *Paul and Jesus*, pp. 51-81.

Wanke, J., 'Die urchristichen Lehrer nach dem Zeugnis des Jakobusbriefes', in Ernst, Schnackenburg and Wanke (eds.), *Die Kirche des Anfangs*, pp. 489-511.

Wansborough, H. (ed.), *Jesus and the Oral Gospel Tradition* (JSNTSup, 64; Sheffield: JSOT Press, 1991).

Ward, R.B., 'The Works of Abraham: James 2.14-26', *HTR* 61 (1968), pp. 283-90.

—'Partiality in the Assembly, Jas 2.2-4', *HTR* 62 (1969), pp. 87-97.

Warrington, K., 'The Significance of Elijah in James 5.13-18', *EvQ* 66 (1994), pp. 217-27.

Watson, D.F., 'James 2 in the Light of Greco-Roman Schemes of Argumentation', *NTS* 39 (1993), pp. 94-121.

—'The Rhetoric of James 3.1-12 and a Classical Pattern of Argumentation', *NovT* 35 (1993), pp. 48-64.

Wedderburn, A.J.M., 'The Soteriology of the Mysteries and Pauline Baptismal Theology', *NovT* 29 (1987), pp. 53-72.

Wedderburn, A.J.M. (ed.), *Paul and Jesus* (JSNTSup, 37; Sheffield: JSOT Press, 1989).

Weiss, K., 'Motiv und Ziel der Frömmigkeit des Jakobusbriefes', *Theologische Versuche* 7 (1976), pp. 107-14.

Wenham, D. (ed.), *The Jesus Tradition outside the Gospels* (Gospel Perspectives, 5; Sheffield: JSOT Press, 1987).

White, J.L., *The Form and Function of the Body of the Greek Letter* (Missoula, MT: Scholars Press, 1972).

—'New Testament Epistolary Literature in the Framework of Ancient Epistolography', *ANRW* 2.25.2, pp. 1751-56.

Wieser, F.E., *Die Abrahamvorstellungen im Neuen Testament* (Frankfurt am Main: Peter Lang, 1987).

Wuellner, W.H., 'Der Jakobusbrief im Licht der Rhetorik und Textpragmatik', *LB* 43 (1978), pp. 5-66.

Zimmermann, A., *Die urchristlichen Lehrer: Studien zum Tradentenkreis der διδάσκαλοι im frühen Urchristentum* (WUNT NS, 12; Tübingen: J.C.B. Mohr [Paul Siebeck], 1984).

Zmijewski, J., 'Christliche "Vollkommenheit": Erwägungen zur Theologie des Jakobusbriefes', *SNTU* 5, Series A (1980), pp. 50-78.

INDEXES

INDEX OF REFERENCES

OLD TESTAMENT

Genesis		19.18	70, 125-	2.8-11	176
1.14-18	153		28, 142,	24.30	46
1.26-28	179		198		
1.26	64, 180			*Judges*	
1.28	180	*Numbers*		2.8	46
4.10	202	11.12	155	18.6	170
15	174	30.3	209		
15.6	173, 174			*1 Samuel*	
18	173	*Deuteronomy*		1.17	170
22	174	5.10	131	12.3	48
22.1	141, 151	6.4-9	57, 198	12.5	48
		6.4-5	126	20.42	170
Exodus		6.4	70, 171,	24.1	151
15.25	141		185, 198	24.7	48
16.4	141	6.5	70, 171,	24.11	48
16.10	60		185	26.9	48
19.22	195	8.2	141	26.11	48
20.5	193	8.16	141	26.16	48
20.6	131	10.18	166	26.23	48
20.7	209	11.14	58, 64,	29.7	170
22.1-2	209		205, 208		
24.2	195	14.28	166	*2 Samuel*	
24.16	60	16.11	166	1.14	48
34.6-7	131	16.14	166	1.16	48
40.34-35	60	16.16	195	6.2	123
		24.17-21	166	15.9	170
Leviticus		24.24-25	202	22.51	48
4.5	48	26.12-13	166	23.1	48
4.16	48	27.19	166		
6.15	48	27.26	129	*1 Kings*	
19	128	32.18	155	8.24-26	46
19.12	209			8.53	46
19.13	202	*Joshua*		8.56	46
19.15	128	2	176	14.8	46

2 Kings
10.10	46
14.25	46
17.13	46
17.23	46
18.12	46
21.8	46
21.10	46

1 Chronicles
| 21.1 | 151 |
| 29.4 | 140 |

2 Chronicles
6.33	123
7.14	123
32.31	141

Esther
| 6.1 | 50 |

Job
1–2	141
5.11	147
5.17	150
12.21	147
38.28	154
42.10-17	207

Psalms
1.1	150
2.2	48
10.14	166
10.18	166
11.3	104
11.7	140
17.51	48
22.9	155
31.1	150
33.9	150
39.5	150
40.2	194
57.5	60
57.11	60
61.5	180
63.2	60
68.5	166
83.3	194

83.6	150
88.4	46
88.21	46
88.39	48
88.52	48
90.2	155
94.6	166
101.18	147
102.8-9	208
102.9	208
104.26	46
111.1	150
131.10	46
138.5	60
146.9	166

Proverbs
1.8	101
1.10	101
3.34	147, 187, 194, 203
8.32	150
8.34	150
10.12	64
16.19	147
23.10	166
24.55	103
24.70	101
27.21	140
30.20	103
31.2	101

Isaiah
1.17	166
5.9	26, 64, 202
25.6	147
40.1-8	148
40.6-7	64
42.8	60
43.7	123
45.1	48
48.11	60
49.13	147
54.10-11	147
55.12	141
56.2	150
66.10	141

Jeremiah
3.8-9	103
7.10-11	123
7.14	123
7.30	123
22.13	202
24	97

Ezekiel
10.18	60
11.23	60
16.32	103
16.38	103
17.24	147
18.12	122
21.31	147
22.7	122, 166
22.29	122
23.37	103
23.43	103
34.23	46
38.17	46
45.8	98
47.13–48.35	98

Hosea
1–3	103
4.13-14	103
6.6	131
12.6-7	195

Joel
| 3.1-5 | 55 |

Amos
3.7	46
8.4	122
9.12	123

Micah
| 2.2 | 122 |

Zephaniah
| 3.12 | 147 |

Zechariah
| 1.3 | 195 |
| 1.6 | 46 |

Zechariah (cont.)
1.13 — 140
3.1-10 — 48
4 — 49
4.1-4 — 48
4.4-10 — 48

4.11-14 — 48
4.14 — 48
6.9-14 — 48
6.14 — 150
7.10 — 166
8.19 — 141

Malachi
3.5 — 103, 122, 202
3.7 — 195
3.24 — 46

APOCRYPHA

Tobit
4 — 31
12 — 31

Judith
8.25-27 — 141
8.35 — 170

Wisdom of Solomon
2.10 — 122
3.4-6 — 141
5.15-16 — 150
6.12-21 — 22
7.7 — 144
7.22-30 — 22
8.21 — 144

Sirach
1.1-30 — 26
2.1-18 — 22, 25, 141
2.1 — 25, 101
2.4 — 25
2.5 — 25
2.6 — 25
2.8 — 25

2.13 — 25
2.14 — 25
4.10 — 166
4.17 — 26, 144, 152
5.9 — 104
5.11-20 — 141
5.13 — 180
7.3 — 101
10.15 — 147
11.14 — 149
14.1 — 150
14.20 — 150
15.11-20 — 25
15.11-12 — 151
15.12 — 25
15.14 — 25
15.17 — 25
15.19 — 25
15.20 — 25
16.11-12 — 132
21.27 — 26, 152
24 — 22, 144
27.5 — 141
27.7 — 141
31.8-11 — 141

32(35).17 — 166
35.17-19 — 147
36.10 — 98
44–50 — 60, 61, 206
44.19 — 60
44.20 — 173
45.2 — 60
45.20 — 60
46.13-20 — 206
47.1 — 206
47.11 — 60
48.1-12 — 206
48.13-14 — 206
48.22 — 206
49.9 — 206

1 Maccabees
2.52 — 173, 174
10.25-45 — 17

2 Maccabees
1.10–2.18 — 99
1.10 — 50
2.17-18 — 99

NEW TESTAMENT

Matthew
3.2 — 205
3.6 — 94
4.17 — 205
5–7 — 64, 70
5.1-2 — 141
5.3-12 — 69
5.3-11 — 150
5.3-6 — 107

5.3 — 28, 63, 67, 69, 80, 107, 113
5.4 — 88
5.5 — 28, 67, 80, 113
5.7 — 71, 82, 131
5.8 — 88

5.9 — 87, 183
5.10-12 — 110
5.11-12 — 67, 70, 76, 207
5.12 — 92
5.17-20 — 129
5.17 — 79
5.18 — 81
5.19 — 178

5.21-48	143	8.18-22	109	18.4	69, 88, 110, 148, 196
5.21-22	130	8.20	108		
5.21	82	9.13	131		
5.22	78, 91	9.37-38	202	18.6-7	178
5.23-24	213	10	54	18.15-17	117
5.27	82	10.2	54	18.15	94
5.33-37	210	10.3	19	18.17	211
5.34-37	63, 93, 209	10.5	54	18.21-35	82, 131
		10.7	54, 205	18.23-34	123
5.43-47	142	10.8	228	19.14	148
5.43-46	128	10.9-10	108, 118, 170	19.16-22	63
5.43	127			19.17	84
5.48	76, 142	10.10	169, 202	19.18	82, 130
6.9-13	65	10.11	110	19.19	127
6.11	71, 83, 110	10.12-13	170	19.21	76, 143
		10.13-14	170	19.22	143
6.12	131, 213	10.21	108	19.28	61, 206
6.13	151	10.22-23	108, 110	19.30	110
6.14-15	82, 213	10.22	70, 92, 207	20.1-16	132
6.14	71, 131			20.1	202
6.19-21	69	10.28	70, 89, 148, 197	20.8	202
6.19-20	70, 90, 202			20.16	110
		10.34-37	108	20.26-27	110
6.20	201	10.39	148	20.26	69
6.24	88, 193	10.40-42	110	21.21-22	71, 110, 145, 212
6.25-34	110	11.5	69, 80, 107		
6.25	84			21.22	93
6.33	78	11.6	150	22.36	126
6.34	71, 89	11.19	87	22.37-39	81, 127, 198
7.1-2	132	11.25	85, 86		
7.1	70, 89, 91, 121, 131, 197	11.29	86	22.37	70
		12.7	131	22.39	70, 126, 127
		12.33-37	180		
7.7-11	110	12.33	86	23.1-36	178
7.7-8	71	12.34-35	85	23.6	119
7.7	63, 71, 76, 87, 144, 145	12.36-37	84	23.7	51
		12.39	87, 103	23.8	101
		13.16	150	23.12	69, 88, 110, 148, 196
7.9-11	151	13.19-23	165		
7.11	71, 78	15.11	85		
7.15-18	180	15.19	80	23.23	82, 129
7.16	86	16.4	87, 103	23.29-39	55
7.21-23	83	16.17-19	225	23.29	207
7.21	79	16.17	150	24	70, 205
7.22	212	16.18	211	24.30-31	206
7.24-27	70, 79	16.25	78	24.3	91
7.24	165	17.20	71, 110	24.13	70, 92, 207

Matthew (cont.)		10.17-20	63	2.46	51
24.26	150	10.18	84	2.52	196
24.27	91, 205	10.19	82	3.11	83
24.30	205	10.21	143	3.12	51
24.33	70, 92,	10.22	143	4.25	94
	206	10.31	110	4.32	165
24.37	91, 205	10.37	61	4.36	165
24.39	91, 205	10.43-44	69, 77,	5.1	165
25	70		110	6.13	193
25.31-46	83	11.22-24	145, 212	6.15	19
25.31-40	110	11.23-24	71, 110	6.16	220
25.31	61, 206	11.23	77	6.17-49	70
25.34	81, 206	11.24-25	93	6.20-26	69
25.35-36	83	11.25	82, 131,	6.20-22	150
25.36	80		213	6.20-21	107
28.19	124	12.1-12	226	6.20	63, 67, 69,
		12.28-34	128		80, 107,
Mark		12.28-31	128		113
1.5	94	12.28	126	6.21	67, 88,
1.15	205	12.29-31	81, 127,		196
1.20	202		198	6.22-23	67, 70, 76,
2.1-12	213	12.29-30	84		110, 207
2.2	165	12.29	70	6.23	92
2.14	19	12.31	70, 126,	6.24-25	67, 69, 90,
3.18	19		127		149
3.32-35	221	12.33	127	6.25	28, 88,
4.14-20	165	12.39	119		196
4.26-29	91, 204	12.40	80, 84,	6.35	82
5.34	84, 170		178	6.36	71, 131,
5.41	220	12.43	107		142
6.3	221	13	205, 208	6.37-38	132
6.8-9	108	13.12	108	6.37	89, 91,
6.8	170	13.13	70, 92,		121, 131,
6.9	169		207		197
6.10	110	13.26-27	205, 206	6.43-45	180
6.11	170	13.26	61	6.43-44	86
6.13	93, 211,	13.29	63, 70, 92,	6.45	85
	228		206	6.46-49	70, 79, 83
7.21	80	15.2	225	6.47	165
7.23	80	17.20	77	7.4-5	119
8.35	78, 148	20.26-27	77	7.22	69, 80,
8.38	61, 87,	21.21-22	77		107
	103	23.12	77	7.23	150
9.35	69, 77,			7.35	87
	110	*Luke*		7.41-42	123
9.38	212	1.45	150	7.50	170
9.42	178	1.46-55	132	8.11-15	165
10.15	148	1.72	83		

8.13	76, 78, 165	12.22-31	110	22.30	206
8.14	191, 192	12.22	84	23.29	150
9.2	228	12.33-34	69, 200, 201	*John*	
9.3	108, 169, 170	12.33	70, 90	3.1	51
9.4	110	12.37-38	150	3.10	51
9.5	170	12.43	150	9.1-3	213
9.24	78	12.47	89		
9.32	61	12.52-53	108	*Acts*	
9.54-56	70	13.1-5	213	1.13	19, 220
9.58	108	13.30	110	1.16	102
10.2	202	14.11	69, 77, 88, 110, 148, 196	2.9-11	97
10.4-7	170			2.17-21	55
10.4	108	14.14-15	150	2.29	102
10.5-8	110	15.7	141	2.37	102
10.5-6	170	15.17	202	2.38	124
10.7	202	15.18	212	3.6	212
10.8-9	110	15.19	202	3.17	102
10.9	205, 228	15.21	202, 212	4.29	46
10.10-11	170	16.13	88	4.30	212
10.11	205	16.17	81, 129	5.11	211
10.17	141, 212	16.19-31	69	6.1	166
10.20	141	16.19	90	6.3	102
10.21	85	17.1-2	178	7.2	102
10.23	150	17.3	94	7.55	61
10.27	70, 81, 126, 127, 198	17.6	71	8.1	211
		18.4	69	8.3	211
		18.9-14	132	9.31	211
10.29-37	128	18.14	77, 88, 110, 148, 196	10.2	119
11.2-4	65			10.48	124
11.3	71, 83, 110	18.16-17	148	11.22	211
11.4	131, 151, 213	18.18-23	63	11.26	211
		18.19	84	11.27-28	53
11.9-13	110	18.20	82, 130	12.1	211
11.9	63, 71, 76, 87, 144, 145	18.22	143	12.2	220
		18.23	143	12.5	211
		20.46	119	13.1-3	54
11.11-13	151	20.47	80, 84, 178	13.1	51, 53, 55, 211
11.13	71, 78	21	205	13.15	102
11.27-28	150	21.3	107	13.26	102
11.28	165	21.19	70, 92, 207	13.38	102
11.37-44	101			15	20
11.43	119	21.27-28	205, 206	15.12-19	35
12.4-7	197	22.26	69, 77, 88, 110, 148	15.13-21	220
12.16-21	69			15.13	19
12.21	201			15.32	54
				16.18	212

Acts (cont.)
16.32-41   53
16.36   170
21   20
21.10   53
21.18   19
23.6-10   101
24.10   210
26.6-7   99
27.22   210
27.25   210
27.26   210

Romans
1.1   45
1.13   102
2   175
3   175
3.20   174
3.28   35, 174, 175
4   172
6.3-4   124
6.4   61
7.4   102
8.12   102
12.4-5   178
13.8-10   126
13.9   127, 130
13.12   190
15.24   34
16.17-18   189

1 Corinthians
1.10-11   102
2.1   102
2.6-9   24
2.8   61
2.14   182
3.1   102
4.6   102
4.14-17   102
6.1-6   117
9.1-5   52
9.2   221
12   52
12.12-27   178

12.28-31   53
12.28   51, 54
14   177
14.1   53
14.3-5   54
14.26-32   53
14.31   54
15   20
15.7   19
15.44-46   182

2 Corinthians
1.8   102
10.4   190

Galatians
1.19   19, 35
2   20
2.9   19, 20, 35, 220
2.11-13   35
2.12   19, 20, 221
2.16   174, 175
3   172
3.2   174
3.5   174
3.10   174
5.3   129
5.14   127

Ephesians
4.11   52
6.11-17   190

Philippians
1.1   45
2.5-11   47

1 Thessalonians
2.11   102
2.19-20   141
5   208
5.23   182

2 Thessalonians
3.14-15   189

1 Timothy
2.7   52
3.16   61

2 Timothy
1.11   52
4.8   150

Titus
1.1   47
3.9-11   189

Philemon
4.10-20   34

Hebrews
3.1   102
3.12   102
10.19   102
10.32-36   141
11.31   176
12.2   141
13.22   102

James
1   63
1.1-12   37
1.1   44-47, 50, 56, 59, 61, 62, 96, 98, 100, 104, 111, 138, 168, 170, 177, 205, 216
1.2–5.11   216
1.2–4.12   173
1.2–3.12   161
1.2-18   22, 25, 26, 137-40, 152, 153, 156, 158-62, 181, 216
1.2-15   35
1.2-12   24, 139
1.2-11   17

1.2-8   138-40,
         147, 150,
         156, 169
1.2-6   194
1.2-5   143
1.2-4   37, 141,
         174, 175,
         205, 207,
         215
1.2   37, 67, 69,
         76, 101,
         138, 139,
         147, 151,
         158, 160,
         165, 200,
         206, 207,
         210, 214
1.3-4   138
1.3   138, 140,
         141, 145,
         165, 172
1.4-13   158
1.4-5   143, 181
1.4   76, 141,
         143, 161,
         203
1.5-8   145, 192,
         194, 210,
         214
1.5-7   37
1.5-6   59, 71
1.5   23, 63, 71,
         76, 144,
         150, 152,
         153, 157,
         161, 181,
         194
1.6-8   104, 145,
         157, 213
1.6   77, 172,
         194
1.7   138, 145,
         205
1.8   104, 146,
         161, 182,
         195

1.9-11   31, 68,
           139, 146,
           147, 150,
           156, 157,
           192
1.9-10   69, 77, 117
1.9   138, 139,
           142, 148,
           192, 194,
           199, 203,
           214
1.10-11   69, 198,
           199, 204
1.10   64, 148
1.11   148
1.12-25   17
1.12-15   150
1.12   37, 69,
           127, 138,
           139, 141,
           142, 150,
           151, 153,
           157, 160,
           171, 192,
           199, 203,
           204, 207,
           214
1.13–5.6   37
1.13-18   194
1.13-15   37, 139,
           150, 153,
           157
1.13-14   138
1.13   138, 151-
           53, 157
1.14-15   37, 152,
           183, 191
1.15   104, 153,
           155, 195
1.16-18   35, 36,
           153
1.16   101, 153,
           158
1.17-25   24
1.17-18   37, 156,
           181

1.17   23, 71, 78,
           143, 153,
           154, 157,
           161, 182,
           185, 194
1.18-12   33
1.18   23, 61,
           155, 157,
           161, 164,
           177
1.19–3.18 158, 161,
           162, 183
1.19-27   35, 158-
           62, 166,
           181, 184,
           216
1.19-20   37, 58,
           162, 163
1.19   101, 158,
           162, 164
1.20   58, 59, 78,
           158, 161
1.21-25   156, 165
1.21   23, 78,
           161, 162,
           164, 165,
           168, 177,
           181, 182,
           185, 214
1.22-25   70, 164
1.22-23   165
1.22   79, 164,
           165, 174
1.23   61
1.25   58, 59, 61,
           79, 130,
           131, 143,
           158, 161,
           164, 165
1.26-27   79, 164,
           166
1.26   158, 161,
           166
1.27   47, 58, 69,
           80, 103,
           112, 158

James (cont.)

Reference	Pages
2	32, 112
2.1–5.11	176
2.1–5.6	18, 35, 160
2.1–3.18	215
2.1–3.12	158, 160-62, 166, 180, 181, 184, 216
2.1–3.10	160
2.1-26	112
2.1-13	31, 35, 63, 111, 112, 114, 125, 130, 133, 134, 137, 138, 146, 158, 161, 165-67, 169, 179, 180, 184, 216
2.1-12	14
2.1-7	114, 133
2.1-6	158
2.1-4	37
2.1	59, 61, 62, 101, 115, 120, 135, 146, 162, 164, 168, 170, 172, 176, 177
2.2-4	114, 116, 164
2.2-3	116, 117, 120, 121, 128, 132, 168, 170, 176-78, 180, 184, 192, 199
2.2	32, 115, 122, 169, 178, 211
2.3	161
2.4-7	168
2.4	61, 80, 120, 121, 130, 131, 197
2.5-7	117, 193
2.5-6	105, 121, 133-35, 146, 170, 176
2.5	28, 42, 63, 67, 69, 80, 101, 106, 112-14, 125, 127, 128, 133, 135, 137, 150, 162, 166, 168, 169, 171, 172, 180, 184, 192, 199, 203
2.6-14	37
2.6-7	117, 121, 122, 125, 148, 198, 204, 209
2.6	114, 122, 139, 142, 164, 197, 203
2.7	62, 123
2.8-13	58, 125, 129, 133, 135, 168, 197
2.8-12	131
2.8-11	126, 184
2.8	25, 59, 70, 81, 125, 127, 130, 131, 158, 168
2.9-12	131
2.9	128, 130, 146, 164
2.10	81, 129
2.11	72, 82, 129, 130, 191
2.12-13	71, 121, 125, 133, 168, 173
2.12	59, 61, 130, 131, 158, 162, 165
2.13	64, 71, 82, 132, 142, 183, 208
2.14-26	14, 24, 33-35, 59, 83, 112, 130, 141, 158, 161, 165, 167, 168, 172, 173, 175-77, 179-81, 184, 217
2.14-17	35
2.14-16	164
2.14	101, 142, 161, 165, 168, 170, 171, 174, 214
2.15-17	169
2.15-16	71, 83, 158, 169, 171, 173, 176-78, 180, 184
2.15	84, 169, 170, 176, 178
2.16	84, 161
2.17-18	142, 161
2.17	170
2.18-26	176
2.18-19	170
2.18	161, 170,

171, 175, 181, 198
2.19-25 — 184
2.19 — 57, 58, 70, 72, 84, 127, 154, 171, 184, 185, 198, 205
2.20-26 — 161
2.20-22 — 142
2.20 — 96, 172
2.21-25 — 176
2.21-23 — 176
2.21 — 59, 151, 172
2.22 — 141, 173-75
2.23-25 — 59, 158
2.23 — 25, 58, 152, 161, 173, 174, 193
2.24-26 — 142
2.24 — 173-75
2.25 — 173, 176
2.26 — 176, 180, 193
2.36 — 183
3.1-12 — 14, 130, 158, 161, 166-68, 177, 179, 181, 184, 217
3.1-10 — 35
3.1 — 33, 34, 44, 50, 51, 72, 84, 101, 130, 162, 177, 178, 184
3.2-12 — 178
3.2-3 — 166
3.2 — 84, 143, 158, 164, 178, 179
3.3–4.10 — 186

3.3-5 — 179
3.5 — 179, 191
3.6-12 — 179
3.6 — 112, 152, 166, 179, 183, 195, 201
3.7-9 — 184
3.7-8 — 179
3.7 — 179
3.8 — 161, 179, 182, 201
3.9-10 — 164, 180, 189
3.9 — 47, 58, 64, 85, 185, 205
3.10-12 — 35, 36
3.10 — 85, 101, 180
3.12–5.6 — 160
3.12 — 86, 101
3.13–5.6 — 160
3.13–4.6 — 35
3.13-18 — 22, 24, 58, 59, 161, 181, 182, 184, 186, 217
3.13-17 — 23, 86, 144
3.13 — 87, 142, 149, 161, 162, 186
3.14 — 161, 164, 182, 186
3.15 — 152, 161, 181, 182, 195
3.16 — 161, 182, 186
3.17 — 23, 59, 161, 183
3.18 — 58, 59, 64, 87, 161
4–5 — 215
4 — 186, 195
4.1–5.20 — 186

4.1-10 — 161, 166, 186-88, 190, 196, 215, 217
4.1-5 — 187, 194, 195
4.1-4 — 164, 187, 190
4.1-3 — 214
4.1 — 186, 190
4.2-3 — 71, 87, 187, 191
4.2 — 152, 186, 191, 192
4.3 — 192
4.4-6 — 215
4.4 — 58, 87, 96, 103, 112, 166, 187, 191, 192, 194, 195
4.5 — 193, 194
4.6 — 25, 147, 186-88, 196, 203, 215
4.7-10 — 35, 69, 71, 187, 194-96, 215
4.7 — 152, 183, 187, 196
4.8 — 88, 96, 103-105, 161, 187, 195
4.9 — 28, 67, 88, 195, 200
4.10 — 88, 186, 187, 196, 199, 205, 215
4.11–5.11 — 70, 161, 186, 188, 190, 197, 208, 215, 217
4.11–5.6 — 35, 197, 215

James (cont.)

Reference	Pages
4.11-12	58, 59, 70, 121, 130, 131, 186, 197, 199, 208
4.11	89, 101, 164, 187, 188
4.12	58, 70, 89, 127, 148, 154, 197, 198, 205, 206, 208, 214
4.13–5.11	187
4.13–5.6	186, 187, 192, 215, 226
4.13-17	31, 32, 71, 89, 188, 199, 203, 226, 227
4.13-16	34
4.13	96, 161, 188, 198-200
4.14-17	32
4.14	200, 209
4.15	58, 199, 205
4.16	199, 200, 209
4.17	64, 89, 183
5	63
5.1-11	187
5.1-6	26, 31, 34, 69, 117, 148, 188, 198, 199, 201, 203, 204, 209, 226, 227
5.1	67, 90, 96, 161, 188, 198, 199
5.2-3	70, 90, 200-202
5.2	201
5.3	201
5.4-6	209
5.4-5	204
5.4	26, 64, 103, 161, 201, 204, 205, 226, 227
5.5	90, 161, 201, 202, 204
5.6	91, 142, 188, 200, 202, 203
5.7-20	35, 37, 187
5.7-11	17, 37, 188, 197, 208, 209, 215
5.7-9	100
5.7-8	62, 70, 204, 207, 208
5.7	58, 64, 91, 101, 154, 188, 199, 204, 208, 226
5.8	91, 161, 204, 205
5.9	63, 70, 91, 101, 130, 189, 199, 206, 208
5.10-11	204, 206, 208
5.12-20	215
5.10	47, 92, 101, 199, 207, 210, 211, 213
5.11	92, 141, 142, 188, 207, 208, 215
5.12-20	161, 186, 188, 190, 209, 215, 217
5.12-18	189
5.12	18, 37, 63, 64, 93, 101, 103, 130, 188, 189, 209, 210, 217
5.13-18	71, 145, 188, 189, 210, 213, 217
5.13-16	18, 93
5.13	210, 213
5.14-20	71
5.14-16	215
5.14-15	62, 212
5.14	62, 93, 210, 211
5.15-18	18, 215
5.15-16	212
5.15	61, 172, 212, 214
5.16	94, 210, 213
5.17-18	213
5.17	94
5.19-20	94, 97, 189, 213, 217
5.19	101, 161
5.20	64, 104, 182, 214

1 Peter

Reference	Pages
1.6-7	141
1.7	140, 141
1.8	141
1.11	61
1.21	61
2.16	46
4.11	61

4.12-14	141	1 2.18	102	*Revelation*	
4.13	61	1 3.13	102	2.10	150
5.4	61, 150	1 5.16-17	189	2.20	46
5.11	61			3.17	107
		Jude		7.4-8	99
2 Peter		5	148	21.12-13	99
3.17	189	19	182		
1 2.1	102	22	189		

PSEUDEPIGRAPHA

1 En.		19.8	141	*T. Iss.*	
103.3	141	19.9	152, 174	7.6-7	146
104.12	141			7.7	195
22.14	60, 61	*Pss. Sol.*			
25.3	60, 61	2.31	60	*T. Jos.*	
27.3	60, 61	11.7	60	2.7	141
27.5	60, 61	17	98	7.4	152
58.2	60	17.26-34	99	7.8	152
61.8	60	17.31	60		
62.16	60	17.32	49	*T. Jud.*	
65.12	60	18.5	49	24	49
91-107	149	18.7	49	25.4	141
				25.5	141
2 Bar.		*T. Abr.*			
5.1-4	60	7.6	154	*T. Levi*	
78–86	99			8.2	150
78.4	99	*T. Ash.*		8.9	150
78.7	99	2	129	17.2	141
		2.5	104	18	49
4 Macc.		3.1-2	104	18.7	60
5.20	129	3.2	152		
17.15	150	4.1-3	104	*T. Naph.*	
		6.4-5	152	8.4	195
4 Ezra		6.6	141		
13.39	99			*T. Reub.*	
13.46-48	99	*T. Benj.*		2.4	152
		4.1	60, 150	4.7-9	152
Jub.		6.1-3	191	5.3-5	141
17	141	6.5	104, 180	6.3-4	152
17.15-18	151	6.7	146	6.8	49
17.16	151	11.2-4	49		
18	141			*T. Sim.*	
18.12	151	*T. Dan*		3.5	195
19.3	141	5.1-2	191	4.5	60
19.8-9	173	5.1	195		

QUMRAN

11QT		5.1	99	*4Q169*	
18	99			3	99
23–24	99	*1QS*			
39	99	5.8-11	209	*CD*	
57	99	9.10-11	48	12.22-23	48
		10.21-24	180	13.20-22	48
1QM				14.18-19	48
2.2-3	99	*1QSa*		15	209
3.14	99	2.11-22	48	16	209

RABBINIC TEXTS

Mishnah		Talmud	
Ab.		*b. Šebu.*	
5.4	173	31	117

PHILO

Abr.		*Ebr.*		*Spec. Leg.*	
167	173	81	154	4.79-91	152
Dec.		*Leg. Gai.*			
142	152	281-82	97		
82–95	209				

JOSEPHUS

Ant.		20.180-81	229	2.135	209
1.223	173	20.182	228	2.139-42	209
1.233-34	173	20.197-203	19	2.218	228
17.305-308	228	20.205-208	229	2.264-65	229
17.305	226	20.212	228	2.272-79	228
17.307	226	20.254-55	228	2.273	228
19.352	228			2.277-78	228
20.124	229	*War*		2.347	163
20.164-65	229	2.85-86	228		

CHRISTIAN SOURCES

1 Clem.		8.5	64	4.5-8	146
31.2	172	9.11	64	6.2	143
		13.4	64	7.1	124
2 Clem.				7.3	124
2.4	64	*Didache*		8.2	65
3.2	64	1	64	9.5	65
4.2	64	1.2–4.14	143	11–15	52
6.12	64	1.2	127	11–13	118

11	53	Eusebius		*Sim.*	
11.1-2	54	*Hist. Eccl.*		2	29
11.4	54	2.23	20, 221		
11.7-12	55	2.23.24-25	11	Ignatius	
11.7-8	54	2.23.25	21	*Pol.*	
11.10	54	3.25.3	11, 21	4.2	115
11.11	54	3.25.5	221		
13	54	3.27.4	221	Jerome	
13.1-2	53			*De vir. ill.*	
13.1	54	*Gospel of Thomas*		2	221
13.2	54	12.2	221		
15.2	54			Polycarp	
16	205	Hermas		*Phil.*	
		Man.		2.3	64
Dio Chrysostom		11.9	115	7.2	64
Disc.		12.1	158	12.3	64
38.4-5	163				
38.6-7	163				

CLASSICAL SOURCES

Aristophanes		3.13.4	159	*Rhetorica ad Herennium*	
Plut.		3.14.1	159	1.3.4	160
193-97	122	3.14.7	160		
353-55	122	3.19.1	160, 190	Tacitus	
754-56	122			*Hist.*	
		Lucian		5.9	228
Aristotle		*Tyr.*			
Rhet.		4	158		
3.13.1-2	159				

INDEX OF AUTHORS

Adamson, J.B. 21, 129
Ahrens, M. 116, 202
Allison, D.C., Jr 128
Alonso Schökel, L. 203
Amstutz, J. 146
Applebaum, S. 202, 226
Aune, D.E. 53, 55

Baasland, E. 24, 34-36, 100, 138, 153,
 160, 161, 175, 186
Baker, W.R. 178, 209, 210
Balch, D.L. 164
Balz, H. 15
Bammel, E. 107
Batten, A. 169
Bauckham, R. 131
Berger, K. 41, 45-47, 127, 176, 189, 190
Berger, P. 39, 41
Betz, O. 34
Beyer, H.W. 123
Blinzer, J. 193
Blondel, J.-L. 15
Blum, E. 126
Boccaccini, G. 34, 100, 132, 152, 175,
 183
Boring, M.E. 56
Boyle, M.O. 129
Brachel, H.U. von 145
Braumann, G. 156, 165
Breytenbach, C. 61
Bultmann, R. 62
Burchard, C. 32, 61, 116, 124, 126, 128,
 172, 175, 198, 206, 211
Busse, U. 125
Byrskog, S. 51

Cargal, T.B. 97
Carson, D.A. 131
Chaine, J. 65

Charlesworth, J.H. 48
Classen, C.J. 159

Dandeker, C. 119
Daube, D. 203
Dautzenberg, G. 210
Davids, P.H. 13, 19, 21, 64, 65, 68, 116,
 123, 124, 127, 129, 140, 142, 144,
 148, 152, 154-56, 163-65, 168, 169,
 171, 173, 177, 178, 180, 182, 190,
 191, 193, 198, 199, 203, 205, 206,
 209-11
Davies, W.D. 62, 67, 203
Delling, G. 142, 155
Dibelius, M. 12-15, 57, 63, 97, 103, 111,
 112, 114, 115, 123, 124, 126, 129,
 138-40, 142, 148, 151, 152, 154-56,
 163-65, 168, 171-73, 178, 180, 182,
 183, 188, 190, 198-201, 203, 205,
 209-11
Donker, C.E. 170
Doty, W.G. 45
Draper, J.A. 53
Duling, D.C. 15
Dungan, D.L. 62

Easton, B.S. 15
Eckart, K.-G. 15
Edwards, R.B. 13
Elliott, J.H. 15, 37, 39, 41, 118, 144, 187
Elliott-Binns, L.E. 12, 27, 155, 227
Ernst, J. 177
Esler, P.F. 102
Evans, C.A. 128
Exler, F.X.J. 45

Ferguson, E. 164
Feuillet, A. 203
Filson, F.V. 55, 56

Fornberg, T. 17
Francis, F.O. 17, 18, 138, 188
Frankemölle, H. 25, 26, 34, 97, 115, 116,
    124, 127, 130, 131, 138, 141, 143-
    45, 148, 149, 151, 156, 164, 165,
    171, 173, 174, 179, 180, 182, 183,
    186, 190, 193, 195, 197, 198, 200-
    203, 205, 206, 210, 212
Frerichs, E.S. 48, 101
Freyne, S. 98, 101, 226, 227
Friedrich, G. 55
Furnish, V.P. 15

Garnsey, P. 118
Gemünden, P. von 148, 180, 204, 205
Gerhardsson, B. 51
Geyser, A.S. 96
Gordon, R.P. 207
Grässer, E. 19
Green, W.S. 48
Greeven, H. 52, 53, 203
Grundmann, W. 147
Gruson, P. 46, 101, 153

Haacker, K. 171
Hadidian, D.Y. 126, 205
Hainthaler, T. 207
Halliday, M.A.K. 39
Hanson, A.T. 176
Hanson, K.C. 102, 118
Harnack, A. 52, 55
Hartin, P.J. 11, 16, 27, 28, 65, 67, 112,
    141, 142, 149, 201
Hasan, R. 39
Hawthorne, G. 34
Heiligenthal, R. 142
Hellholm, D. 17
Hengel, M. 19, 23, 34, 51, 108, 226
Hoffmann, P. 107, 110
Hoppe, R. 11, 16, 22-24, 46, 116, 123,
    125-27, 130, 138, 140-42, 144, 155,
    171, 173, 174, 177, 183, 186, 198,
    209
Horsley, R. 98, 99, 109, 122
Hort, F.J.A. 20, 115, 139, 155
Hübner, H. 172
Hutchinson Edgar, D. 58, 127, 131

Jackson-McCabe, M. 67, 98
Jacobson, A.D. 151
Jefford, C.N. 53
Jeremias, J. 202, 226
Johnson, L.T. 35, 112, 128, 164, 175,
    186, 195
Johnson, T. 119

Karrer, M. 61, 127, 212
Keck, L.E. 111
Kee, H.C. 115
Kelber, W.H. 64
Kertelge, K. 165
Kirk, J.A. 144
Kittel, G. 27
Kleinheyer, B. 156
Kloppenborg, J.S. 68, 125, 227
Koester, H. 64
Koskenniemi, H. 45
Kuhn, H.W. 62
Kümmel, W.G. 15
Kuss, O. 193

Lautenschlager, M. 172
Laws, S. 11, 28, 57, 68, 115, 116, 123,
    127, 140, 148, 151, 152, 154, 155,
    164, 169, 171, 173, 177, 187, 190,
    193, 194, 198, 201, 203, 206, 208,
    209, 211
Lindemann, A. 172
Lips, H. von 24, 59, 138, 173
Llewelyn, S.R. 44
Lohse, E. 124
Luck, U. 22-24
Luckman, T. 39, 41
Ludwig, M. 126, 155, 156
Lührmann, D. 32, 176

Macholz, C. 126
Malina, B.J. 39-41, 49, 60, 95, 102, 106,
    108, 109, 113, 118, 119, 122, 132,
    167, 169, 194, 200, 202, 212
Marcus, J. 152
Marshall, S.S.C. 104
Martin, D.B. 45, 46
Martin, R.A. 15
Martin, R.P. 11, 19, 21, 46, 116, 123,
    130, 140, 142, 144, 147, 148, 152,

154-56, 164, 165, 169, 172, 177,
    178, 180, 190, 191, 193, 198, 199,
    201, 203, 206, 209-11, 213
Massebieau, L. 26
Massynbaerde Ford, J. 176
Maur, H. auf der 156
Maurer, C. 98
Maynard-Reid, P. 30, 115, 116, 122, 139,
    148, 199, 201-203
Mayor, J.B. 20, 26, 65, 96, 103, 115, 116,
    122, 123, 126, 129, 154, 155, 158,
    169, 174, 190, 203, 210, 211
Mayordomo-Marín, M. 200
McKenzie, J.L. 23
Meeks, W.A. 164
Merk, O. 19
Merklein, H. 15
Mette, N. 145
Michl, J., 193
Moxnes, H. 60, 106, 118
Mussies, G. 225
Mussner, F. 11, 15, 16, 20, 34, 61-63, 65,
    98, 103, 111, 114, 123, 126, 138,
    141, 148, 152, 154-56, 165, 168,
    171, 177, 182, 186, 189, 190, 193,
    194, 198, 199, 201, 203, 206, 210,
    211

Neitzel, H. 171
Neusner, J. 48, 101
Neyrey, J.H. 95, 102
Niederwimmer, K. 143
Nissen, A. 127
Noack, B. 199

O Fearghail, F. 138, 188
Oakman, D.E. 102, 118, 122, 201, 226
Öhler, M. 213
Olbricht, T.H. 159

Patterson, S.J. 53, 111, 114, 116, 118,
    169, 173, 177
Paulsen, H. 13, 61
Pearson, B.A. 182
Penner, T. 13, 67, 98, 120, 138
Perdue, L.G. 16, 29, 195
Perrin, N. 15
Pilch, J. 41, 113, 212

Piper, R.A. 169
Pitt-Rivers, J. 102
Popkes, W. 13, 17, 32, 33, 156, 171, 177
Porter, S.E. 104, 159, 225
Pratscher, W. 19
Prockter, L.J. 193

Rad, G. von 60
Ramsey, A.M. 61
Rebell, W. 145
Reed, J.T. 159
Reese, J.M. 178
Reicke, B. 119, 130, 178
Rendall, G.H. 189
Rengstorf, K.H. 50, 104, 195
Riesner, R. 51
Robbins, V.K. 40
Roberts, J.J.M. 48
Rohrbaugh, R.L. 41, 102, 106, 113, 118,
    119, 132, 167, 169, 202, 212
Ropes, J.H. 12-14, 46, 57, 97, 102, 103,
    115, 116, 122, 123, 126, 139, 140,
    154, 155, 174, 186, 189, 191, 193,
    198, 200, 201, 203, 209-11
Rordorf, W. 65

Saller, R. 119
Sanders, E.P. 98, 99, 104, 175
Sato, M. 32, 53, 56, 198
Schammberger, H. 155
Schiffman, L. 48
Schille, G. 145
Schlatter, A. 65, 96, 102, 115, 126, 129,
    138, 165, 190, 193
Schmidt, K.L. 97, 211
Schmitt, J.J. 103
Schnackenburg, R. 177
Schnider, F. 171
Schottroff, L. 107, 109-11, 121, 142, 169,
    229
Schrage, W. 15
Schroeder, D. 17
Schürmann, H. 56
Schweizer, E. 115
Segovia, F. 112
Seitz, O.J.F. 104, 126
Sevenster, J.N. 225
Shepherd, M.H. 67

Sherwin-White, A.N. 226
Sigal, P. 126, 165
Siker, J.S. 173
Simon, L. 97
Smit, D.J. 122
Soden, H. von 102
Soucek, J. 148
Spitta, F. 26, 63
Stählin, G. 191
Stegemann, E. 126
Stegemann, W. 107, 109-11, 121, 142
Stegner, W.R. 128
Stern, M. 97
Strecker, G. 32, 176
Strobel, A. 207

Taatz, I. 98, 99
Talmon, S. 48
Tamez, E. 97, 107, 111, 113, 115, 122, 126, 127, 145, 148, 211
Theissen, G. 41, 107-11, 116, 124, 177, 229
Thurén, L. 138, 160
Tollefson, K.D. 37
Townsend, M.J. 190
Trocmé E. 177
Tuttle, G.A. 21

Verseput, D. 154, 172
Vouga, F. 47, 62, 97, 123, 129, 154, 155, 164, 165, 169, 180, 188, 190, 191, 193, 199, 203, 205, 208, 209, 212

Walker, R. 175
Wall, R.W. 116, 148, 200
Wallace-Hadrill, A. 119
Walter, N. 62
Wanke, J. 177
Wansborough, H. 65
Ward, R.B. 116, 117, 173
Warrington, K. 213
Watson, D.F. 112, 161
Wedderburn, A.J.M. 62, 124
Weiss, K. 112
Wenham, D. 64
White, J.L. 45
Wieser, F.E. 172, 173
Williamson, H.G.M. 131
Wintermute, O.S. 174
Woolf, G. 118
Wuellner, W.H. 36, 37, 138, 139, 186

Zimmermann, A. 52, 55, 177
Zmijewski, J. 126, 143, 165

JOURNAL FOR THE STUDY OF THE NEW TESTAMENT
SUPPLEMENT SERIES

129   Carl Judson Davis, *The Names and Way of the Lord: Old Testament Themes, New Testament Christology*

130   Craig S. Wansink, *Chained in Christ: The Experience and Rhetoric of Paul's Imprisonments*

131   Stanley E. Porter and Thomas H. Olbricht (eds.), *Rhetoric, Scripture and Theology: Essays from the 1994 Pretoria Conference*

132   J. Nelson Kraybill, *Imperial Cult and Commerce in John's Apocalypse*

133   Mark S. Goodacre, *Goulder and the Gospels: An Examination of a New Paradigm*

134   Larry J. Kreitzer, *Striking New Images: Roman Imperial Coinage and the New Testament World*

135   Charles Landon, *A Text-Critical Study of the Epistle of Jude*

136   Jeffrey T. Reed, *A Discourse Analysis of Philippians: Method and Rhetoric in the Debate over Literary Integrity*

137   Roman Garrison, *The Graeco-Roman Context of Early Christian Literature*

138   Kent D. Clarke, *Textual Optimism: A Critique of the United Bible Societies' Greek New Testament*

139   Yong-Eui Yang, *Jesus and the Sabbath in Matthew's Gospel*

140   Thomas R. Yoder Neufeld, *Put on the Armour of God: The Divine Warrior from Isaiah to Ephesians*

141   Rebecca I. Denova, *The Things Accomplished among Us: Prophetic Tradition in the Structural Pattern of Luke–Acts*

142   Scott Cunningham, *'Through Many Tribulations': The Theology of Persecution in Luke–Acts*

143   Raymond Pickett, *The Cross in Corinth: The Social Significance of the Death of Jesus*

144   S. John Roth, *The Blind, the Lame and the Poor: Character Types in Luke–Acts*

145   Larry Paul Jones, *The Symbol of Water in the Gospel of John*

146   Stanley E. Porter and Thomas H. Olbricht (eds.), *The Rhetorical Analysis of Scripture: Essays from the 1995 London Conference*

147   Kim Paffenroth, *The Story of Jesus According to L*

148   Craig A. Evans and James A. Sanders (eds.), *Early Christian Interpretation of the Scriptures of Israel: Investigations and Proposals*

149   J. Dorcas Gordon, *Sister or Wife?: 1 Corinthians 7 and Cultural Anthropology*

150   J. Daryl Charles, *Virtue amidst Vice: The Catalog of Virtues in 2 Peter 1.5-7*

151   Derek Tovey, *Narrative Art and Act in the Fourth Gospel*

152   Evert-Jan Vledder, *Conflict in the Miracle Stories: A Socio-Exegetical Study of Matthew 8 and 9*

153   Christopher Rowland and Crispin H.T. Fletcher-Louis (eds.), *Understanding, Studying and Reading: New Testament Essays in Honour of John Ashton*

154 Craig A. Evans and James A. Sanders (eds.), *The Function of Scripture in Early Jewish and Christian Tradition*

155 Kyoung-Jin Kim, *Stewardship and Almsgiving in Luke's Theology*

156 I.A.H. Combes, *The Metaphor of Slavery in the Writings of the Early Church: From the New Testament to the Begining of the Fifth Century*

157 April D. DeConick, *Voices of the Mystics: Early Christian Discourse in the Gospels of John and Thomas and Other Ancient Christian Literature*

158 Jey. J. Kanagaraj, *'Mysticism' in the Gospel of John: An Inquiry into its Background*

159 Brenda Deen Schildgen, *Crisis and Continuity: Time in the Gospel of Mark*

160 Johan Ferreira, *Johannine Ecclesiology*

161 Helen C. Orchard, *Courting Betrayal: Jesus as Victim in the Gospel of John*

162 Jeffrey T. Tucker, *Example Stories: Perspectives on Four Parables in the Gospel of Luke*

163 John A. Darr, *Herod the Fox: Audience Criticism and Lukan Characterization*

164 Bas M.F. Van Iersel, *Mark: A Reader-Response Commentary*

165 Alison Jasper, *The Shining Garment of the Text: Gendered Readings of John's Prologue*

166 G.K. Beale, *John's Use of the Old Testament in Revelation*

167 Gary Yamasaki, *John the Baptist in Life and Death: Audience-Oriented Criticism of Matthew's Narrative*

168 Stanley E. Porter and D.A. Carson (eds.), *Linguistics and the New Testament: Critical Junctures*

169 Derek Newton, *Deity and Diet: The Dilemma of Sacrificial Food at Corinth*

170 Stanley E. Porter and Jeffrey T. Reed (eds.), *Discourse Analysis and the New Testament: Approaches and Results*

171 Stanley E. Porter and Anthony R. Cross (eds.), *Baptism, the New Testament and the Church: Historical and Contemporary Studies in Honour of R.E.O. White*

172 Casey Wayne Davis, *Oral Biblical Criticism: The Influence of the Principles of Orality on the Literary Structure of Paul's Epistle to the Philippians*

173 Stanley E. Porter and Richard S. Hess (eds.), *Translating the Bible: Problems and Prospects*

174 J.D.H. Amador, *Academic Constraints in Rhetorical Criticism of the New Testament: An Introduction to a Rhetoric of Power*

175 Edwin K. Broadhead, *Naming Jesus: Titular Christology in the Gospel of Mark*

176 Alex T. Cheung, *Idol Food in Corinth: Jewish Background and Pauline Legacy*

177 Brian Dodd, *Paul's Paradigmatic 'I': Personal Examples as Literary Strategy*

178 Thomas B. Slater, *Christ and Community: A Socio-Historical Study of the Christology of Revelation*

179   Alison M. Jack, *Texts Reading Texts, Sacred and Secular: Two Postmodern Perspectives*

180   Stanley E. Porter and Dennis L. Stamps (eds.), *The Rhetorical Interpretation of Scripture: Essays from the 1996 Malibu Conference*

181   Sylvia C. Keesmaat, *Paul and his Story: (Re)Interpreting the Exodus Tradition*

182   Johannes Nissen and Sigfred Pedersen (eds.), *New Readings in John: Literary and Theological Perspectives. Essays from the Scandinavian Conference on the Fourth Gospel in Århus 1997*

183   Todd D. Still, *Conflict at Thessalonica: A Pauline Church and its Neighbours*

184   David Rhoads and Kari Syreeni (eds.), *Characterization in the Gospels: Reconceiving Narrative Criticism*

185   David Lee, *Luke's Stories of Jesus: Theological Reading of Gospel Narrative and the Legacy of Hans Frei*

186   Stanley E. Porter, Michael A. Hayes and David Tombs (eds.), *Resurrection*

187   David A. Holgate, *A Prodigality, Liberality and Meanness: The Prodigal Son in Graeco-Roman Perspective*

188   Jerry L. Sumney, *'Servants of Satan', 'False Brothers' and Other Opponents of Paul: A Study of those Opposed in the Letters of the Pauline Corpus*

189   Steve Moyise (ed.), *The Old Testament in the New Testament: Essays in Honour of J.L. North*

190   John M. Court, *The Book of Revelation and the Johannine Apocalyptic Tradition*

191   Stanley E. Porter, *The Criteria for Authenticity in Historical-Jesus Research. Previous Discussion and New Proposals*

192   Stanley E. Porter and Brook W.R. Pearson (eds.), *Christian–Jewish Relations through the Centuries*

193   Stanley E. Porter (ed.), *Diglossia and other Topics in New Testament Linguistics*

196   J.M. Holmes, *Text in a Whirlwind: A Critique of Four Exegetical Devices at 1 Timothy 2.9-15*

197   F. Gerald Downing, *Making Sense in (and of) the First Christian Century*

198   Greg W. Forbes, *The God of Old: The Role of the Lukan Parables in the Purpose of Luke's Gospel*

199   Kieran O'Mahony, O.S.A., *Pauline Persuasion: A Sounding in 2 Corinthians 8–9*

200   F. Gerald Downing, *Doing Things with Words in the First Christian Century*

202   Gustavo Martín-Asensio, *Transitivity-Based Foregrounding in the Acts of the Apostles: A Functional-Grammatical Approach*

203   H. Benedict Green, CR, *Matthew, Poet of the Beatitudes*

204   Warren Carter, *Matthew and the Margins: A Socio-Political and Religious Commentary*

206   David Hutchinson Edgar, *Has God Not Chosen the Poor? The Social Setting of the Epistle of James*